Ran and the Gray World 6

Story and Art by **Aki Irie**

Contents

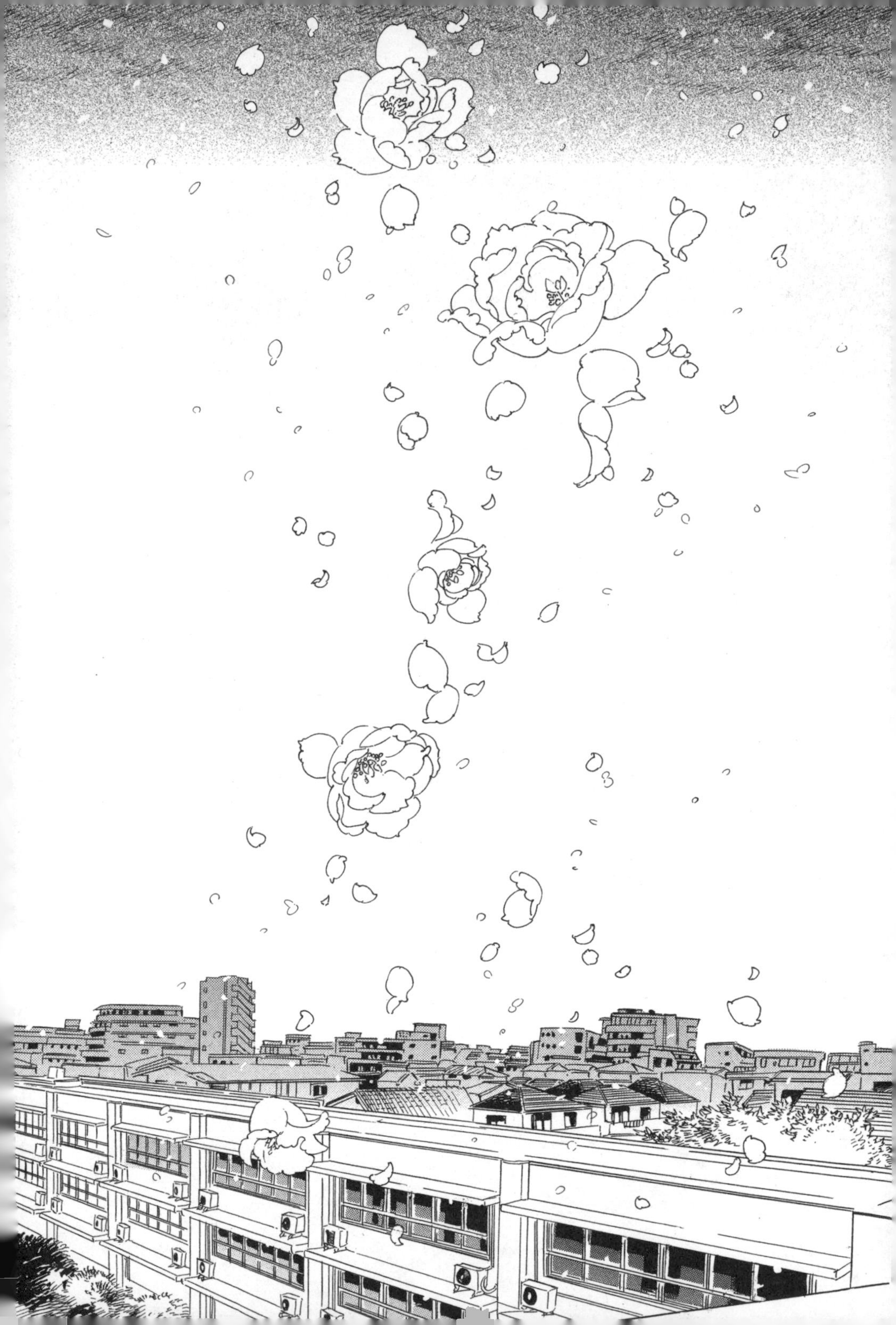

Chapter 30

Tonight's Feast Shall Drive Away Evil

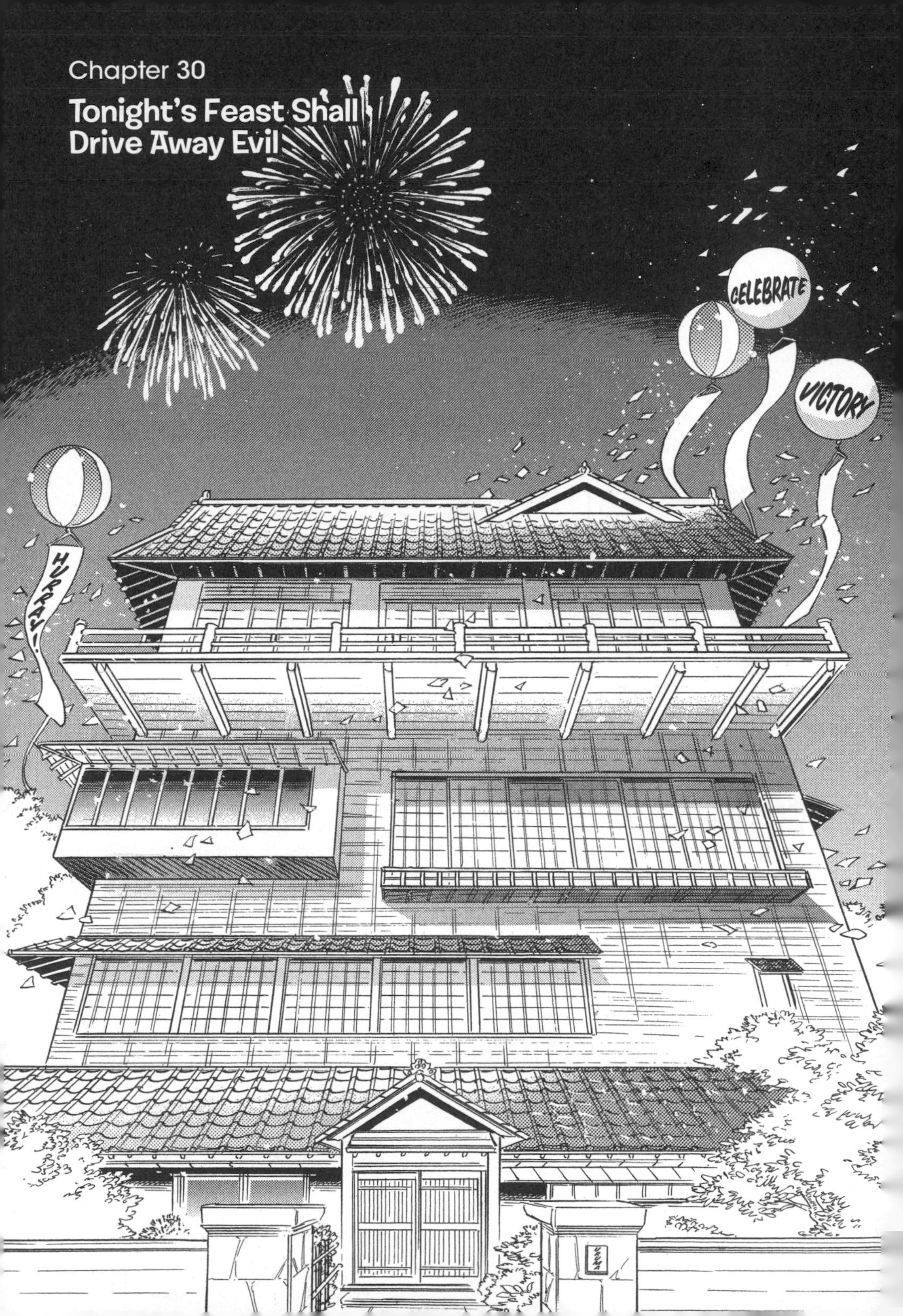
CELEBRATE
VICTORY
HURRAY!

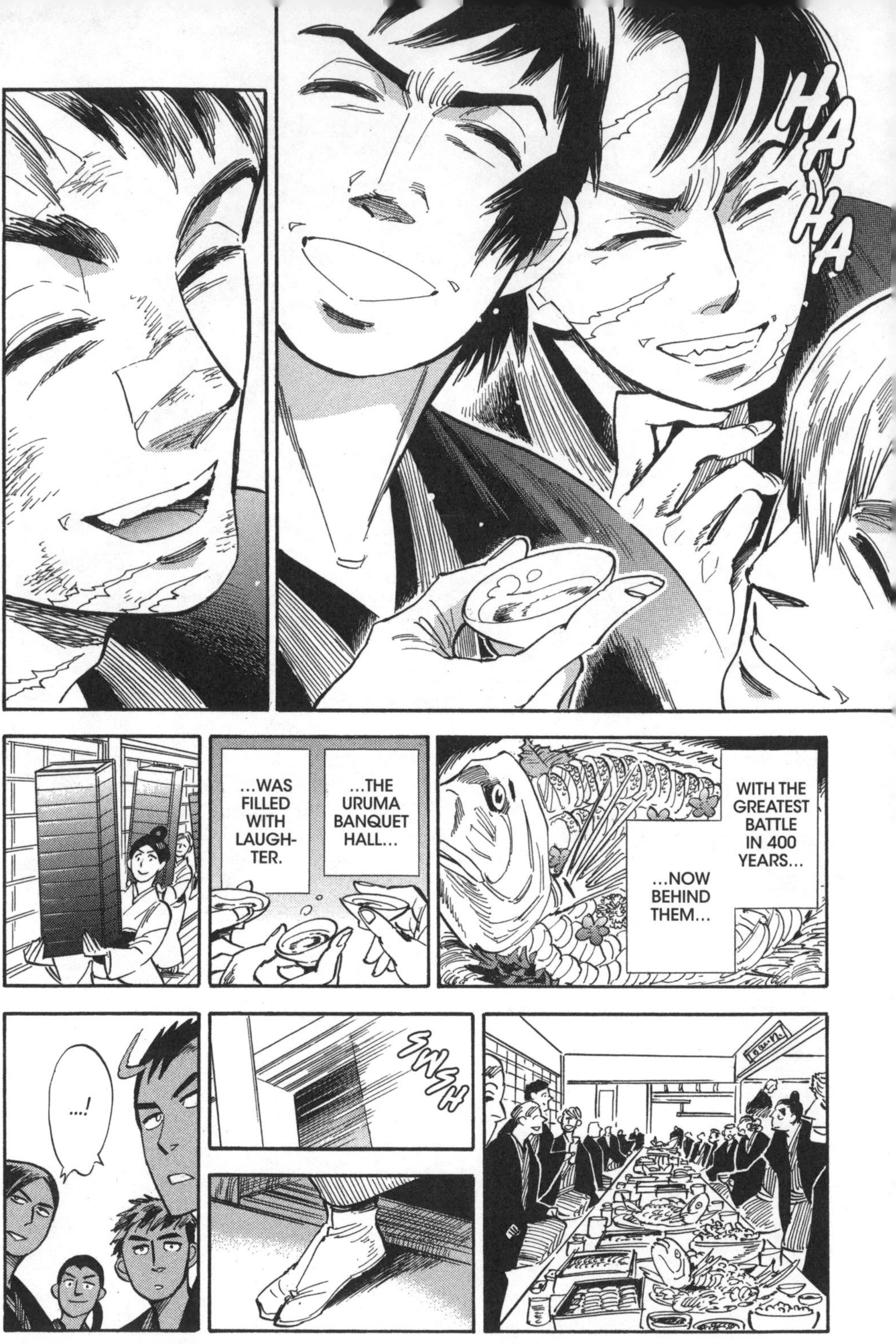
HA HA HA
WITH THE GREATEST BATTLE IN 400 YEARS...
...NOW BEHIND THEM...
...THE URUMA BANQUET HALL...
...WAS FILLED WITH LAUGH-TER.
SWSH
...!

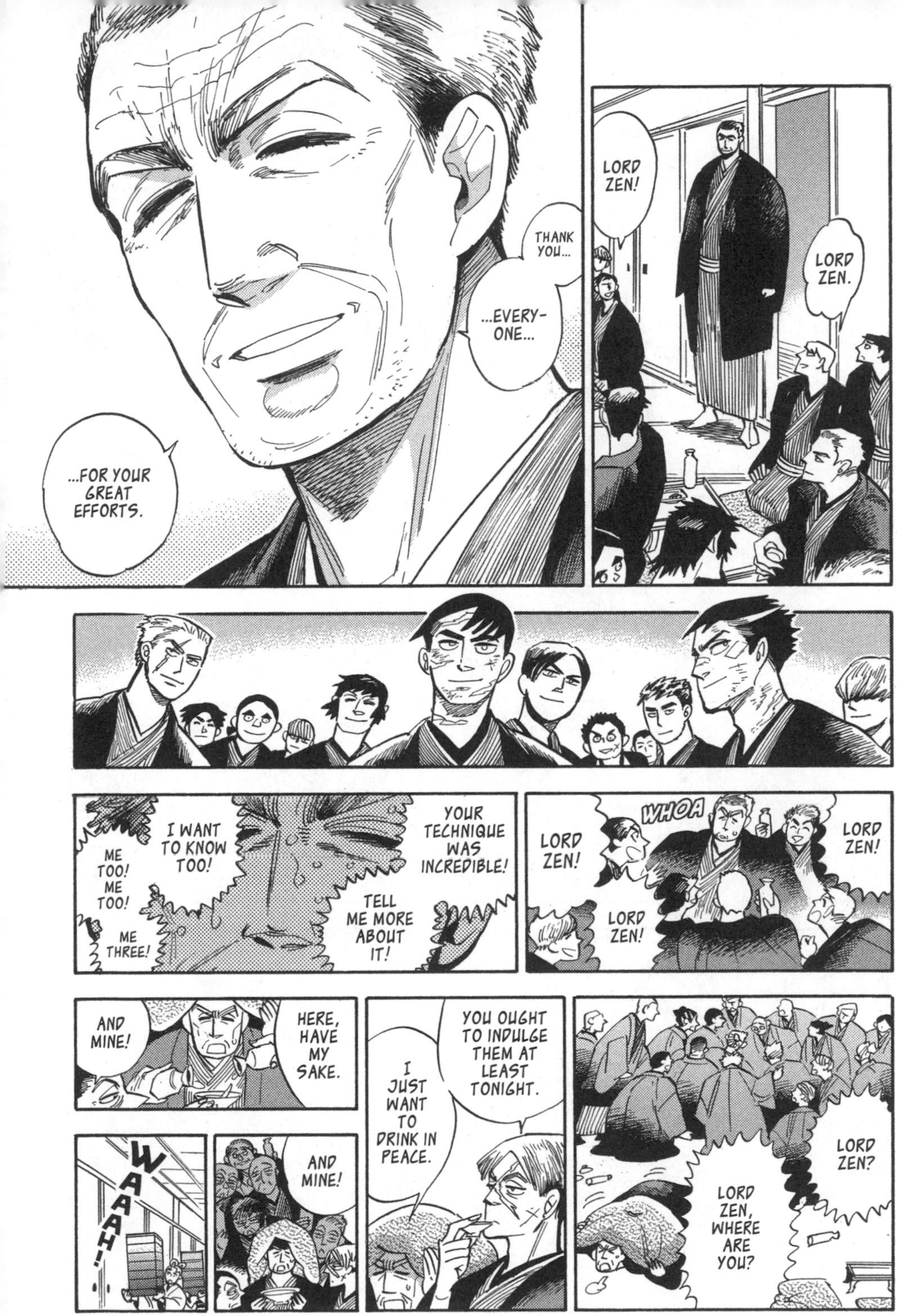
LORD ZEN!
LORD ZEN.
THANK YOU...
...EVERY-ONE...
...FOR YOUR GREAT EFFORTS.
WHOA
LORD ZEN!
LORD ZEN!
LORD ZEN!
YOUR TECHNIQUE WAS INCREDIBLE!
I WANT TO KNOW TOO!
TELL ME MORE ABOUT IT!
ME TOO! ME TOO!
ME THREE!
LORD ZEN?
LORD ZEN, WHERE ARE YOU?
YOU OUGHT TO INDULGE THEM AT LEAST TONIGHT.
I JUST WANT TO DRINK IN PEACE.
HERE, HAVE MY SAKE.
AND MINE!
AND MINE!
WAAAAH!

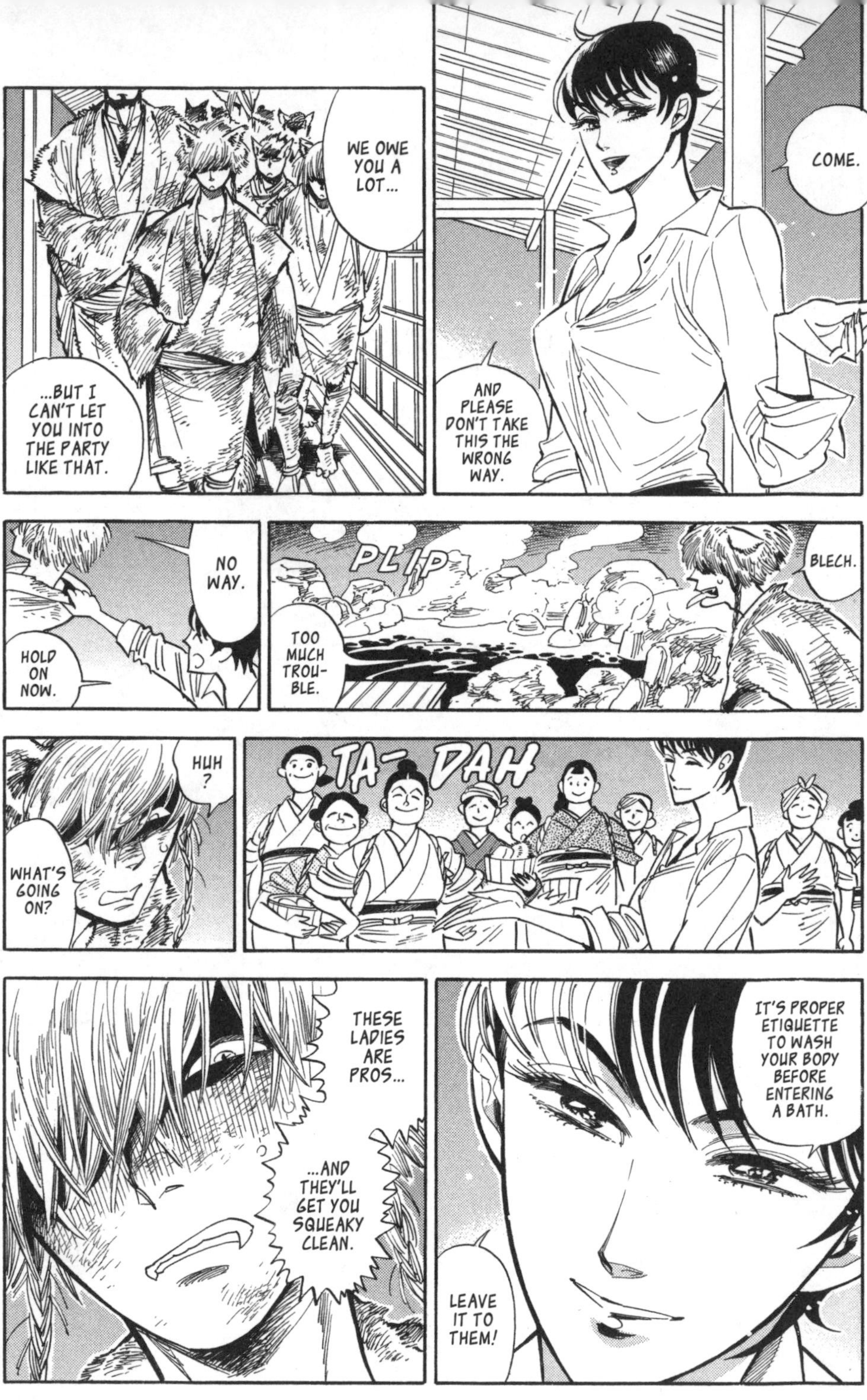
COME.
AND PLEASE DON'T TAKE THIS THE WRONG WAY.
WE OWE YOU A LOT...
...BUT I CAN'T LET YOU INTO THE PARTY LIKE THAT.
BLECH.
PLIP
TOO MUCH TROUBLE.
NO WAY.
HOLD ON NOW.
TA-DAH
HUH?
WHAT'S GOING ON?
IT'S PROPER ETIQUETTE TO WASH YOUR BODY BEFORE ENTERING A BATH.
LEAVE IT TO THEM!
THESE LADIES ARE PROS...
...AND THEY'LL GET YOU SQUEAKY CLEAN.

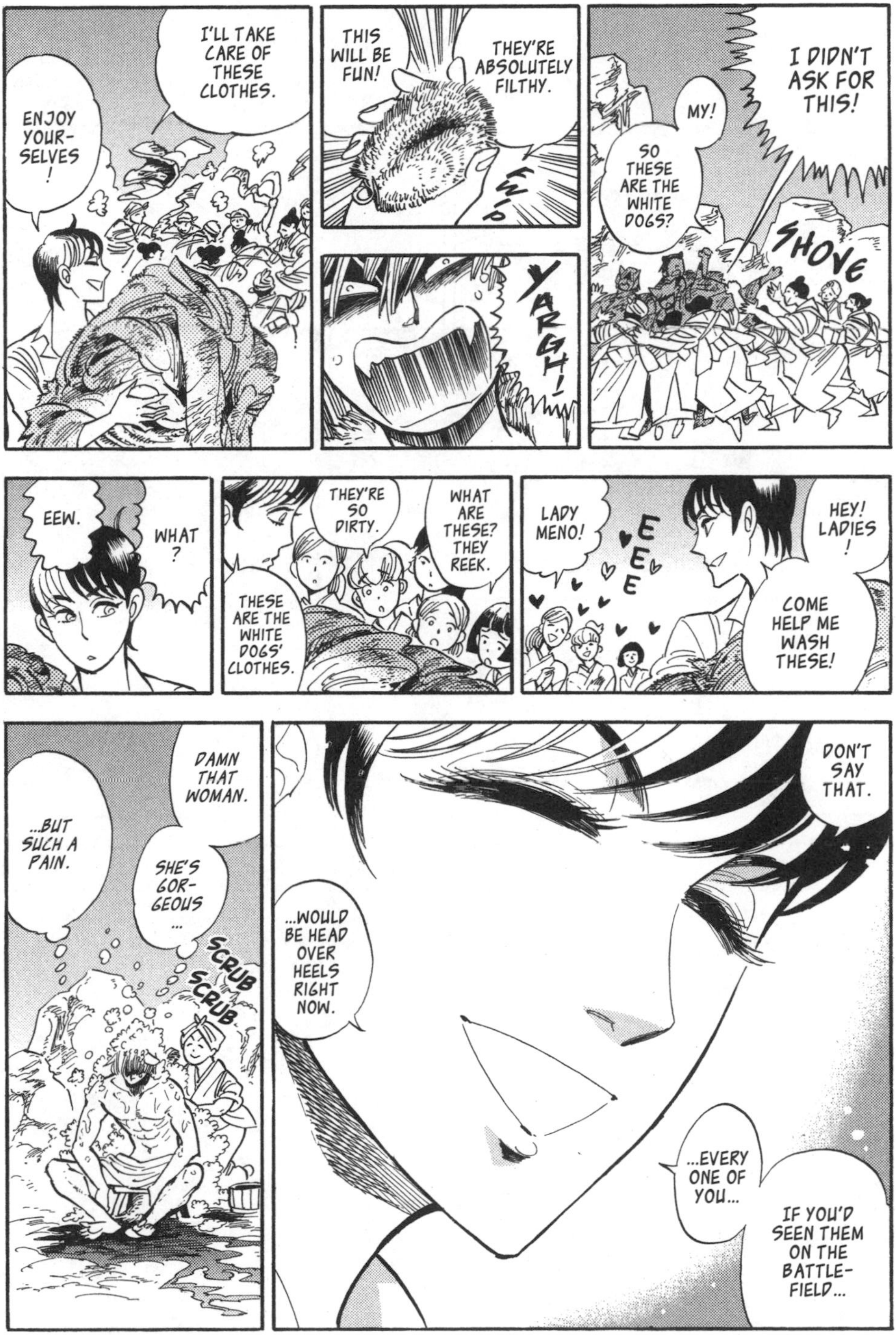
I DIDN'T ASK FOR THIS!
MY!
SO THESE ARE THE WHITE DOGS?
SHOVE
THEY'RE ABSOLUTELY FILTHY.
THIS WILL BE FUN!
FWIP
YARGH!
I'LL TAKE CARE OF THESE CLOTHES.
ENJOY YOUR-SELVES!
HEY! LADIES!
COME HELP ME WASH THESE!
LADY MENO!
EEE
WHAT ARE THESE? THEY REEK.
THEY'RE SO DIRTY.
THESE ARE THE WHITE DOGS' CLOTHES.
WHAT?
EEW.
DON'T SAY THAT.
IF YOU'D SEEN THEM ON THE BATTLE-FIELD...
...EVERY ONE OF YOU...
...WOULD BE HEAD OVER HEELS RIGHT NOW.
DAMN THAT WOMAN.
SHE'S GOR-GEOUS...
...BUT SUCH A PAIN.
SCRUB SCRUB

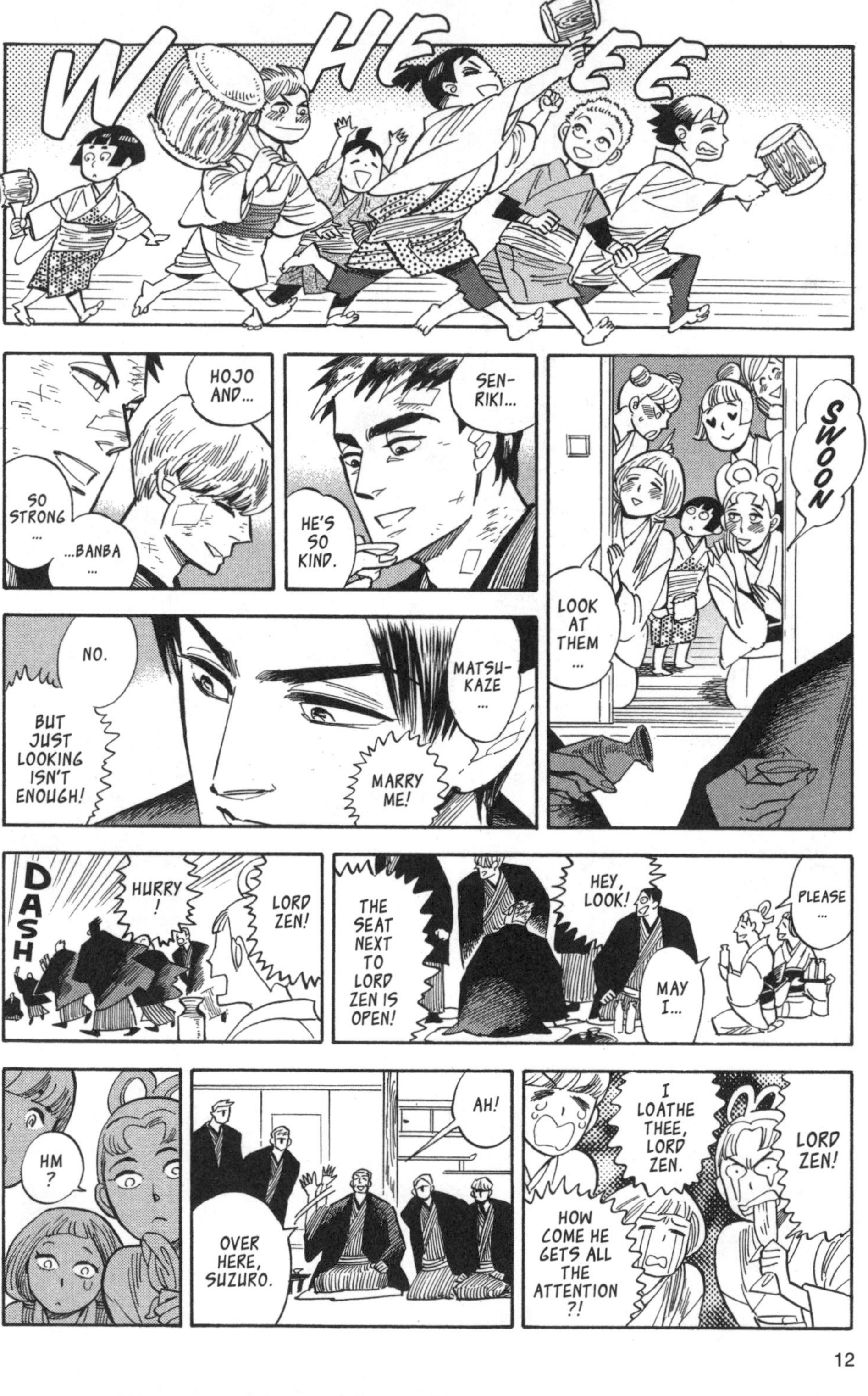
WHEEE
SWOON
LOOK AT THEM...
SEN-RIKI...
HE'S SO KIND.
HOJO AND...
SO STRONG...
...BANBA...
MATSU-KAZE...
MARRY ME!
NO.
BUT JUST LOOKING ISN'T ENOUGH!
PLEASE...
HEY, LOOK!
MAY I...
THE SEAT NEXT TO LORD ZEN IS OPEN!
LORD ZEN!
HURRY!
DASH
LORD ZEN!
I LOATHE THEE, LORD ZEN.
HOW COME HE GETS ALL THE ATTENTION?!
AH!
OVER HERE, SUZURO.
HM?

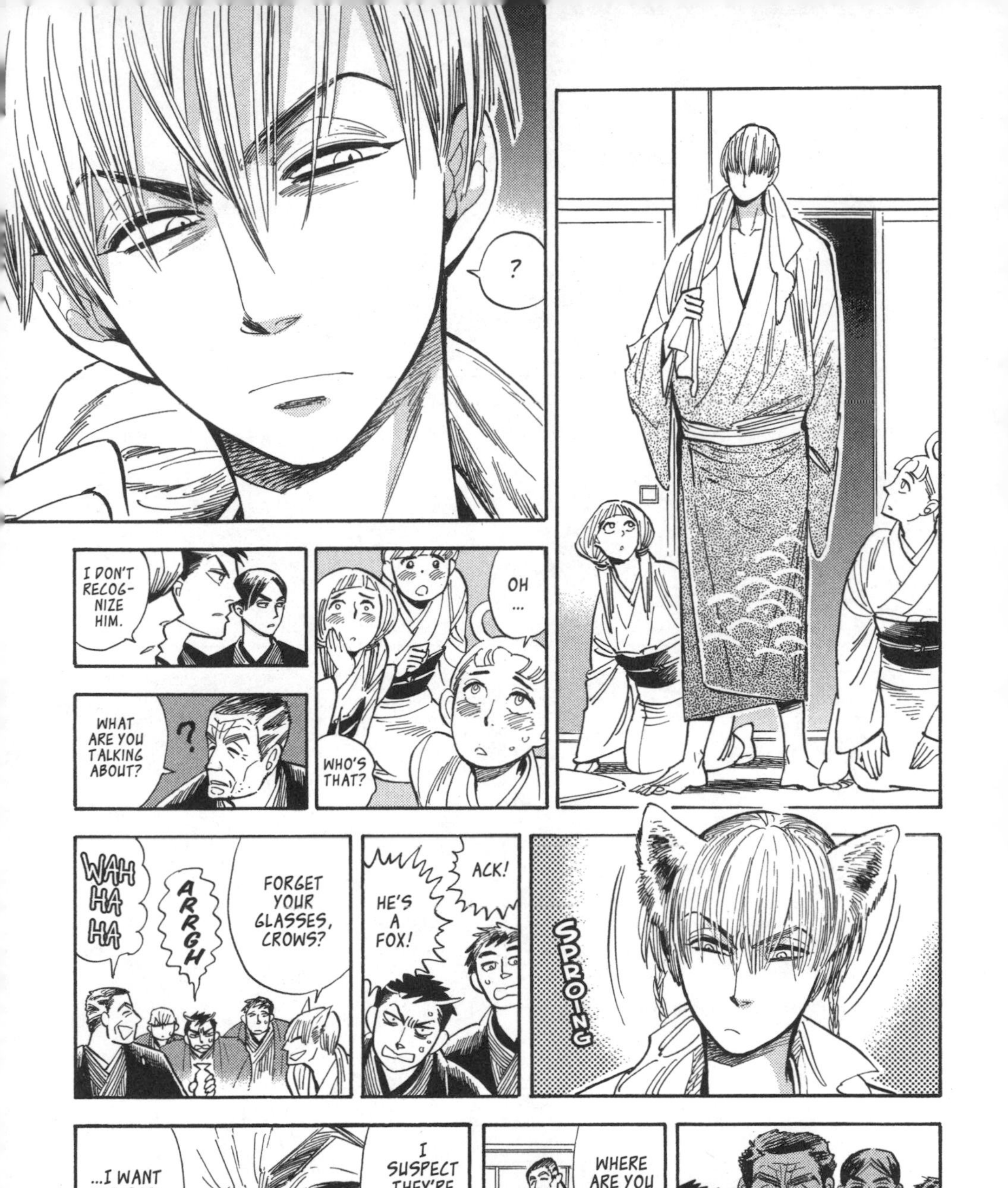
?
OH ...
WHO'S THAT?
I DON'T RECOG-NIZE HIM.
?
WHAT ARE YOU TALKING ABOUT?
SPROING
ACK!
HE'S A FOX!
FORGET YOUR GLASSES, CROWS?
ARRGH
WAH HA HA
WE COULDN'T HAVE DONE IT WITHOUT THE WHITE DOGS.
PLEASE, RELAX AND ENJOY YOUR-SELVES.
WHERE ARE YOU GOING?
I'LL BE RIGHT BACK.
I SUSPECT THEY'RE ASLEEP BY NOW, BUT...
...I WANT TO SEE MY KIDS.

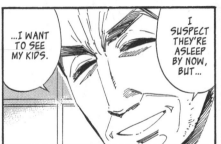

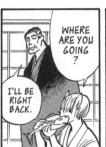

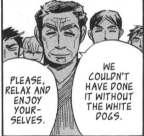

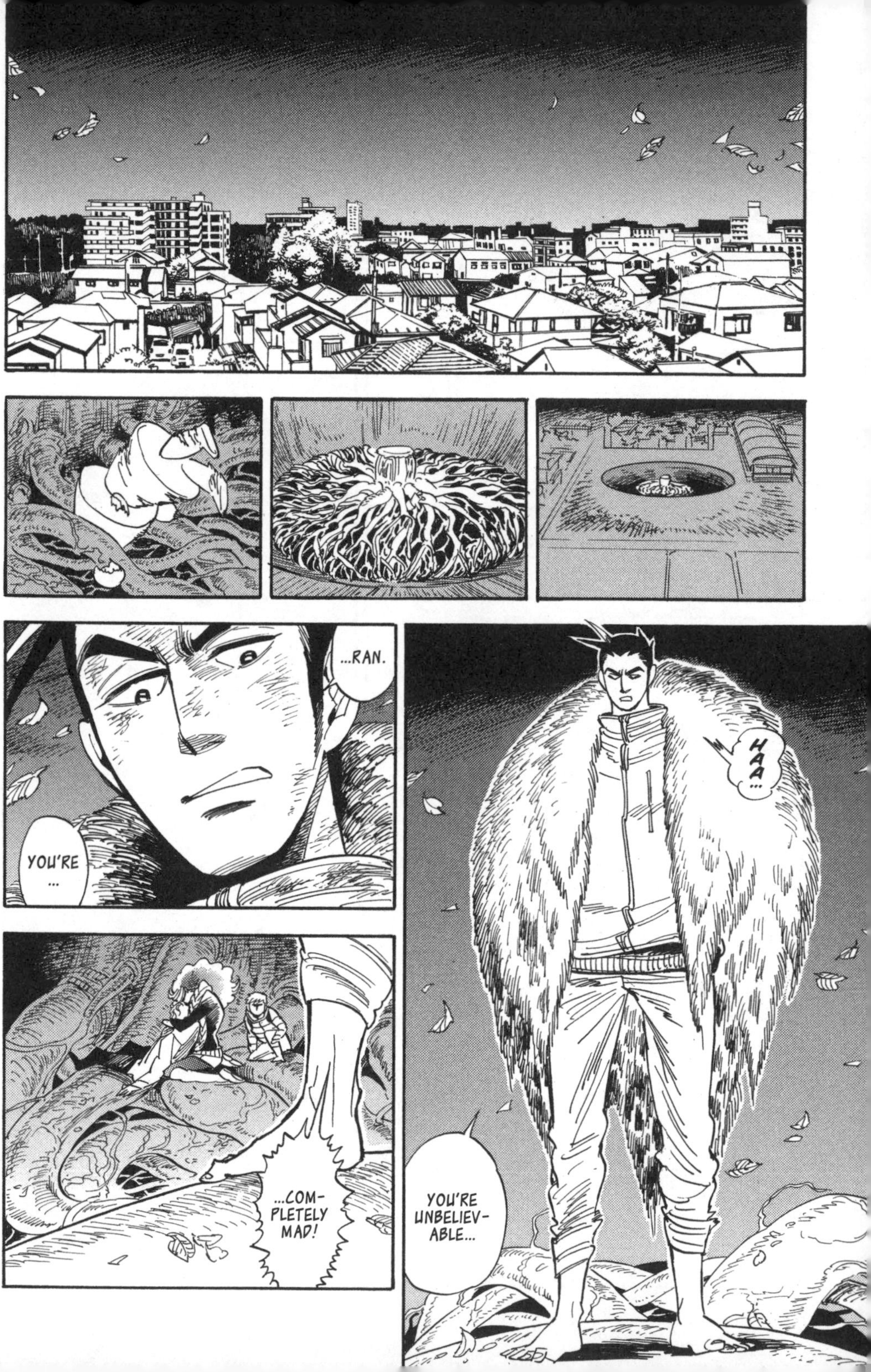
HAA...
YOU'RE UNBELIEV-ABLE...
...RAN.
YOU'RE ...
...COM-PLETELY MAD!

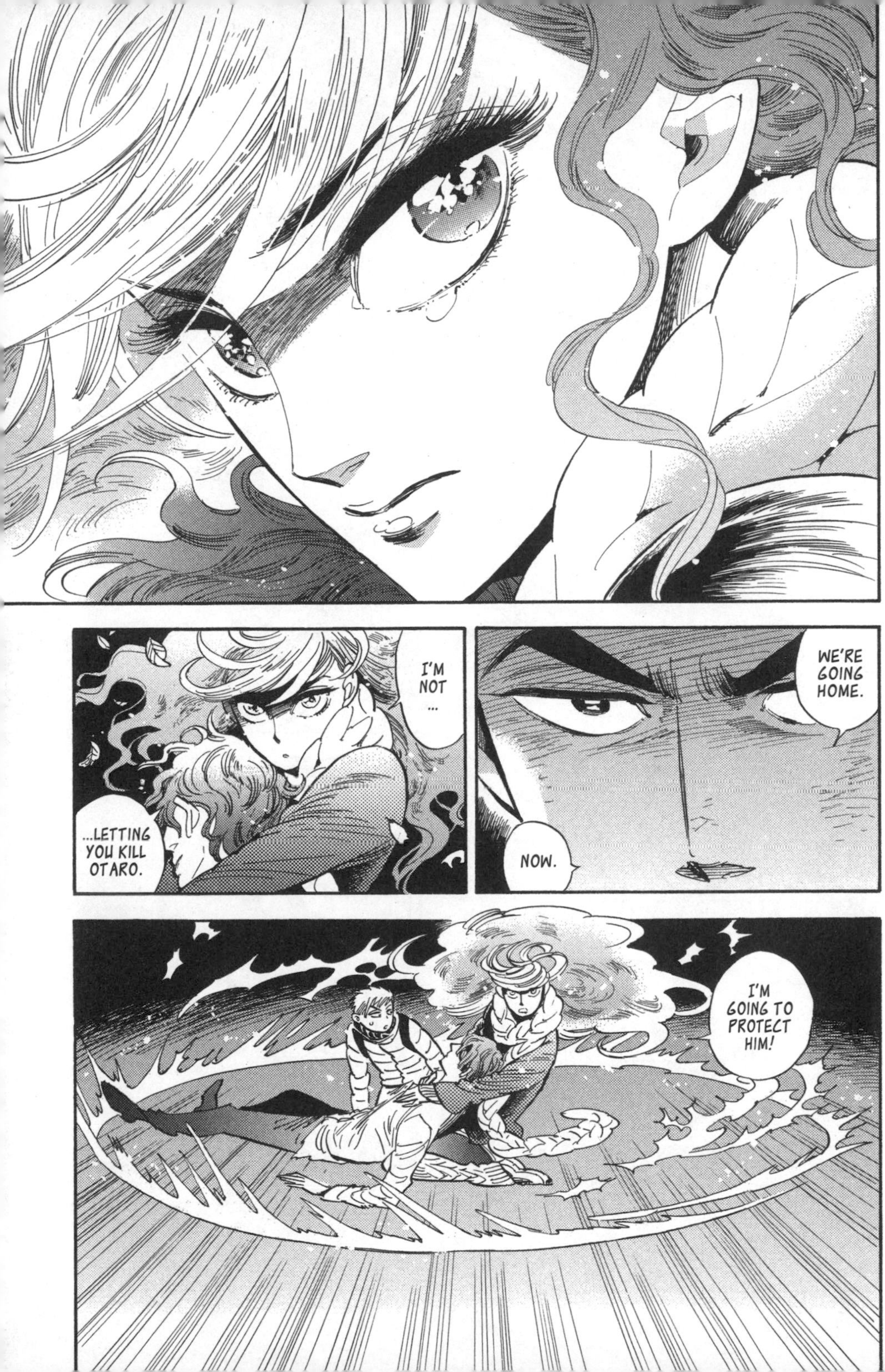
WE'RE GOING HOME.
NOW.
I'M NOT ...
...LETTING YOU KILL OTARO.
I'M GOING TO PROTECT HIM!

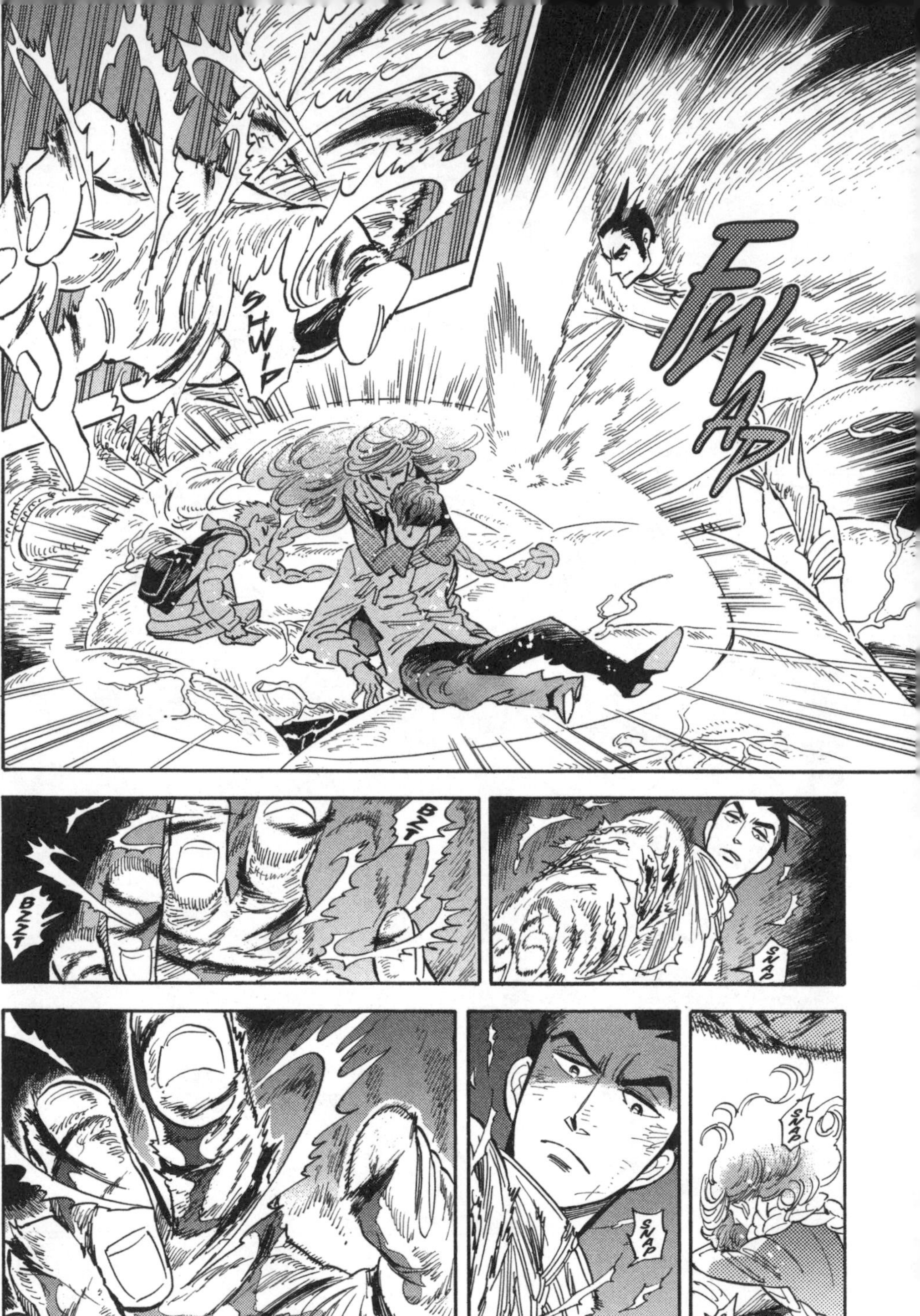
FWAP
SHWAP
SNAP
BZZT
BZZT
SNAP
SNAP
SNAP

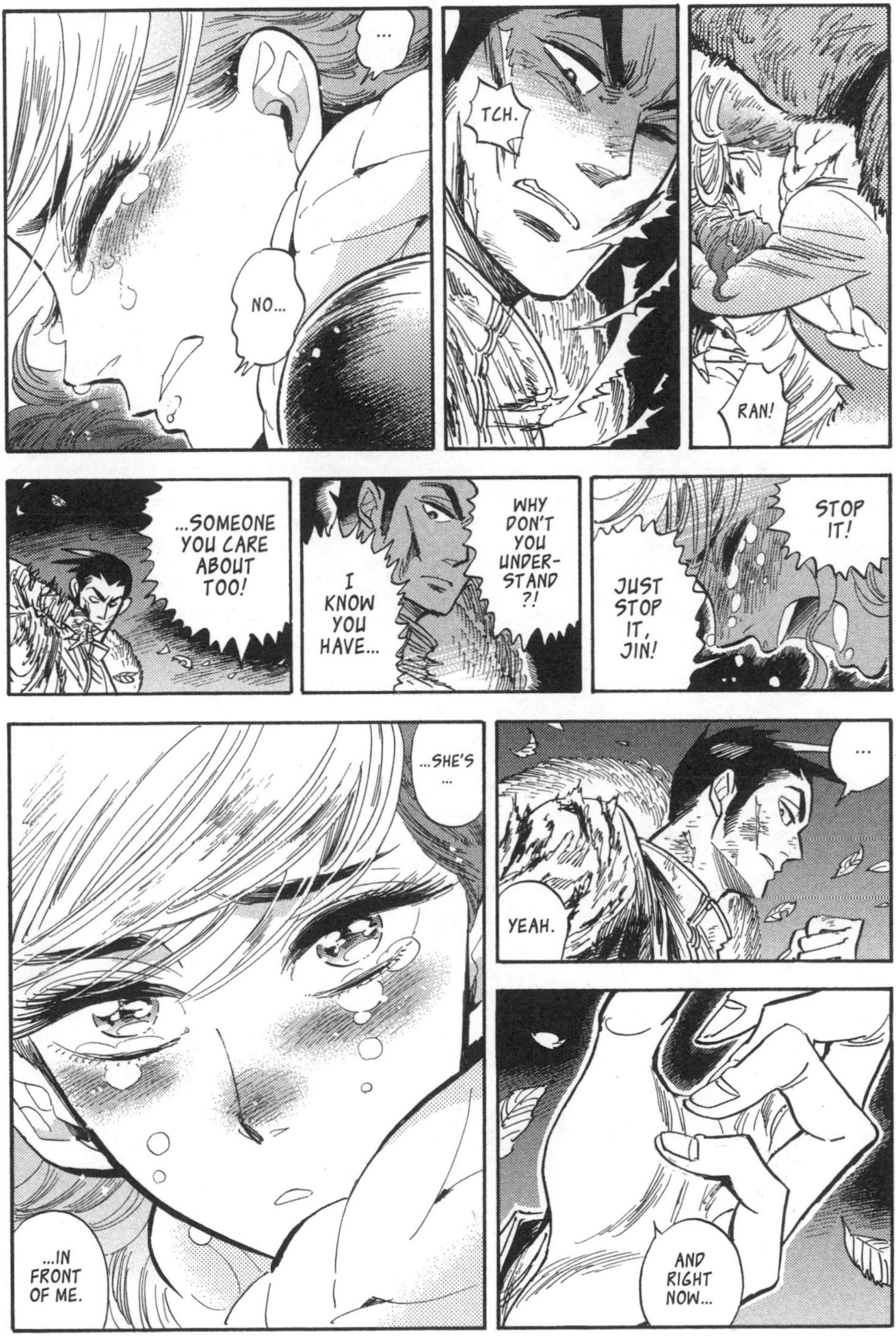
RAN!
TCH.
...
NO...
STOP IT!
JUST STOP IT, JIN!
WHY DON'T YOU UNDERSTAND?!
I KNOW YOU HAVE...
...SOMEONE YOU CARE ABOUT TOO!
...
YEAH.
AND RIGHT NOW...
...SHE'S...
...IN FRONT OF ME.

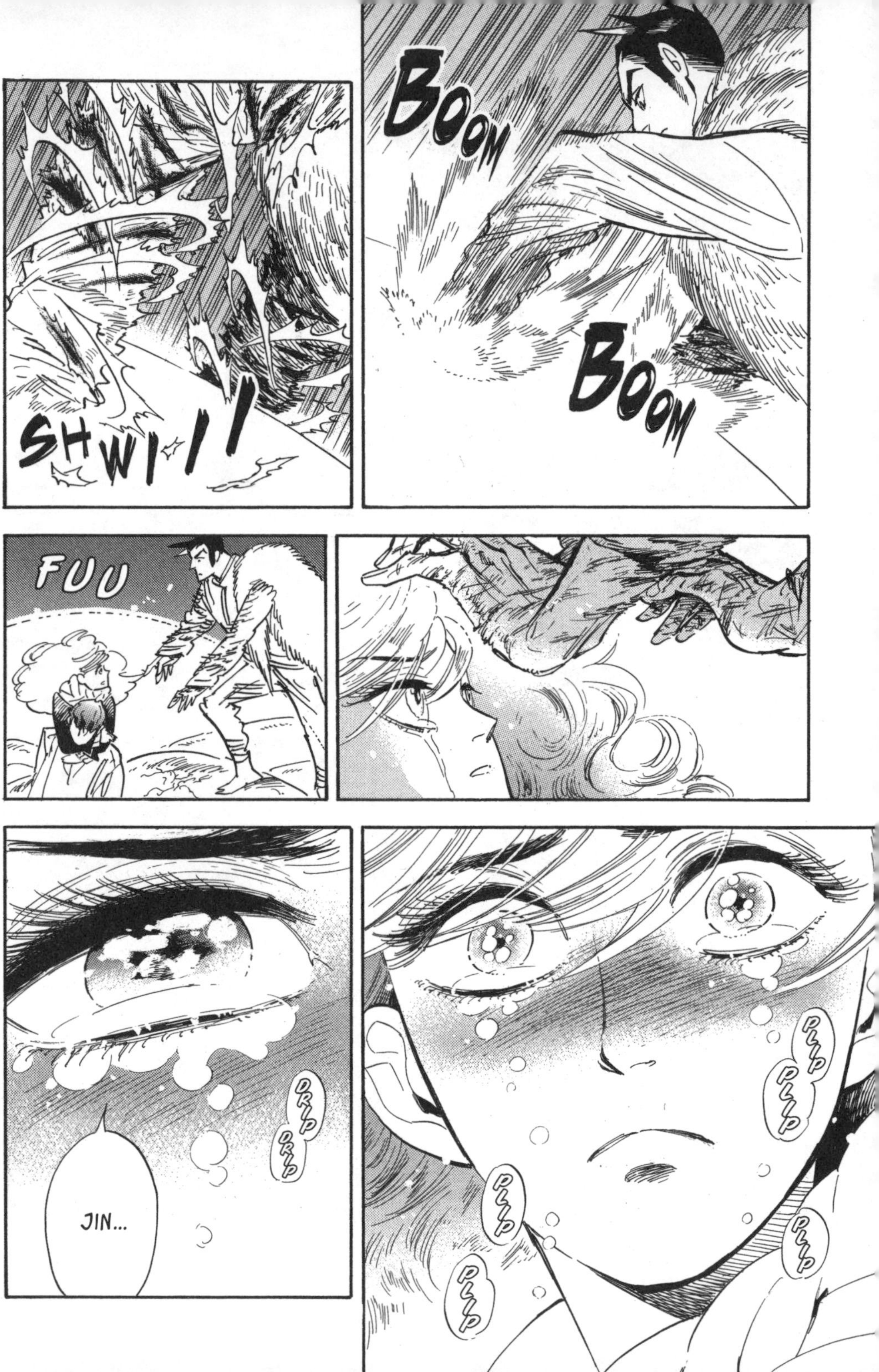
BOOM
BOOM
SHWI!!
FUU
PLIP PLIP
PLIP
PLIP
PLIP
DRIP DRIP
JIN...

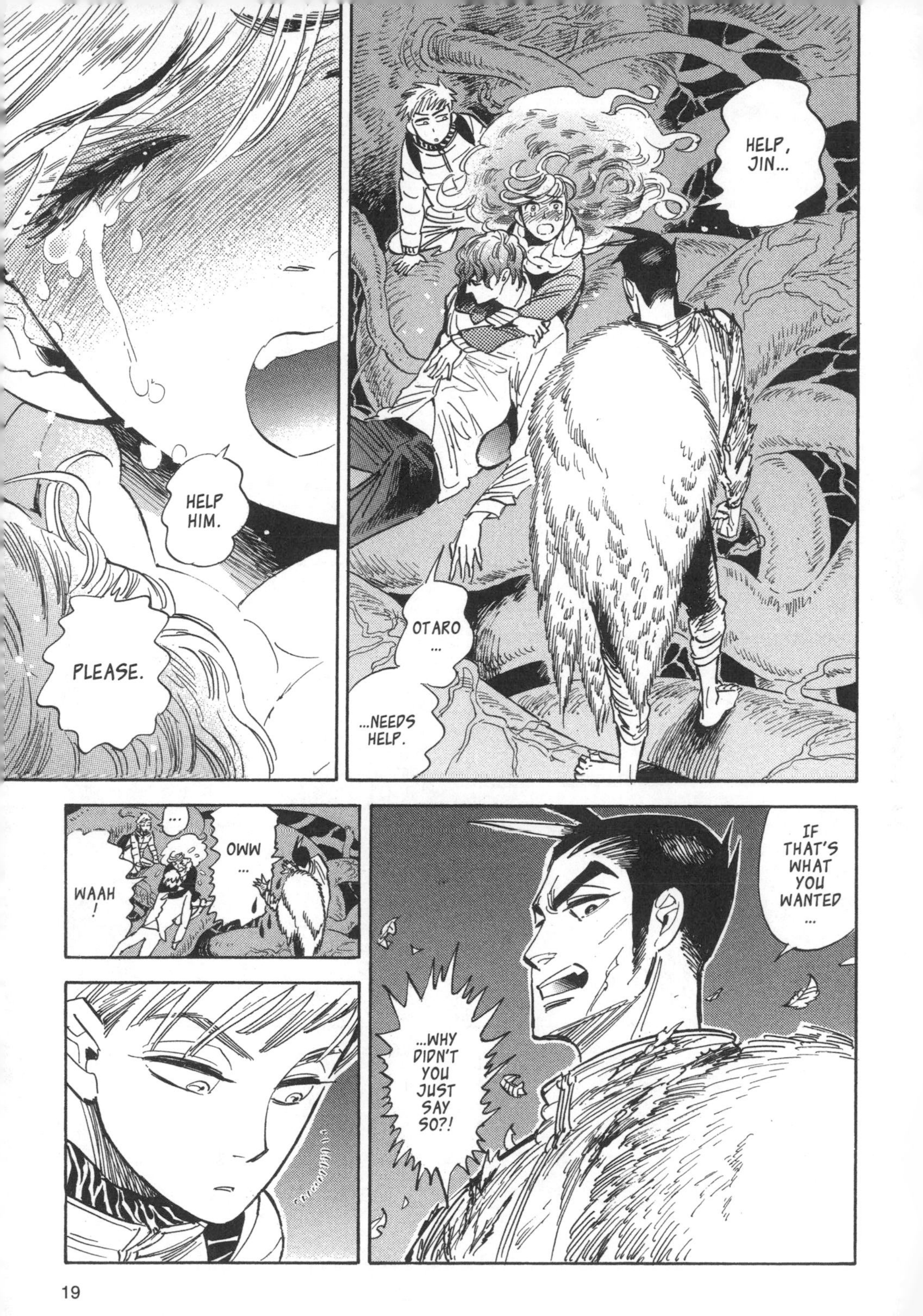
HELP, JIN...
OTARO ...
...NEEDS HELP.
HELP HIM.
PLEASE.
IF THAT'S WHAT YOU WANTED ...
...WHY DIDN'T YOU JUST SAY SO?!
...
OWW ...
WAAH !

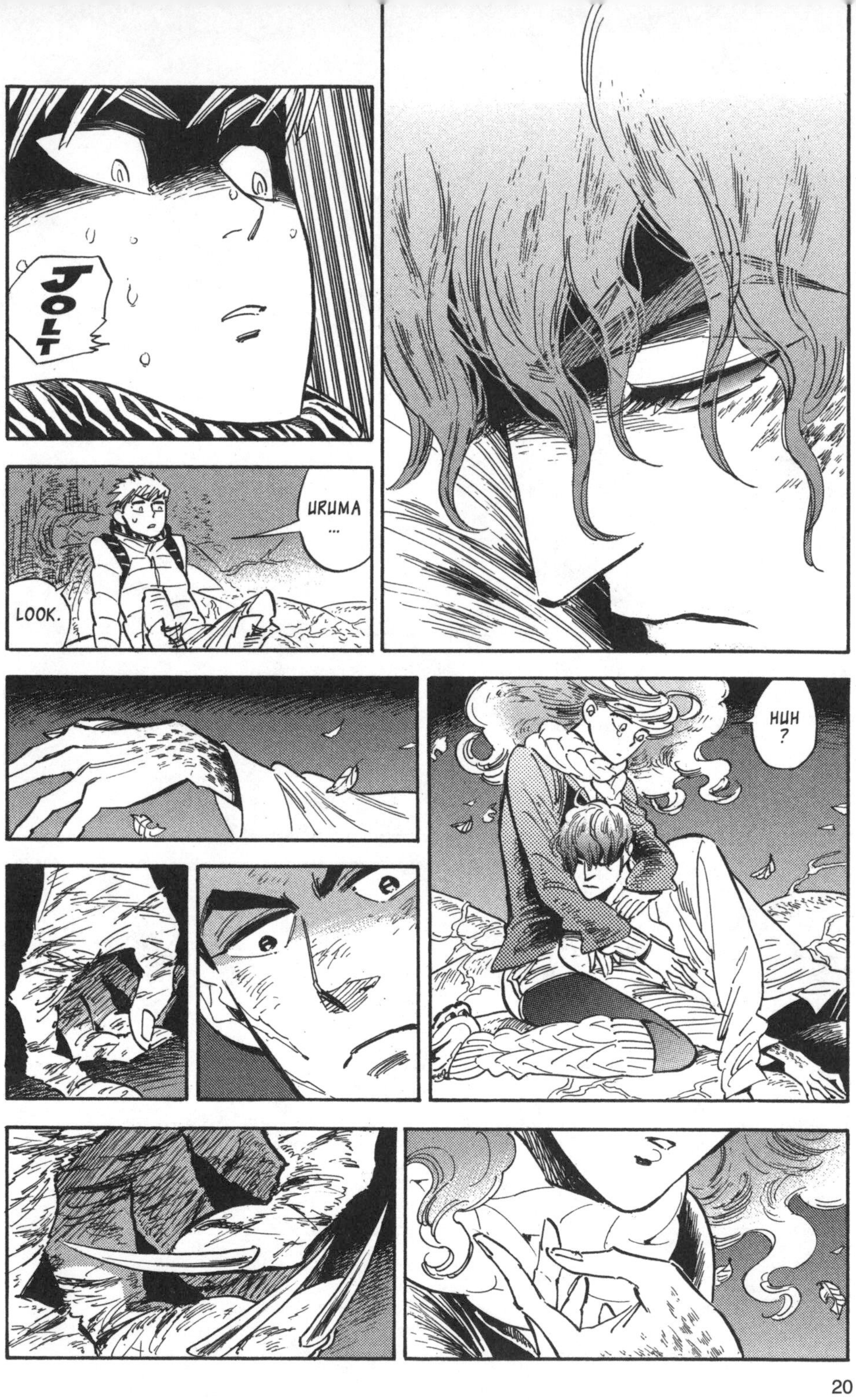
JOLT
URUMA ...
LOOK.
HUH ?

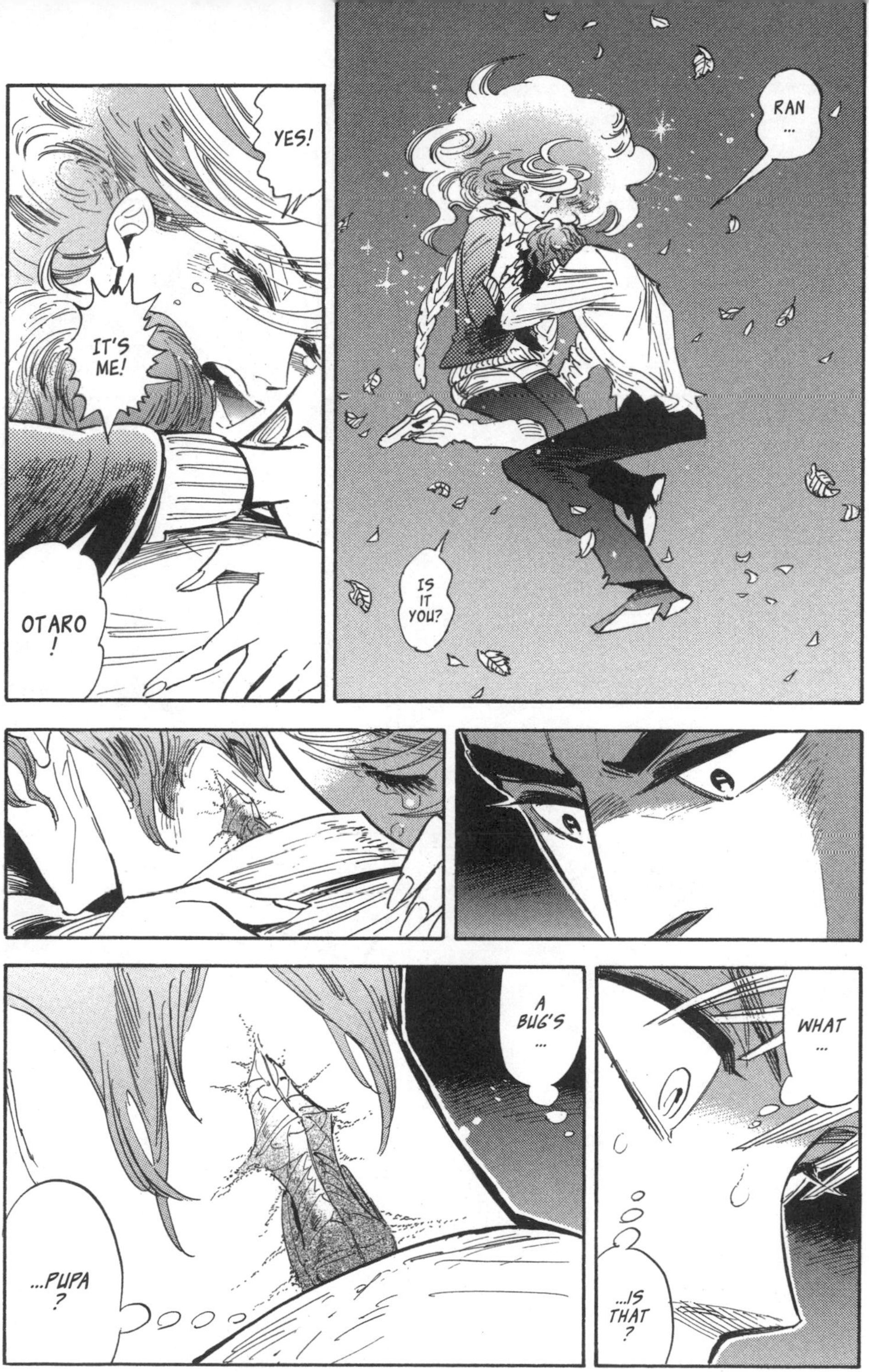
RAN ...
IS IT YOU?
YES!
IT'S ME!
OTARO!
WHAT ...
...IS THAT ?
A BUG'S ...
...PUPA ?

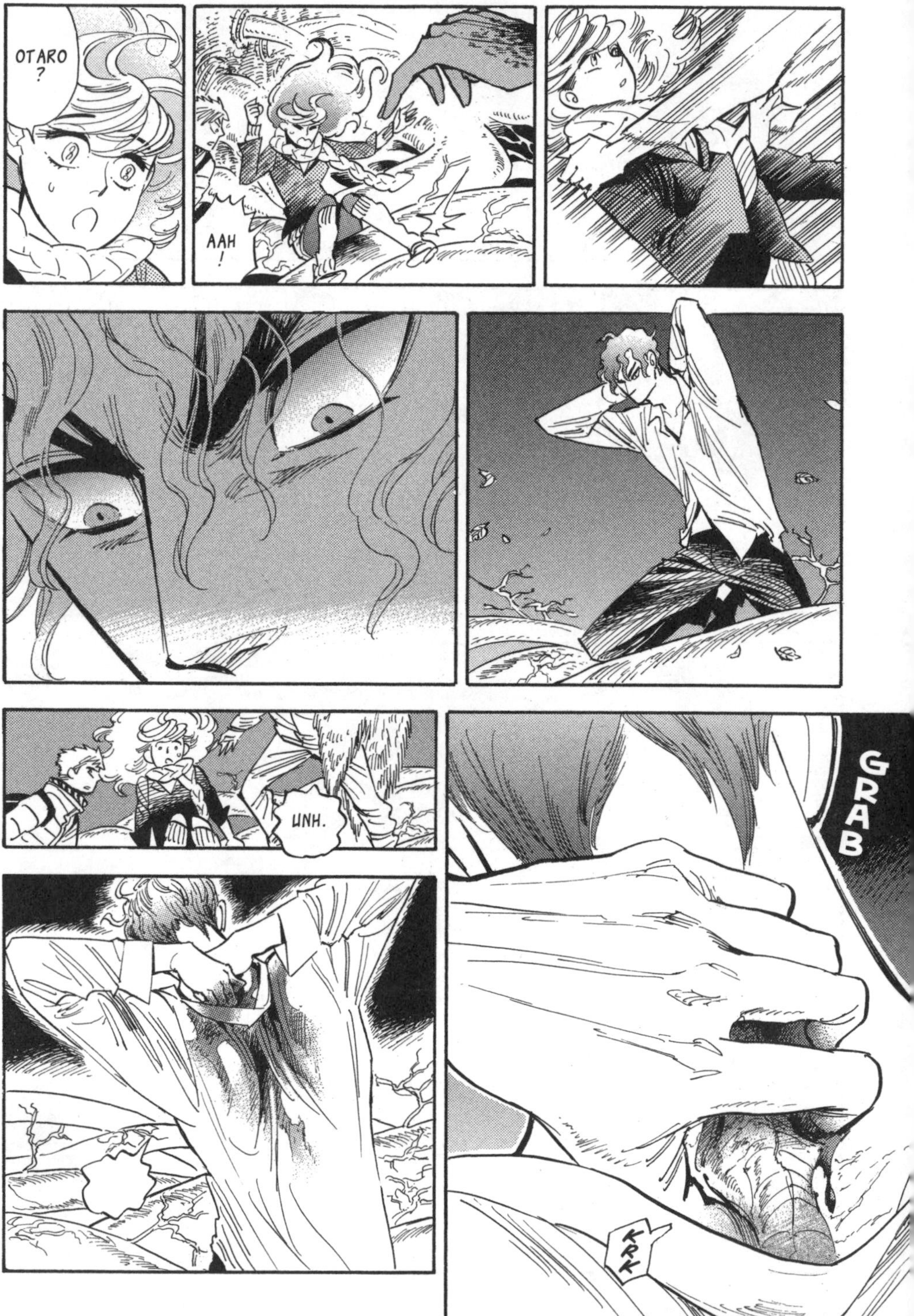
AAH!
OTARO?
GRAB
KRK
UNH.

ZRCH
NGH!
RRIP
RRP
RRP
RRP
UHN...
RRP
NN...
UHN...
NHN...
NGH...

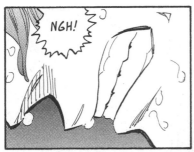

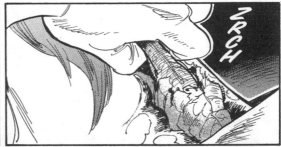

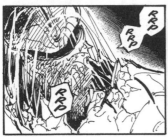

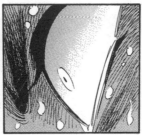

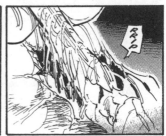

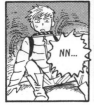

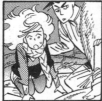

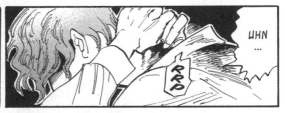

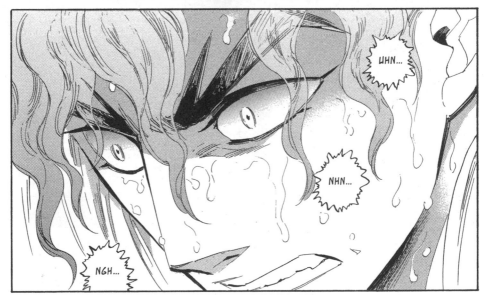

GRRAH!

AA...

AAH!

UNGH.

...

HAA...

HAA...

HAA...

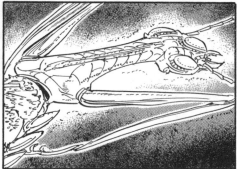

RAN...

WAIT!

OTARO...

24

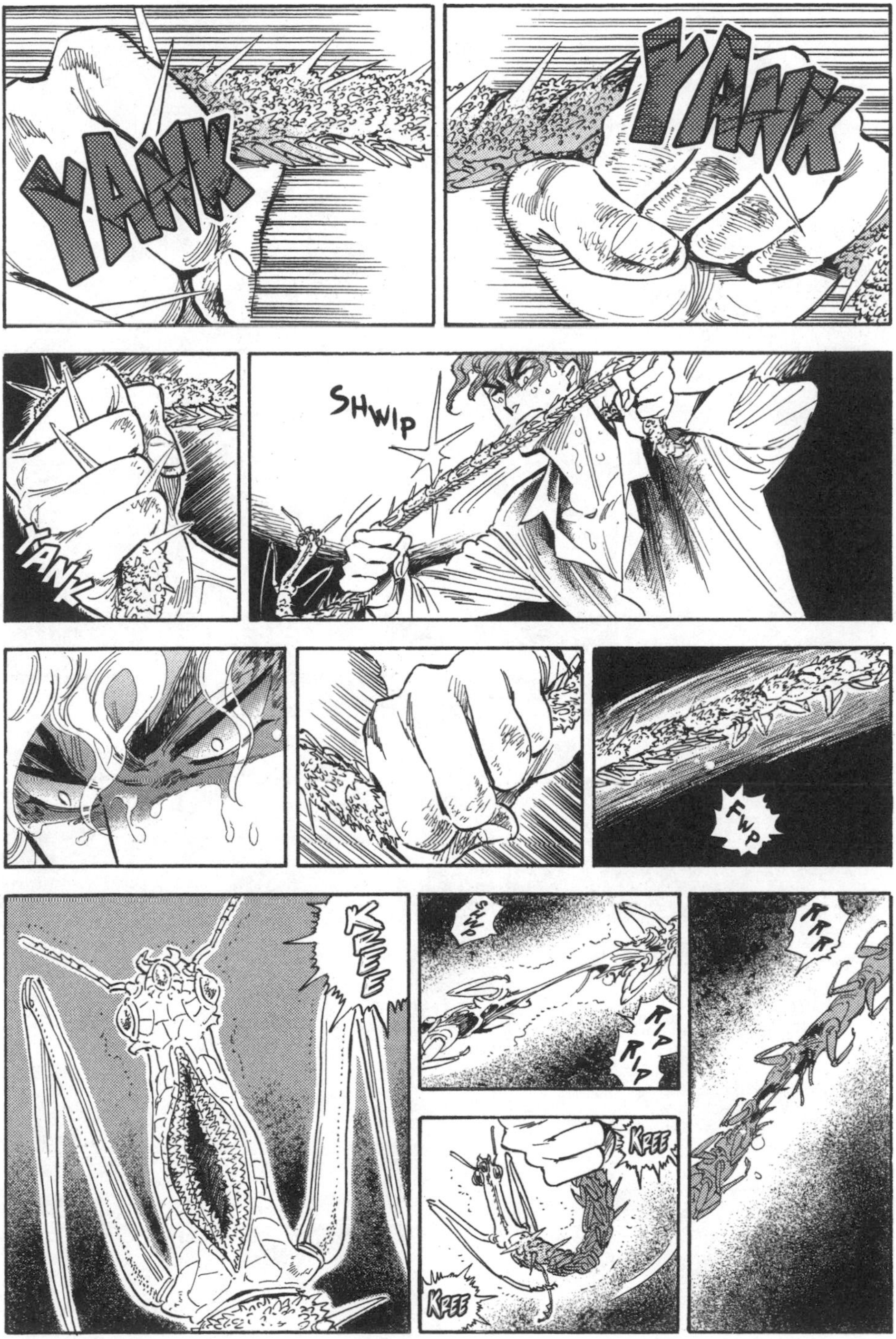
YANK
YANK
SHWIP
YANK
FWP
RRR
SHWP
RIP
RIP
KREE
KREE
KREEE

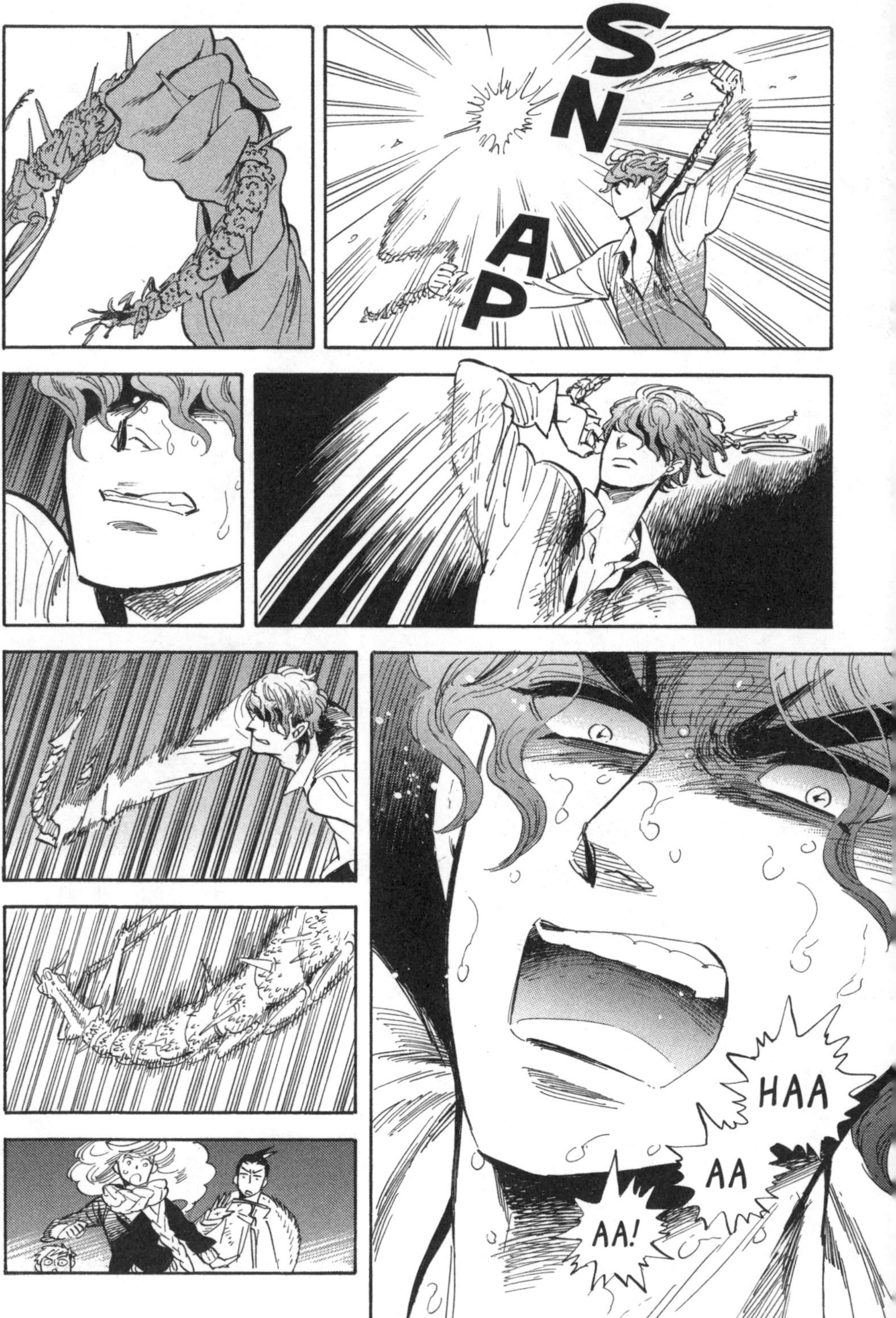
SNAP
HAA
AA
AA!

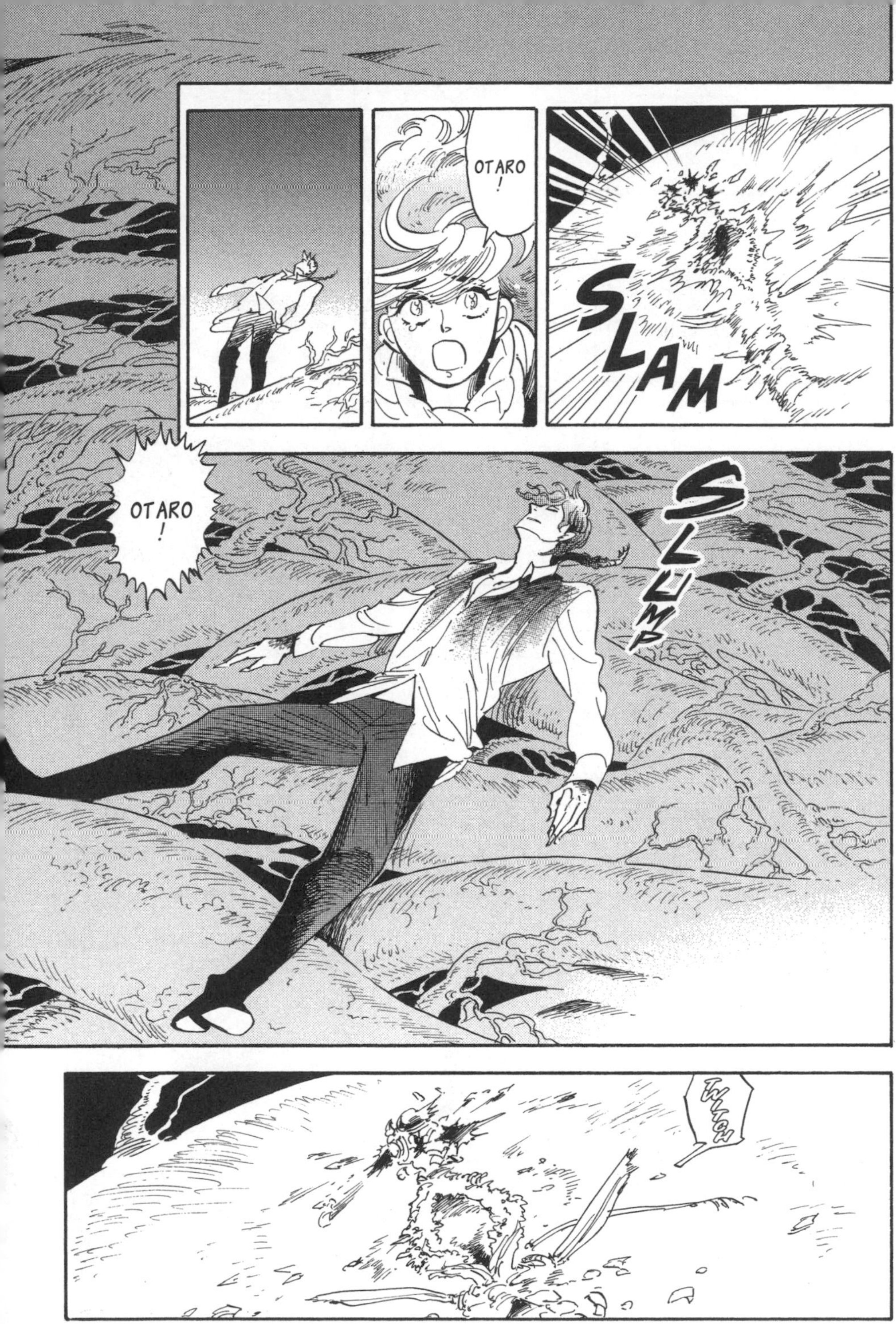
SLAM
OTARO!
OTARO!
SLUMP
TWITCH

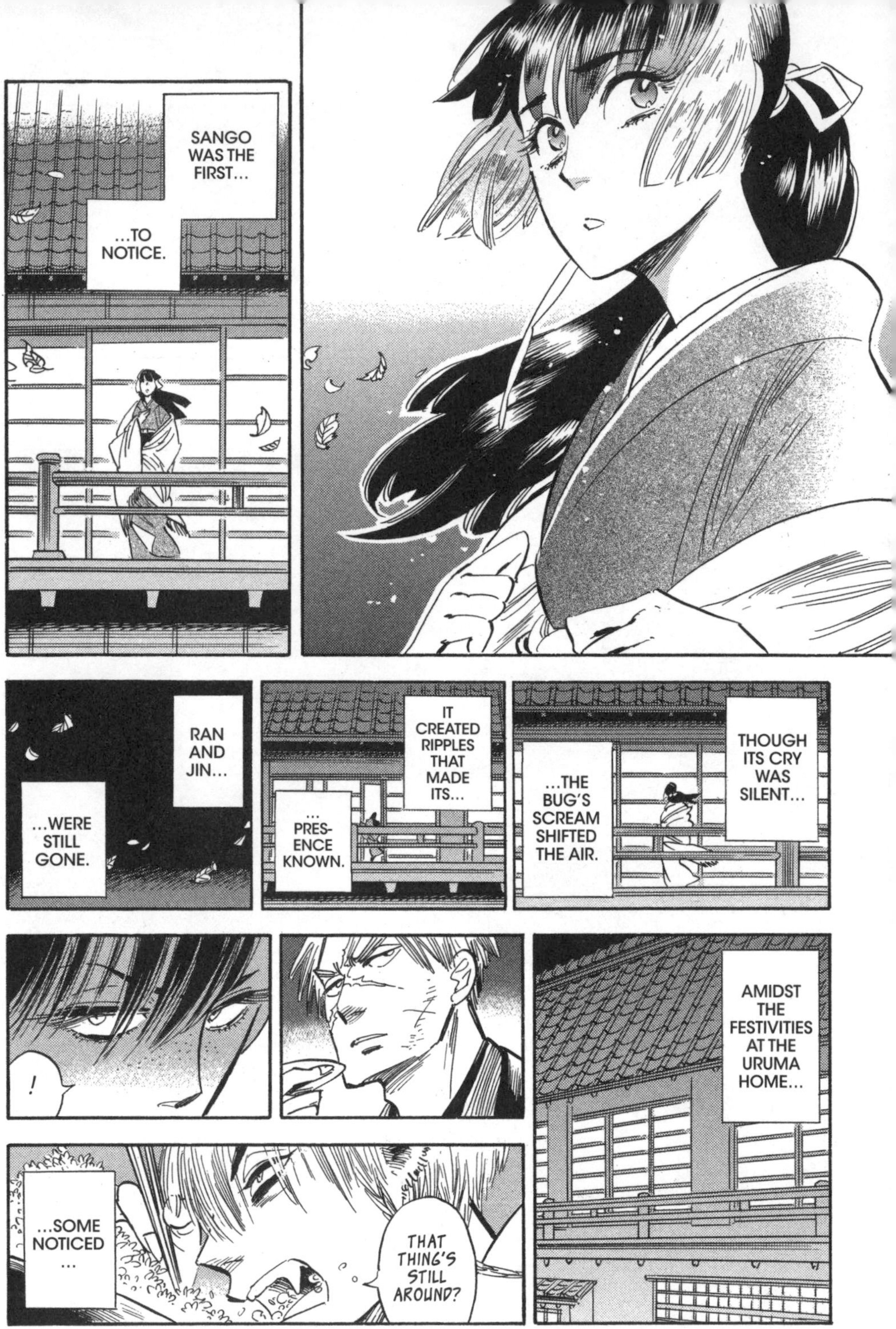
SANGO WAS THE FIRST...
...TO NOTICE.
THOUGH ITS CRY WAS SILENT...
...THE BUG'S SCREAM SHIFTED THE AIR.
IT CREATED RIPPLES THAT MADE ITS...
...PRESENCE KNOWN.
RAN AND JIN...
...WERE STILL GONE.
AMIDST THE FESTIVITIES AT THE URUMA HOME...
!
...SOME NOTICED...
THAT THING'S STILL AROUND?

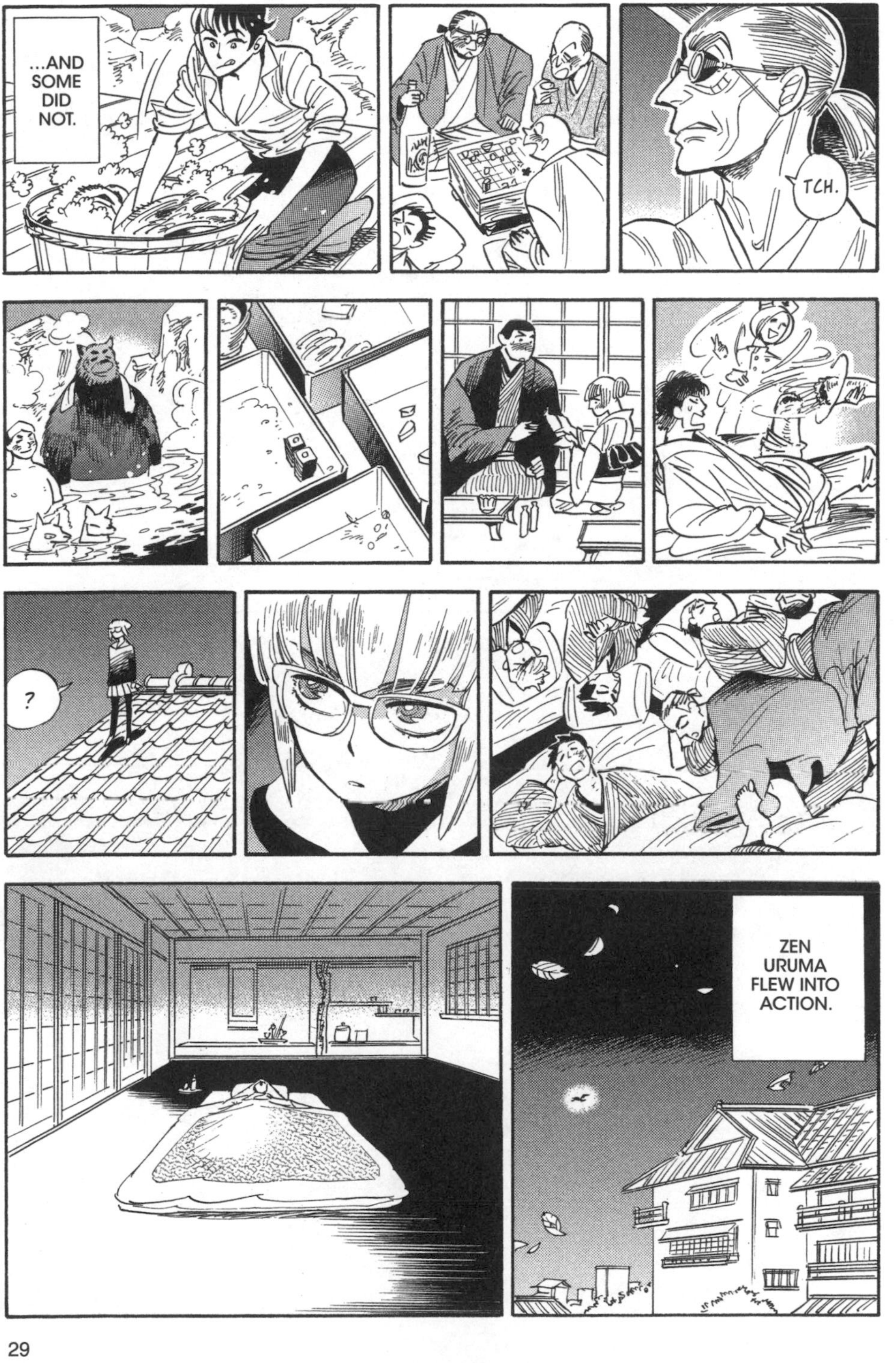
TCH.
...AND SOME DID NOT.
?
ZEN URUMA FLEW INTO ACTION.

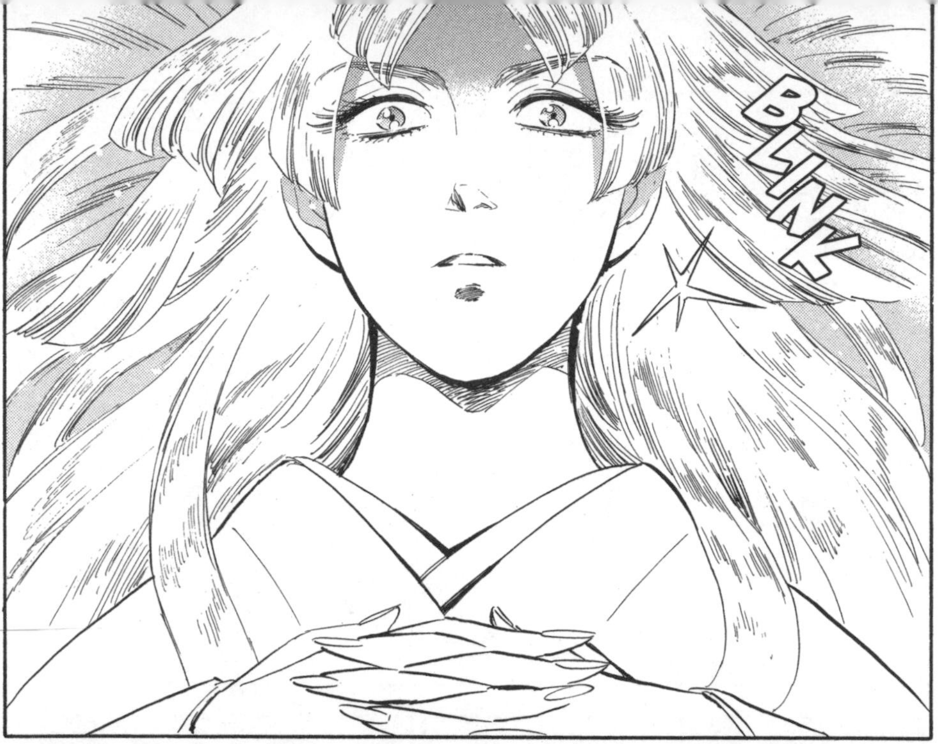
BLINK

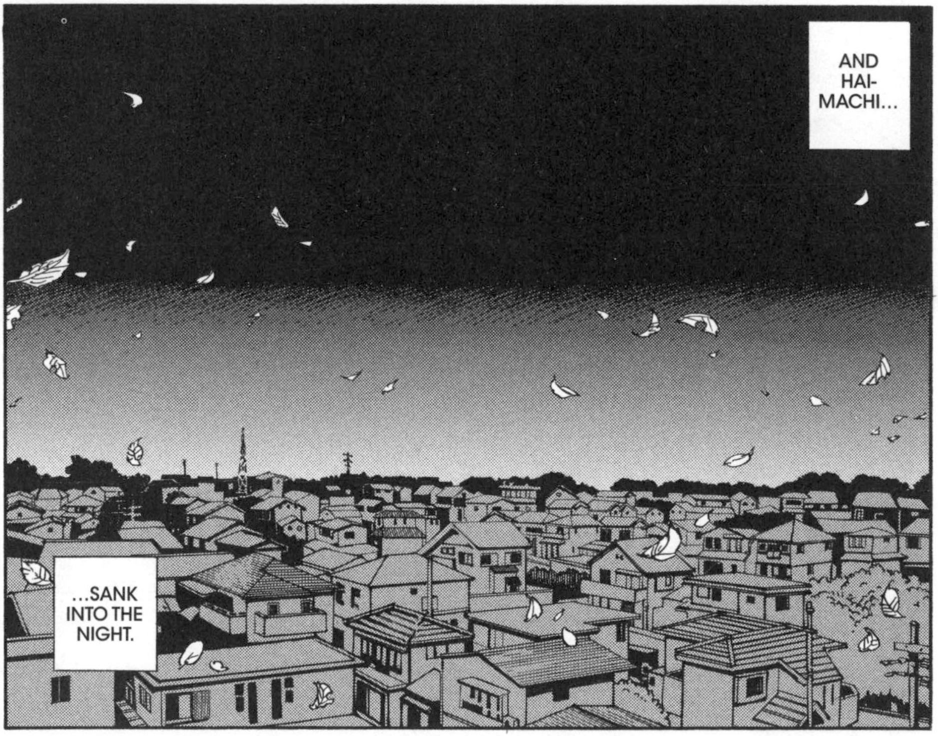
AND HAI-MACHI...
...SANK INTO THE NIGHT.

Chapter 30 / The End

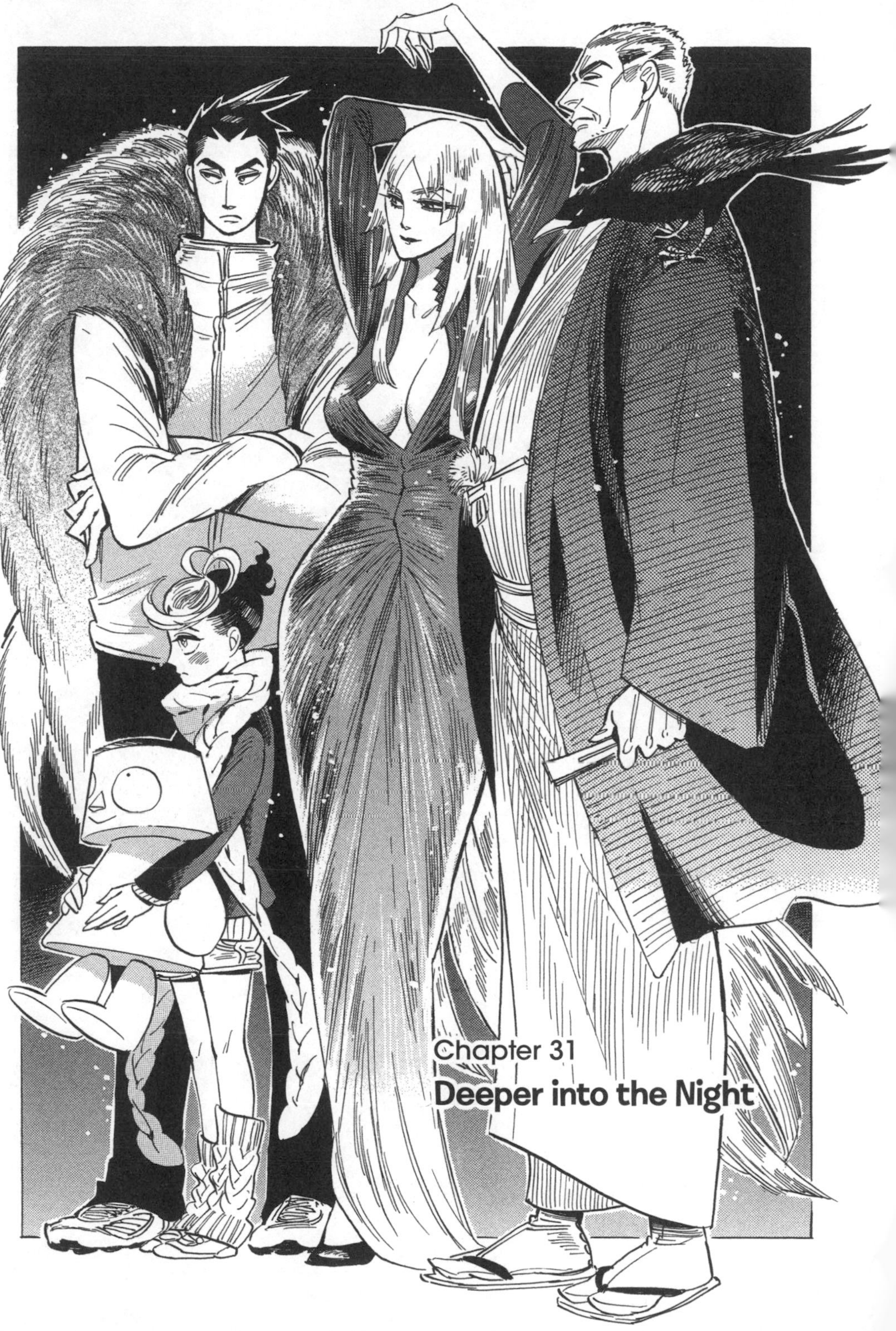

Chapter 31
Deeper into the Night

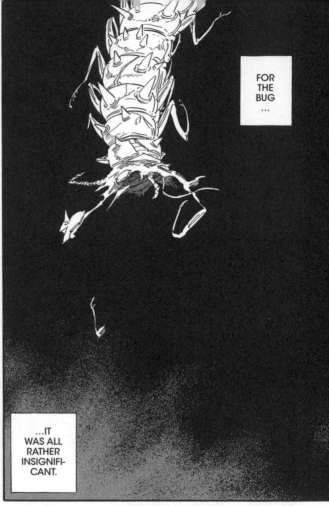

FOR THE BUG ...
...IT WAS ALL RATHER INSIGNIFICANT.
A SEVERED BODY...
... COULD ...
...EASILY REGENERATE.
AND EVEN IF ITS HOST RETAINED ...
...ITS CONSCIOUSNESS...
...THAT COULD ...
...EASILY BE ERASED AGAIN.

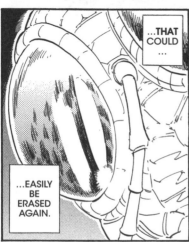

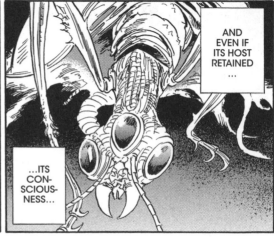

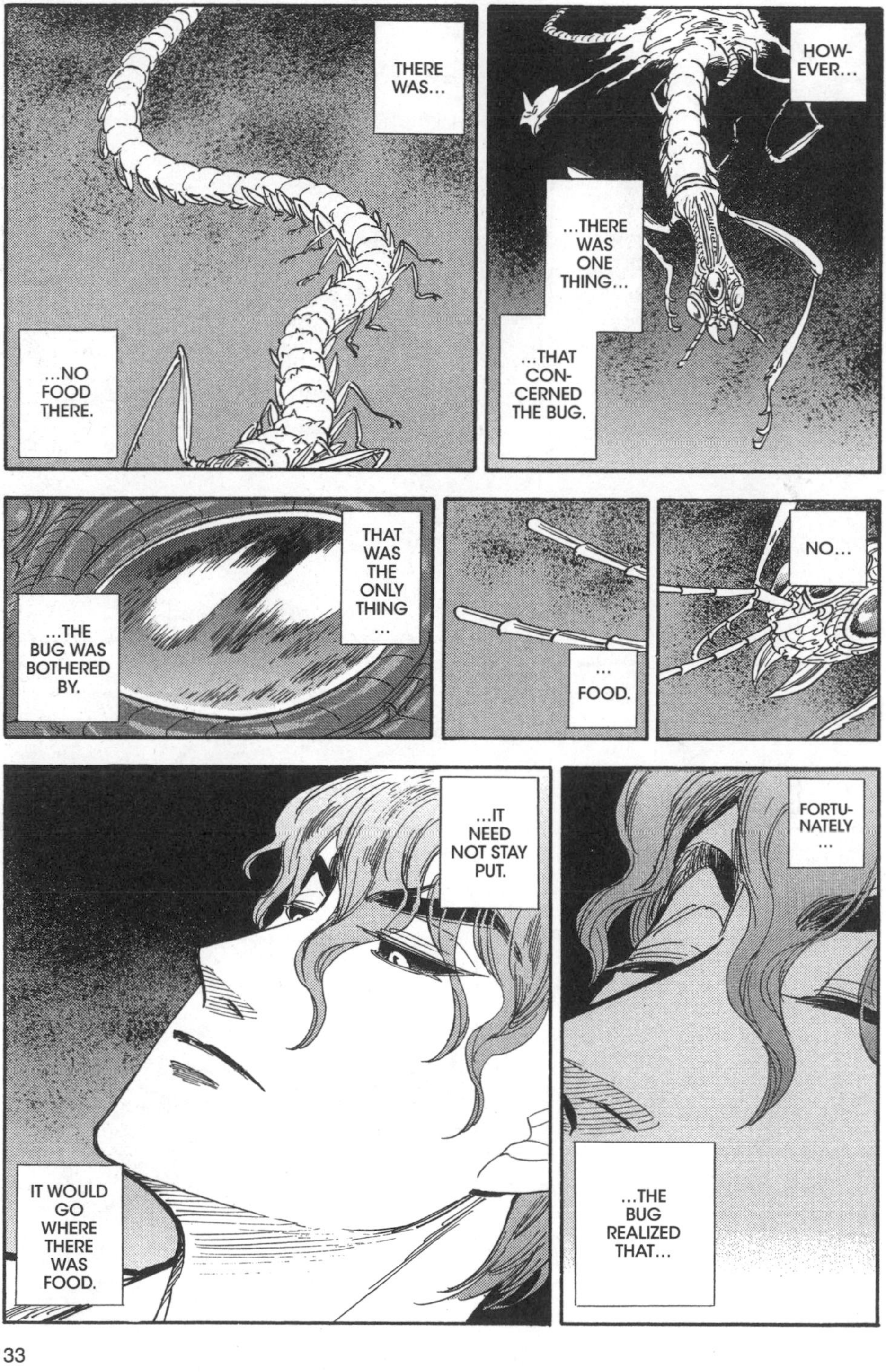
HOW-EVER…
…THERE WAS ONE THING…
…THAT CON-CERNED THE BUG.
THERE WAS…
…NO FOOD THERE.
NO…
… FOOD.
THAT WAS THE ONLY THING …
…THE BUG WAS BOTHERED BY.
FORTU-NATELY …
…THE BUG REALIZED THAT…
…IT NEED NOT STAY PUT.
IT WOULD GO WHERE THERE WAS FOOD.

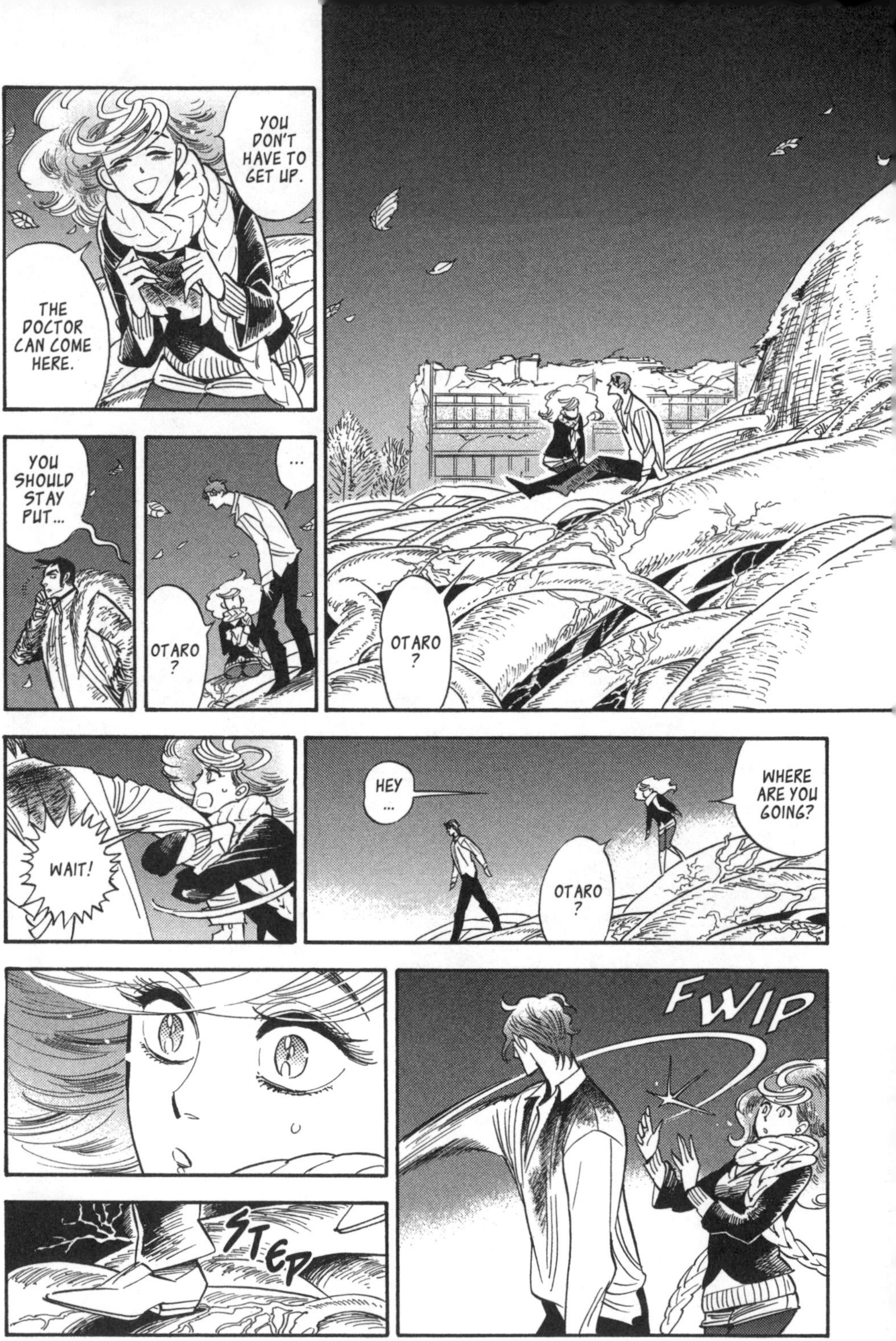
OTARO?
YOU DON'T HAVE TO GET UP.
THE DOCTOR CAN COME HERE.
...
OTARO?
YOU SHOULD STAY PUT...
WHERE ARE YOU GOING?
HEY ...
OTARO?
WAIT!
FWIP
STEP

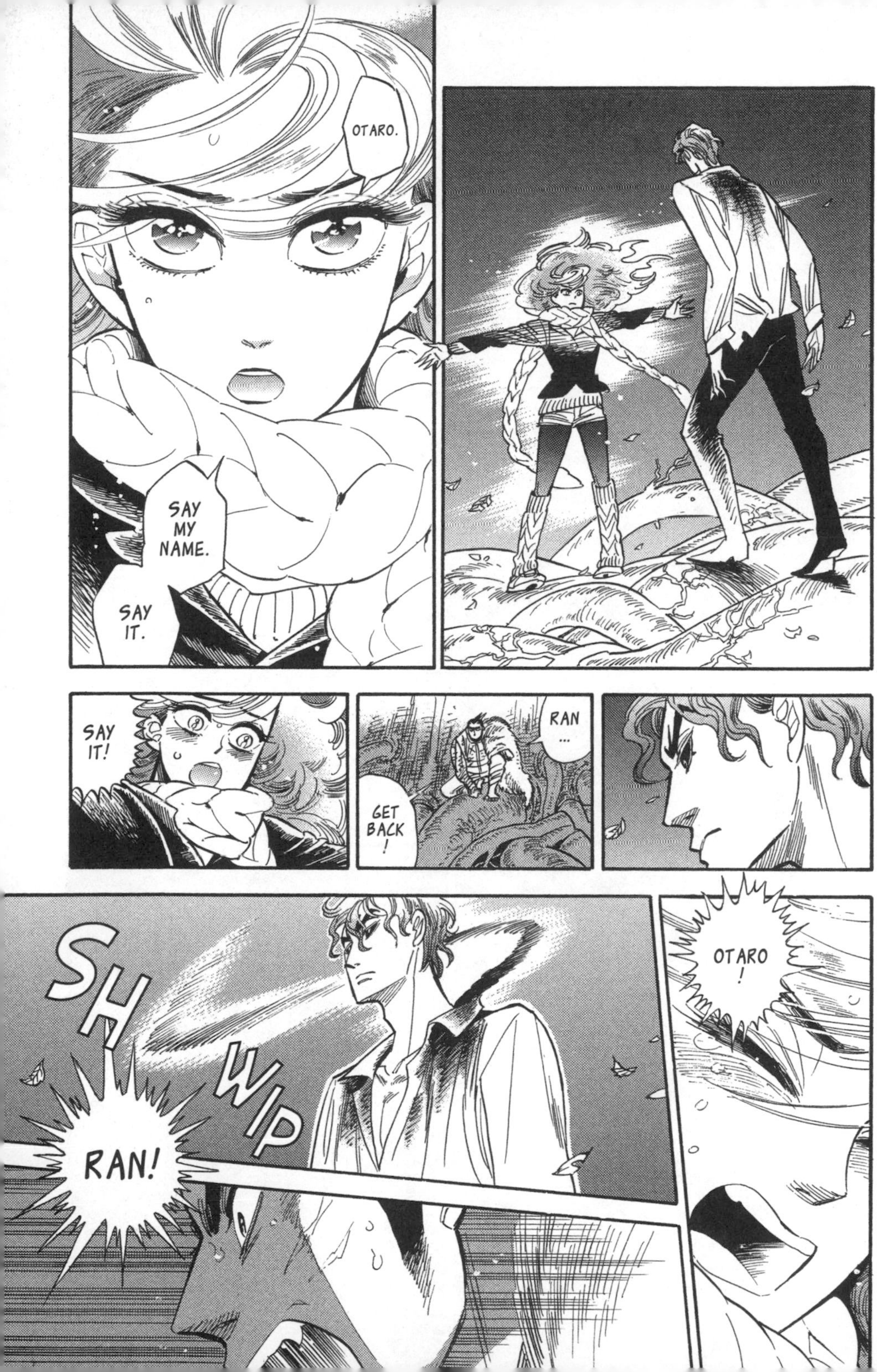
OTARO.
SAY MY NAME.
SAY IT.
RAN ...
GET BACK!
SAY IT!
OTARO!
SHWIP
RAN!

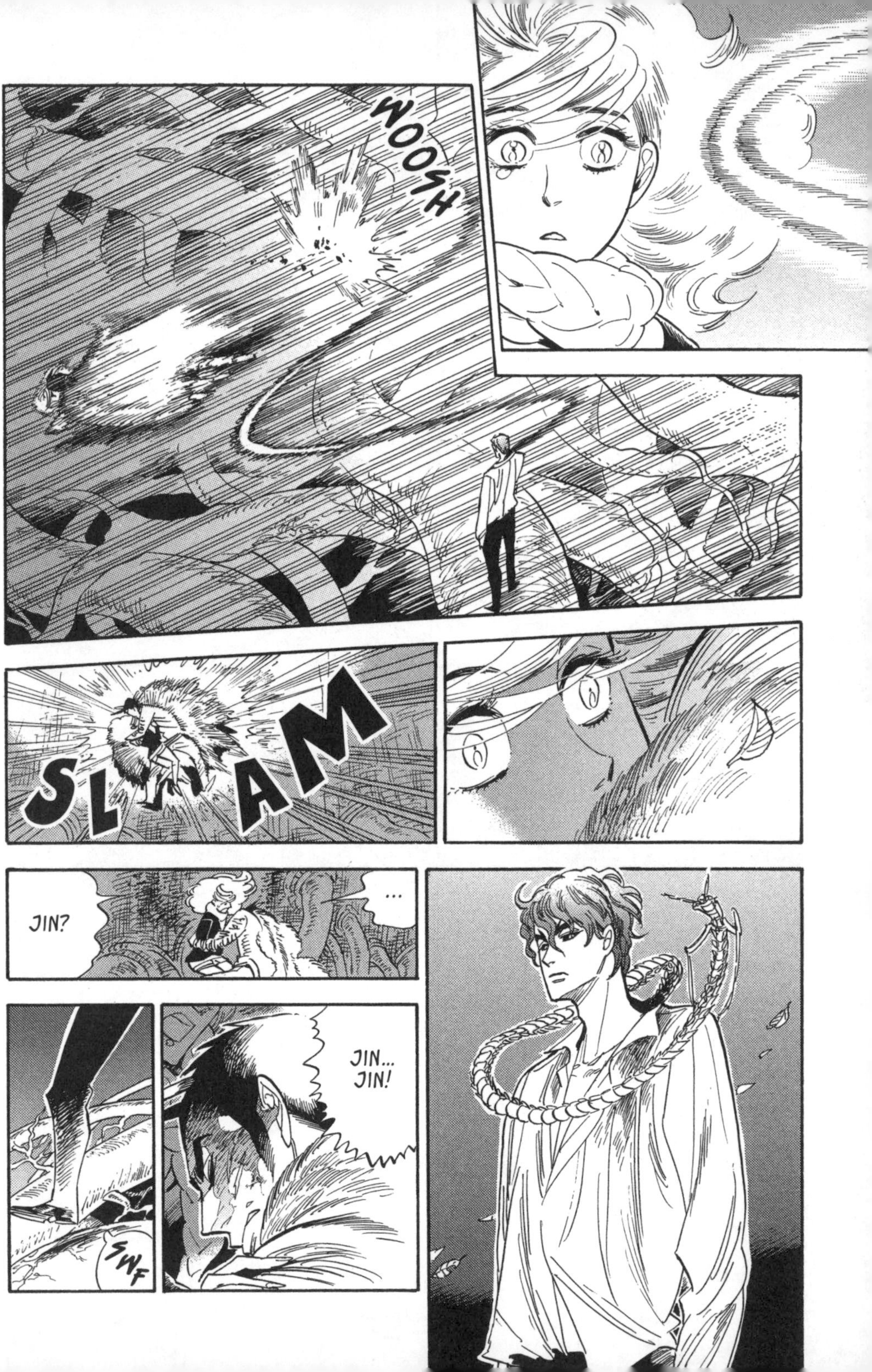
WOOSH
SLAM
...
JIN?
JIN... JIN!
SWF

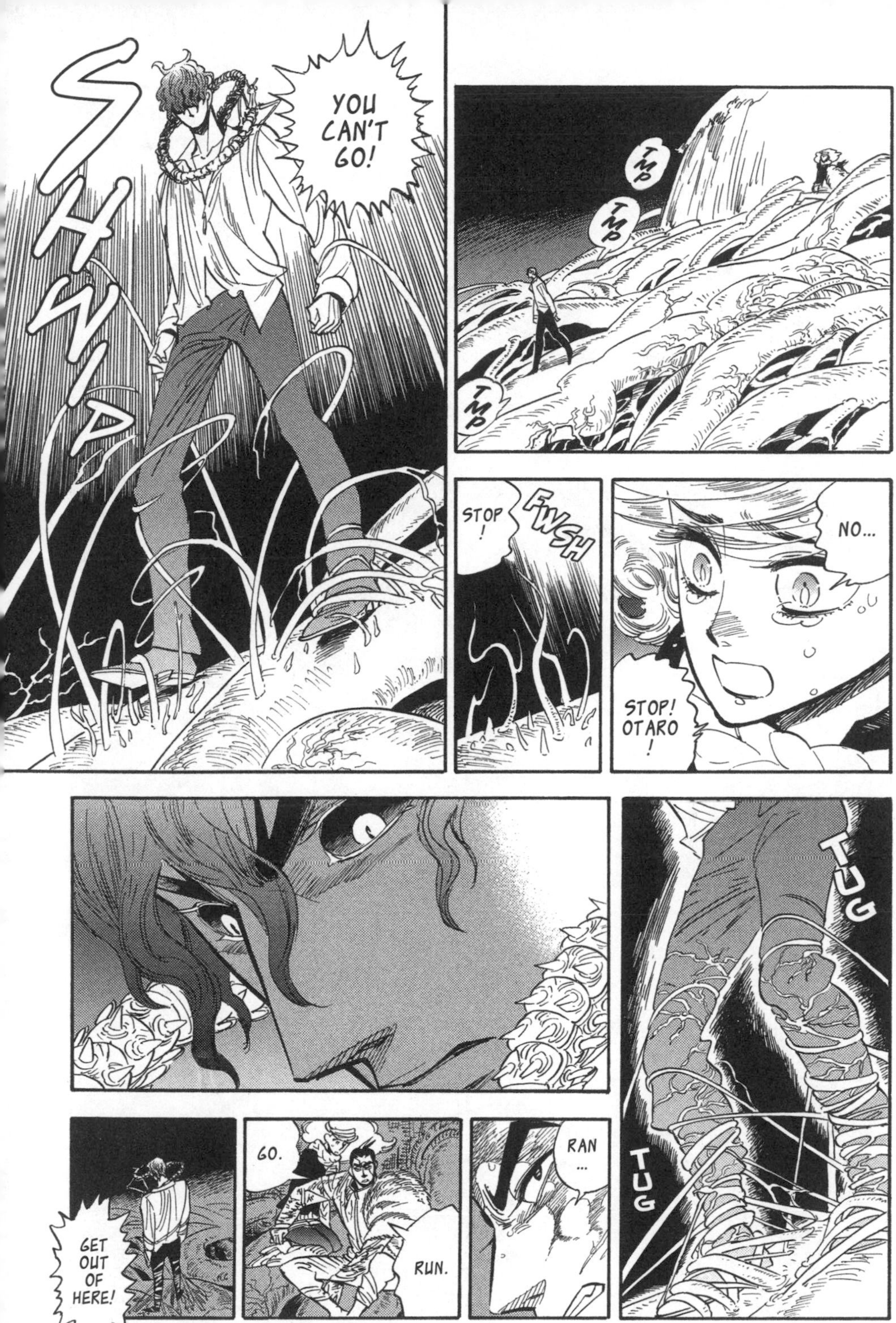
TMP
TMP
TMP
NO...
STOP! OTARO!
STOP!
FWSH
SHWIP
YOU CAN'T GO!
TUG
TUG
RAN...
GO.
RUN.
GET OUT OF HERE!

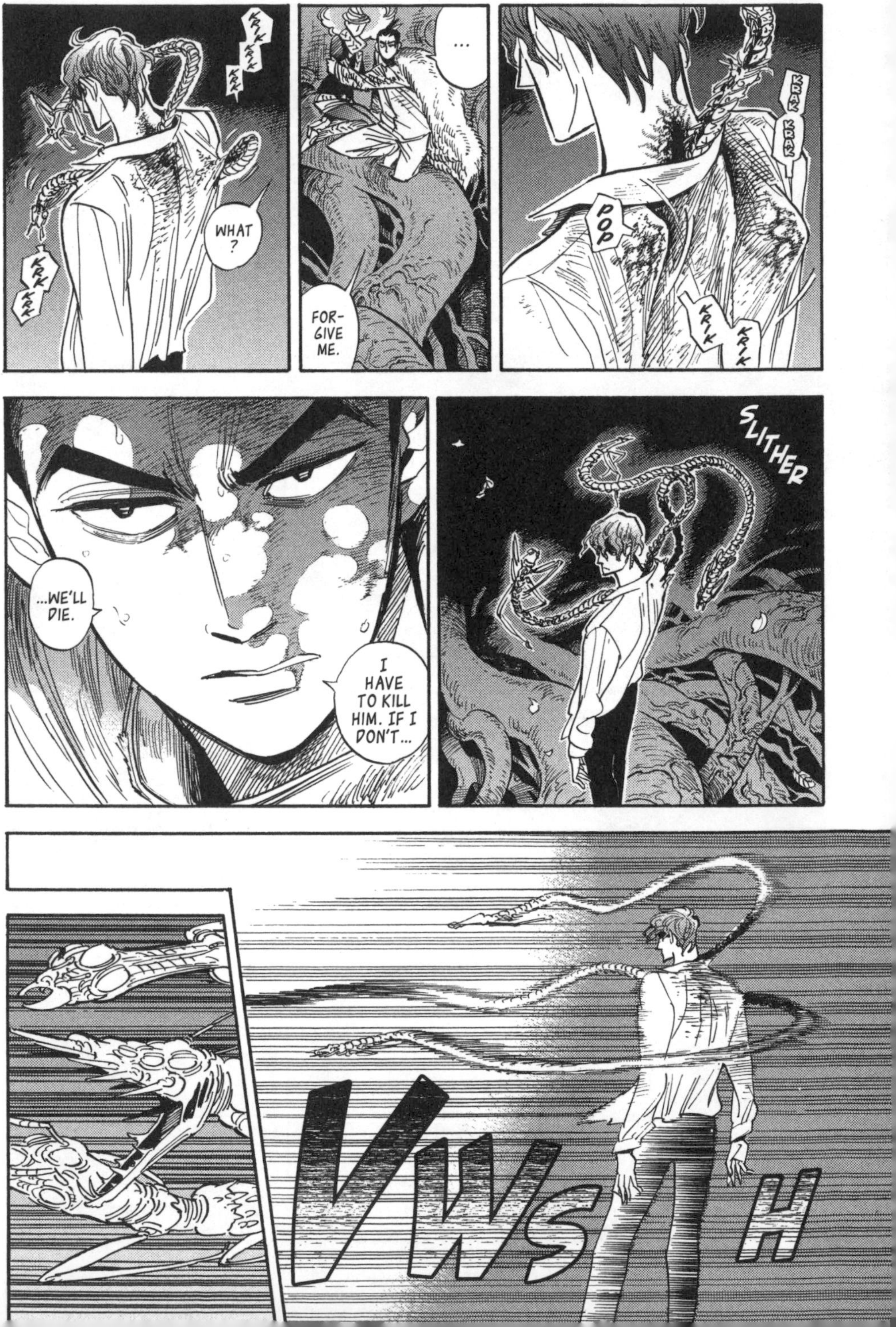
KRAK KRAK
POP
KRIK KRIK
...
FOR-GIVE ME.
KRIK KRIK KRIK
WHAT ?
KRIK KRIK
SLITHER
I HAVE TO KILL HIM. IF I DON'T...
...WE'LL DIE.
VWSH

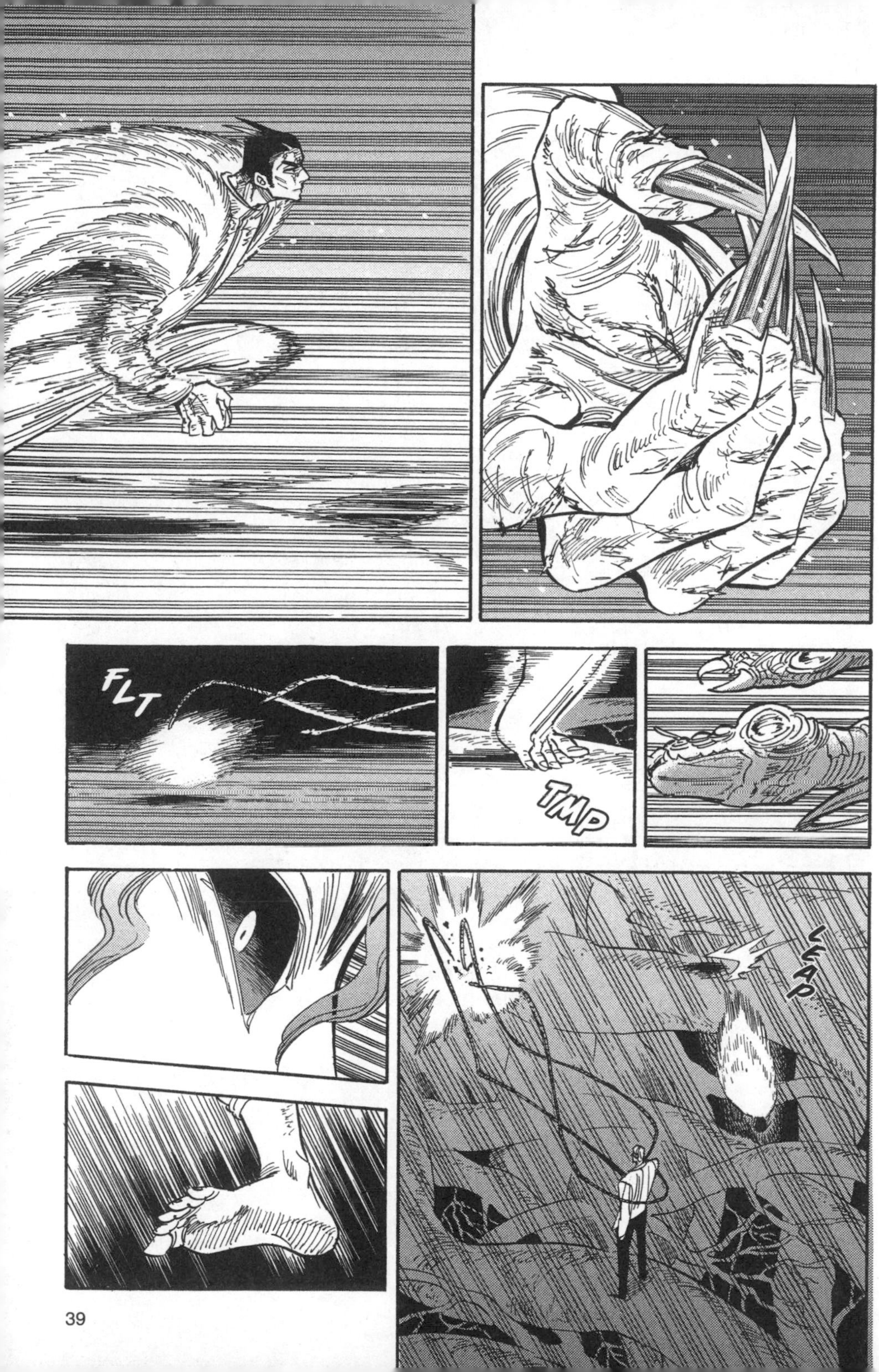
TMP
FLT
LEAP

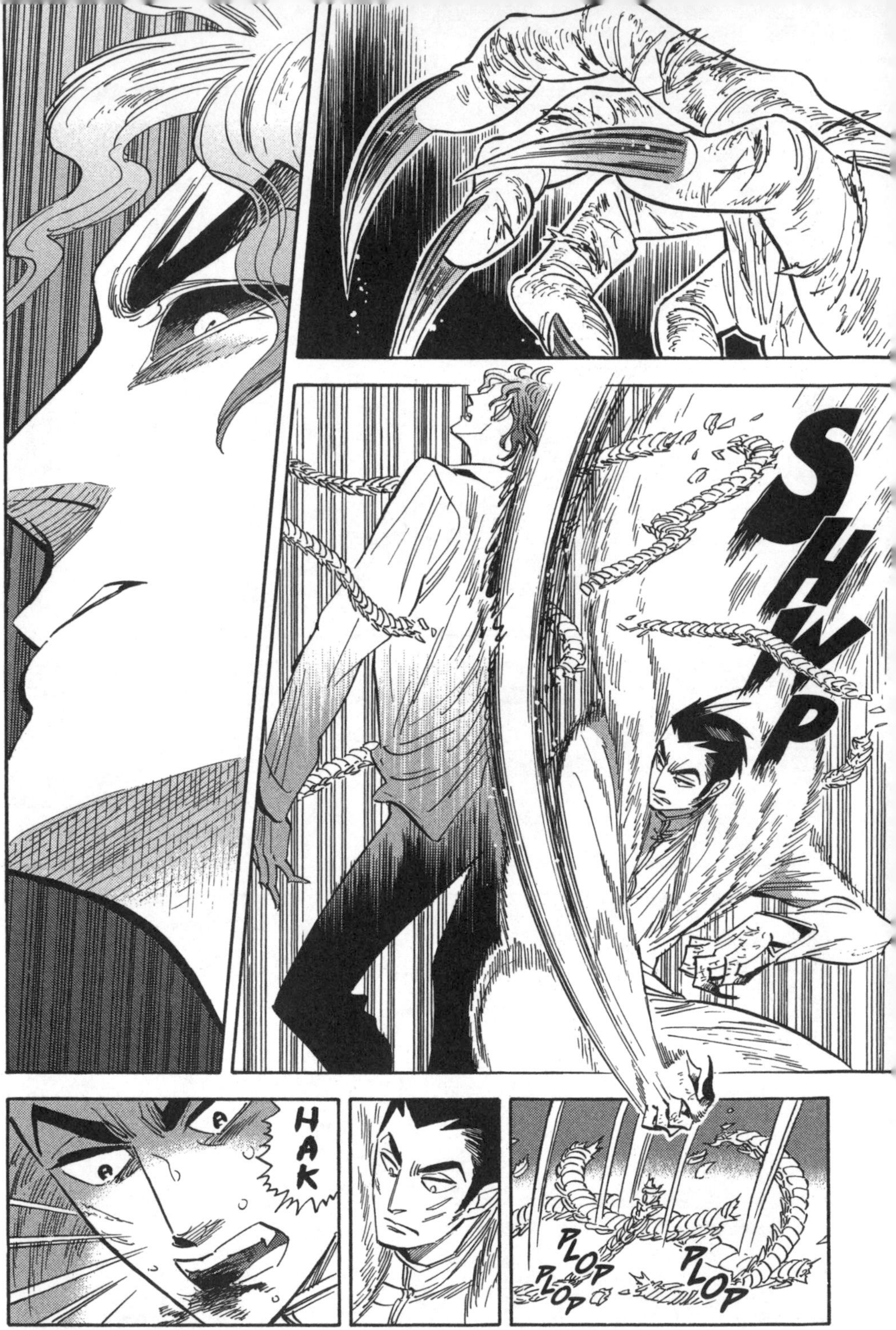
SHWIP
PLOP PLOP
PLOP PLOP
HAK

YOU'RE
...

...

...A
MON-
STER!

UNH
...

GET
AWAY
...

...
FROM
...

RAN!

FLY!

SLUMP

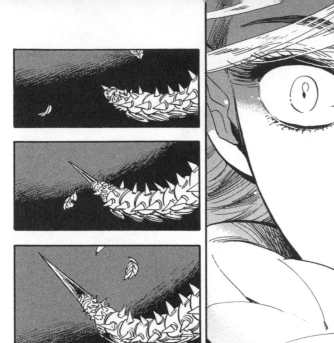

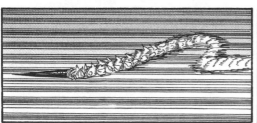

VWOO

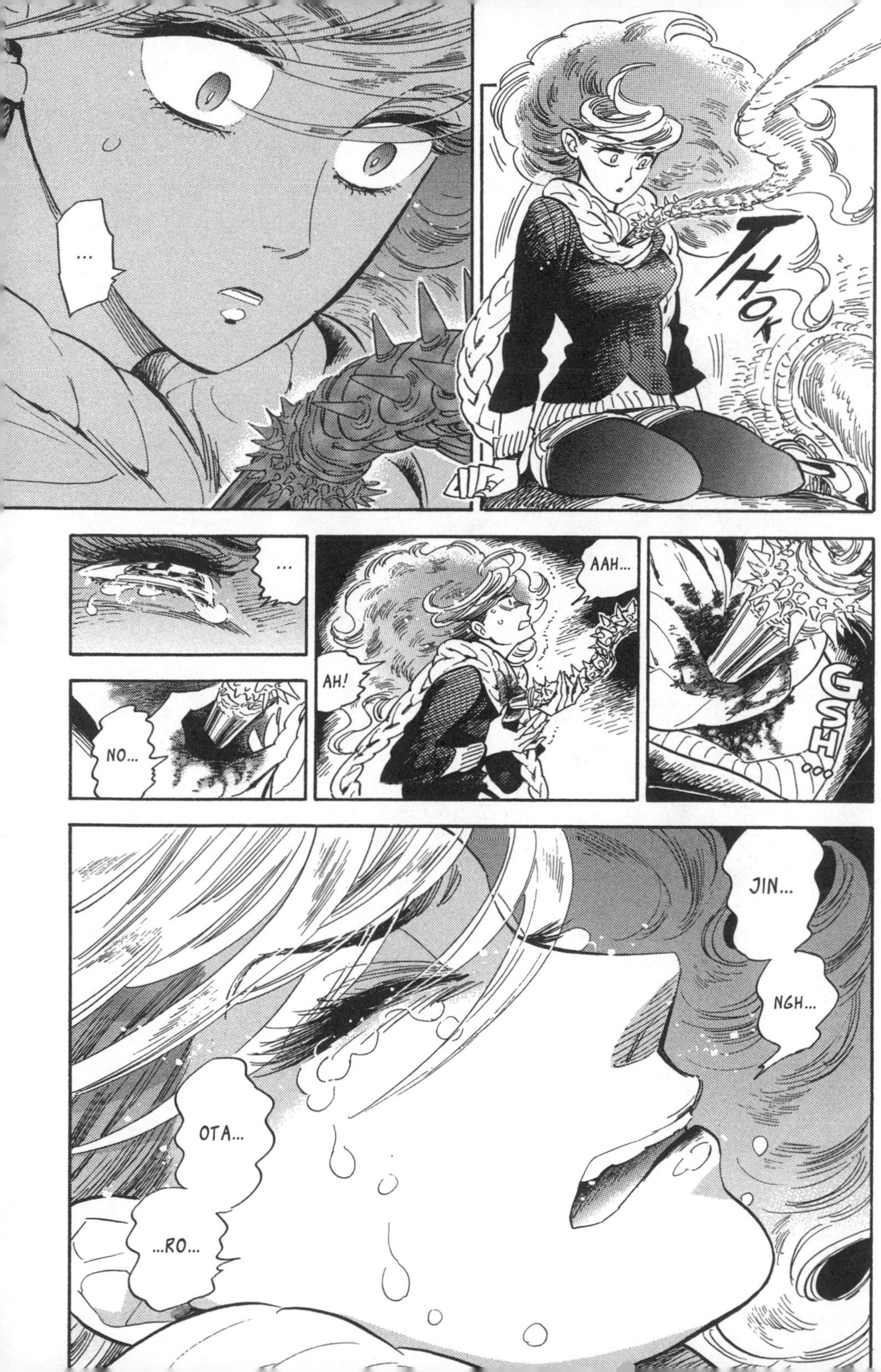
THOK
...
GSH...
AAH...
AH!
...
NO...
JIN...
NGH...
OTA...
...RO...

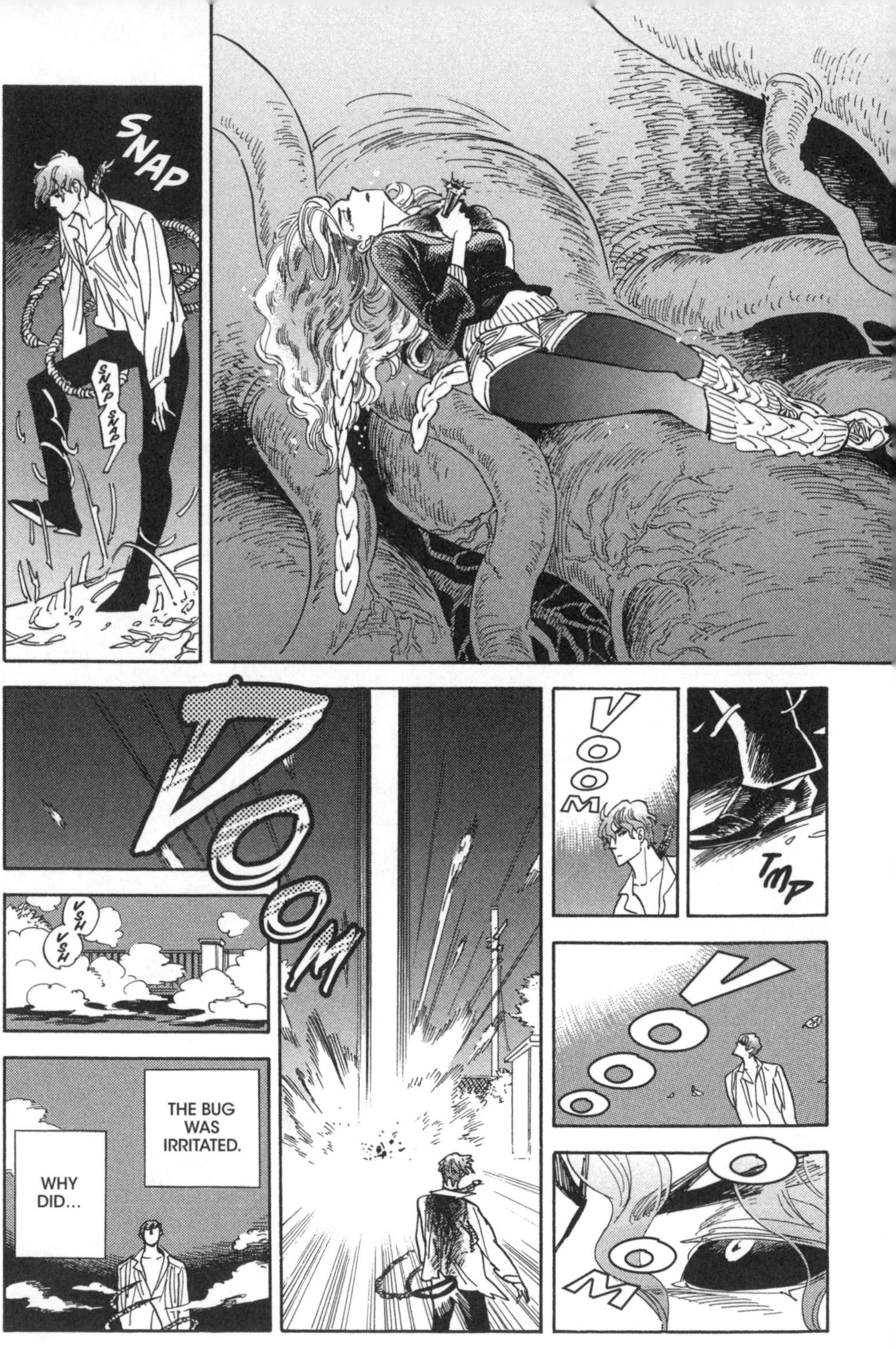
SNAP
SNAP SNAP
TMP
VOOOM
VOOOO
OOM
DOOM
VSH VSH
THE BUG WAS IRRITATED.
WHY DID…

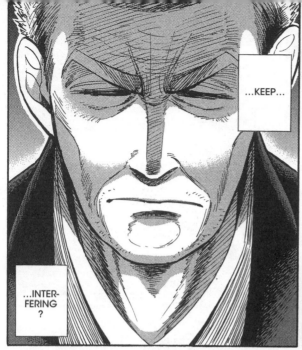

...KEEP...

...INTER-FERING?

...EVERY-ONE...

STEP

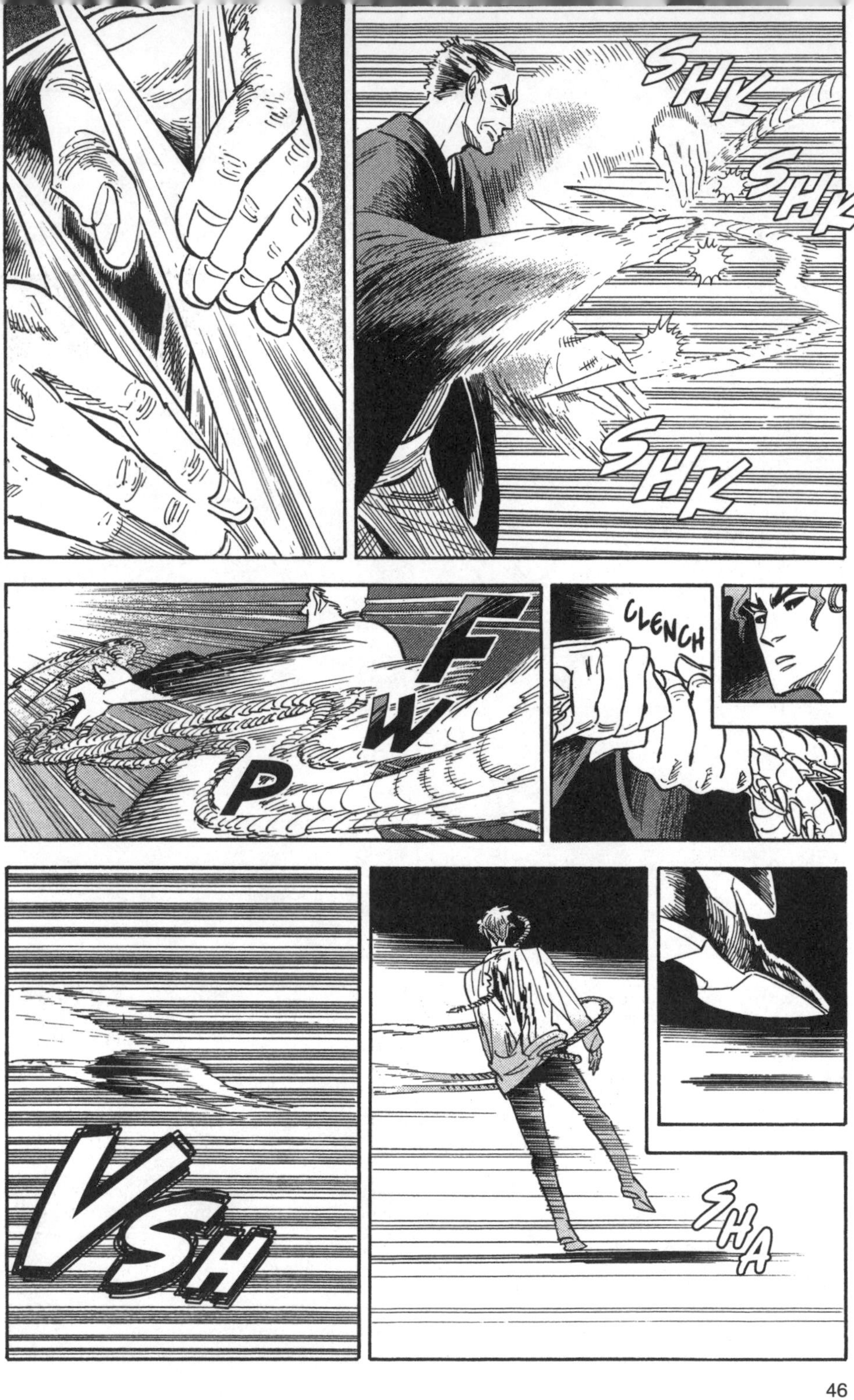
SHK
SHK
SHK
CLENCH
FWP
SHA
VSH

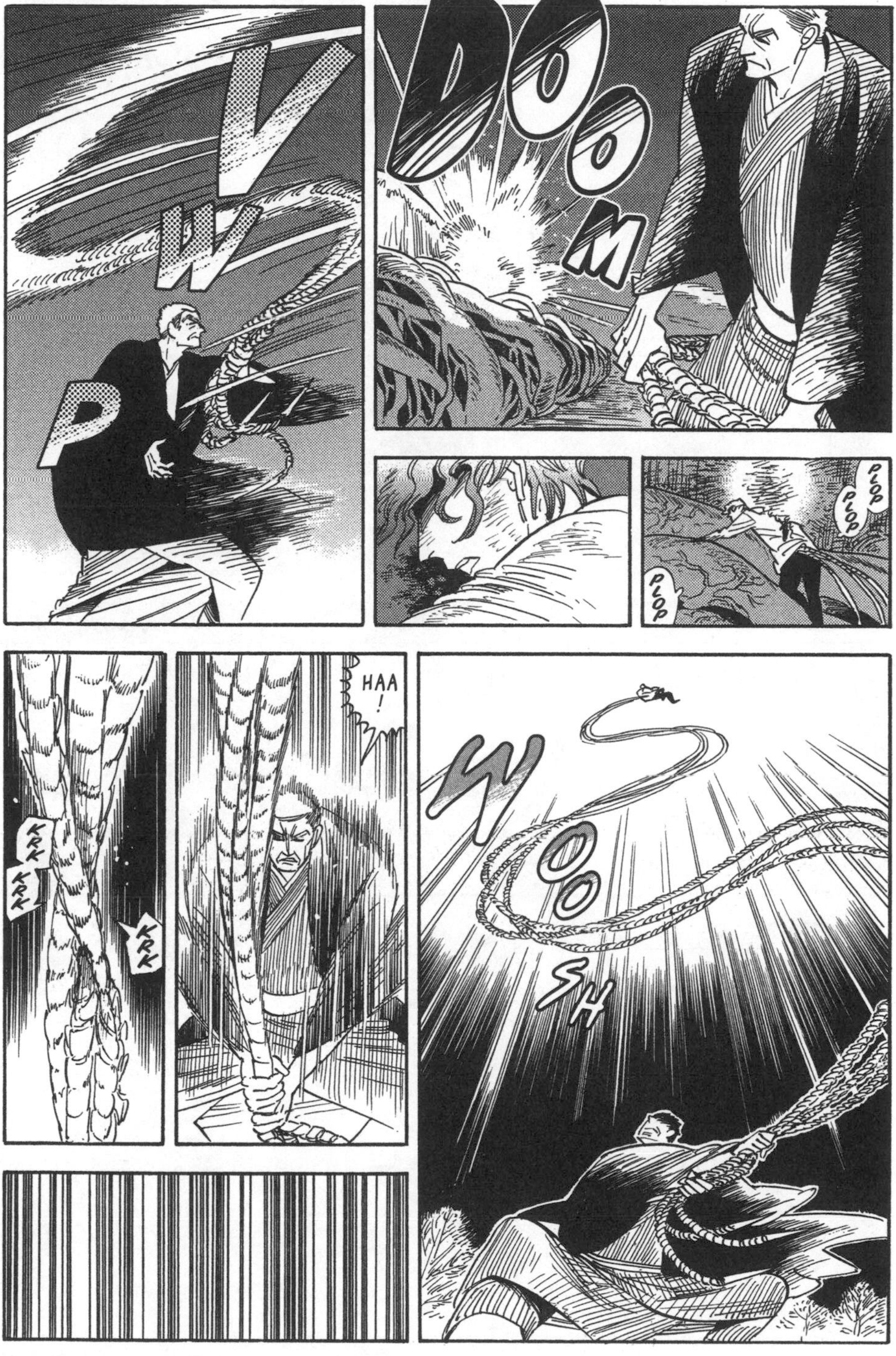
DOOOM
PLOP PLOP
PLOP
VWW
P
WOOOSH
HAA!
KRK KRK
KRK

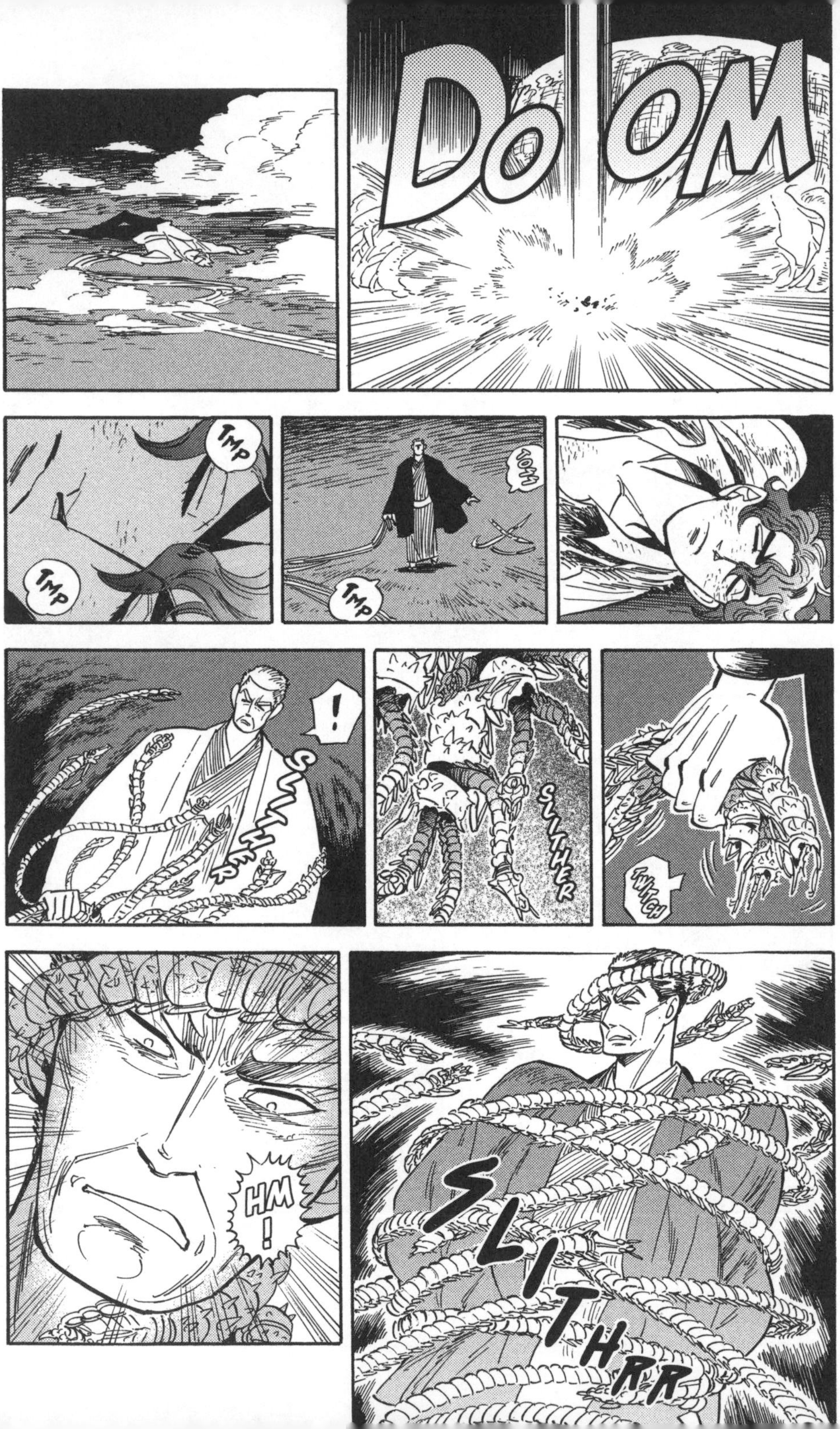
DOOM
TMP
TMP
TMP
!
SLITHER
SLITHER
TWITCH
HM!
SLITHRR

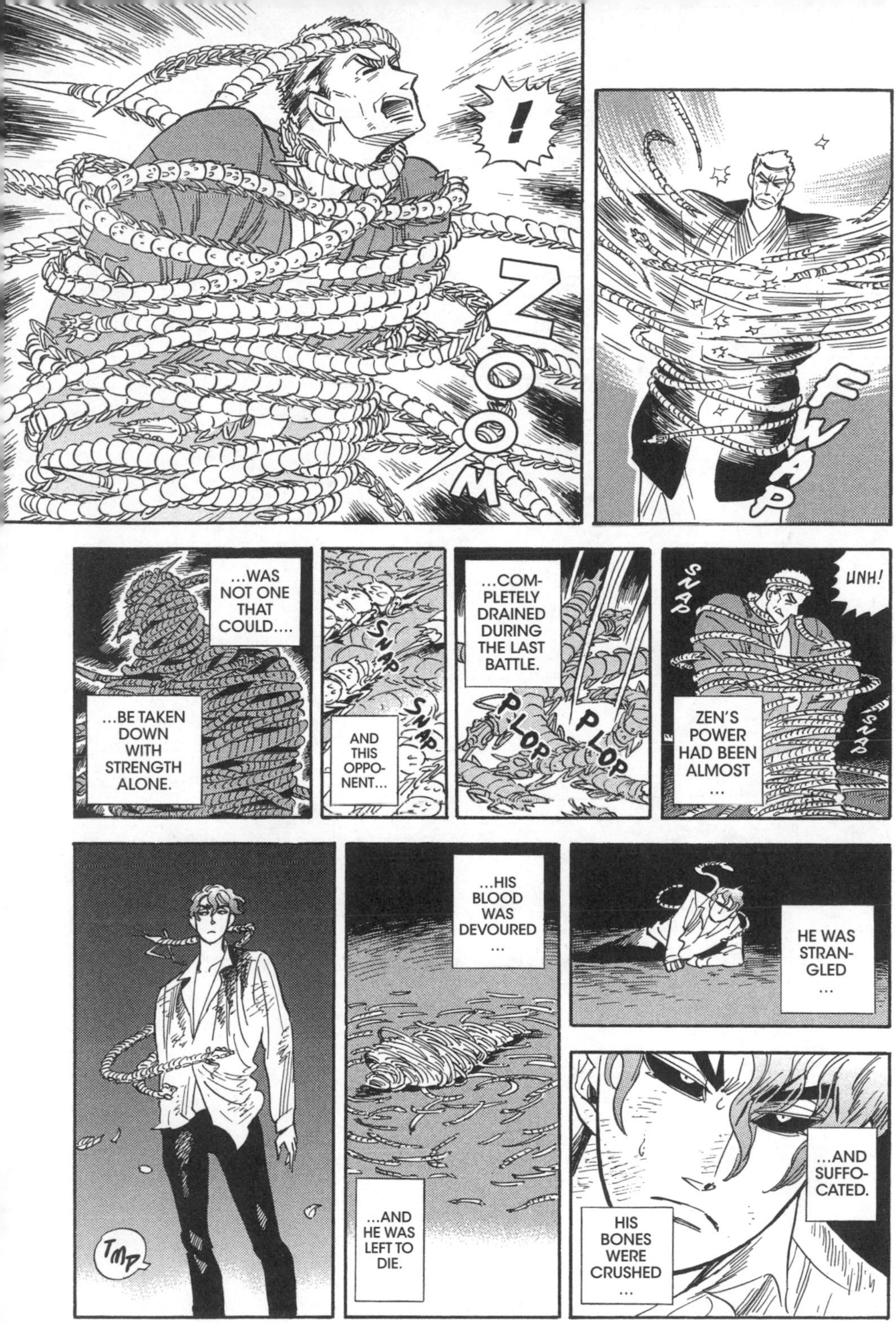
FWAP
!
ZOOM
UNH!
SNAP
SNAP
ZEN'S POWER HAD BEEN ALMOST ...
...COMPLETELY DRAINED DURING THE LAST BATTLE.
PLOP
PLOP
SNAP
SNAP
AND THIS OPPONENT...
...WAS NOT ONE THAT COULD....
...BE TAKEN DOWN WITH STRENGTH ALONE.
HE WAS STRANGLED ...
...AND SUFFOCATED.
HIS BONES WERE CRUSHED ...
...HIS BLOOD WAS DEVOURED ...
...AND HE WAS LEFT TO DIE.
TMP

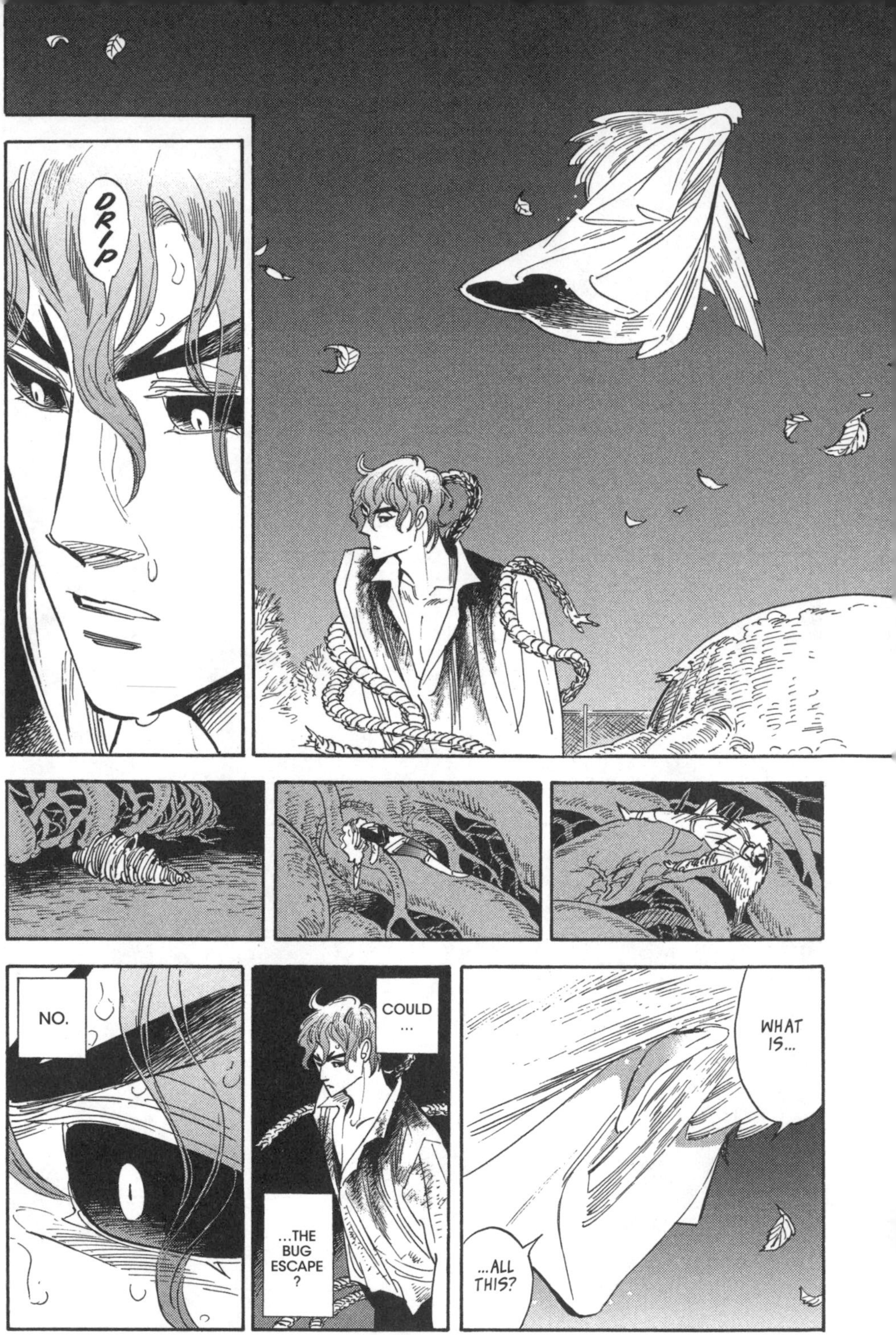
DRIP
WHAT IS...
...ALL THIS?
COULD ...
...THE BUG ESCAPE ?
NO.

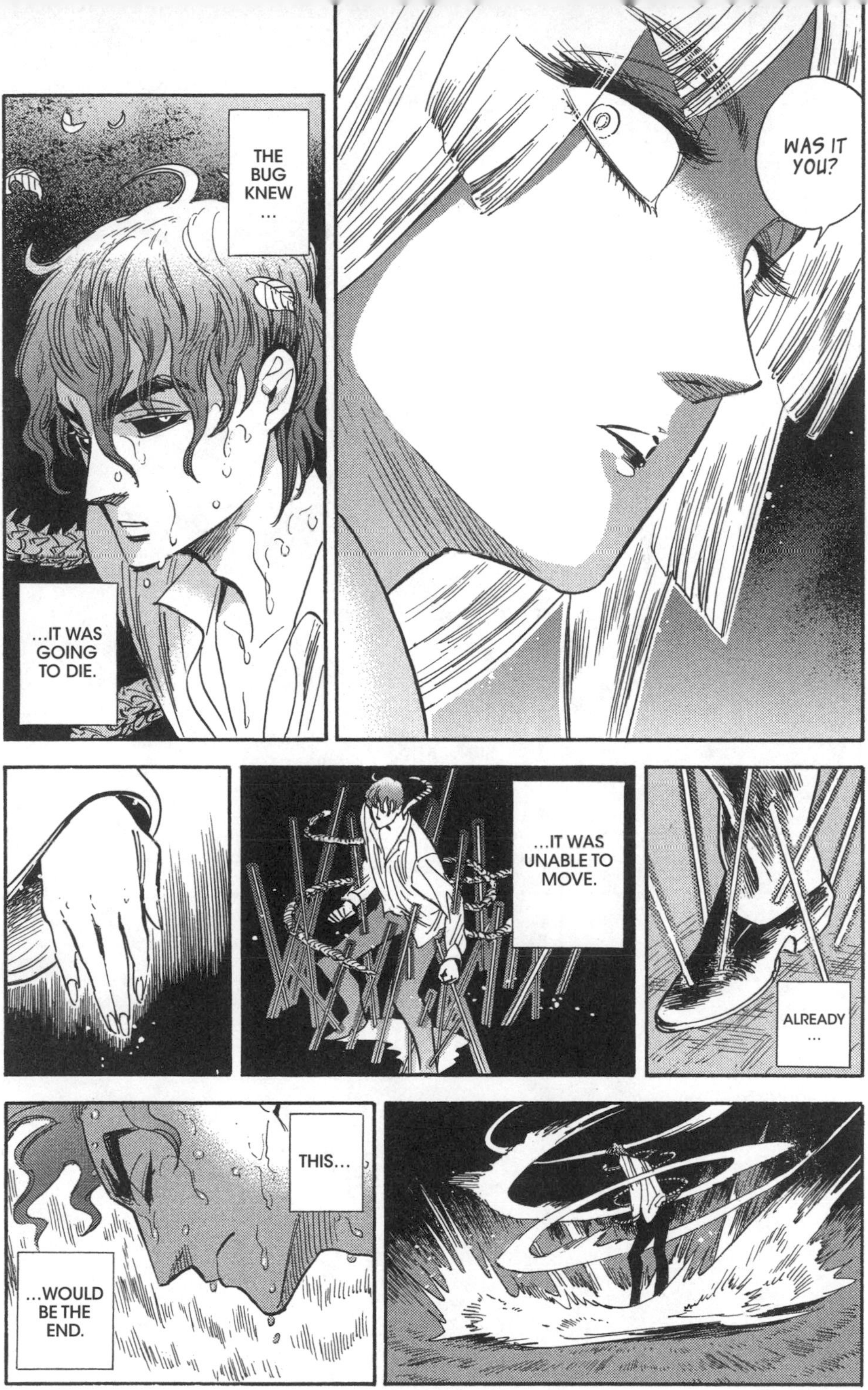
WAS IT YOU?
THE BUG KNEW ...
...IT WAS GOING TO DIE.
ALREADY ...
...IT WAS UNABLE TO MOVE.
THIS...
...WOULD BE THE END.

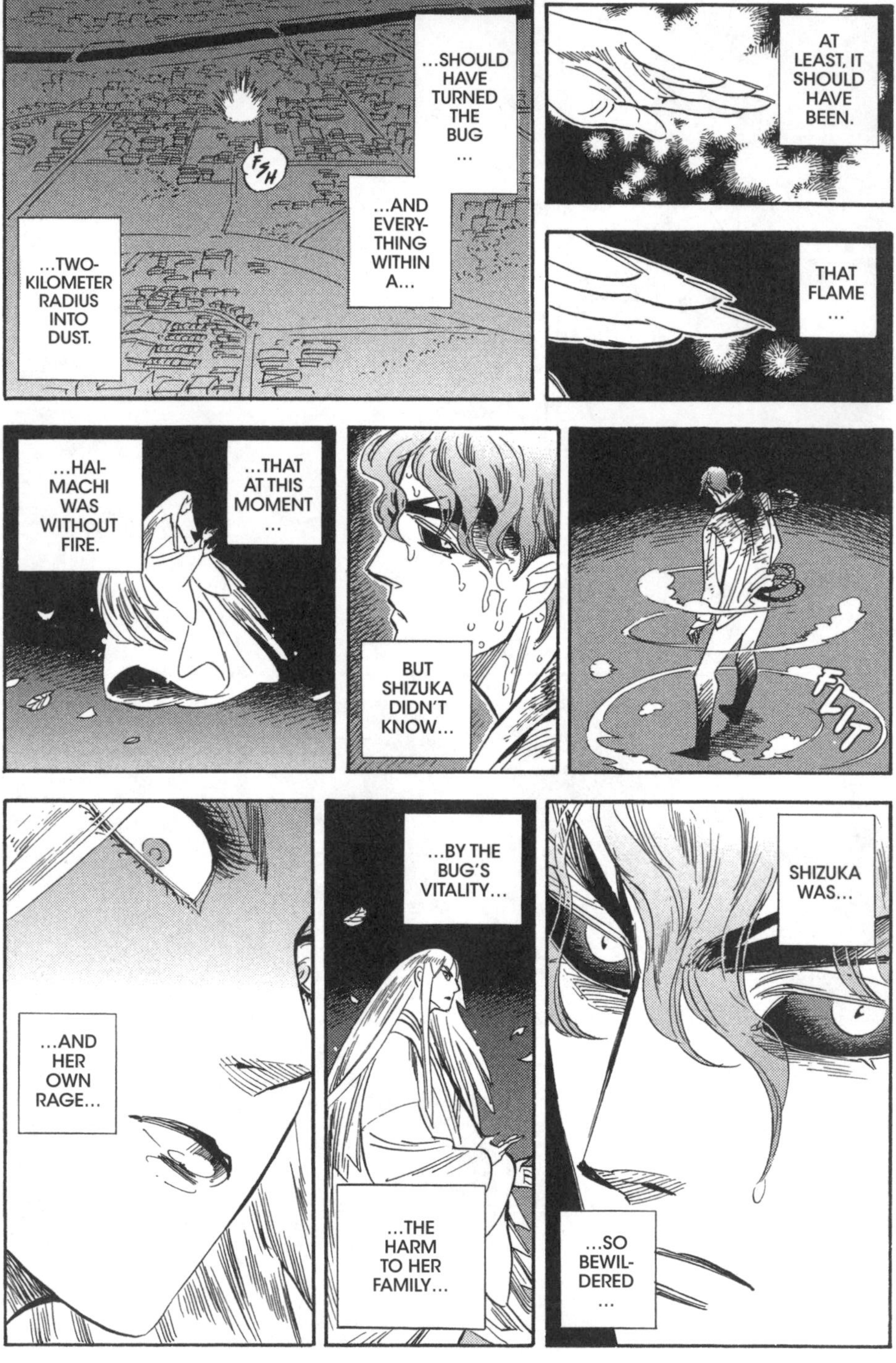
AT LEAST, IT SHOULD HAVE BEEN.
THAT FLAME ...
...SHOULD HAVE TURNED THE BUG ...
...AND EVERY-THING WITHIN A...
FSH
...TWO-KILOMETER RADIUS INTO DUST.
FLIT
BUT SHIZUKA DIDN'T KNOW...
...THAT AT THIS MOMENT ...
...HAI-MACHI WAS WITHOUT FIRE.
SHIZUKA WAS...
...SO BEWIL-DERED ...
...BY THE BUG'S VITALITY...
...THE HARM TO HER FAMILY...
...AND HER OWN RAGE...

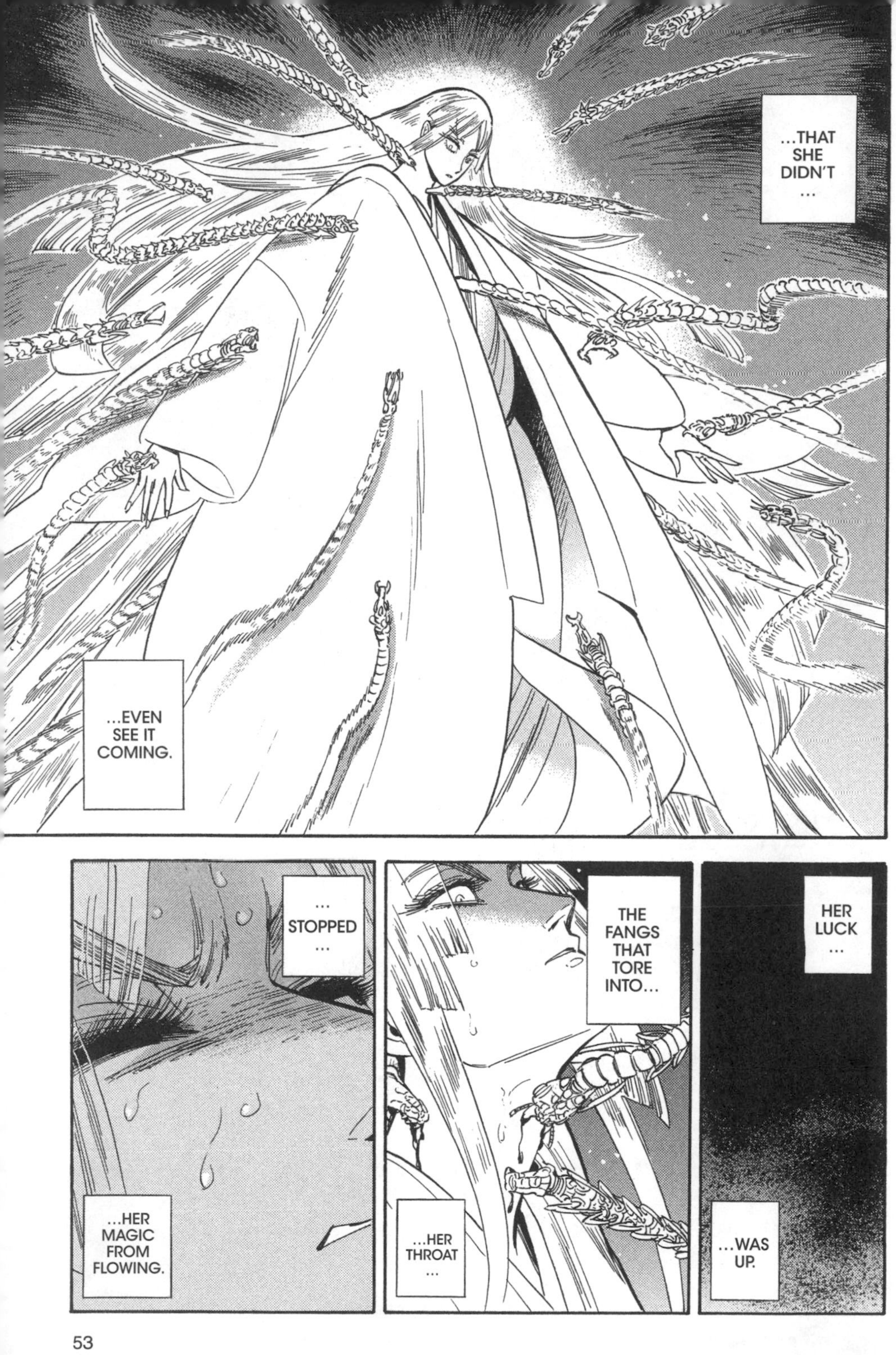
...THAT SHE DIDN'T ...
...EVEN SEE IT COMING.
HER LUCK ...
...WAS UP.
THE FANGS THAT TORE INTO...
...HER THROAT ...
... STOPPED ...
...HER MAGIC FROM FLOWING.

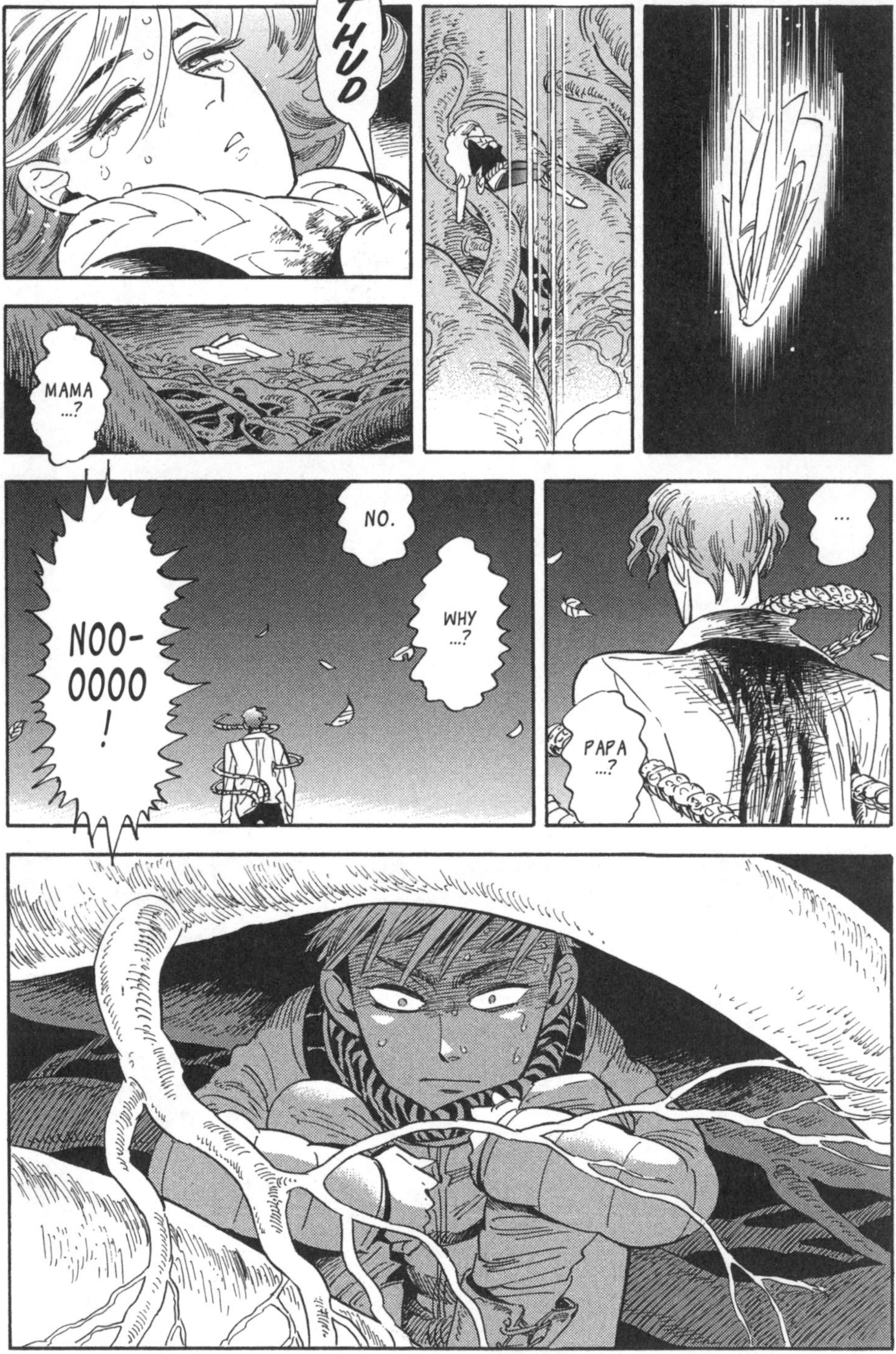
THUD
MAMA ...?
...
PAPA ...?
NO.
WHY ...?
NOO-OOOO!

Chapter 31 / The End

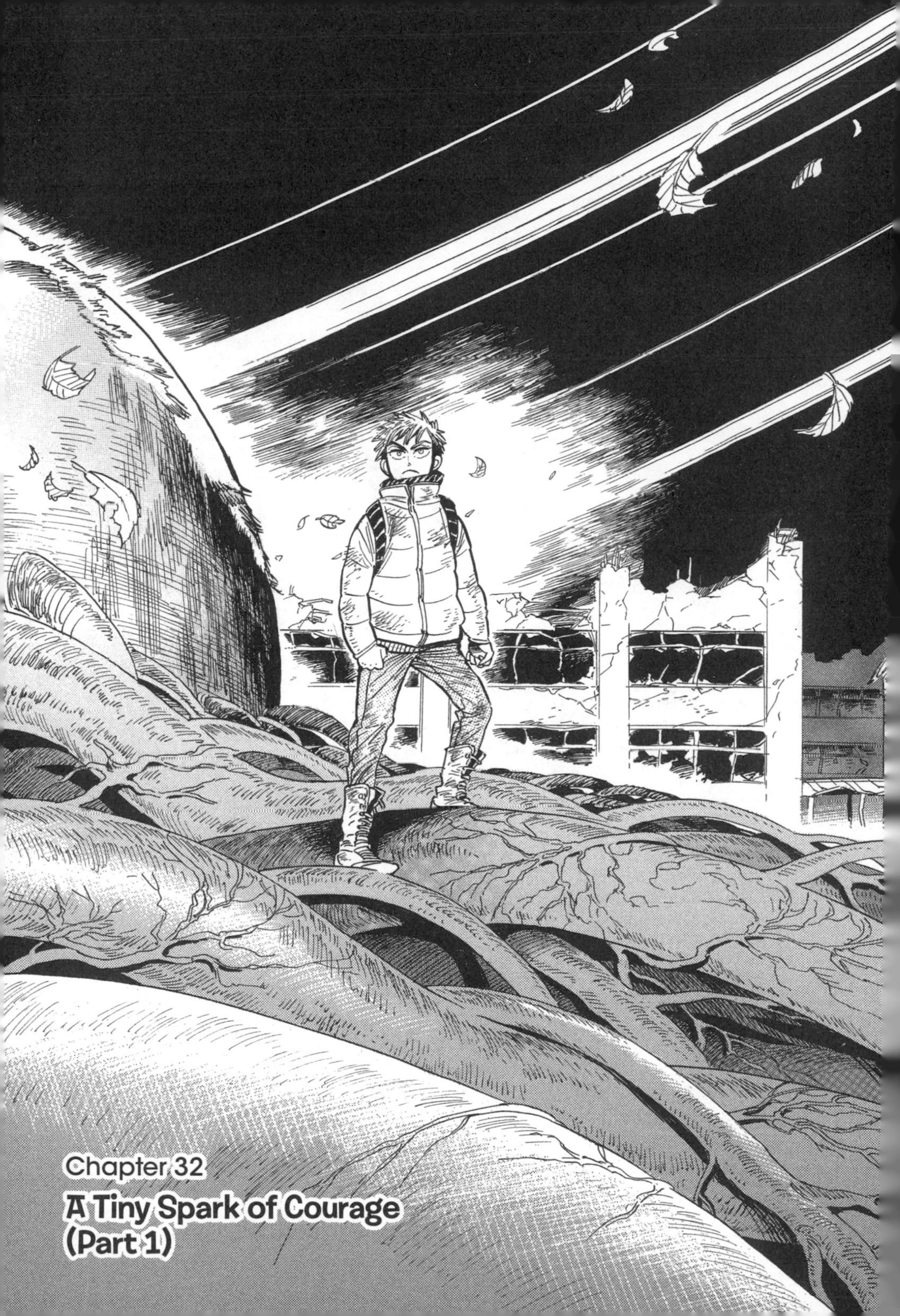
Chapter 32
A Tiny Spark of Courage
(Part 1)

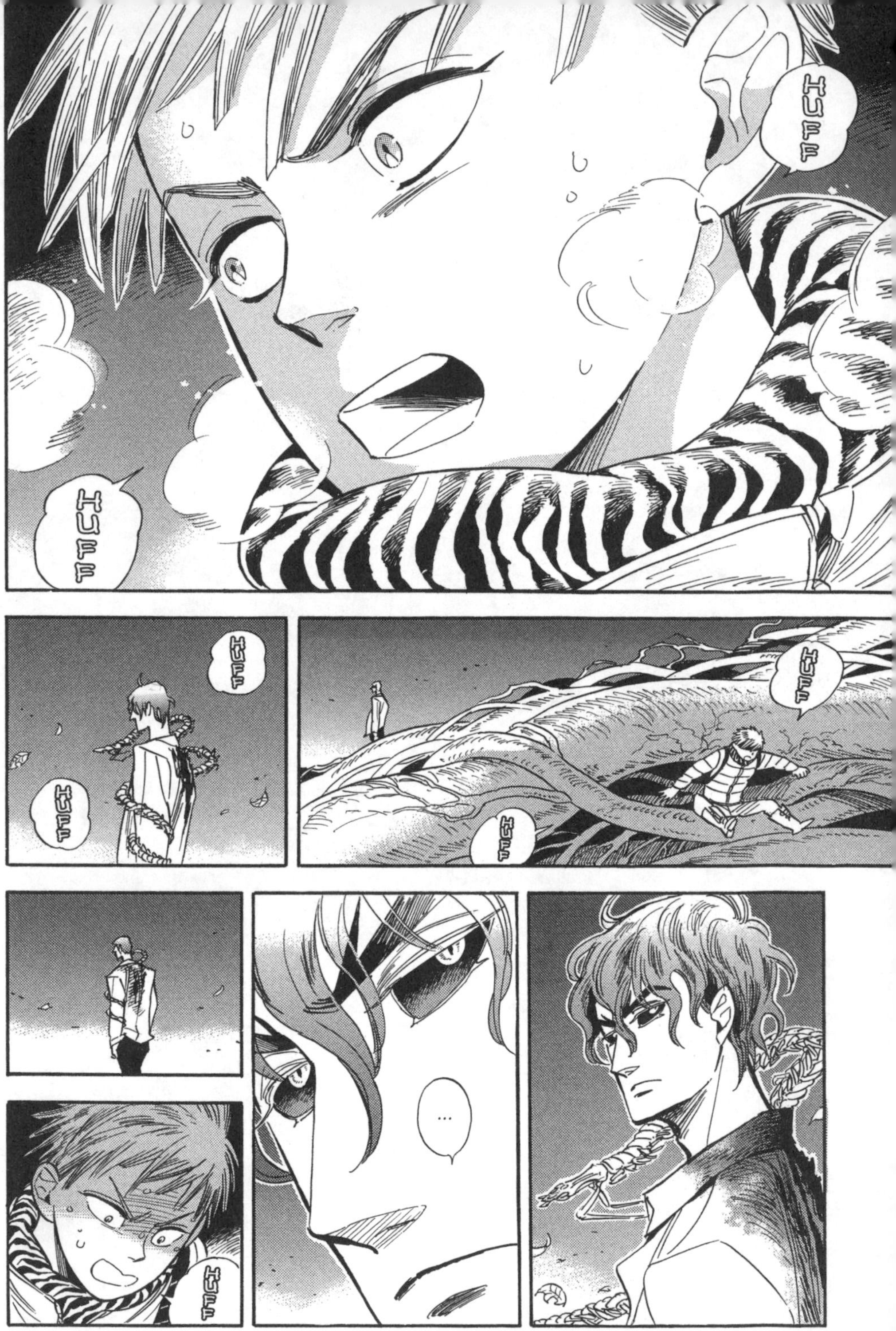
HUFF
HUFF
HUFF
HUFF
HUFF
HUFF
...
HUFF

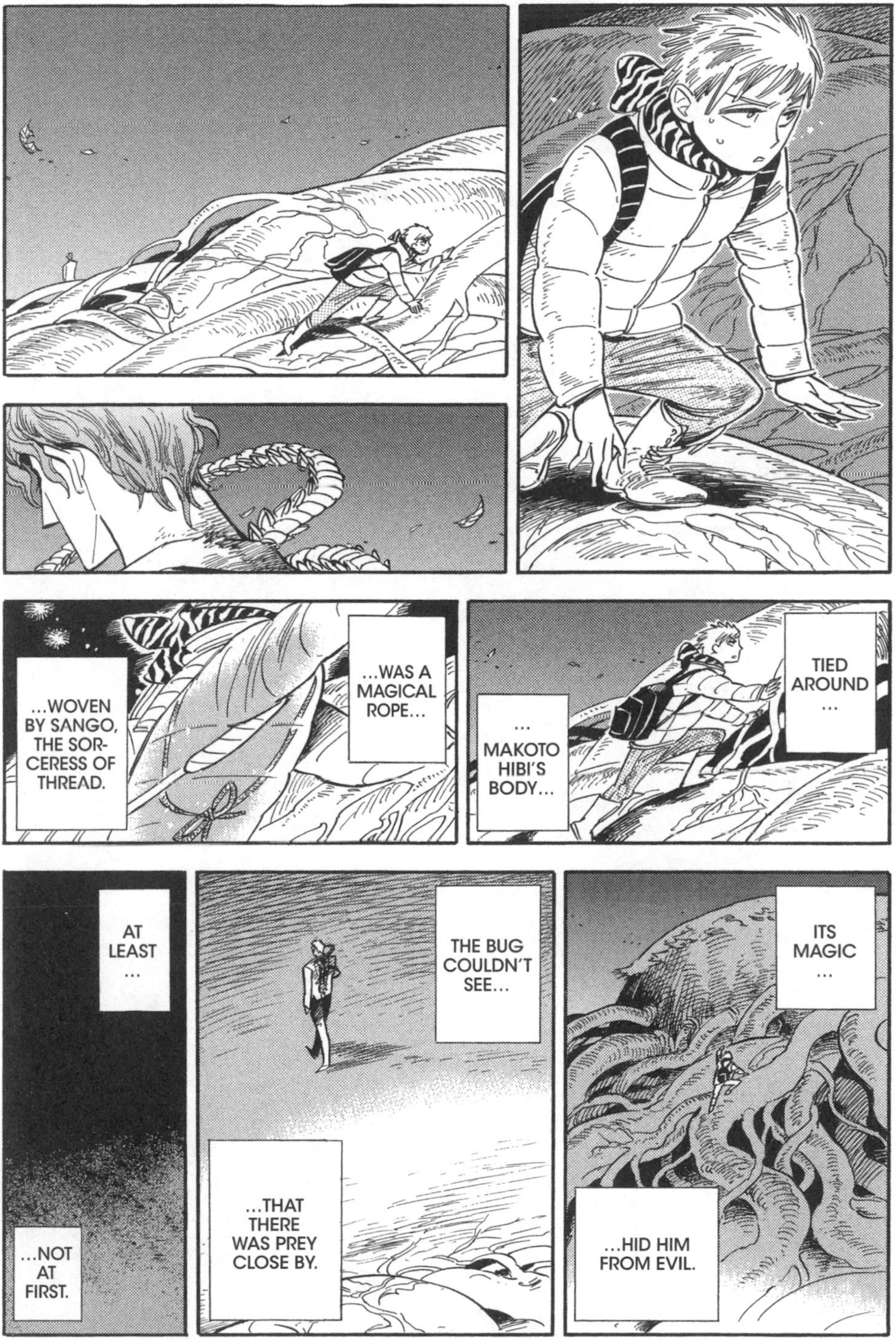
TIED AROUND ...
... MAKOTO HIBI'S BODY...
...WAS A MAGICAL ROPE...
...WOVEN BY SANGO, THE SORCERESS OF THREAD.
ITS MAGIC ...
...HID HIM FROM EVIL.
THE BUG COULDN'T SEE...
...THAT THERE WAS PREY CLOSE BY.
AT LEAST ...
...NOT AT FIRST.

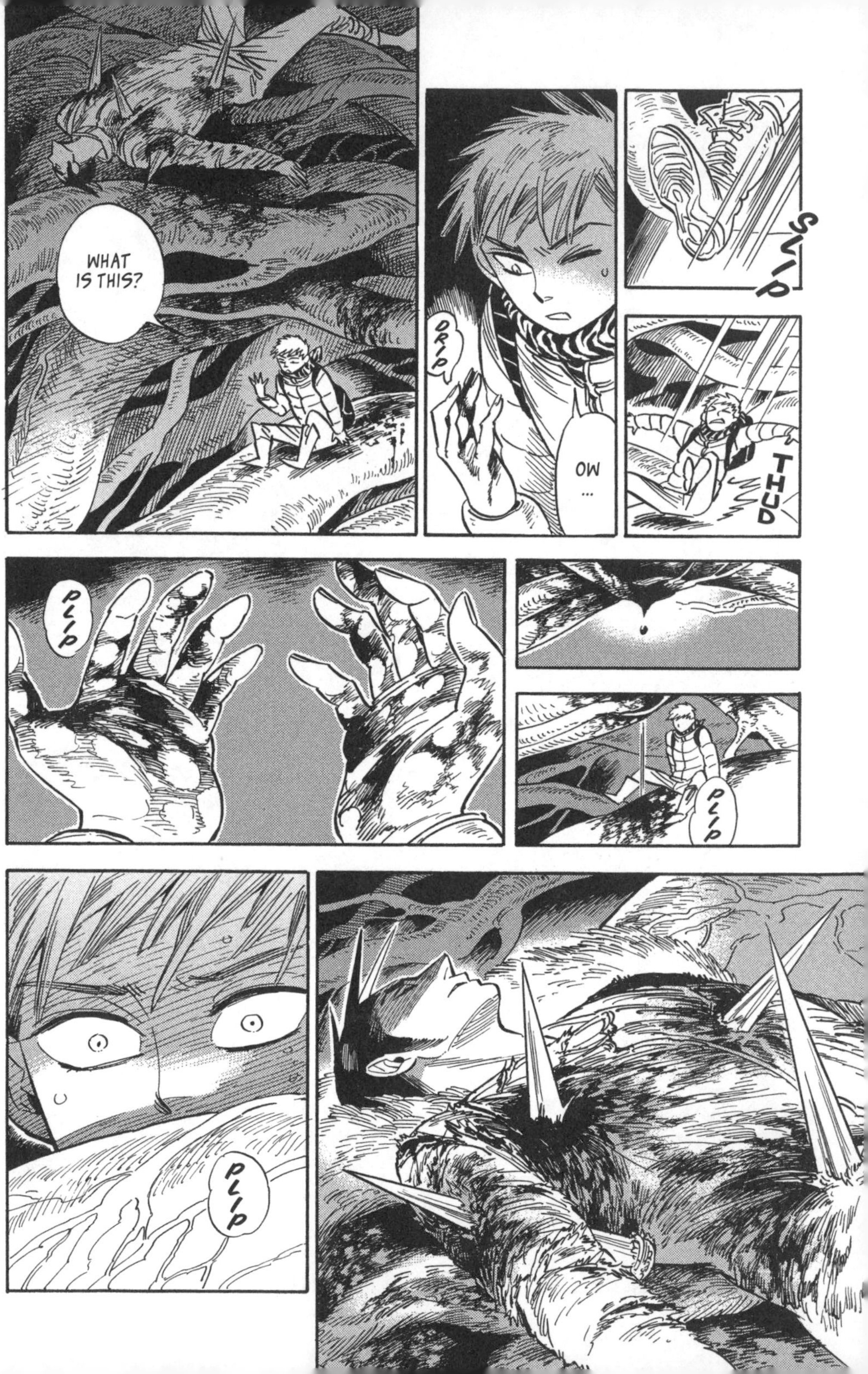
SLIP
THUD
DRIP
OW ...
WHAT IS THIS?
PLIP
PLIP
PLIP

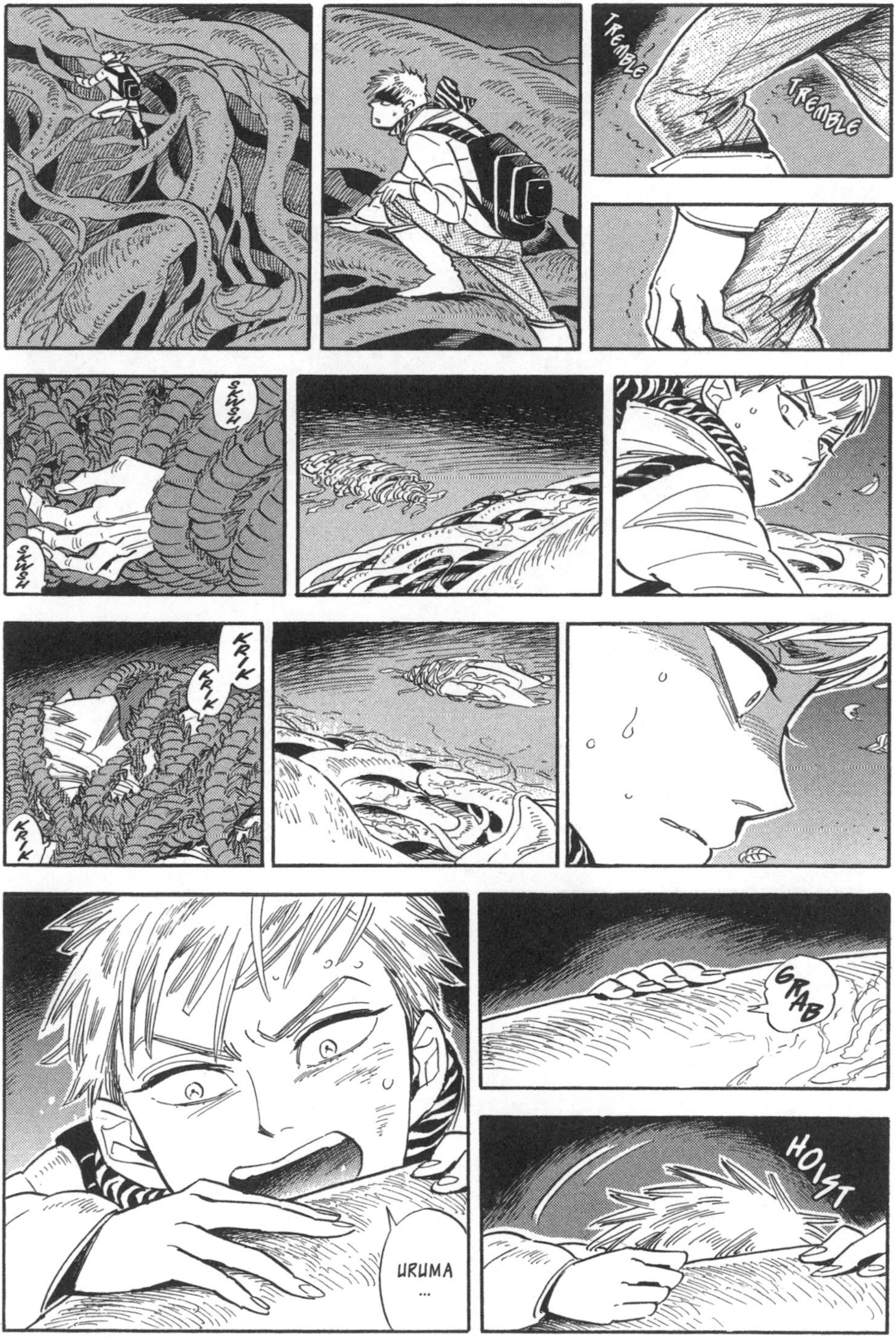
TREMBLE
TREMBLE
SWSH
SWSH
KRIK
KRIK
KRIK
GRAB
HOIST
URUMA
...

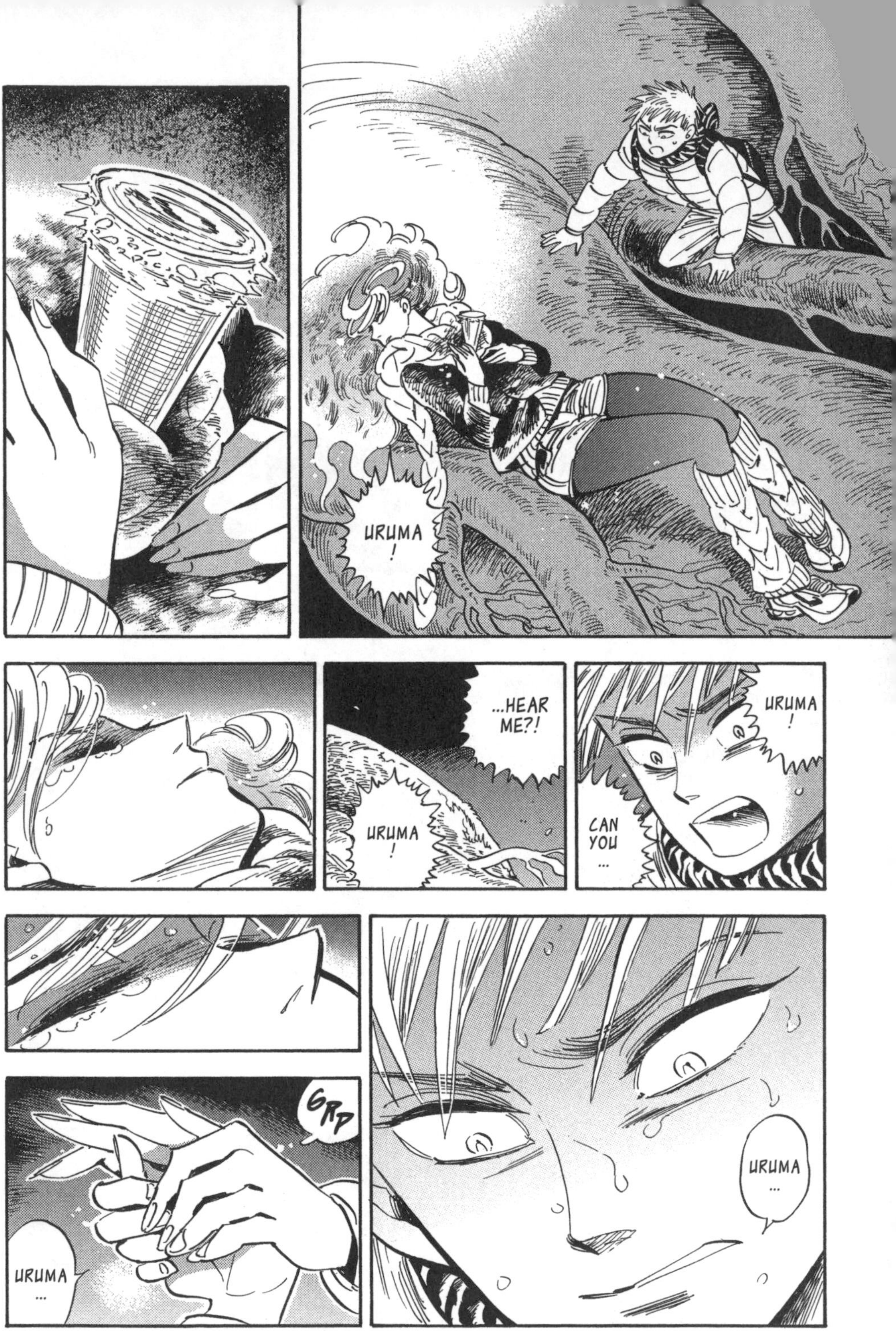
URUMA!
URUMA!
CAN YOU ...
...HEAR ME?!
URUMA!
URUMA ...
GRP
URUMA ...

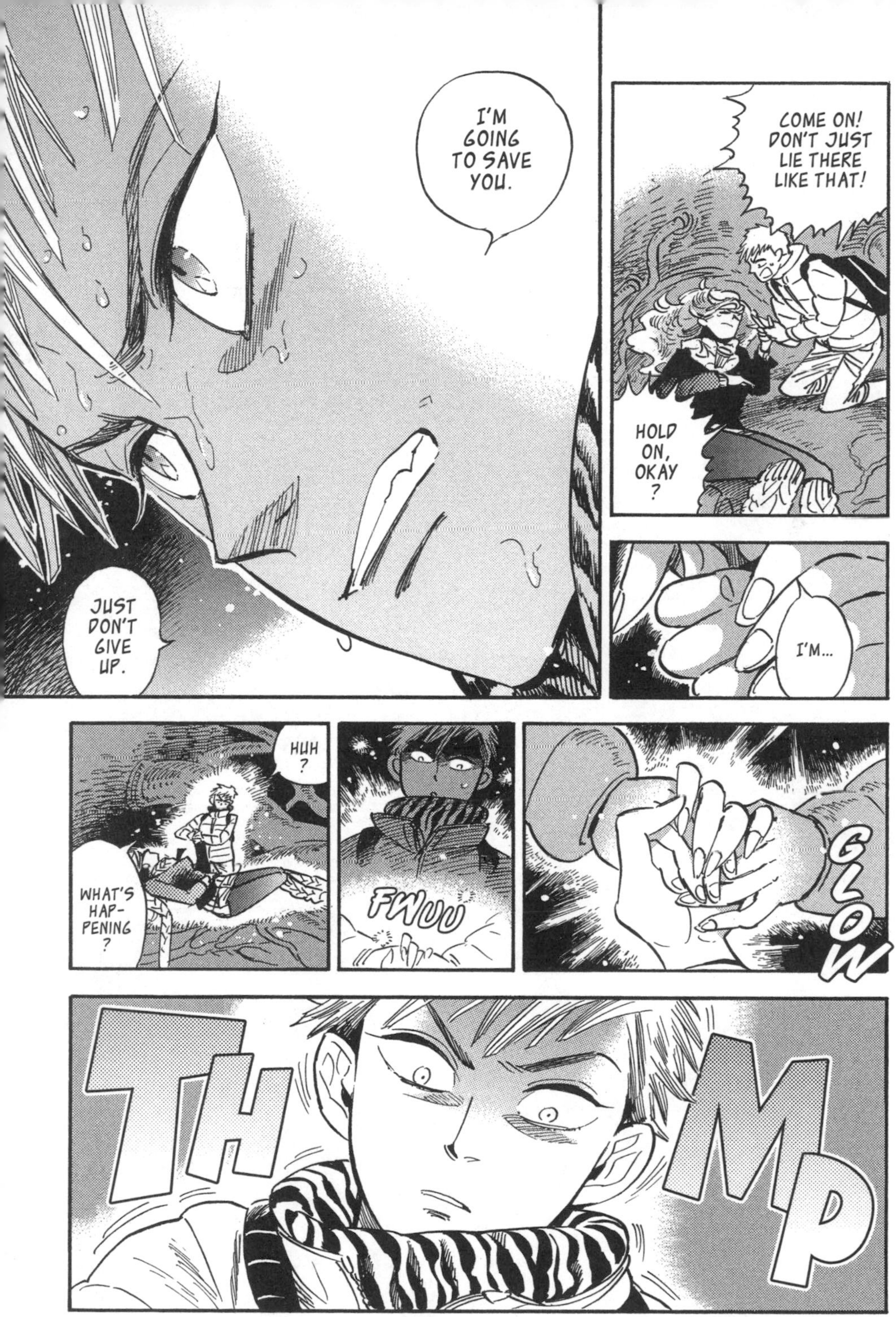

COME ON! DON'T JUST LIE THERE LIKE THAT!
HOLD ON, OKAY?
I'M...
I'M GOING TO SAVE YOU.
JUST DON'T GIVE UP.
GLOW
FWUU
HUH?
WHAT'S HAP-PENING?
THMP

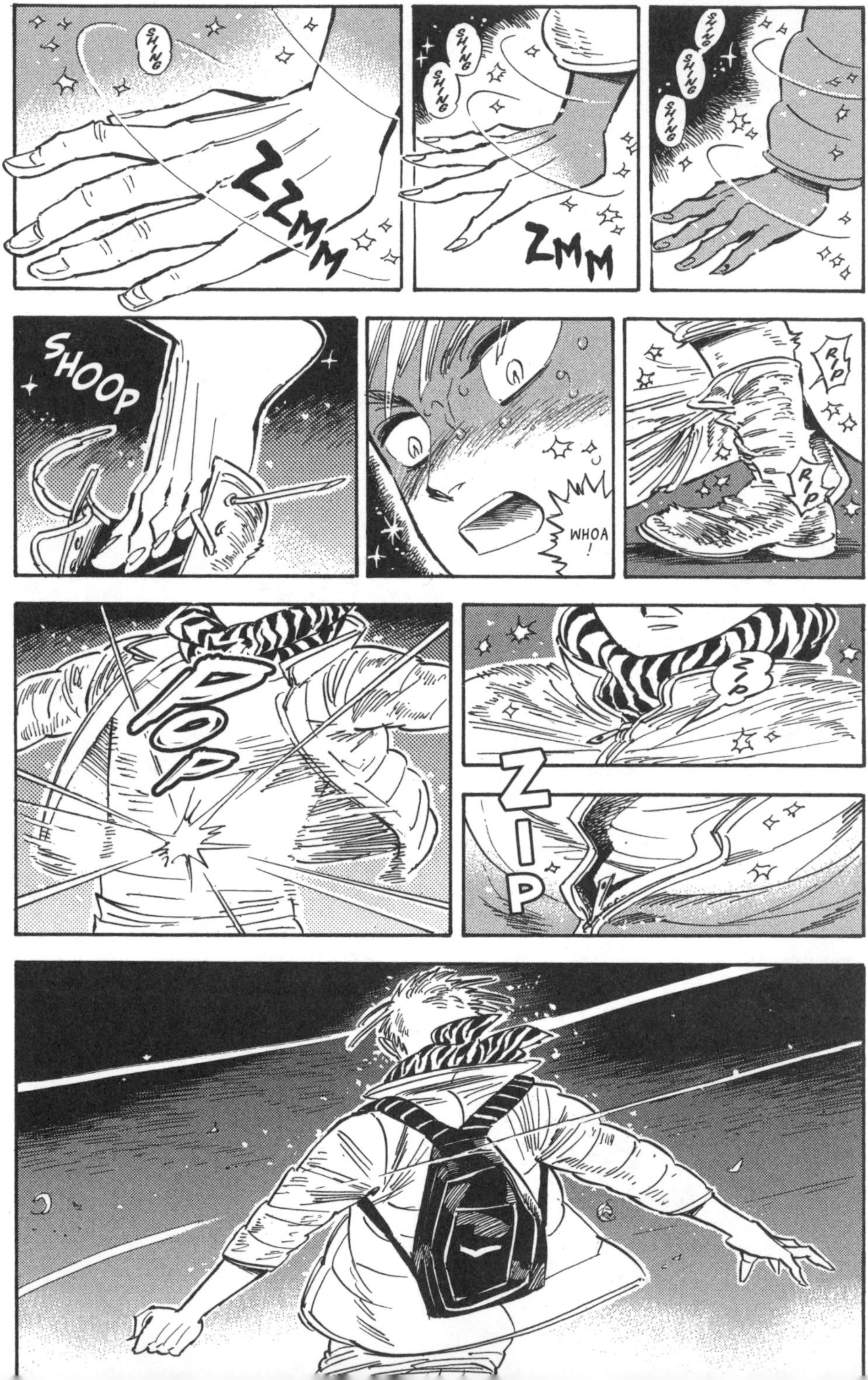
SHING
SHING
SHING
SHING
SHING
ZMM
SHING
ZZMM
RIP
RIP
WHOA!
SHOOP
ZIP
ZIP
POP

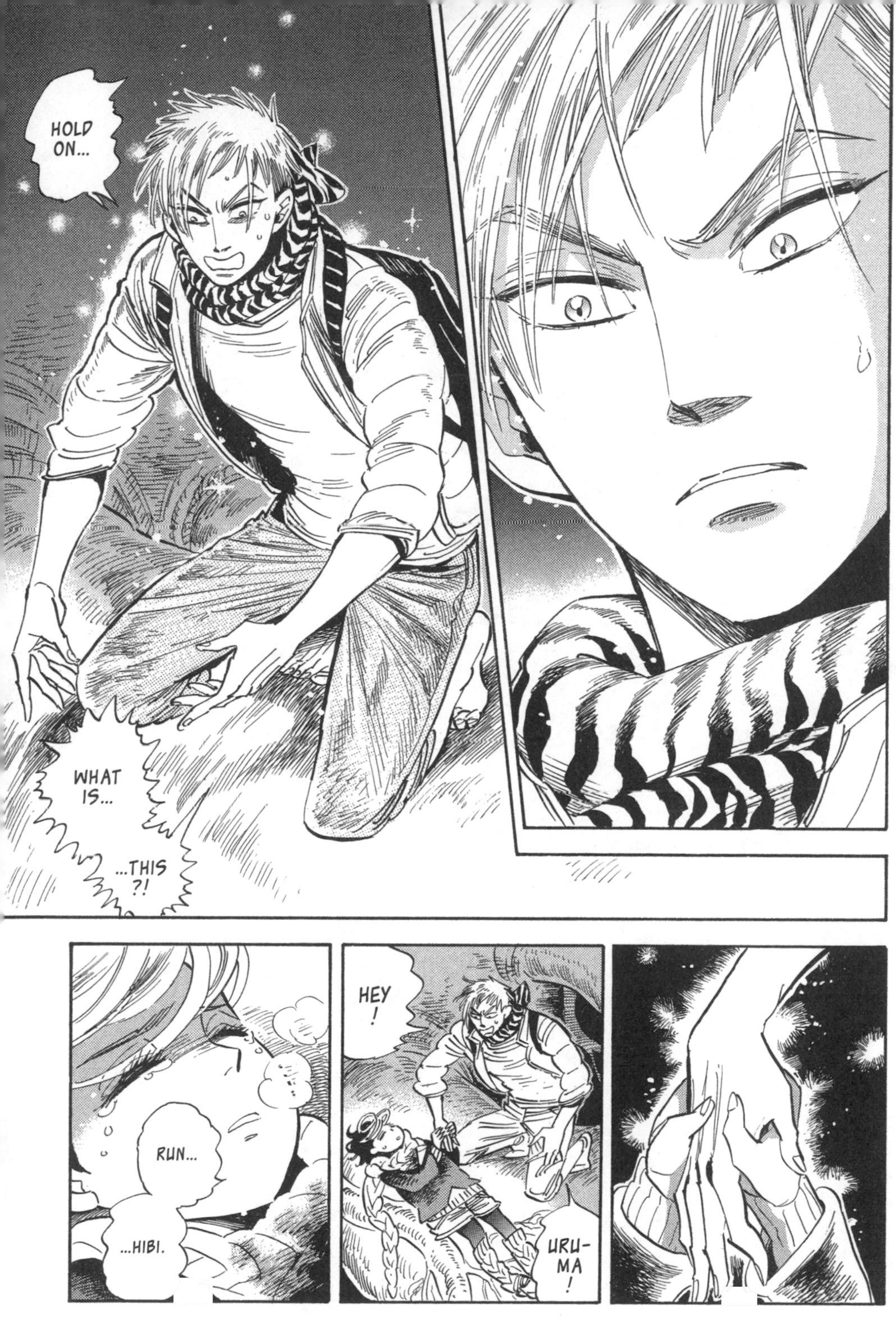
HOLD ON...
WHAT IS...
...THIS ?!
HEY !
URU-MA !
...
RUN...
...HIBI.

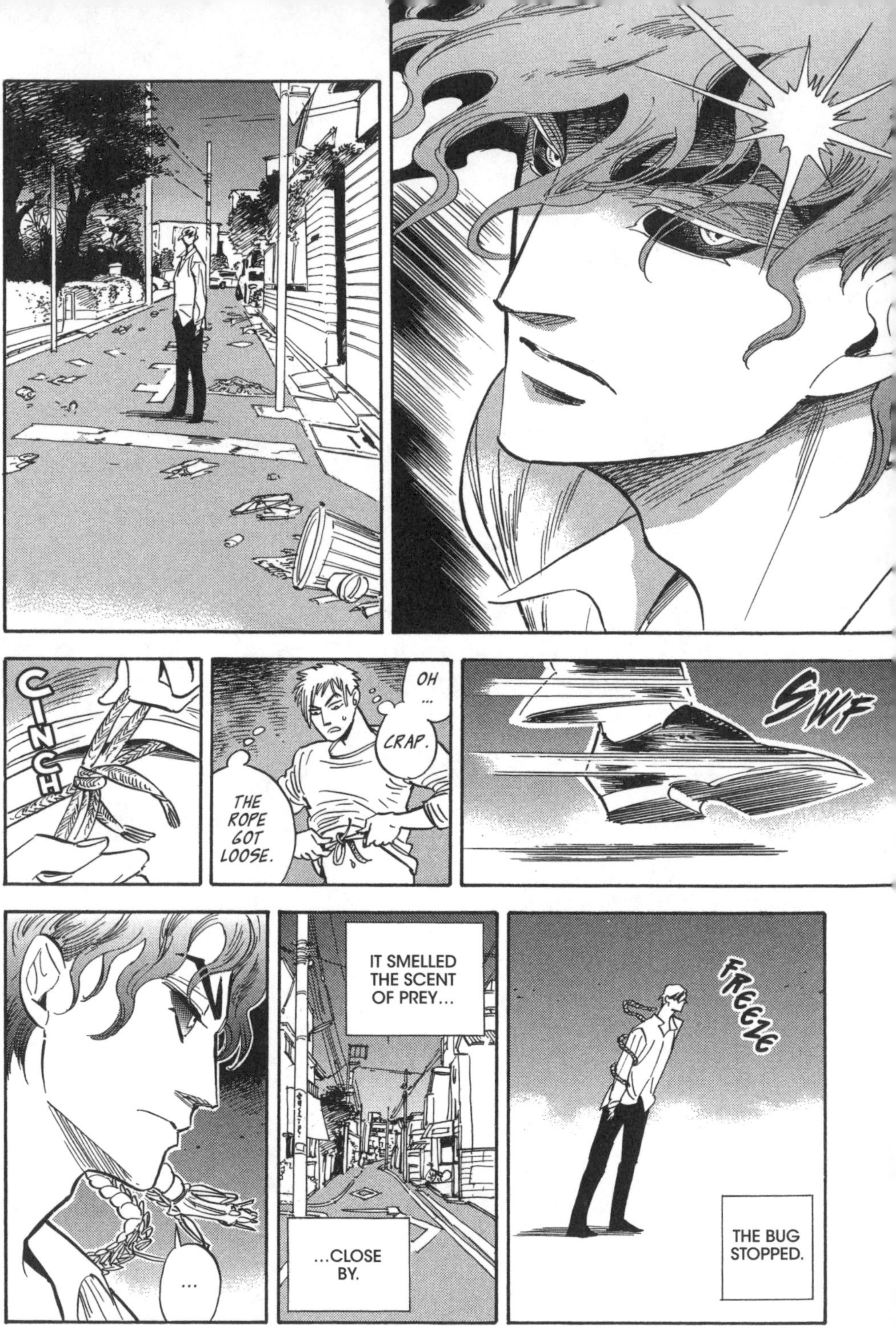
SWF
OH ...
CRAP.
THE ROPE GOT LOOSE.
CINCH
FREEZE
THE BUG STOPPED.
IT SMELLED THE SCENT OF PREY...
...CLOSE BY.
...

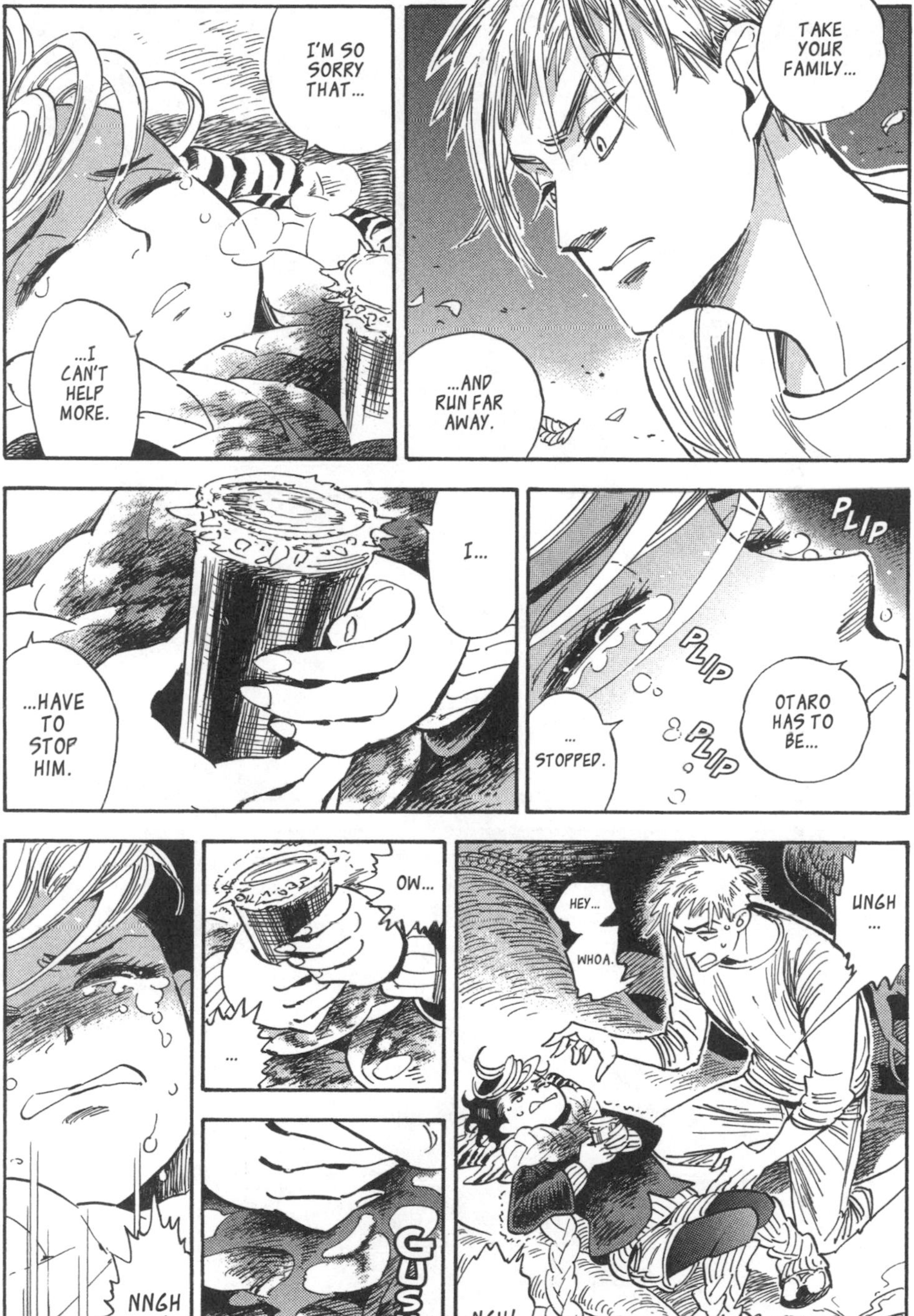
TAKE YOUR FAMILY...
...AND RUN FAR AWAY.
I'M SO SORRY THAT...
...I CAN'T HELP MORE.
PLIP
PLIP
PLIP
OTARO HAS TO BE...
...STOPPED.
I...
...HAVE TO STOP HIM.
UNGH ...
HEY...
WHOA.
NGH!
OW...
...
GUSH
NNGH ...!

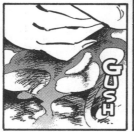

HAA

HAA

IT'S OKAY.

IDIOT!

STOP!

IF YOU DO THAT, YOU'LL...

... BLEED OUT...

IF I CAN...

...PULL IT OUT...

HAA

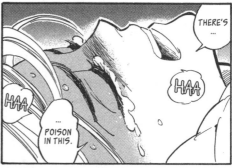

THERE'S...

HAA

HAA

... POISON IN THIS.

GRP

NGH!

NGH...

OKAY.

I BELIEVE YOU.

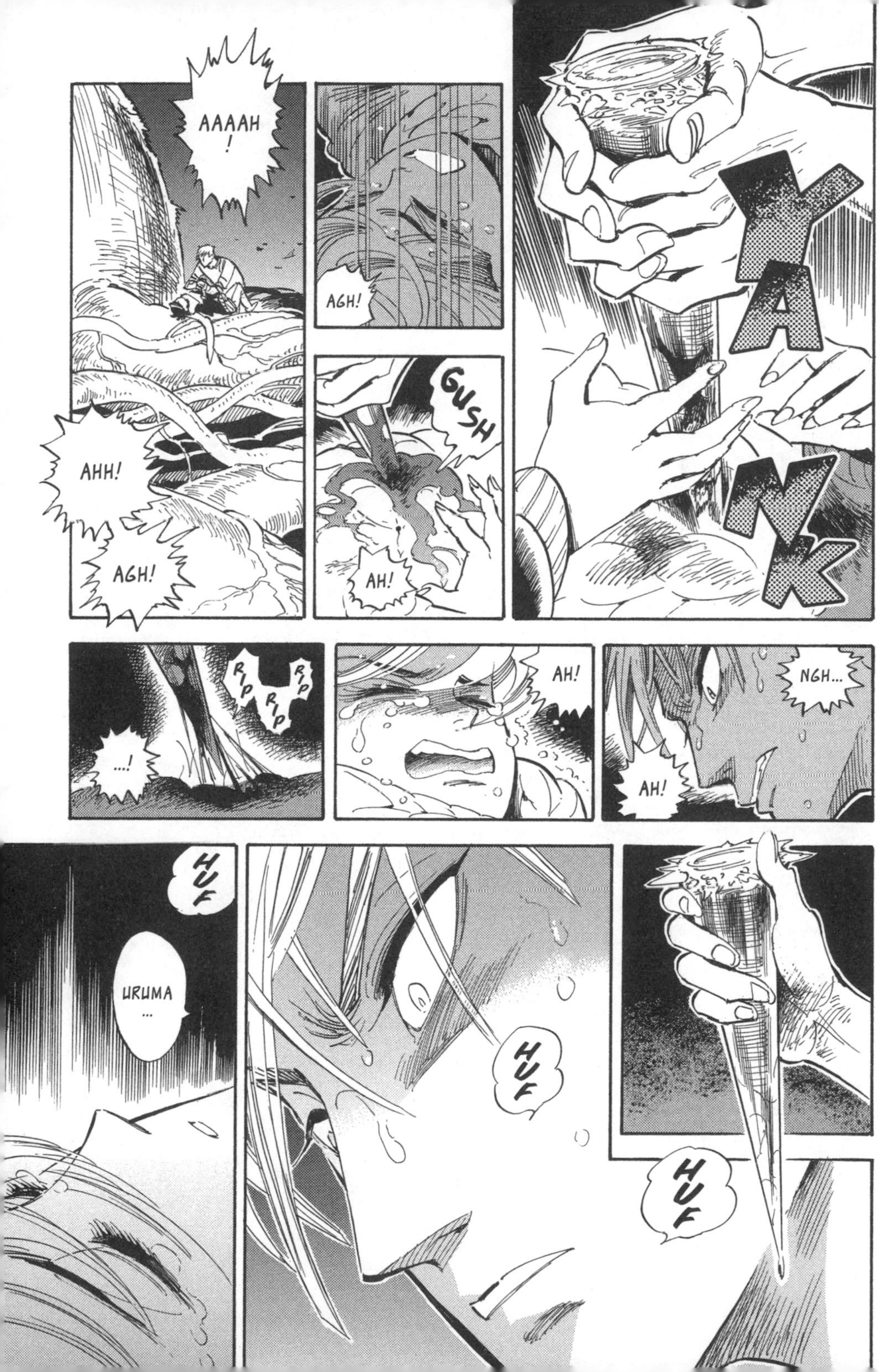
YANK
AGH!
GUSH
AH!
AAAAH!
AHH!
AGH!
NGH...
AH!
AH!
RIP RIP RIP
...!
HUF
HUF
HUF
URUMA...

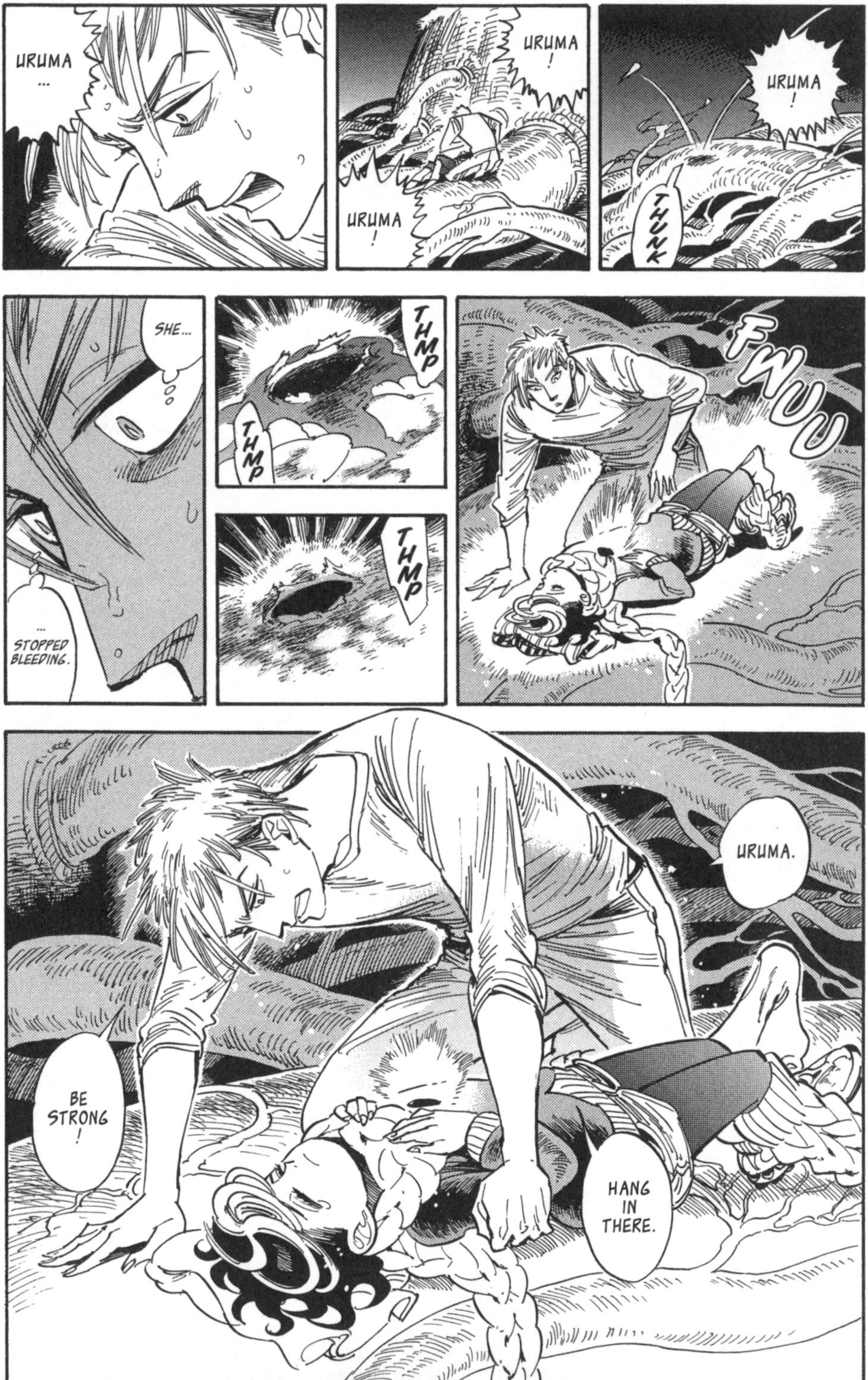
URUMA !
THUNK
URUMA !
URUMA !
URUMA ...
FWUU
THMP
THMP
THMP
SHE...
... STOPPED BLEEDING.
URUMA.
HANG IN THERE.
BE STRONG !

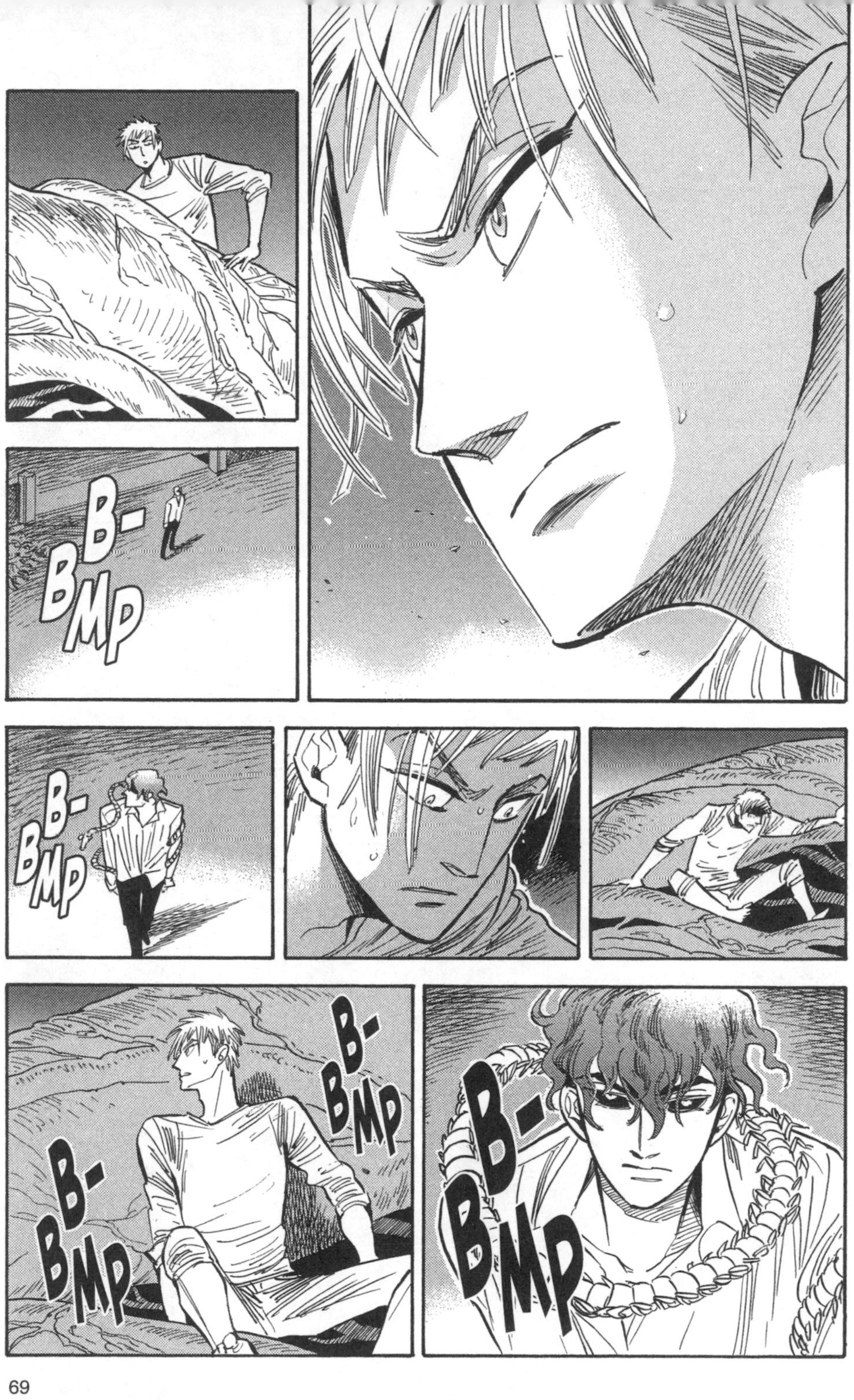
B-BMP
B-BMP
B-BMP
B-BMP
B-BMP

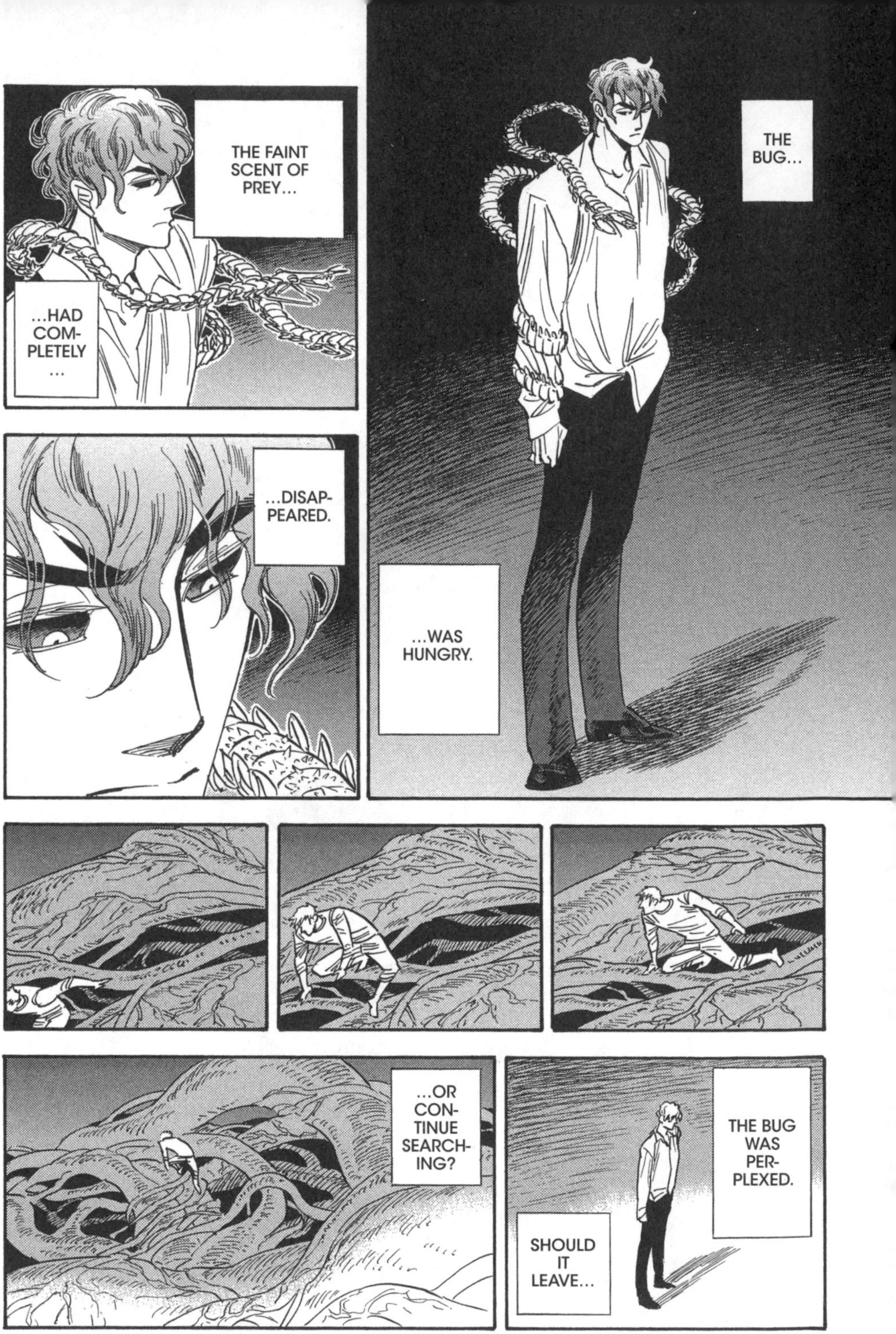
THE BUG...
...WAS HUNGRY.
THE FAINT SCENT OF PREY...
...HAD COMPLETELY...
...DISAPPEARED.
THE BUG WAS PERPLEXED.
SHOULD IT LEAVE...
...OR CONTINUE SEARCHING?

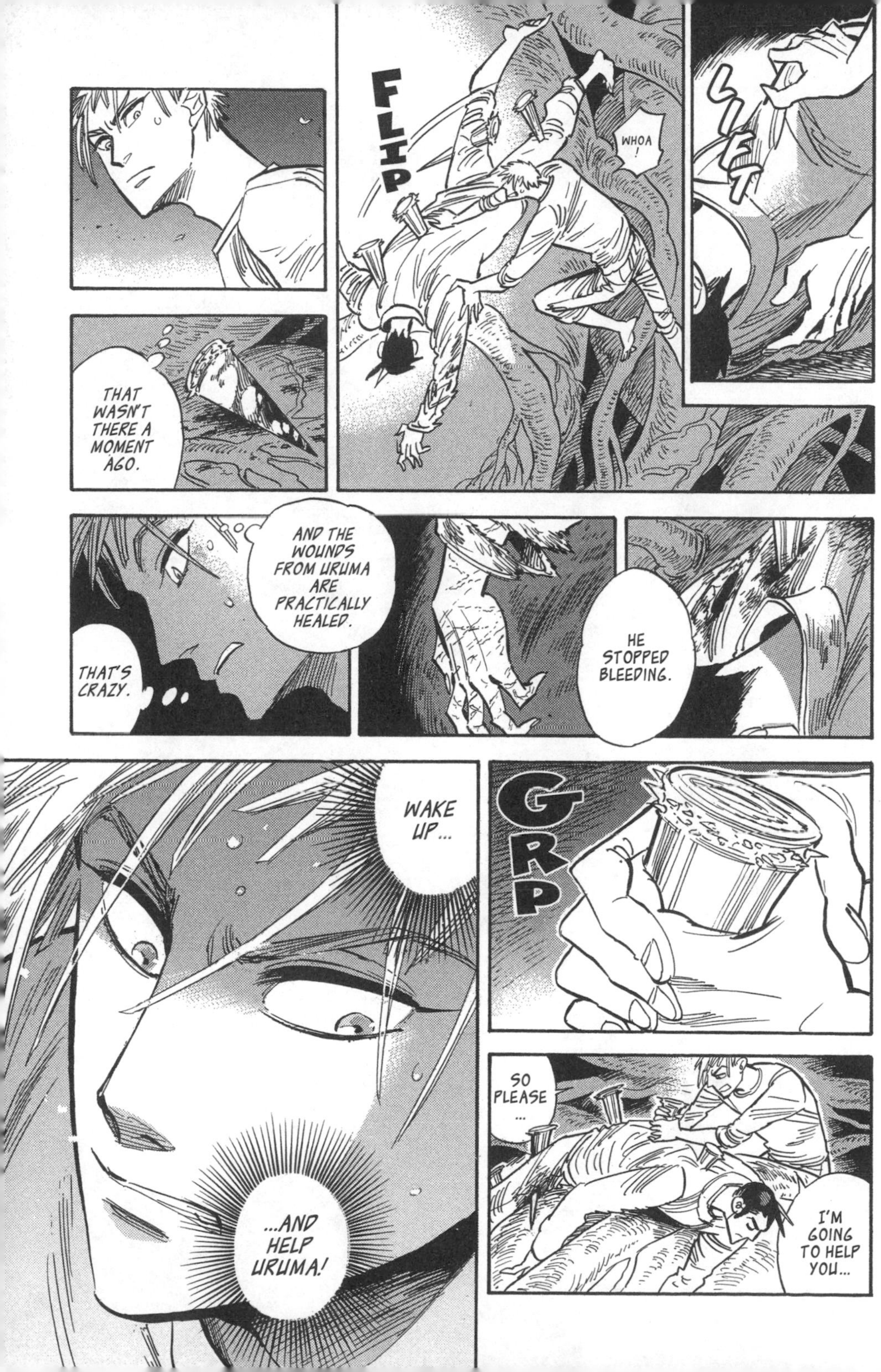
LIFT
WHOA!
FLIP
THAT WASN'T THERE A MOMENT AGO.
HE STOPPED BLEEDING.
AND THE WOUNDS FROM URUMA ARE PRACTICALLY HEALED.
THAT'S CRAZY.
GRP
I'M GOING TO HELP YOU...
SO PLEASE...
WAKE UP...
...AND HELP URUMA!

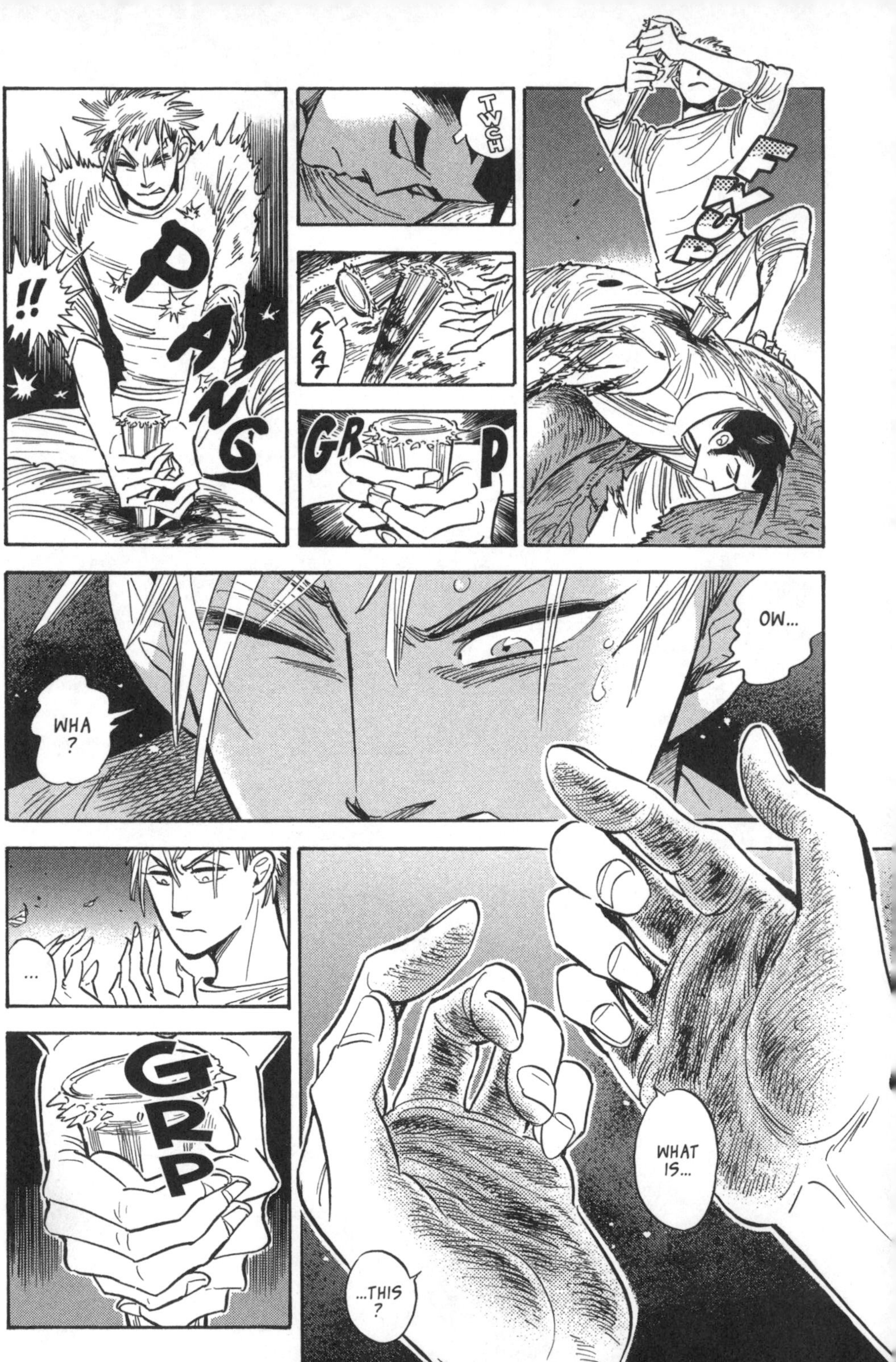
FWUP
TWCH
KLAT
GR P
!!
PANG
OW...
WHA?
WHAT IS...
...THIS?
...
GRP

...

WHO CARES ?!

....!

"THERE'S...

"...POISON IN THIS."

ZZT

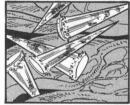

FWUP

FWUP

ROLL

TRMBL

TRMBL TRMBL

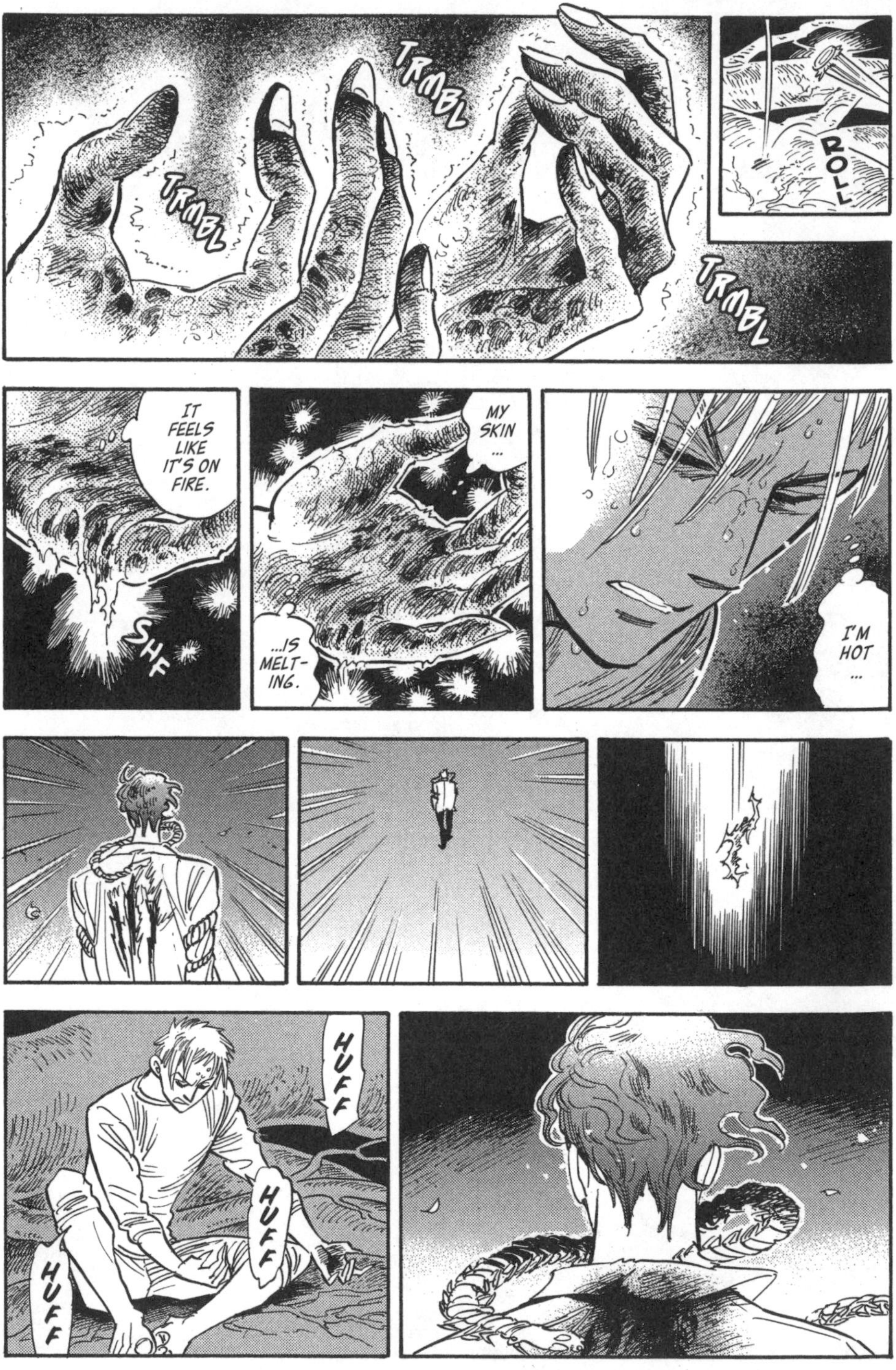
ROLL
TRMBL
TRMBL
TRMBL
I'M HOT ...
MY SKIN ...
...IS MELTING.
IT FEELS LIKE IT'S ON FIRE.
SHF
HUFF
HUFF
HUFF

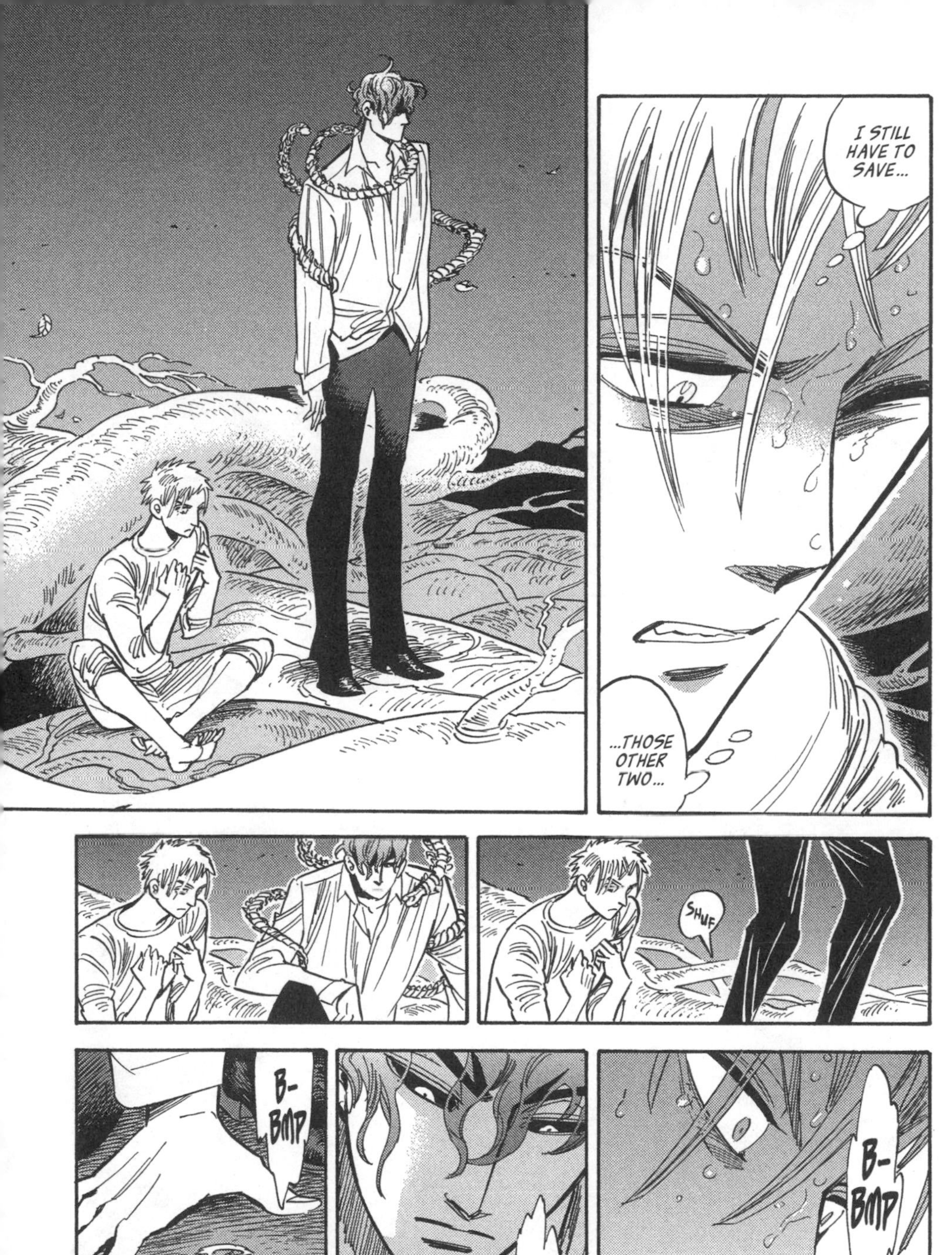
I STILL HAVE TO SAVE...
...THOSE OTHER TWO...
SHUF
B-BMP
B-BMP
B-BMP

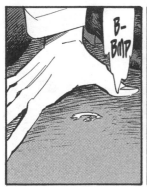

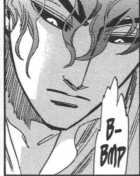

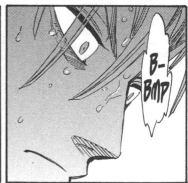

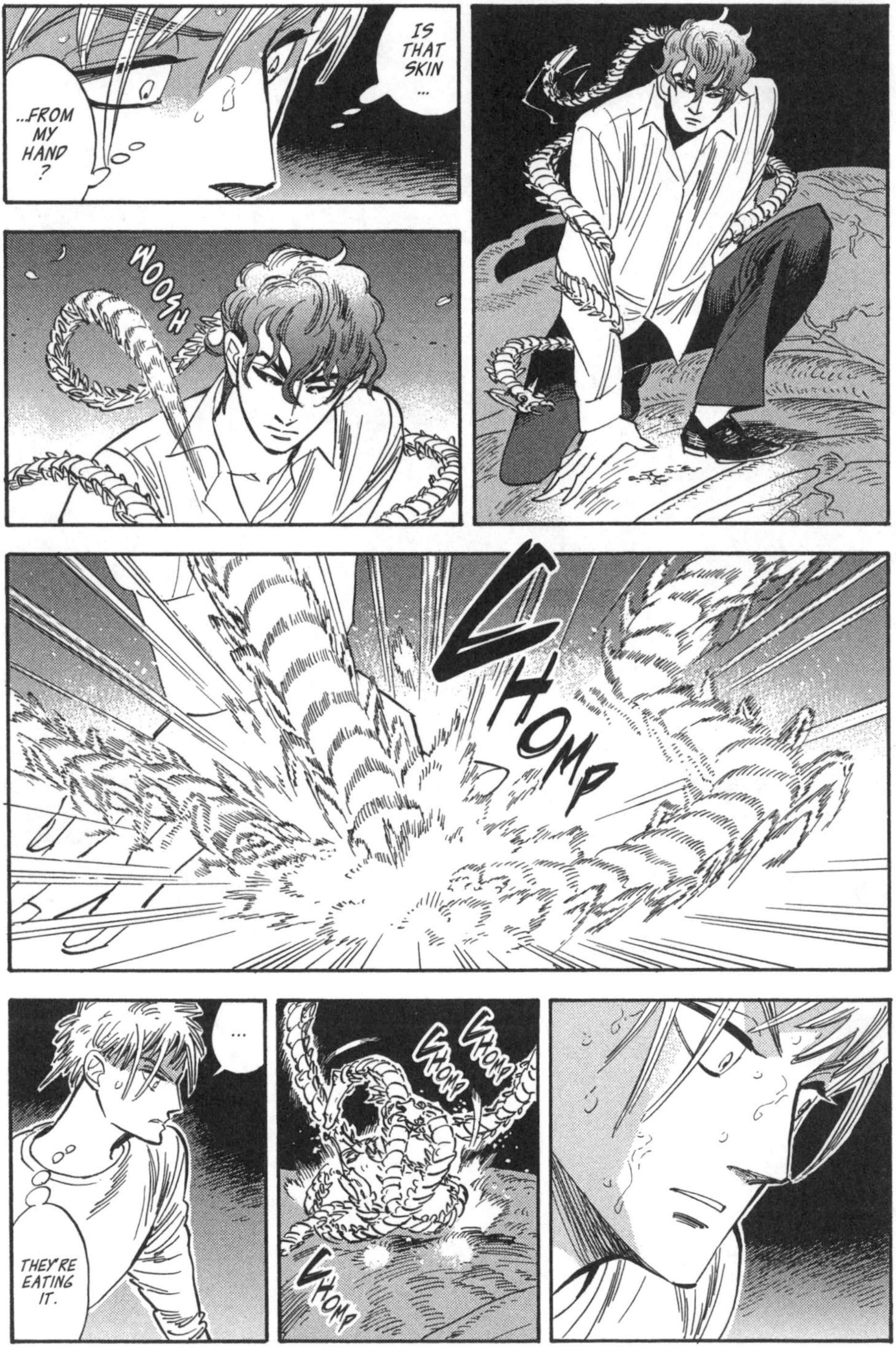
IS THAT SKIN ...
...FROM MY HAND ?
WOOSH
CHOMP
CHOMP
CHOMP
CHOMP
...
THEY'RE EATING IT.

HIBI'S BODY...

...WAS HIDDEN FROM THE BUG.

...AND...

...CAST HER MAGIC WITHIN IT.

SANGO'S ROPE...

...COULD SEAL OFF A SPACE...

...

BUT...

...THAT WAS NOT THE CASE FOR THAT WHICH...

...LEFT HIS BODY.

IT BE-LONGED...

...TO SOME-ONE ELSE.

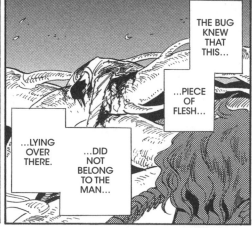

THE BUG KNEW THAT THIS...

...PIECE OF FLESH...

...LYING OVER THERE.

...DID NOT BELONG TO THE MAN...

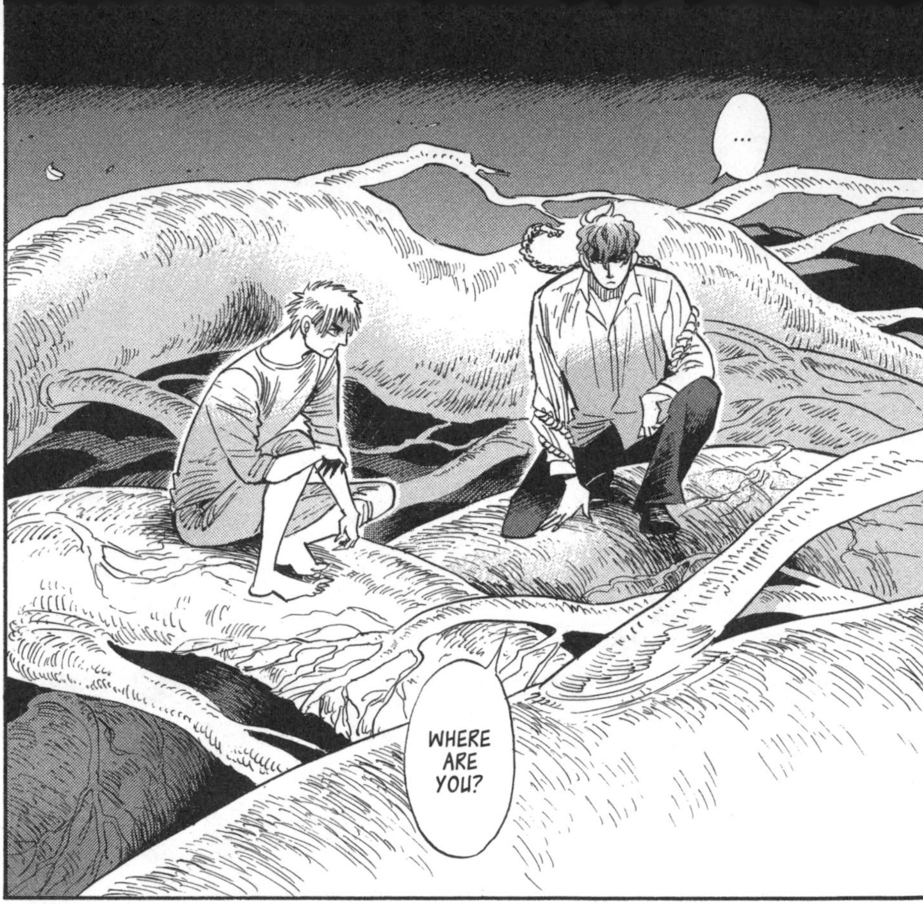
...
WHERE ARE YOU?
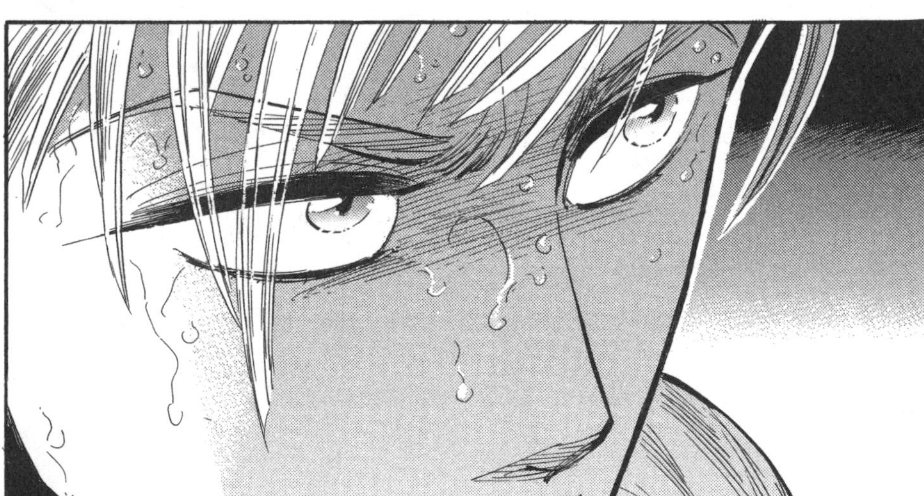

Chapter 32 / The End

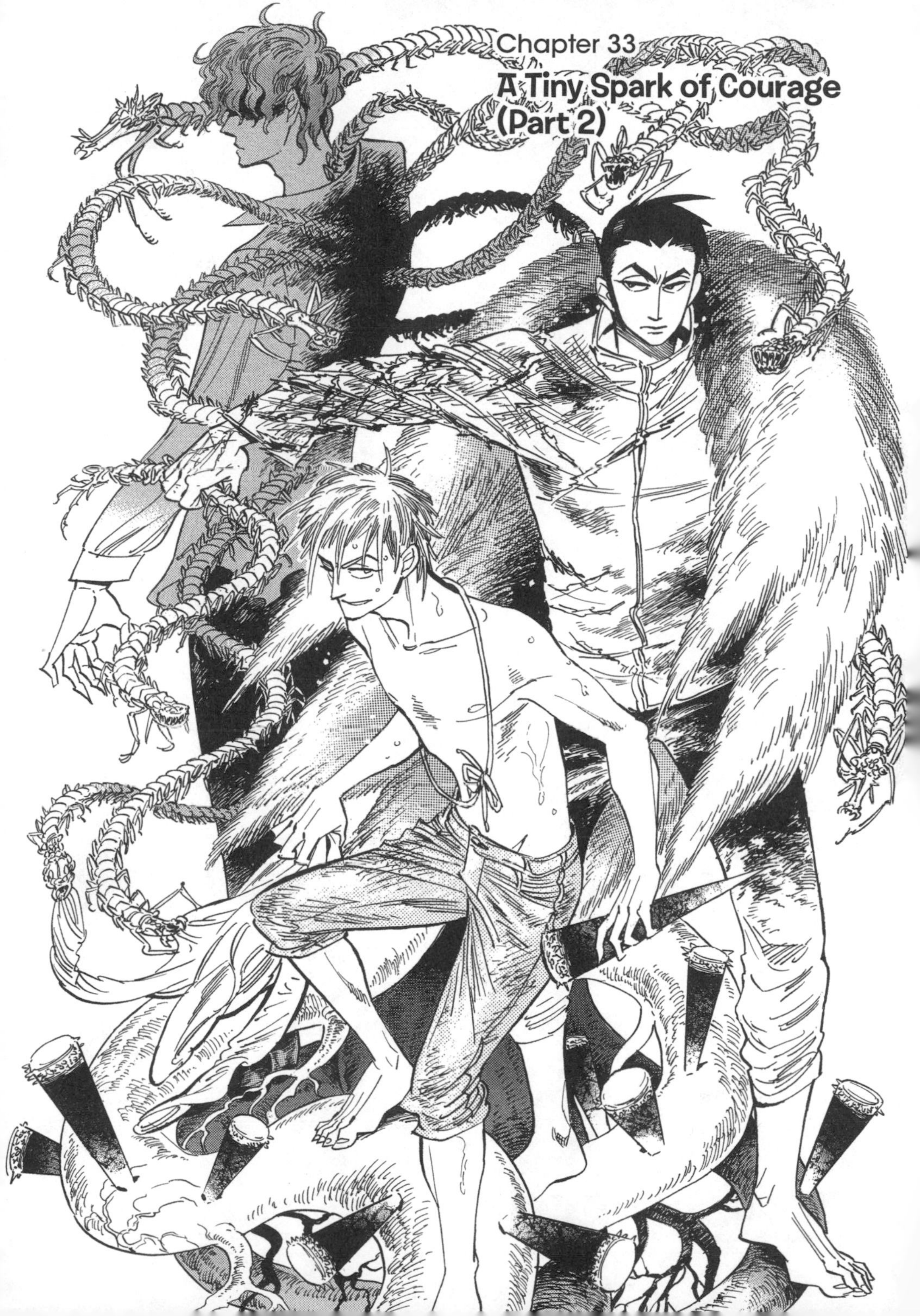
Chapter 33
A Tiny Spark of Courage
(Part 2)

ALL
THAT
FOR A
DROP OF
SWEAT
...

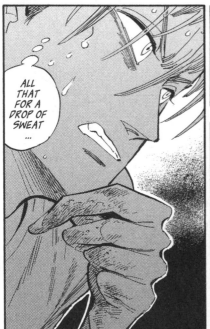

D-ZOOM

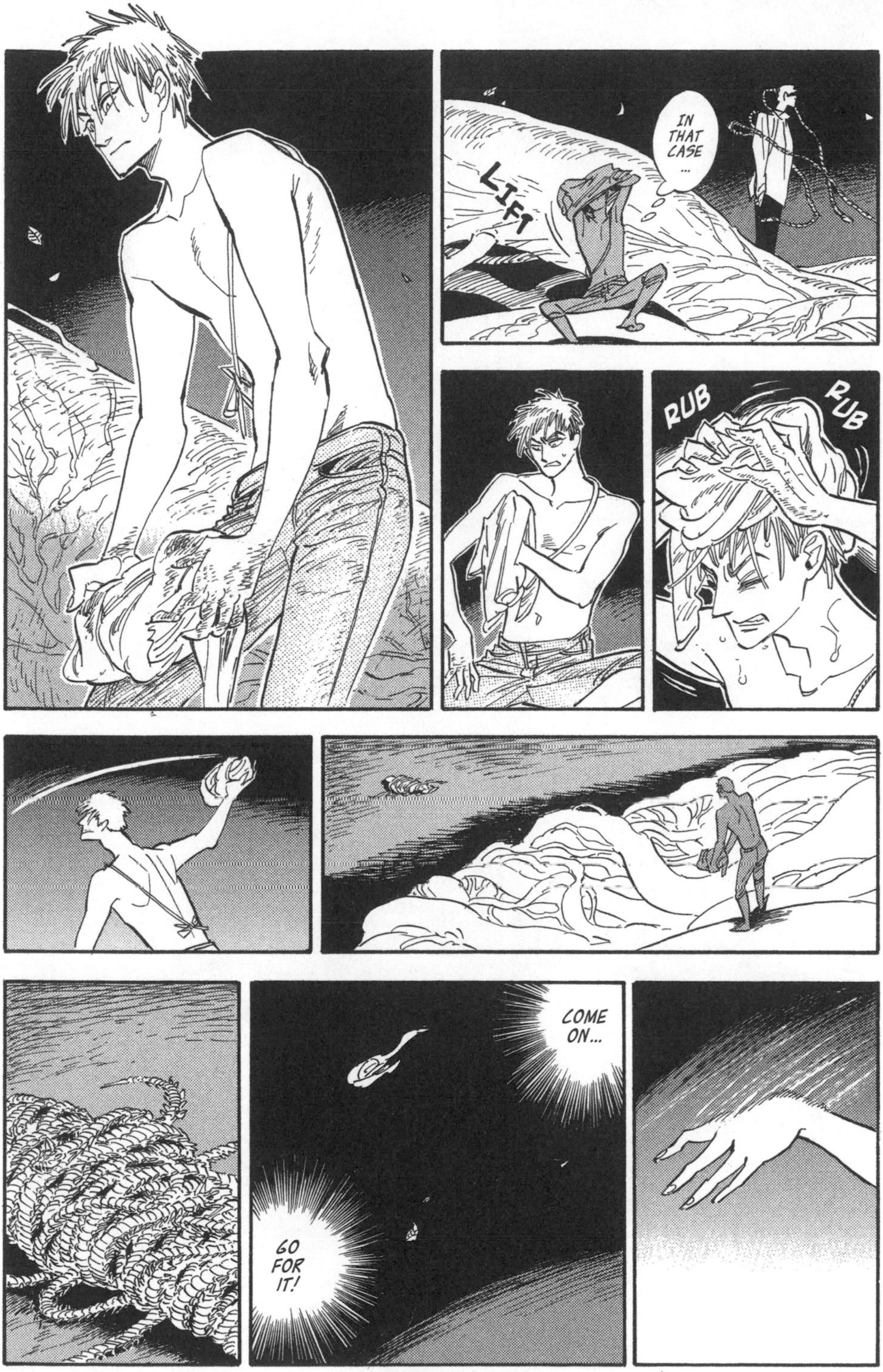
IN THAT CASE ...
LIFT
RUB RUB
COME ON...
GO FOR IT!

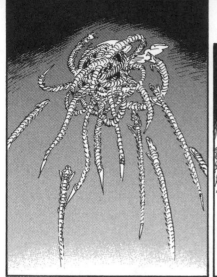

ZOOM

THUNK

GRIP

THROB

B-BMP

B-BMP

PLEASE
BE
ALIVE.

MR.
URUMA
...

NOW'S
MY
CHANCE
...

HE
MOVED!

YES!

...TO GET
AWAY
FROM
THAT
GUY.

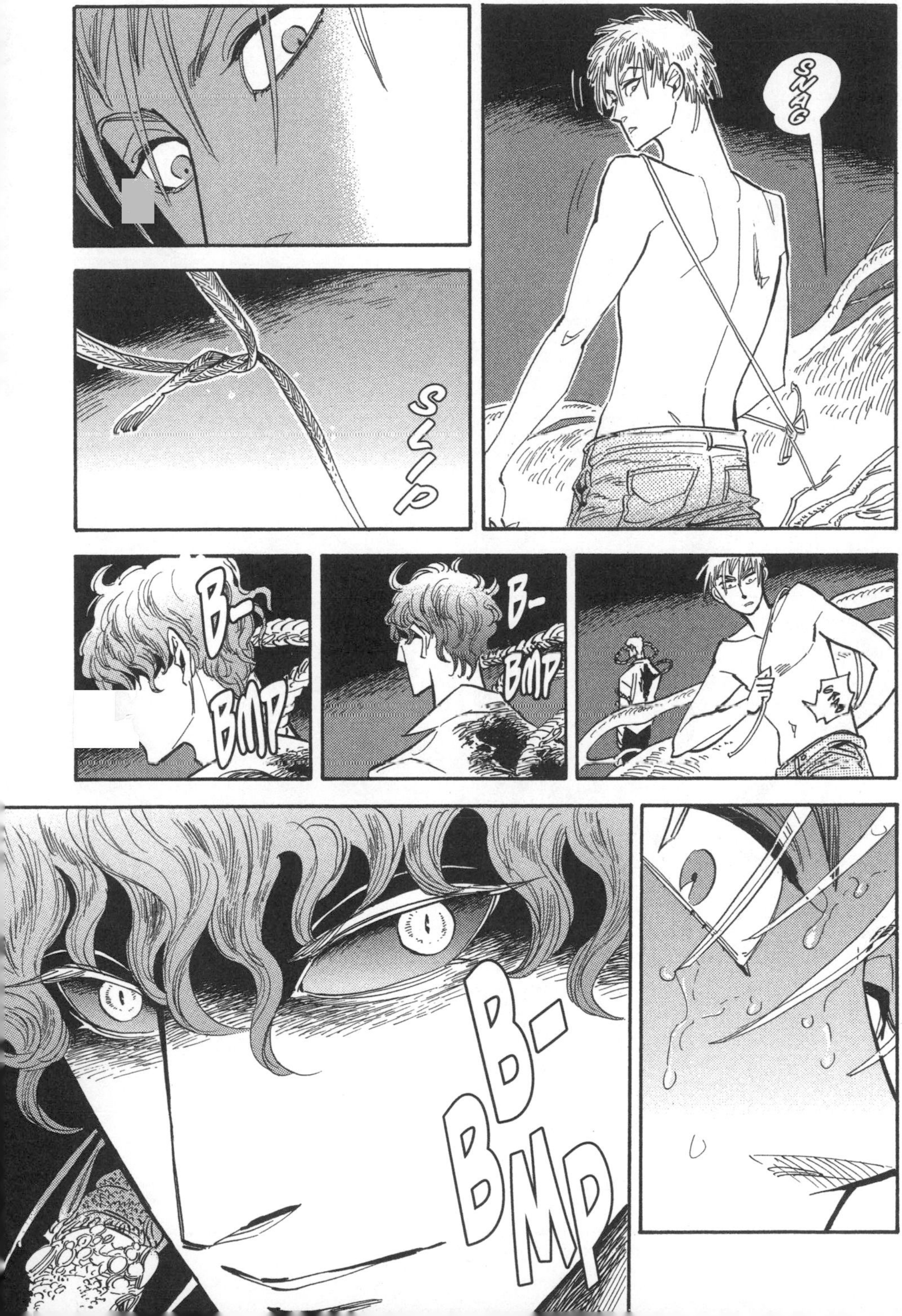
SNAG
SLIP
GRAB
B-BMP
B-BMP
B-BMP

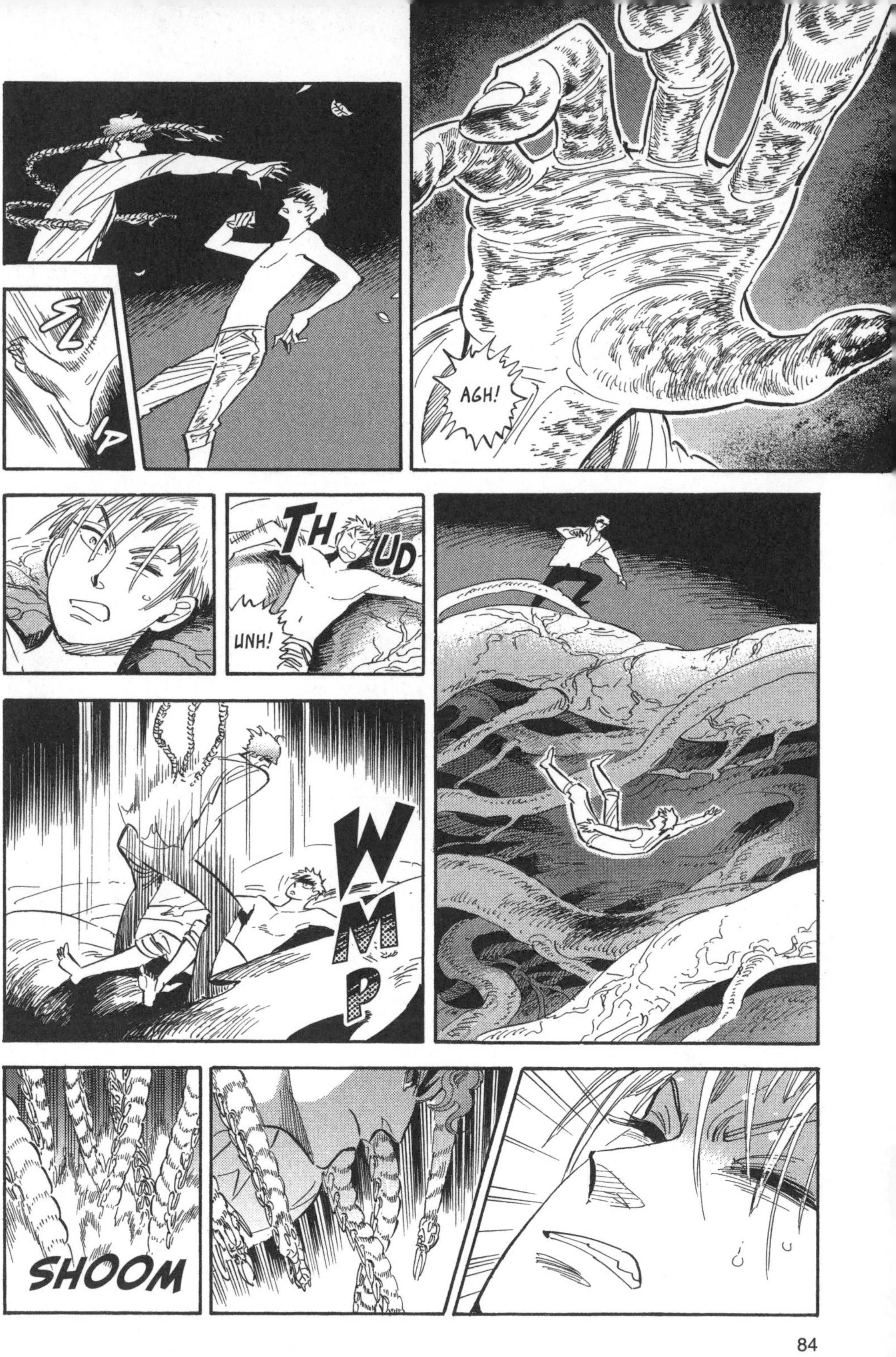
AGH!
SLIP
THUD
UNH!
WMP
SHOOM

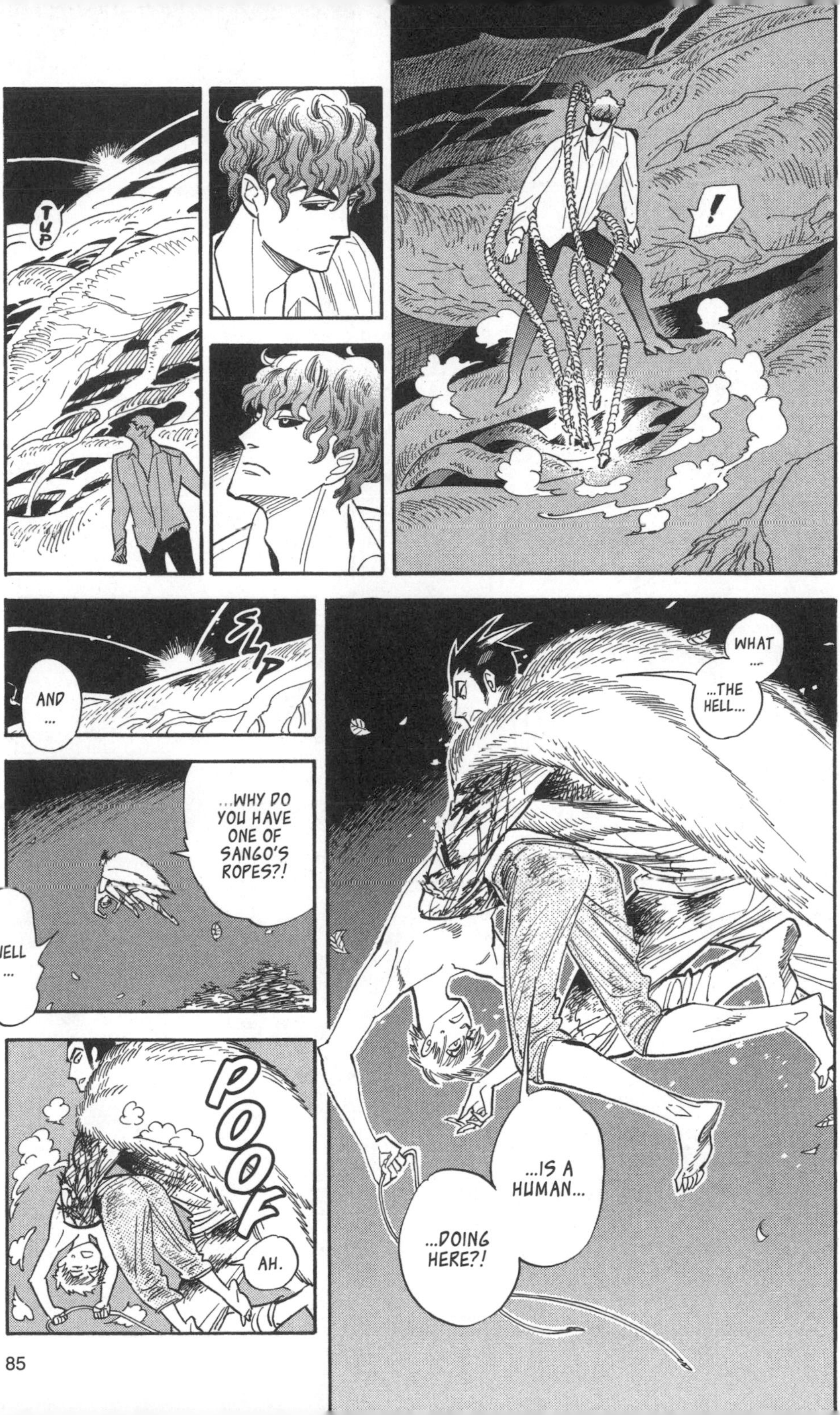
!
TUP
WHAT ...
...THE HELL...
...IS A HUMAN...
...DOING HERE?!
SLIP
AND ...
...WHY DO YOU HAVE ONE OF SANGO'S ROPES?!
WELL ...
POOF
AH.

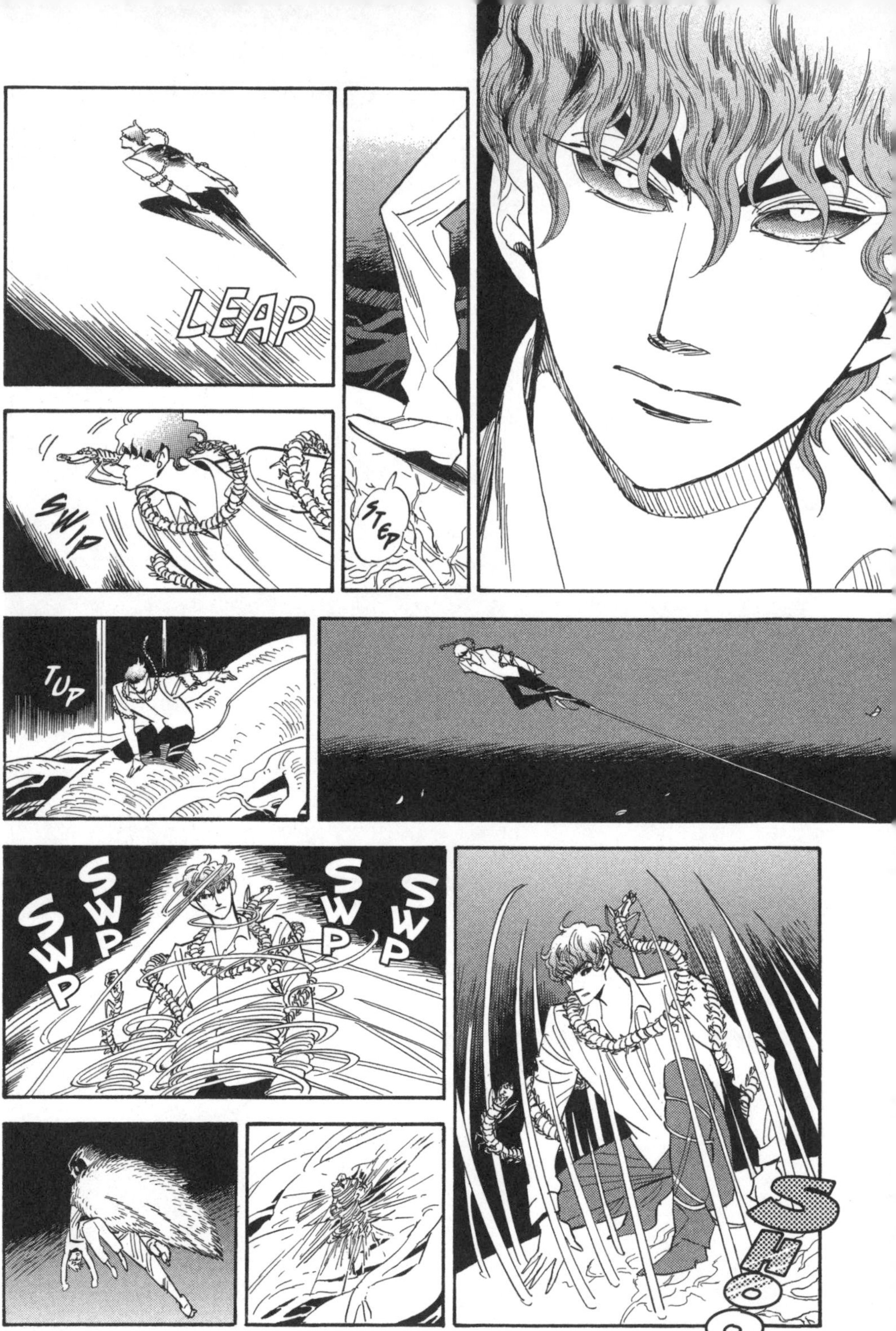
STEP
LEAP
SWIP
TUP
SHOOO
SWP
SWP
SWP
SWP

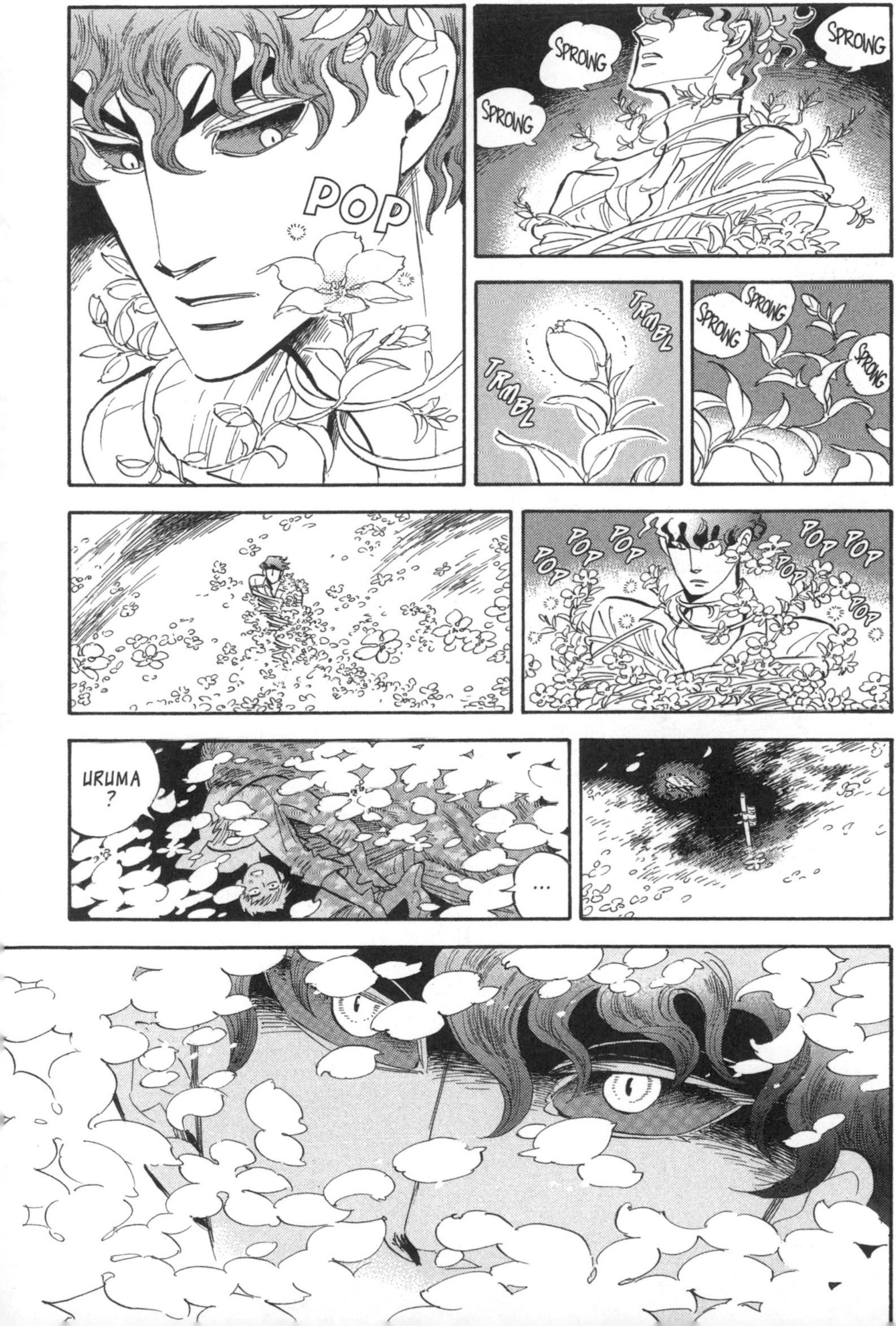
SPROING
SPROING
SPROING
SPROING
SPROING
SPROING
TRMBL
TRMBL
POP
POP
POP
POP
POP
POP
POP
POP
POP
URUMA?
...

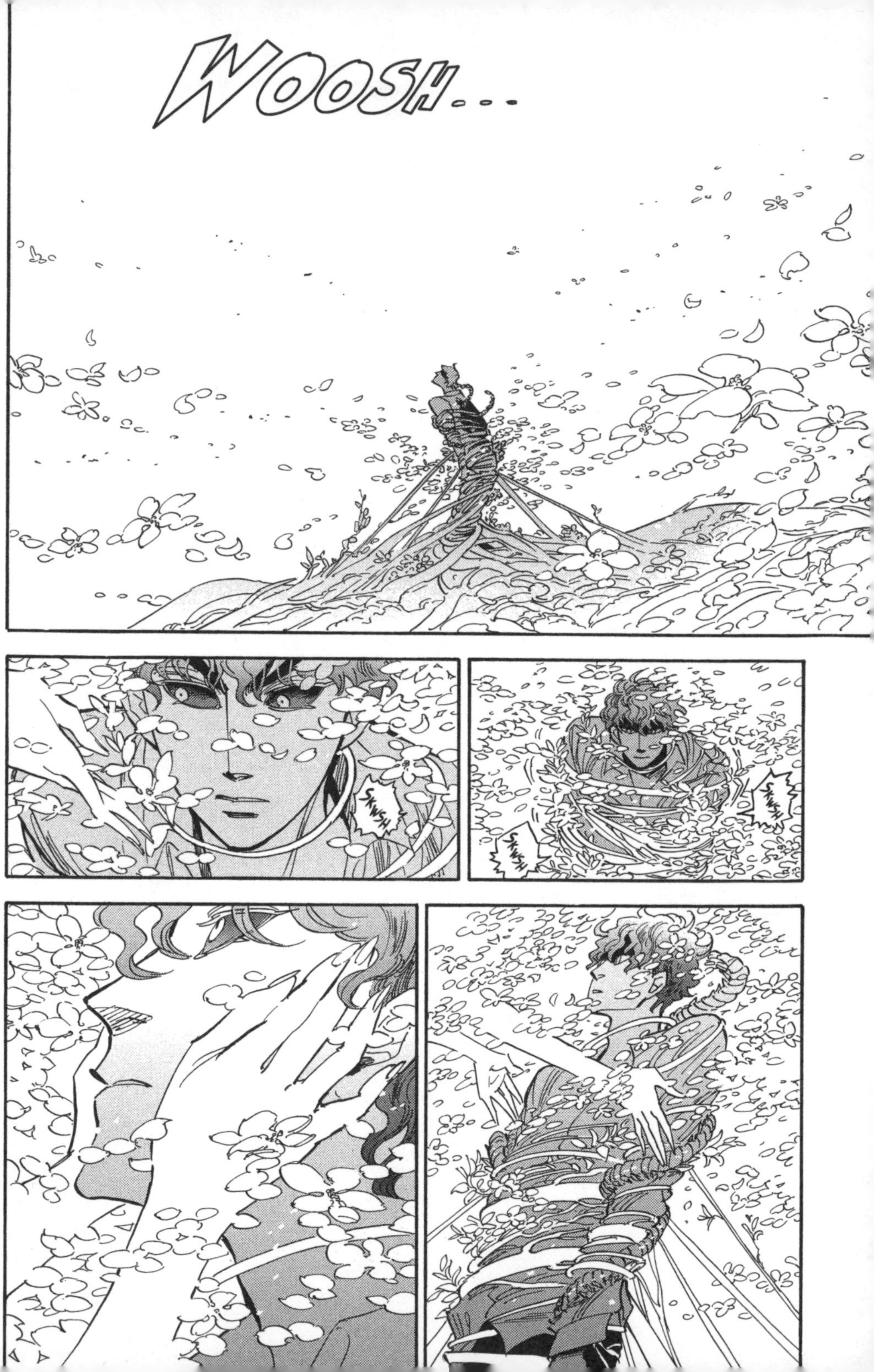
WOOSH...
SKWISH
SKWISH
SKWISH

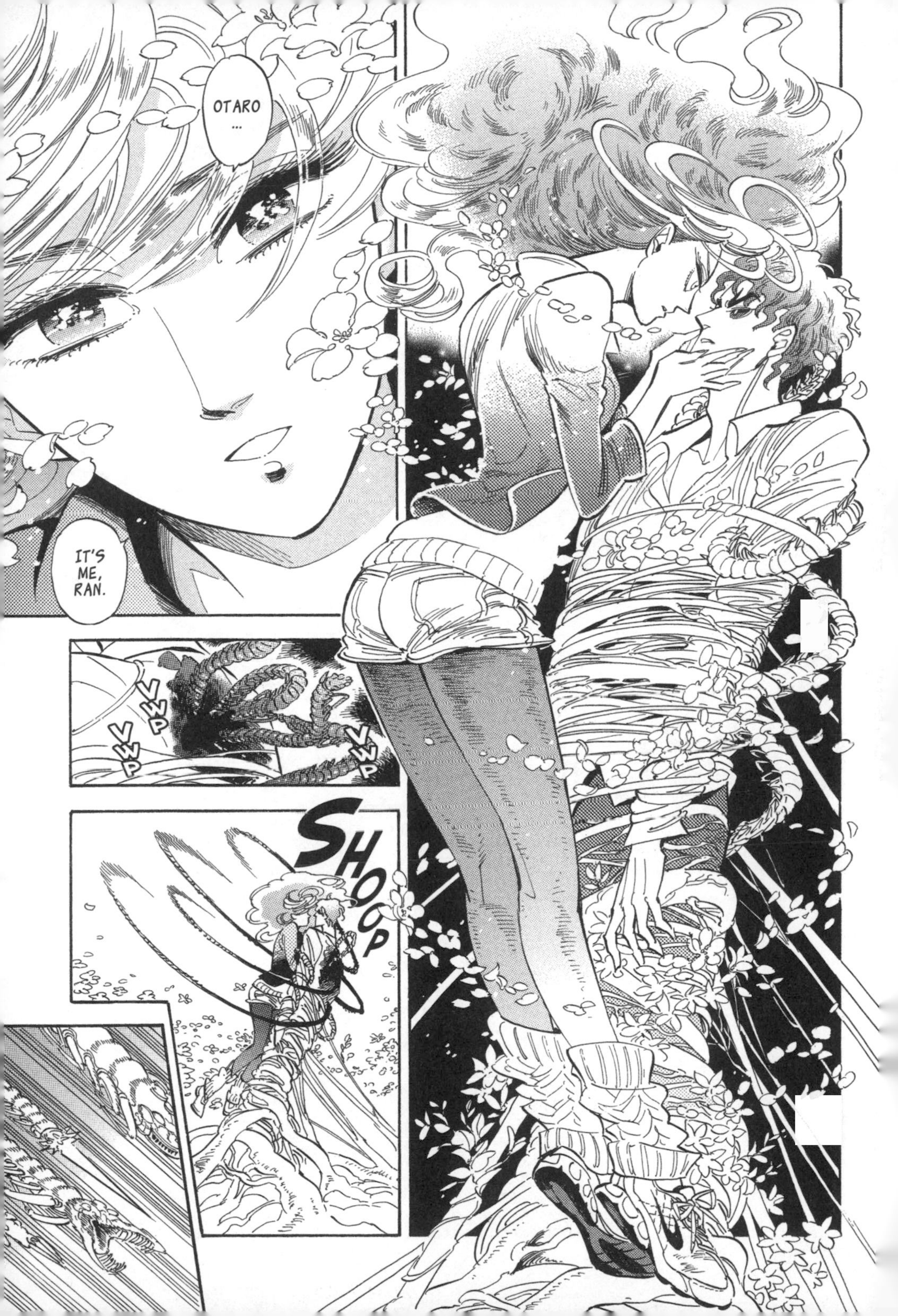
OTARO ...
IT'S ME, RAN.
VWP VWP VWP
SHOOP

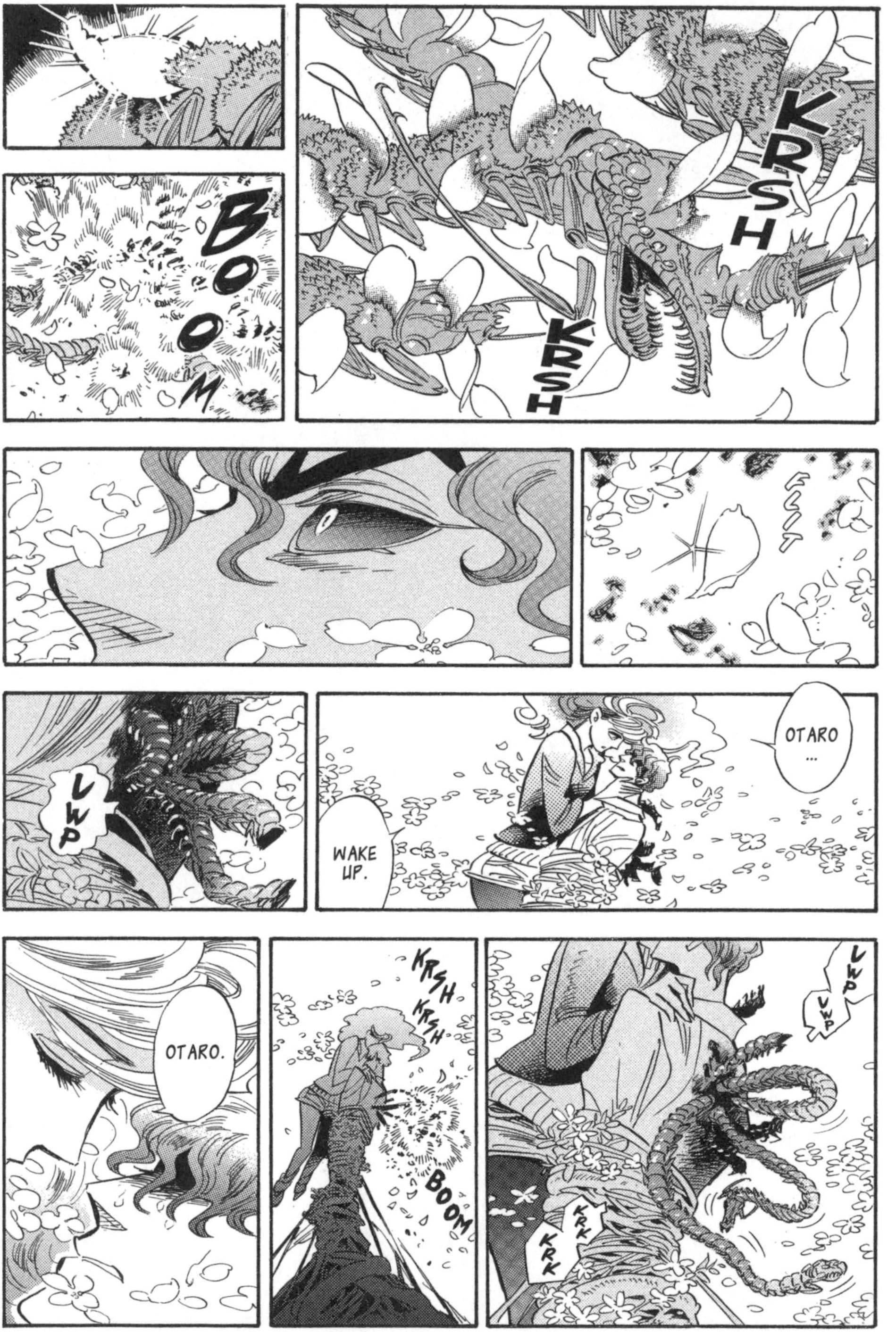
KRSH
KRSH
BOOOM
FLIT
OTARO ...
WAKE UP.
UWP
UWP
UWP
KRK
KRK
KRSH
KRSH
BOOM
OTARO.

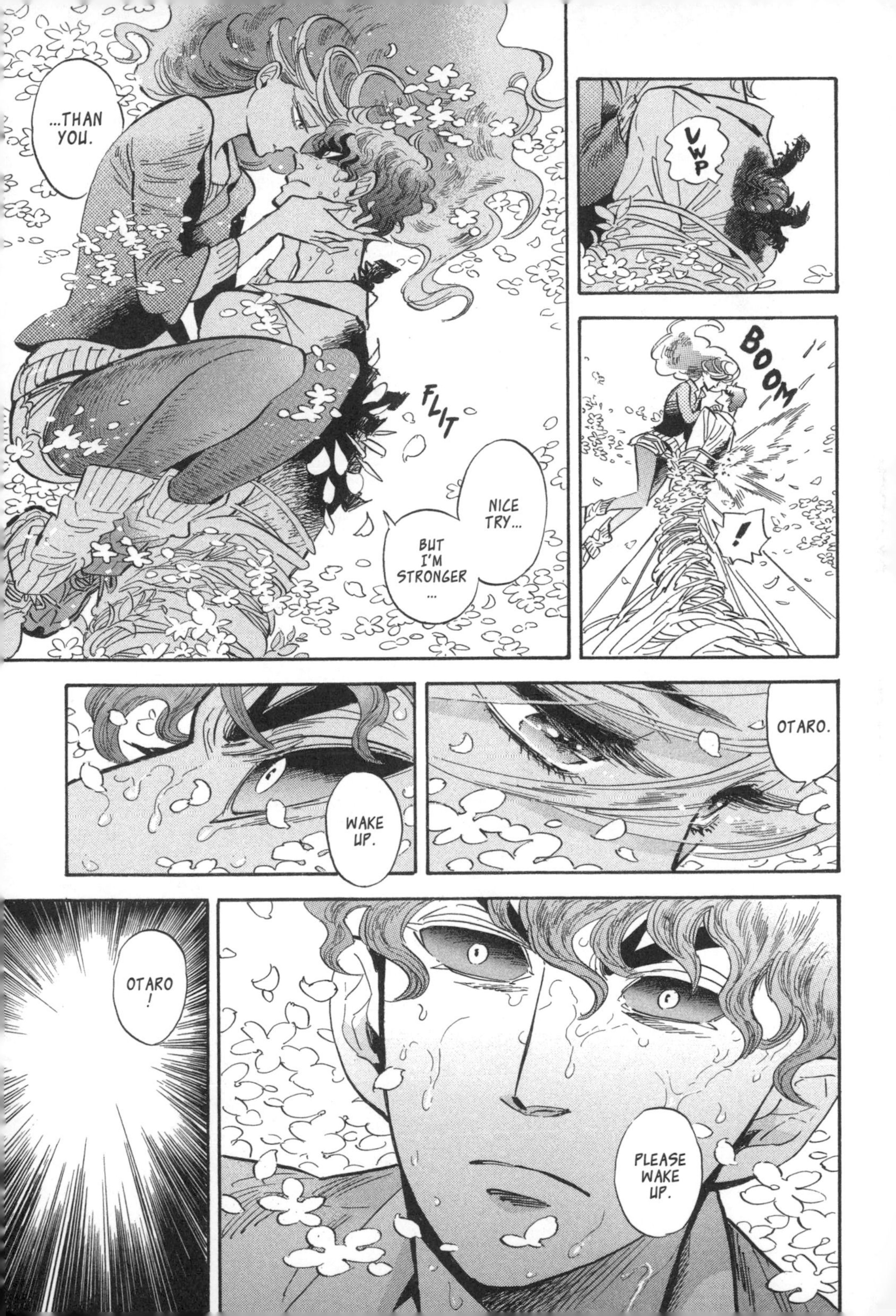
UWP
BOOM
!
...THAN YOU.
FLIT
NICE TRY...
BUT I'M STRONGER ...
OTARO.
WAKE UP.
PLEASE WAKE UP.
OTARO!

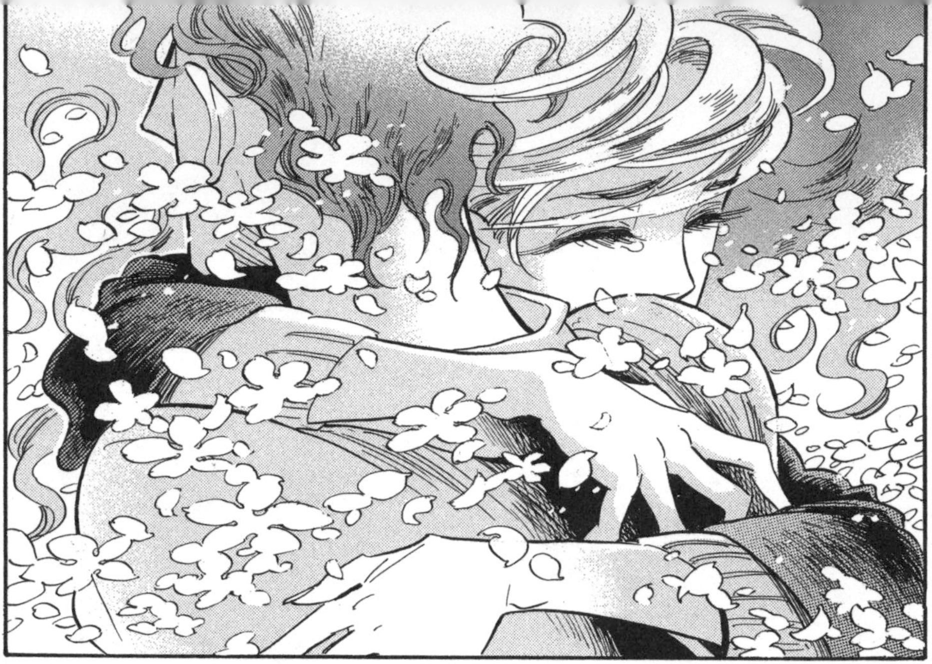
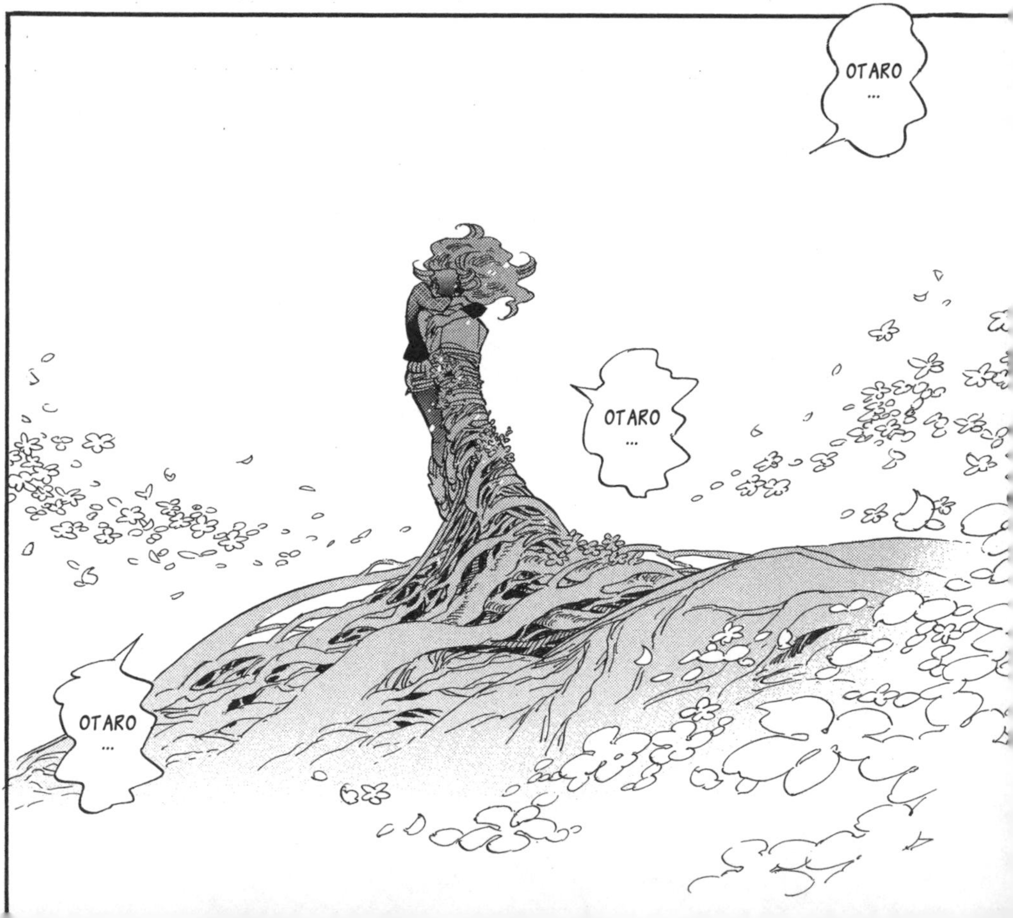
OTARO
...
OTARO
...
OTARO
...

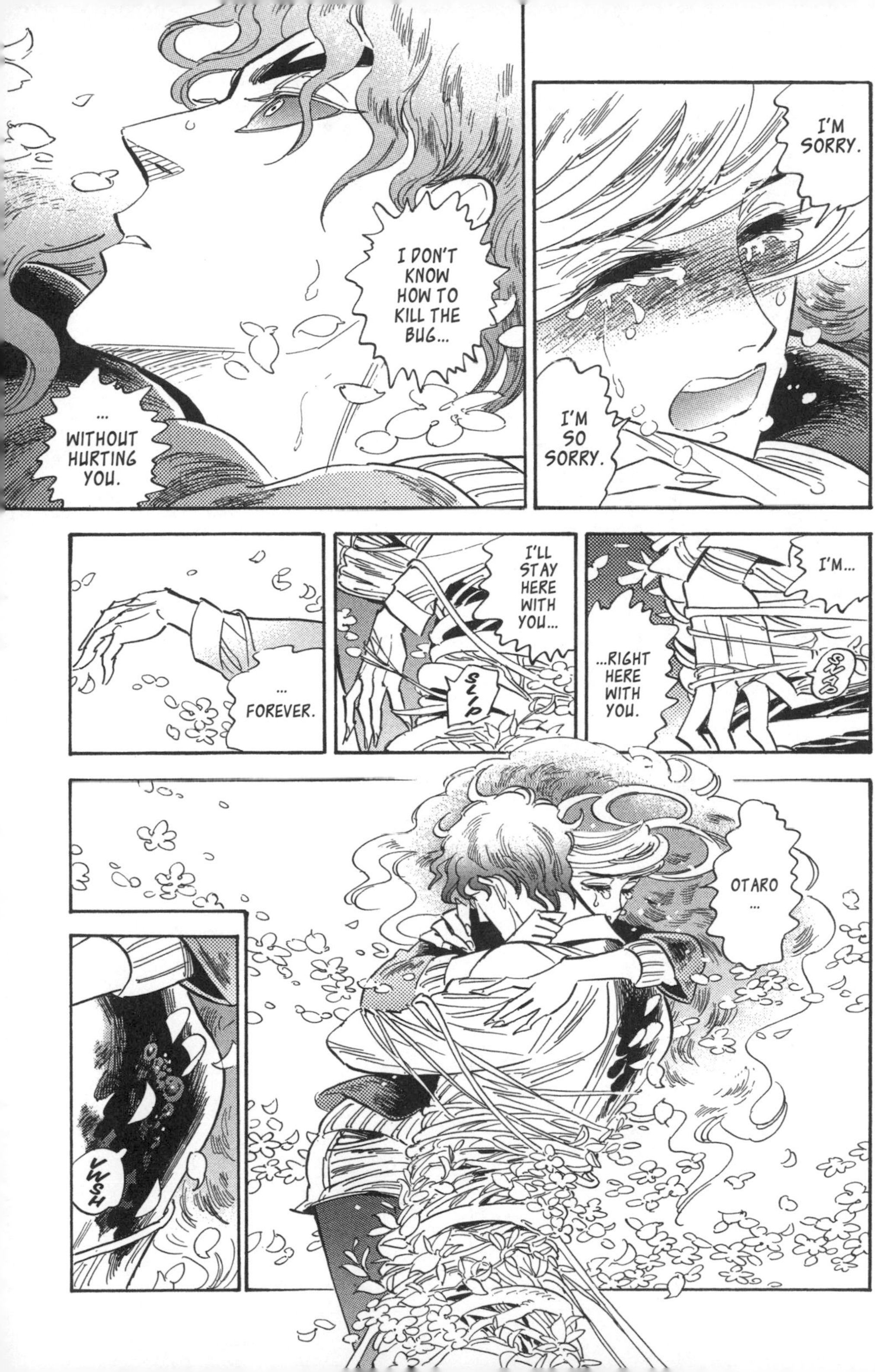
I'M SORRY.
I'M SO SORRY.
I DON'T KNOW HOW TO KILL THE BUG...
... WITHOUT HURTING YOU.
I'M...
...RIGHT HERE WITH YOU.
SNAP
I'LL STAY HERE WITH YOU...
SLIP
... FOREVER.
OTARO ...
VWSH

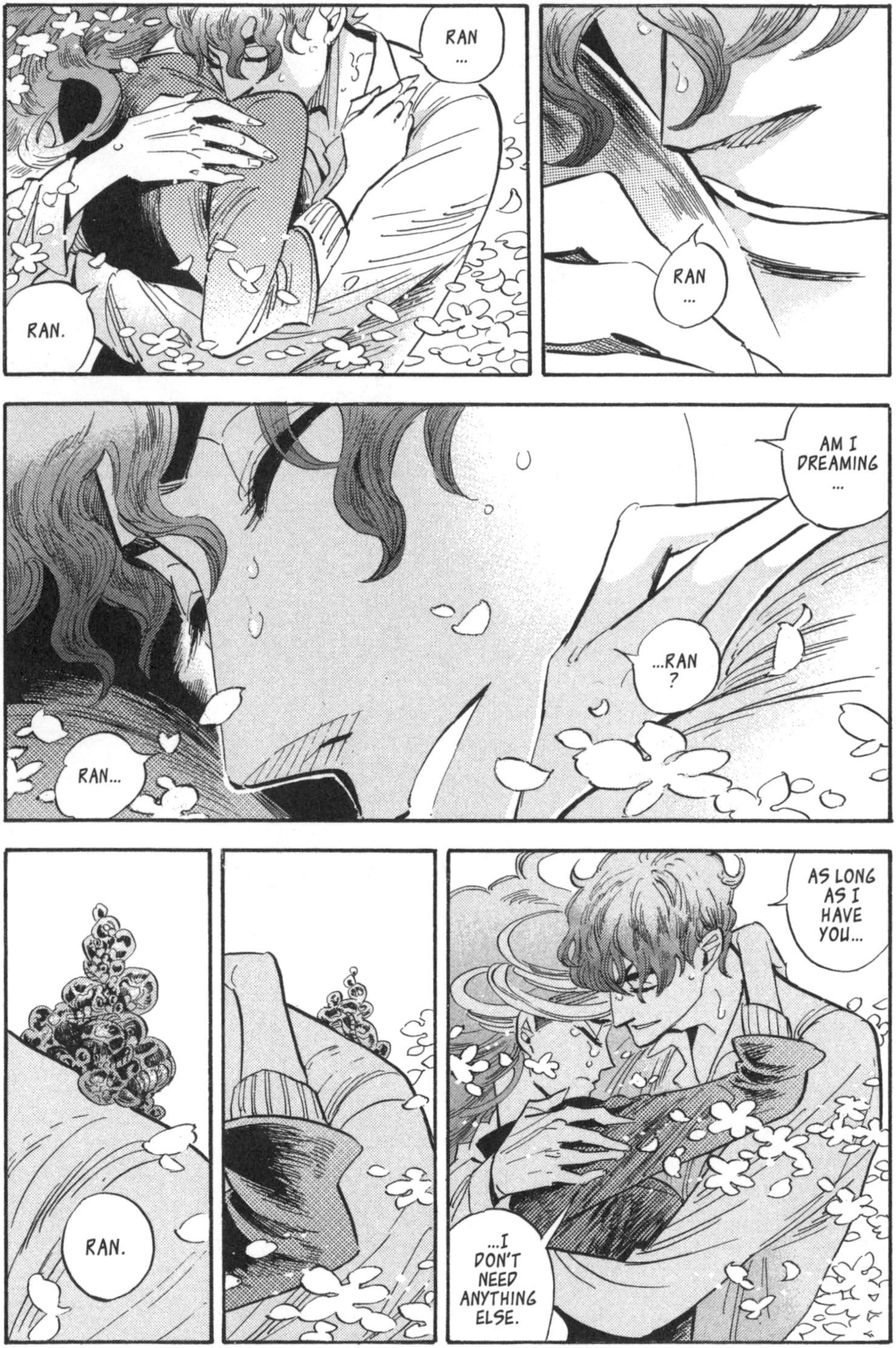
RAN ...
RAN ...
RAN.
AM I DREAMING ...
...RAN ?
RAN...
AS LONG AS I HAVE YOU...
...I DON'T NEED ANYTHING ELSE.
RAN.

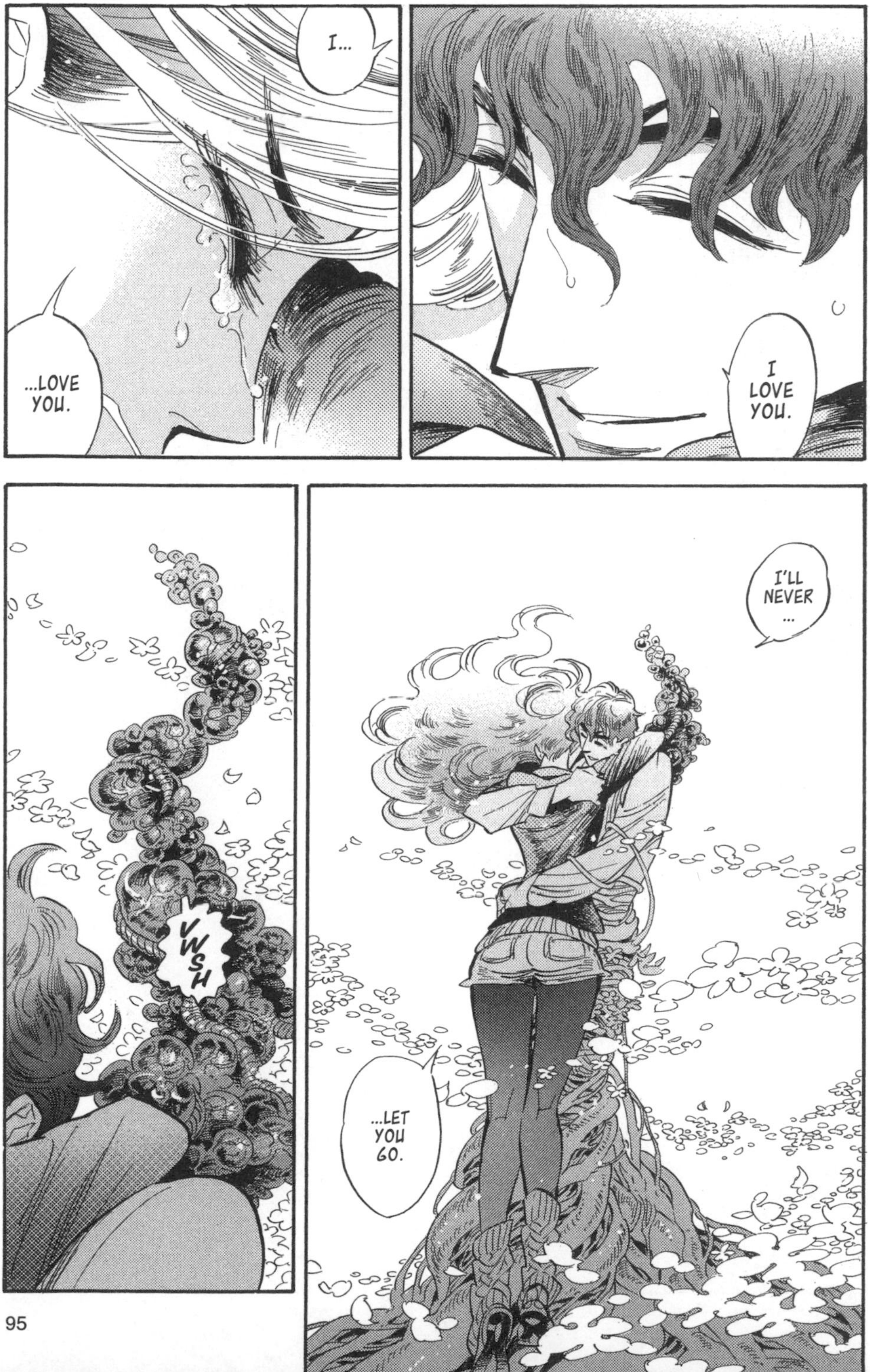
I LOVE YOU.
I...
...LOVE YOU.
I'LL NEVER ...
...LET YOU GO.
VWSH

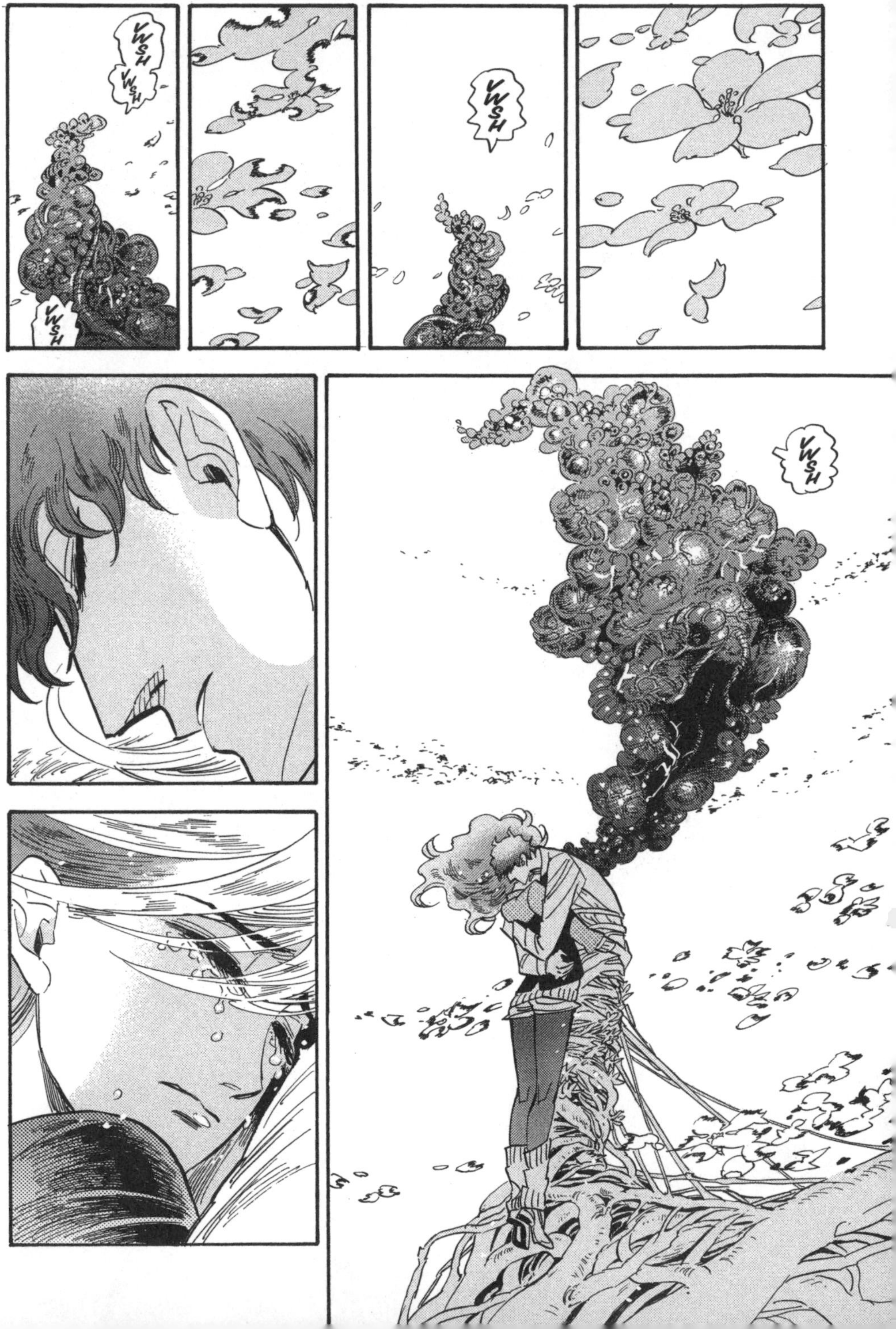
VWSH
VWSH
VWSH
VWSH
VWSH

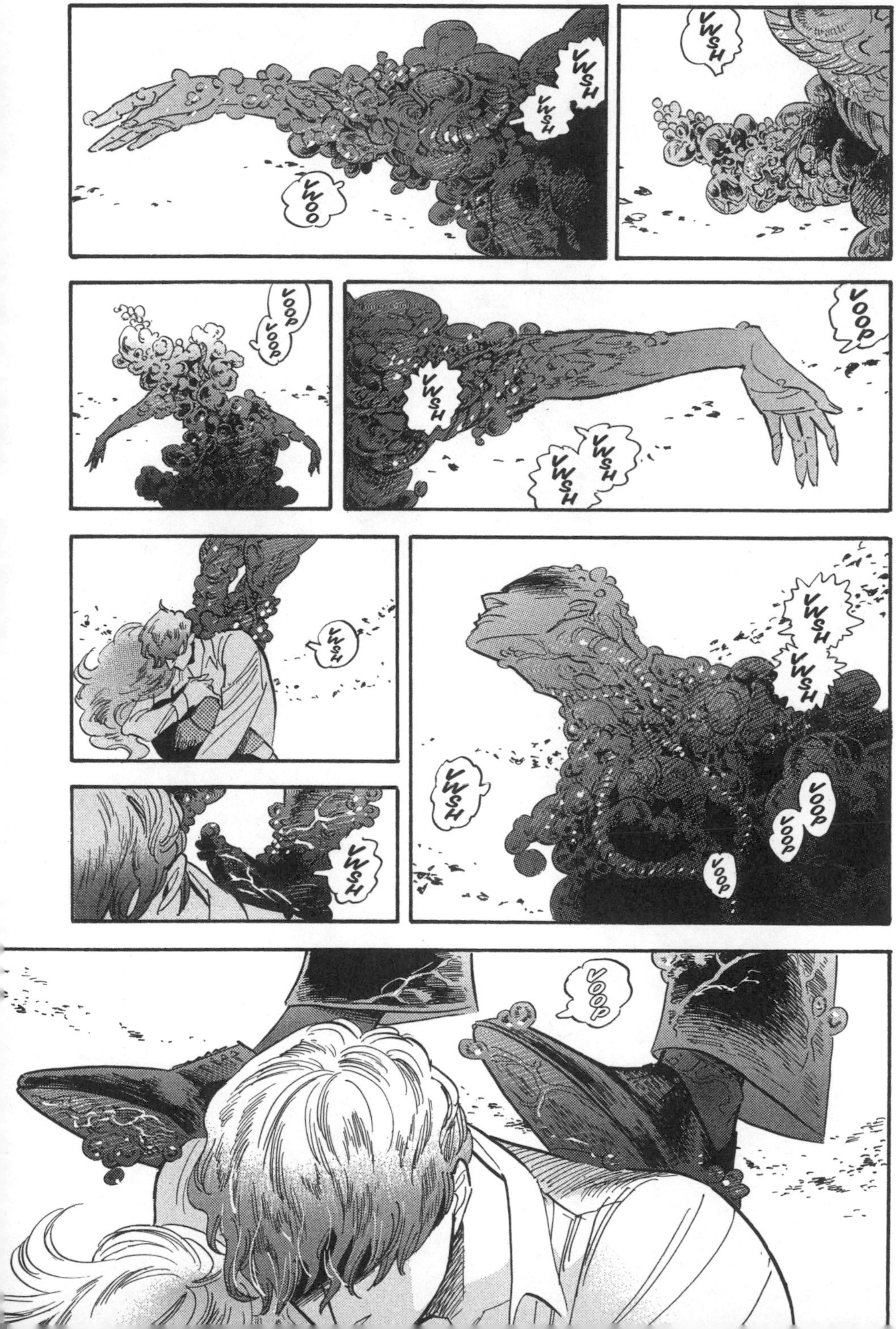
VWSH
VWSH
VWSH
VWOO
VOOP
VWSH
VWSH
VWSH
VOOP
VOOP
VWSH
VWSH
VWSH
VOOP
VOOP
VOOP
VWSH
VWSH
VOOP

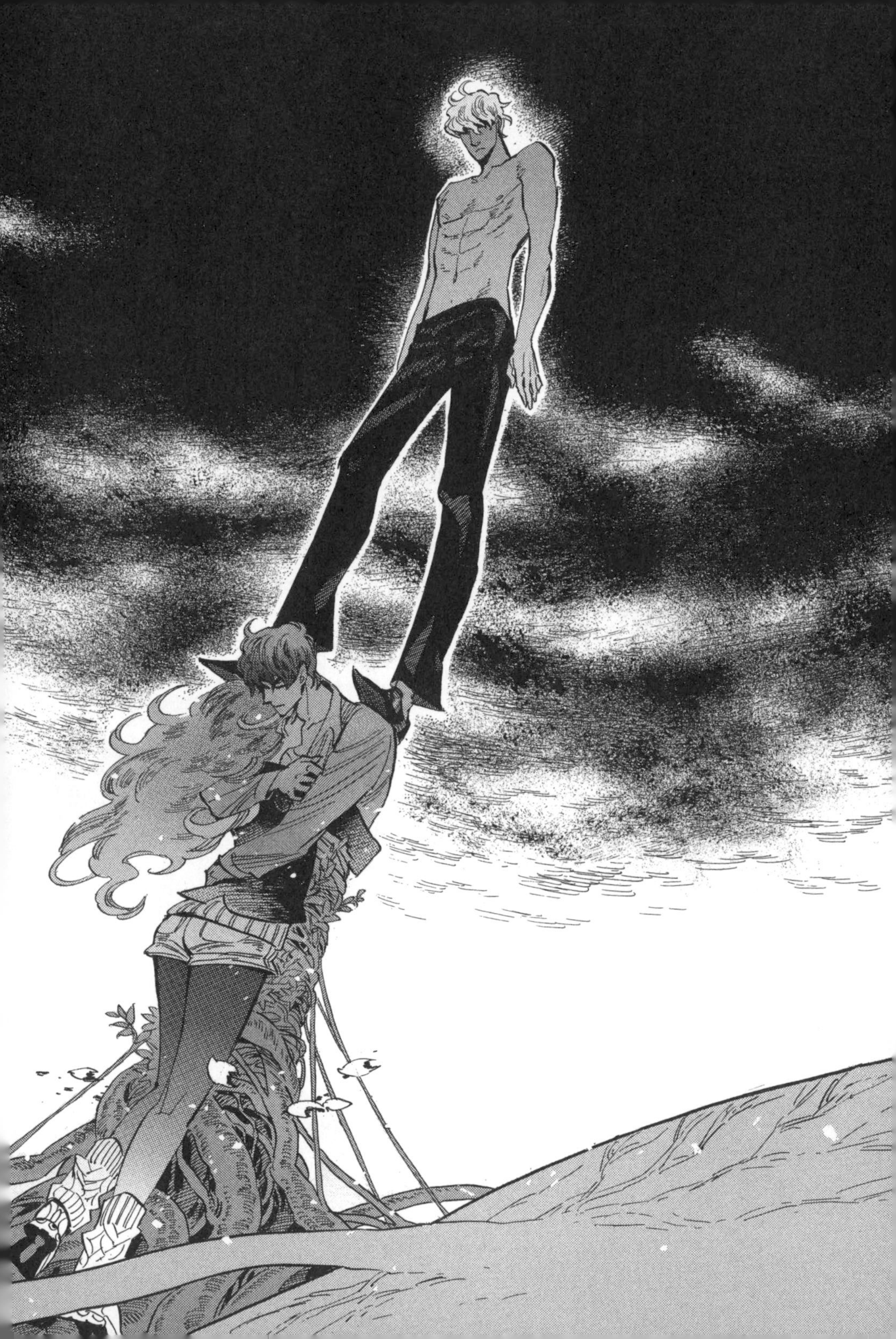

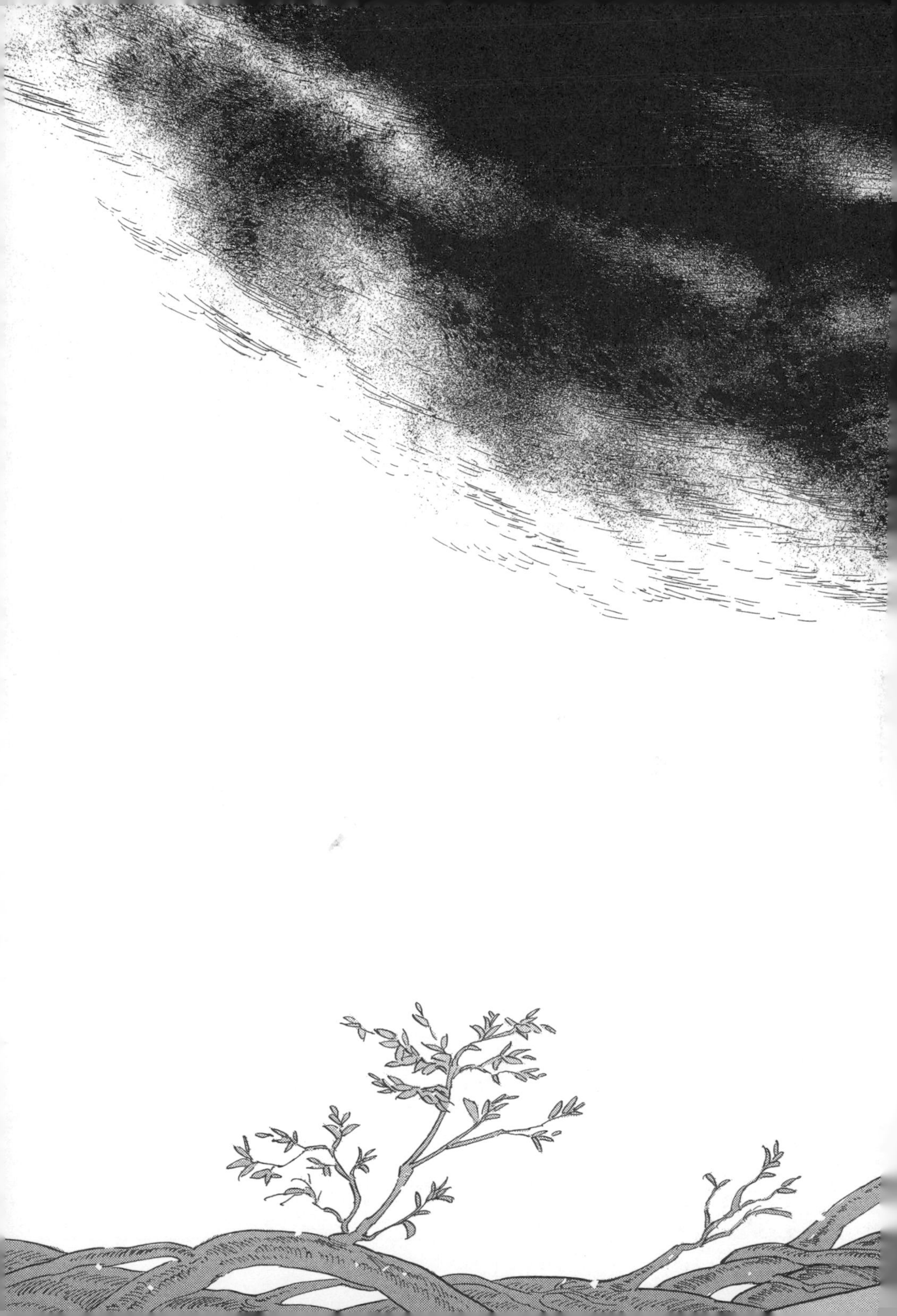

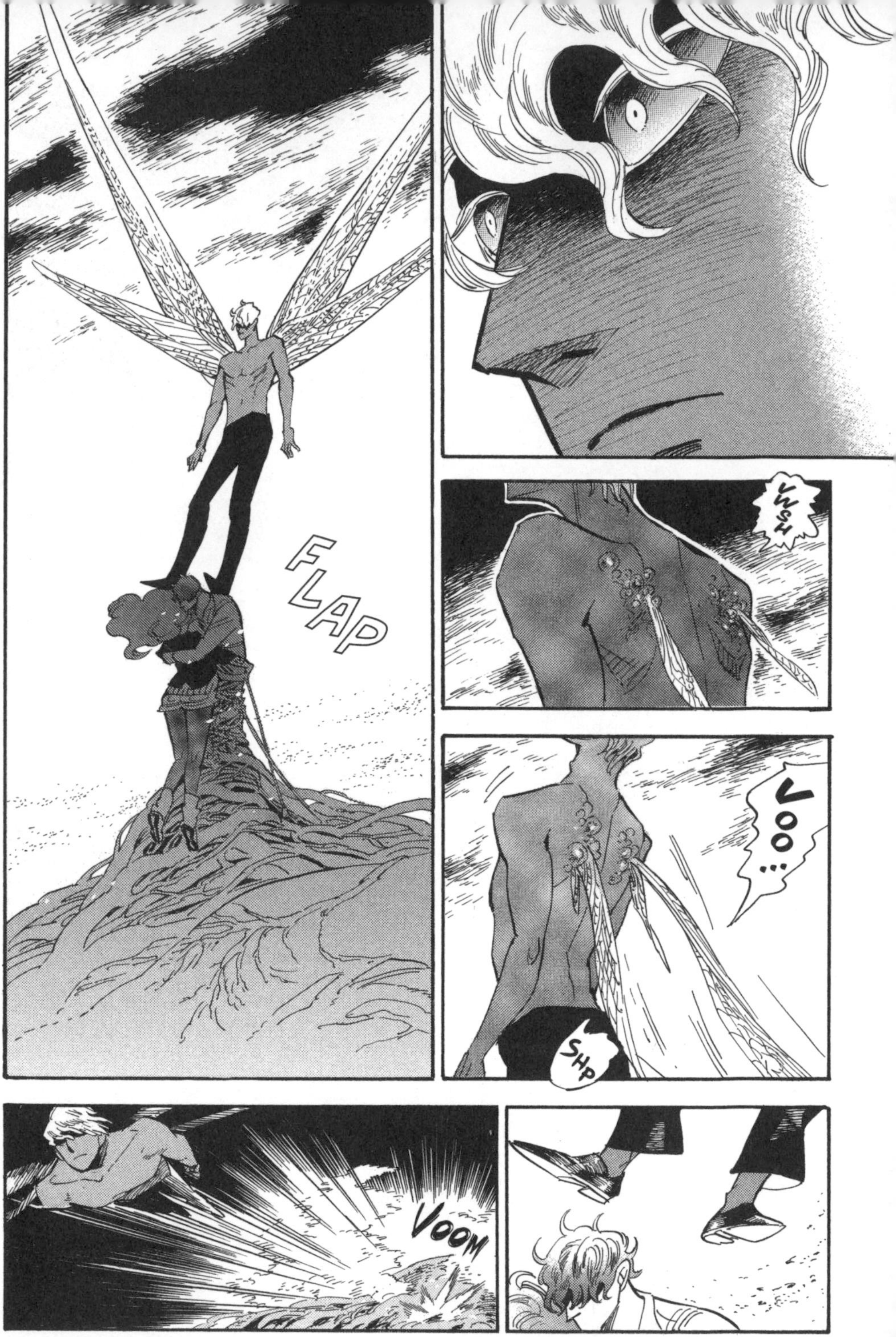
VWSH
VOO...
SHP
FLAP
VOOM

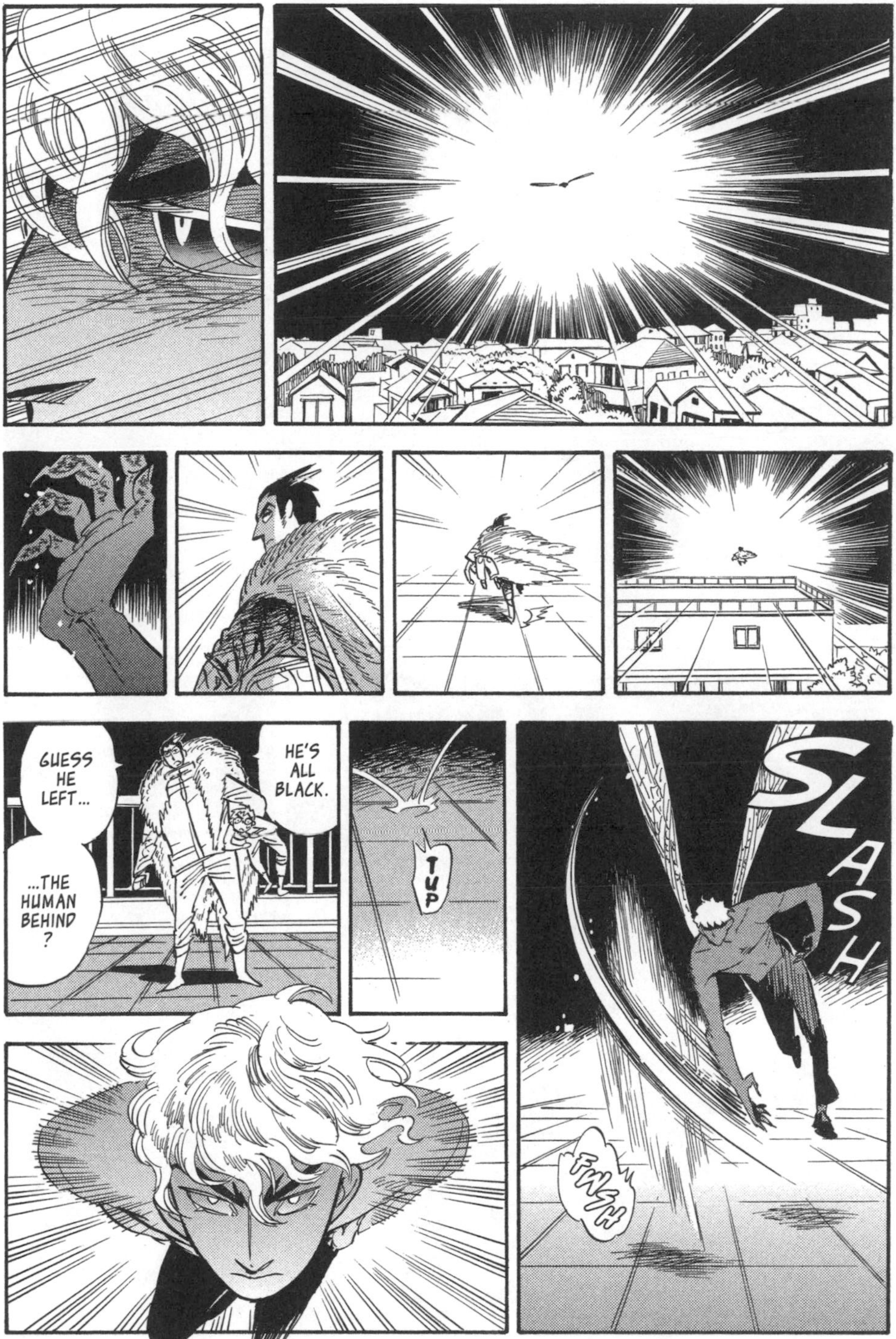
SLASH
FWSH
TUP
HE'S ALL BLACK.
GUESS HE LEFT...
...THE HUMAN BEHIND?

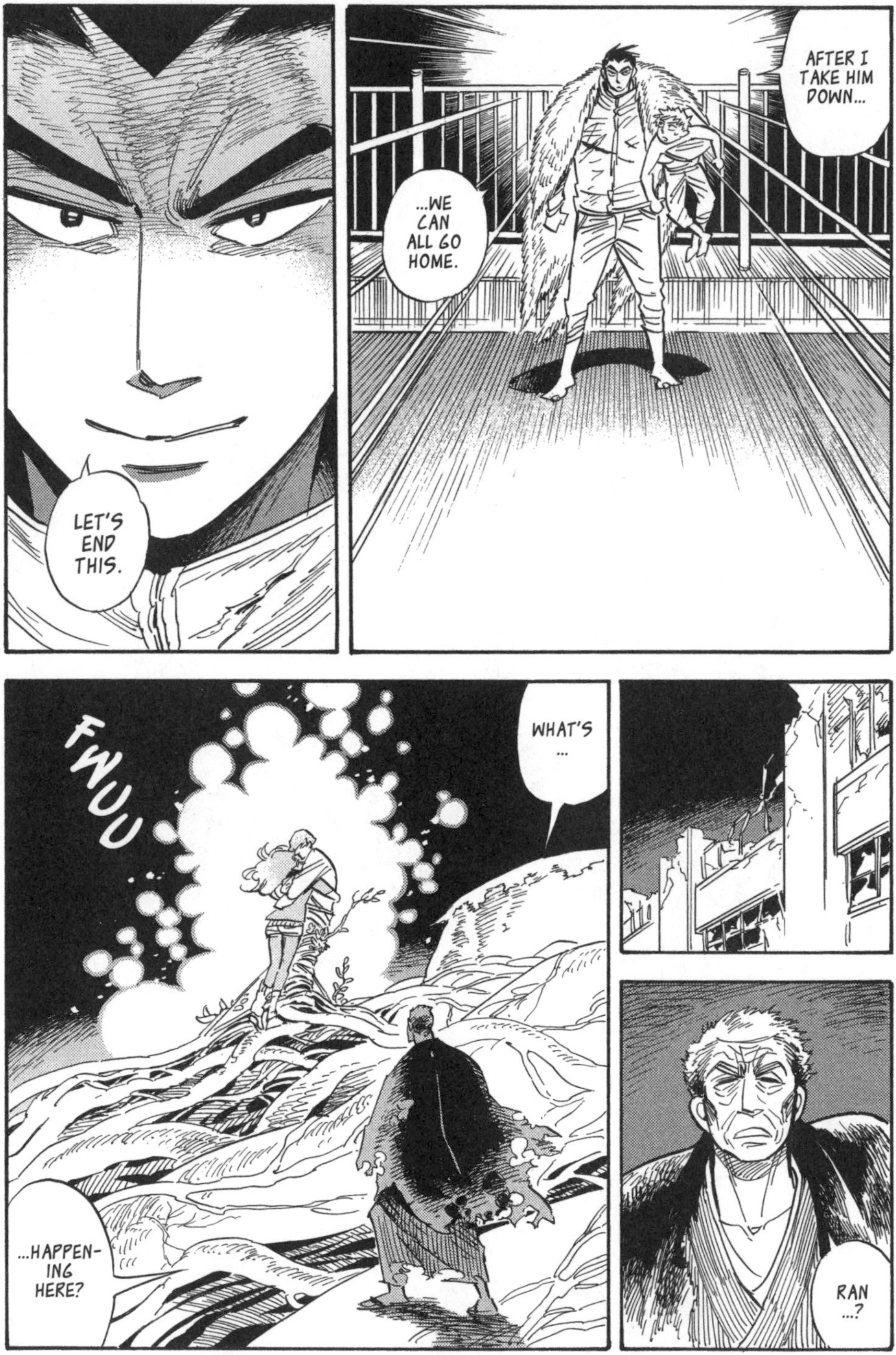
AFTER I TAKE HIM DOWN...
...WE CAN ALL GO HOME.
LET'S END THIS.
RAN ...?
FWUU
WHAT'S ...
...HAPPENING HERE?

Chapter 33 / The End

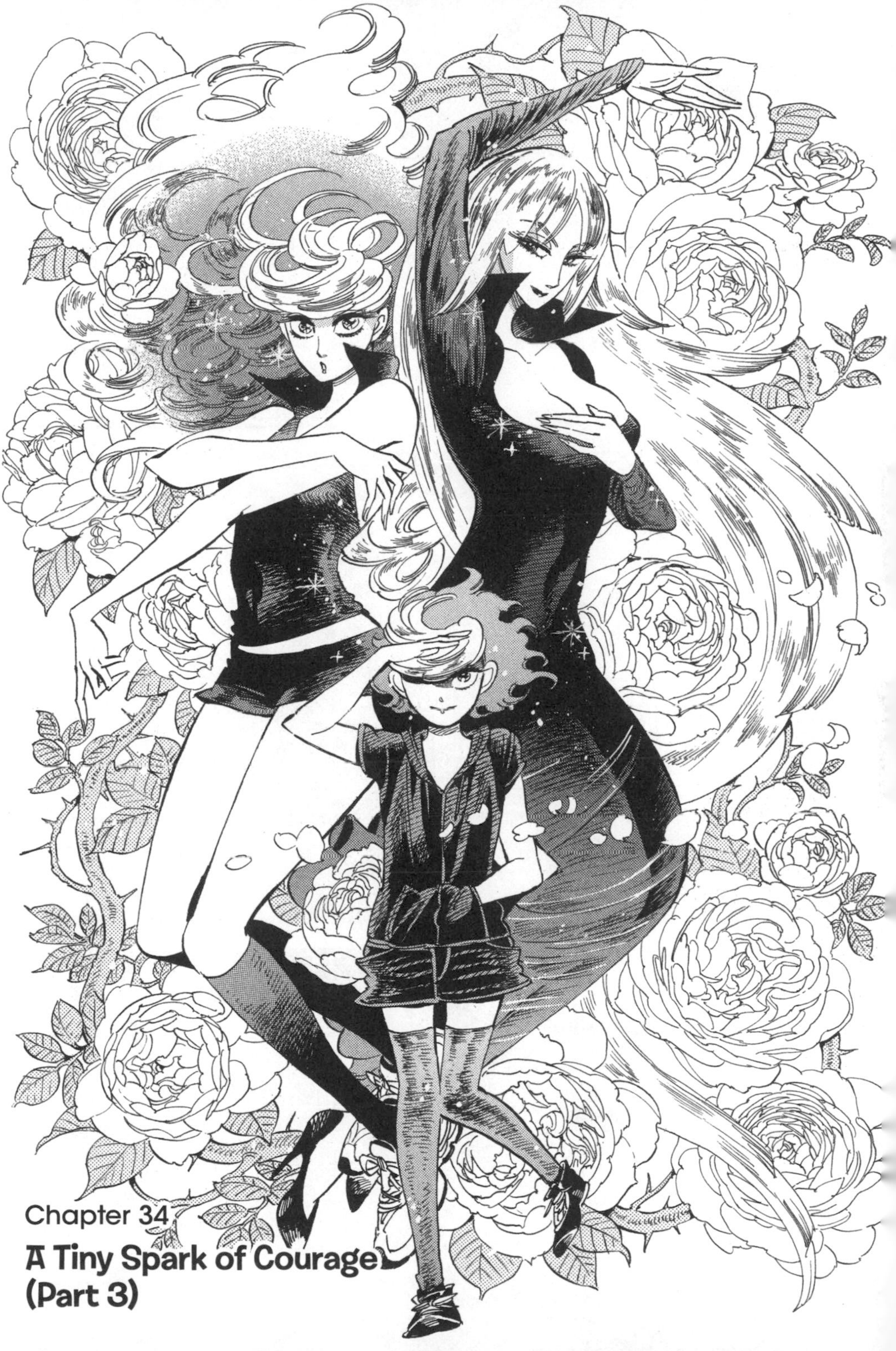

Chapter 34

A Tiny Spark of Courage (Part 3)

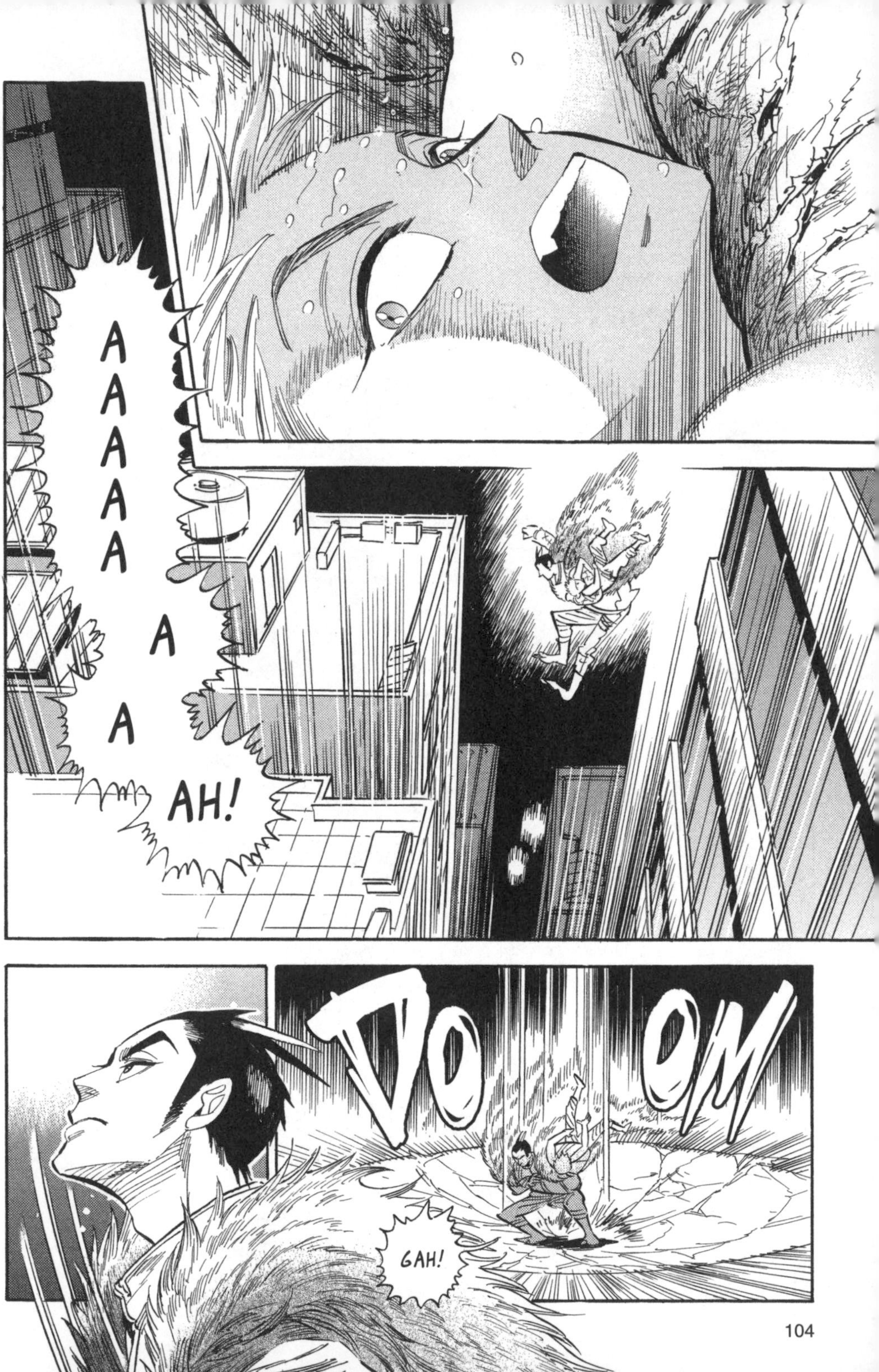

AAAAAAAAAAH!
DO OM
GAH!

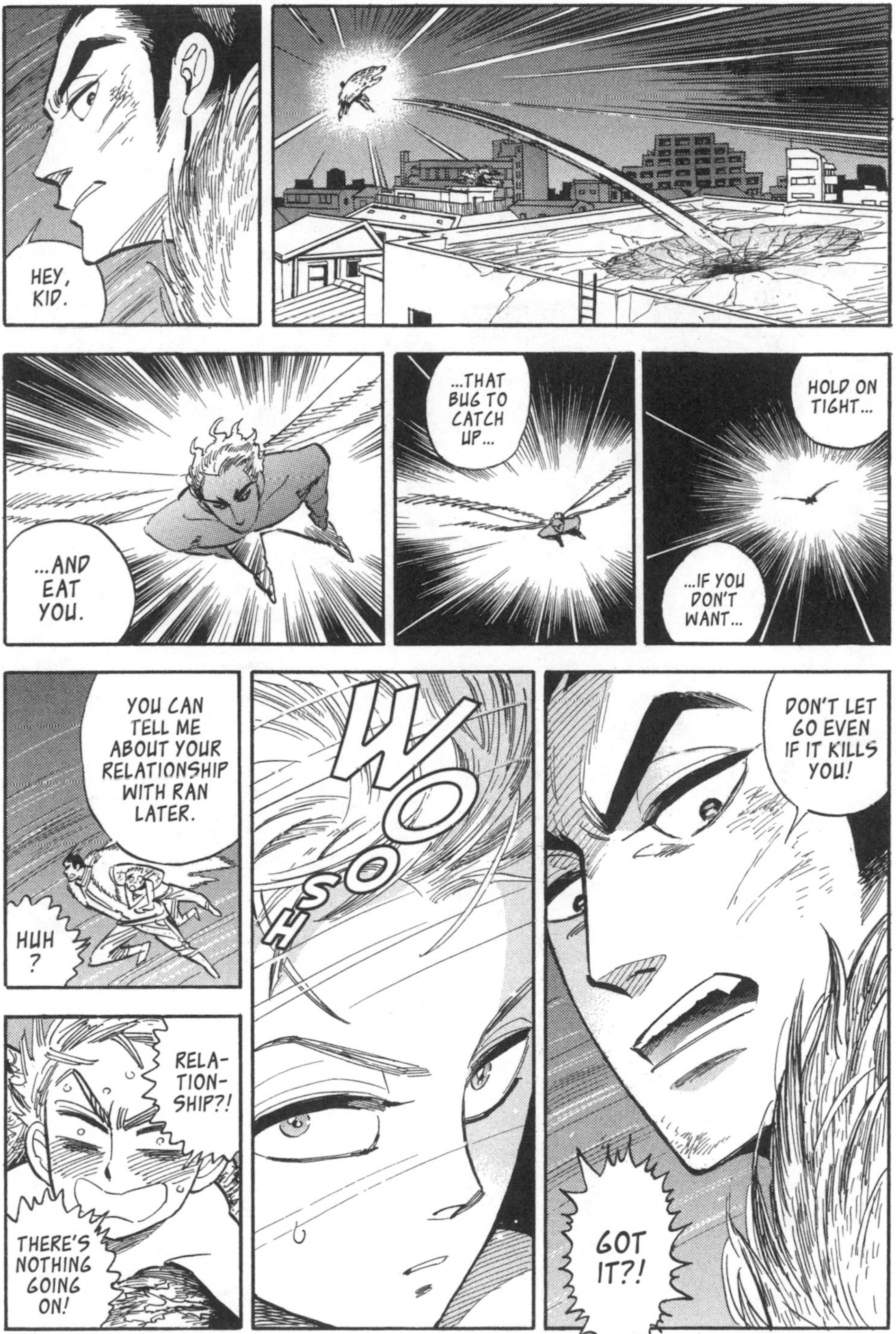
HEY, KID.
HOLD ON TIGHT...
...IF YOU DON'T WANT...
...THAT BUG TO CATCH UP...
...AND EAT YOU.
DON'T LET GO EVEN IF IT KILLS YOU!
GOT IT?!
WOOSH
YOU CAN TELL ME ABOUT YOUR RELATIONSHIP WITH RAN LATER.
HUH?
RELA-TION-SHIP?!
THERE'S NOTHING GOING ON!

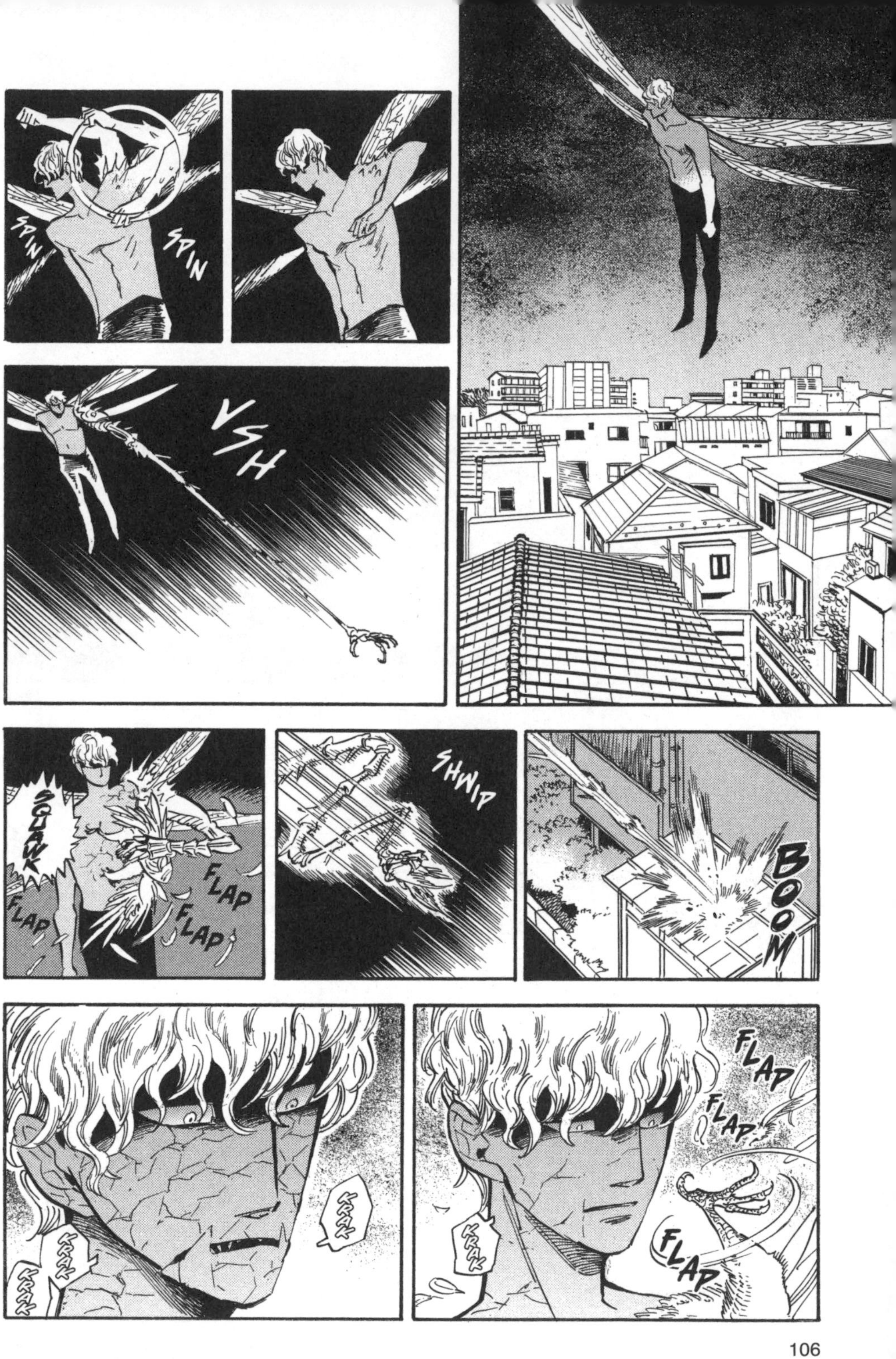
SPIN
SPIN
VSH
BOOM
SHWIP
SQUAWK
FLAP
FLAP
FLAP
FLAP
FLAP
FLAP
KRAK
KRAK
KRAK
KRAK

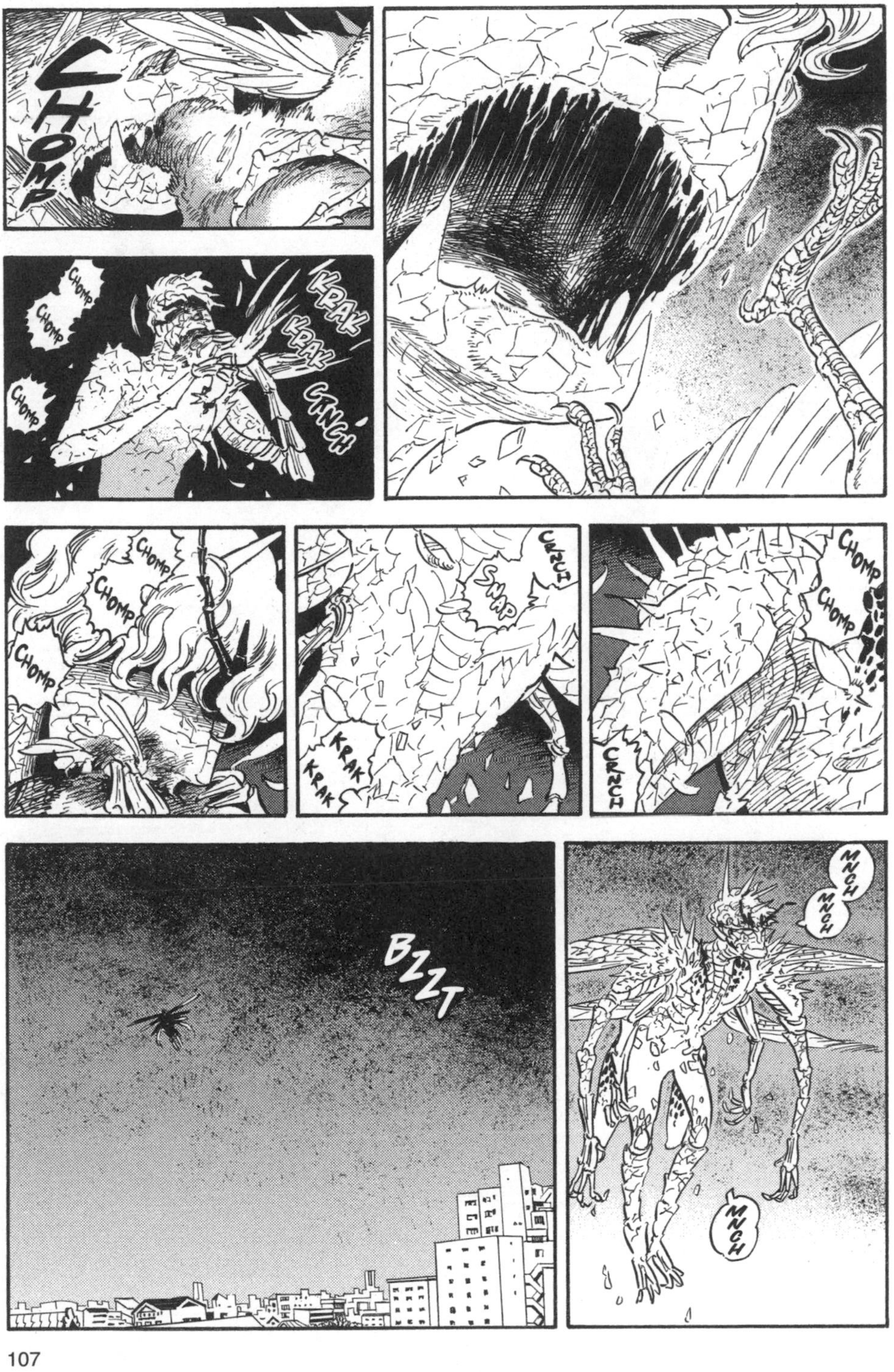
CHOMP
CHOMP
CHOMP
CHOMP
KRAK
KRAK
CRNCH
CHOMP
CHOMP
CRNCH
CRNCH
SNAP
KRAK
KRAK
CHOMP
CHOMP
CHOMP
MNCH
MNCH
MNCH
BZZT

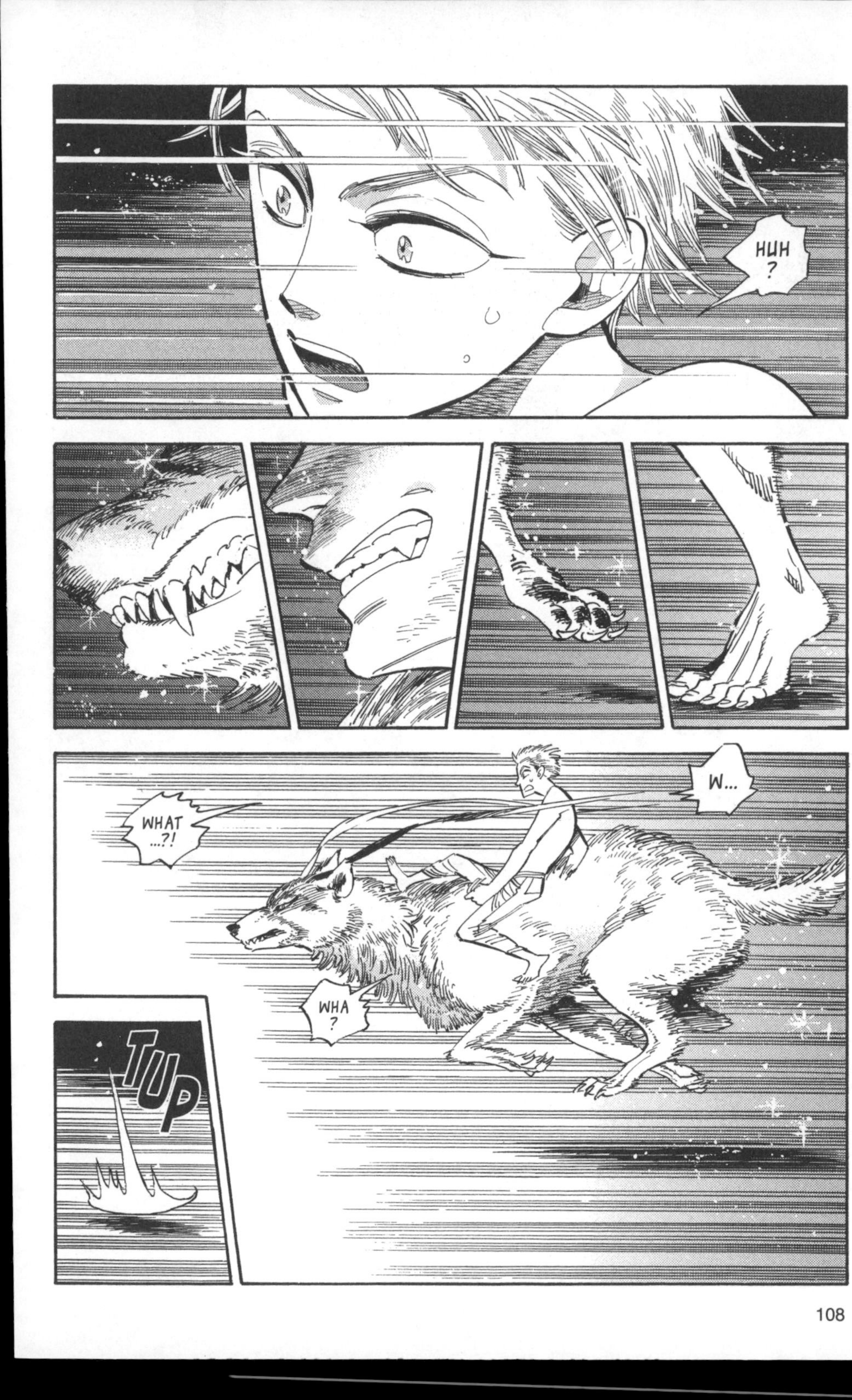
HUH?
W...
WHAT...?!
WHA?
TUP

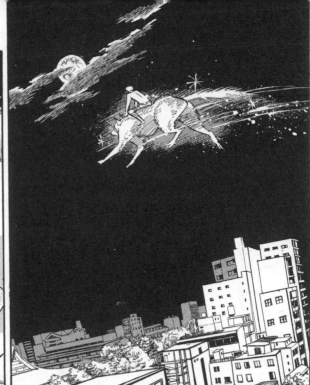

WOOOSH

TUP

TUP

TUP

TMP

WHOA!

...IS
...

...TOTALLY
...

...AWE-
SOME
!!

TH...

THIS
...

TUP

109

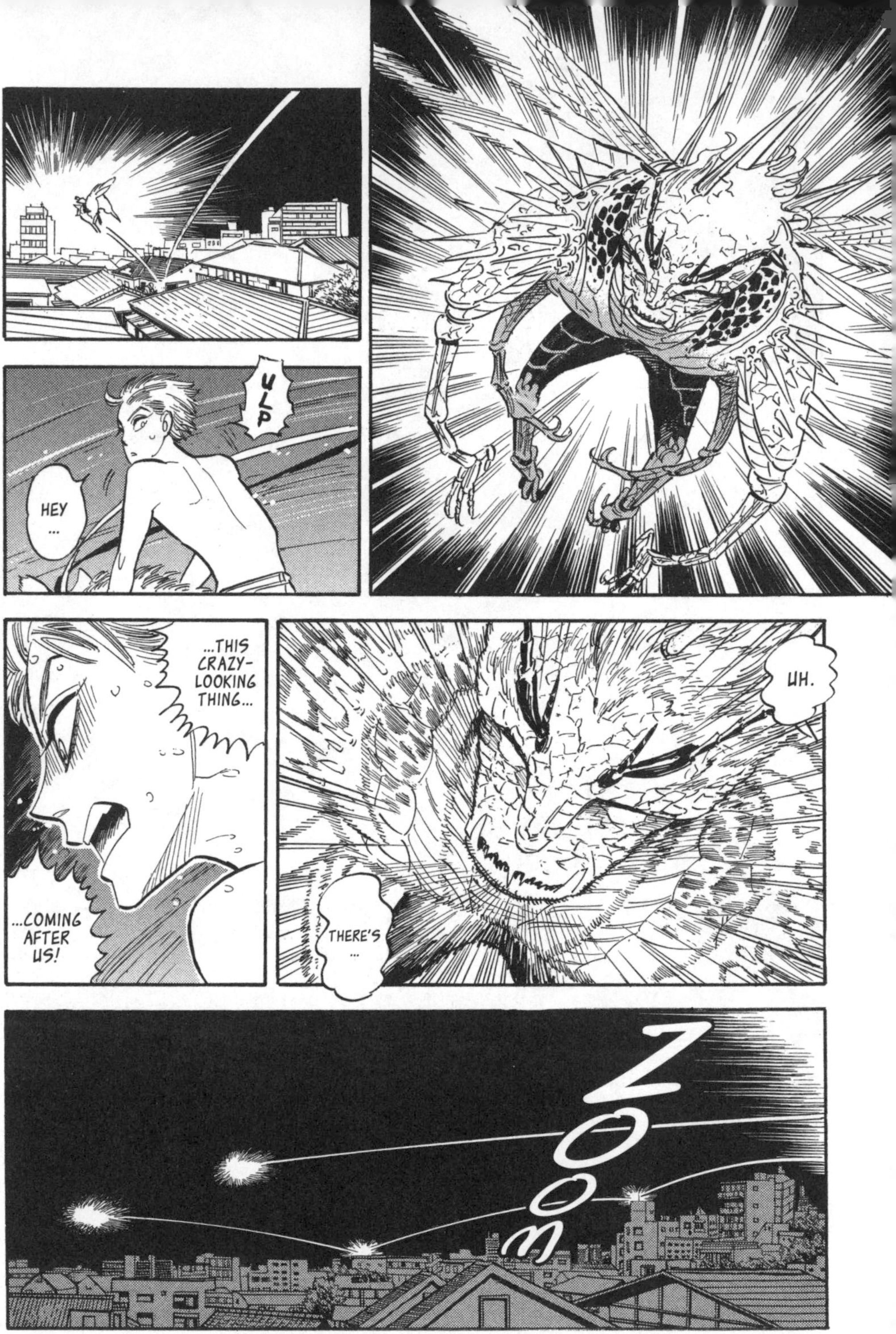
ULP
HEY ...
UH.
THERE'S ...
...THIS CRAZY-LOOKING THING...
...COMING AFTER US!
ZOOOM

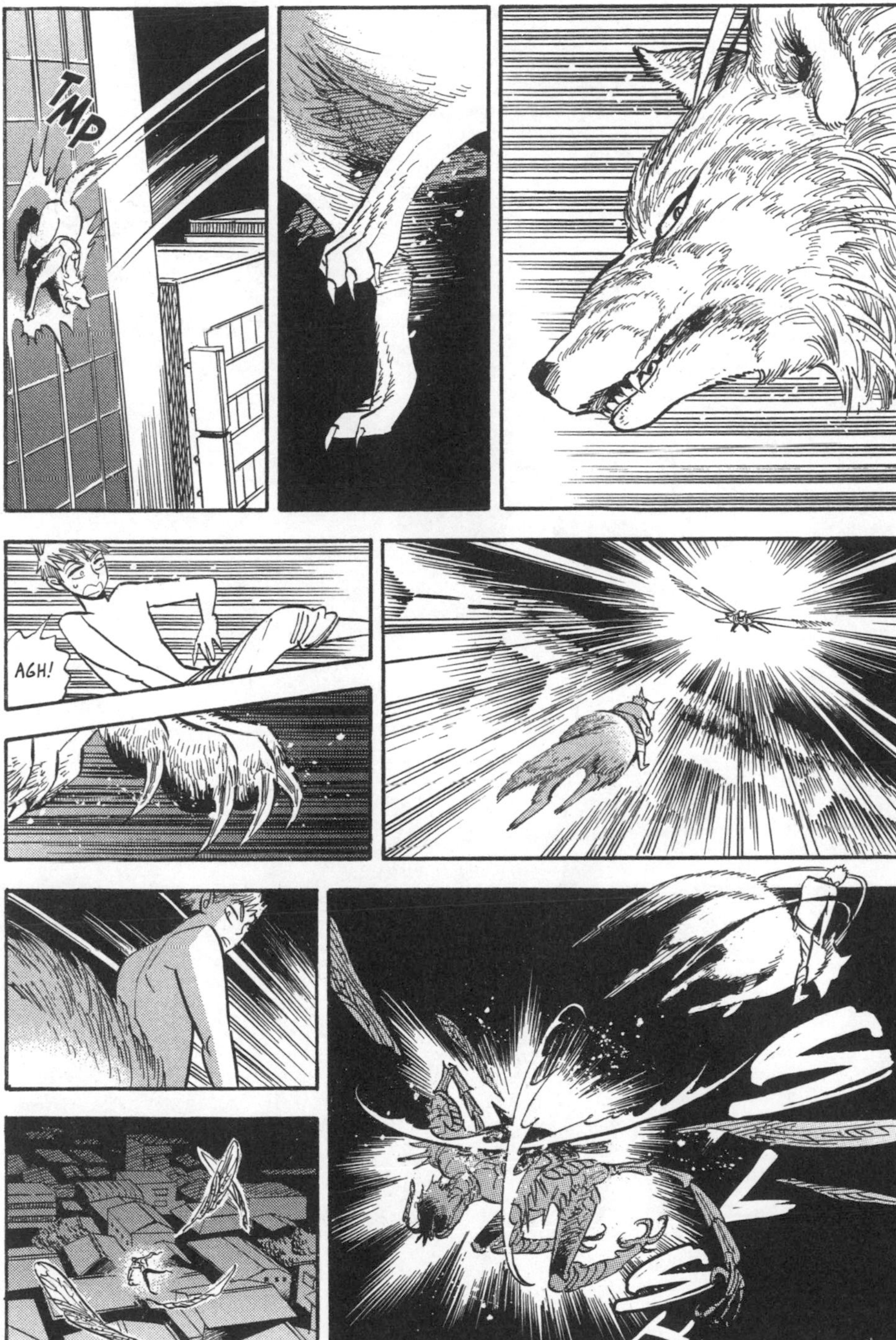
TMP
AGH!
SLSH

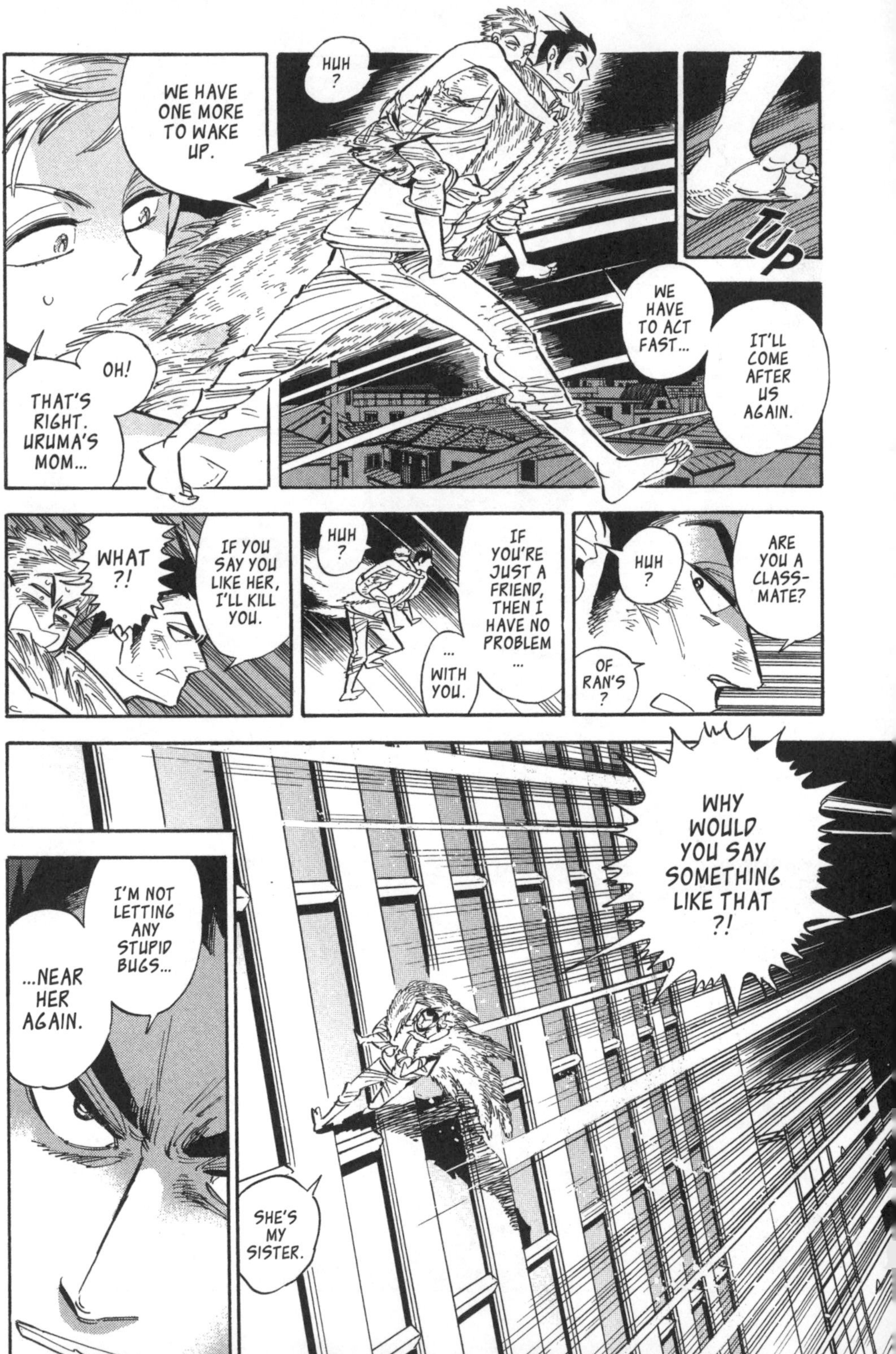
TUP
HUH?
WE HAVE TO ACT FAST...
IT'LL COME AFTER US AGAIN.
WE HAVE ONE MORE TO WAKE UP.
OH!
THAT'S RIGHT. URUMA'S MOM...
ARE YOU A CLASSMATE?
HUH?
OF RAN'S?
IF YOU'RE JUST A FRIEND, THEN I HAVE NO PROBLEM...
HUH?
...WITH YOU.
IF YOU SAY YOU LIKE HER, I'LL KILL YOU.
WHAT?!
WHY WOULD YOU SAY SOMETHING LIKE THAT?!
I'M NOT LETTING ANY STUPID BUGS...
...NEAR HER AGAIN.
SHE'S MY SISTER.

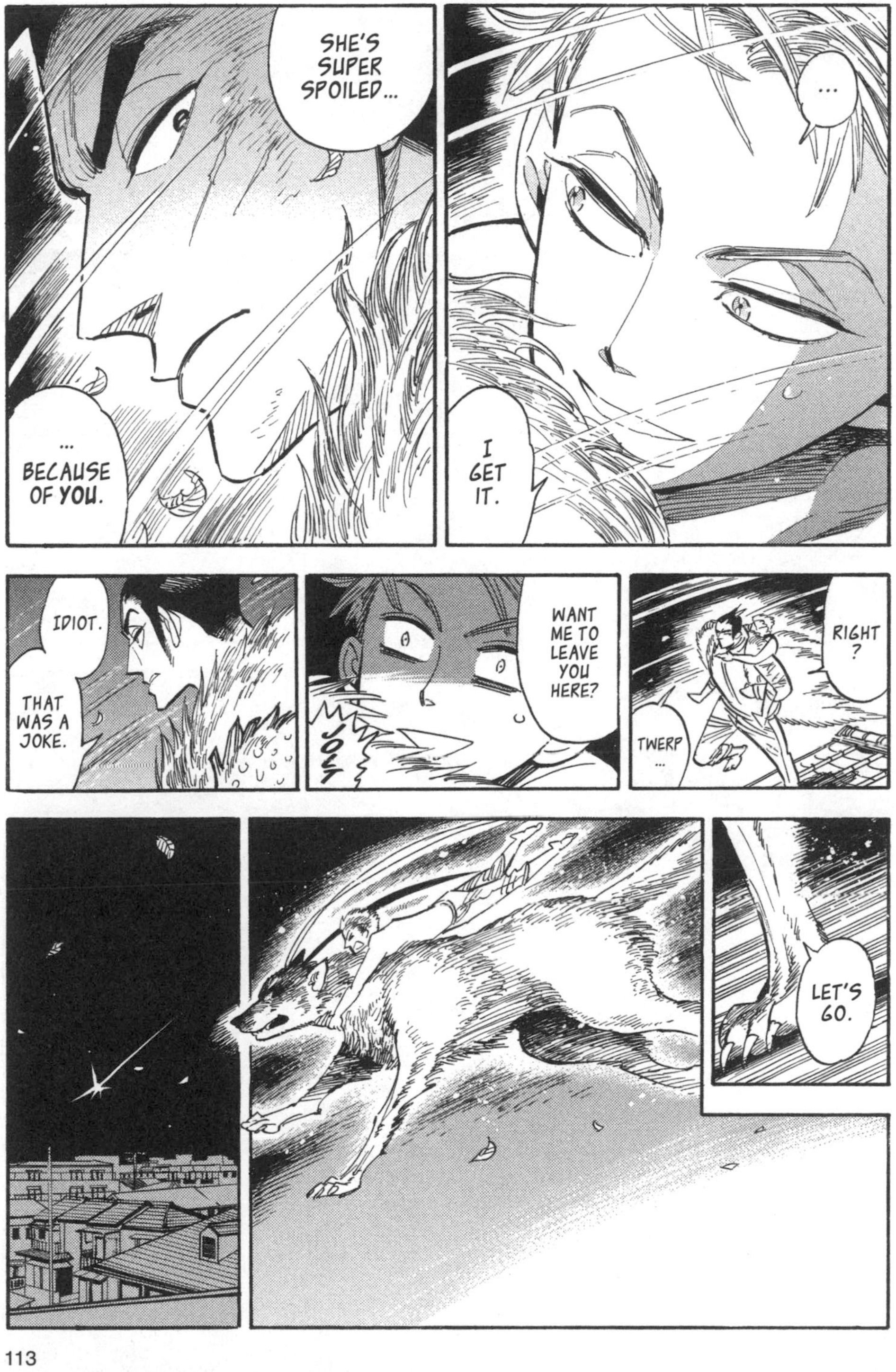
...
I GET IT.
SHE'S SUPER SPOILED...
... BECAUSE OF YOU.
RIGHT?
TWERP ...
WANT ME TO LEAVE YOU HERE?
JOLT
IDIOT.
THAT WAS A JOKE.
LET'S GO.

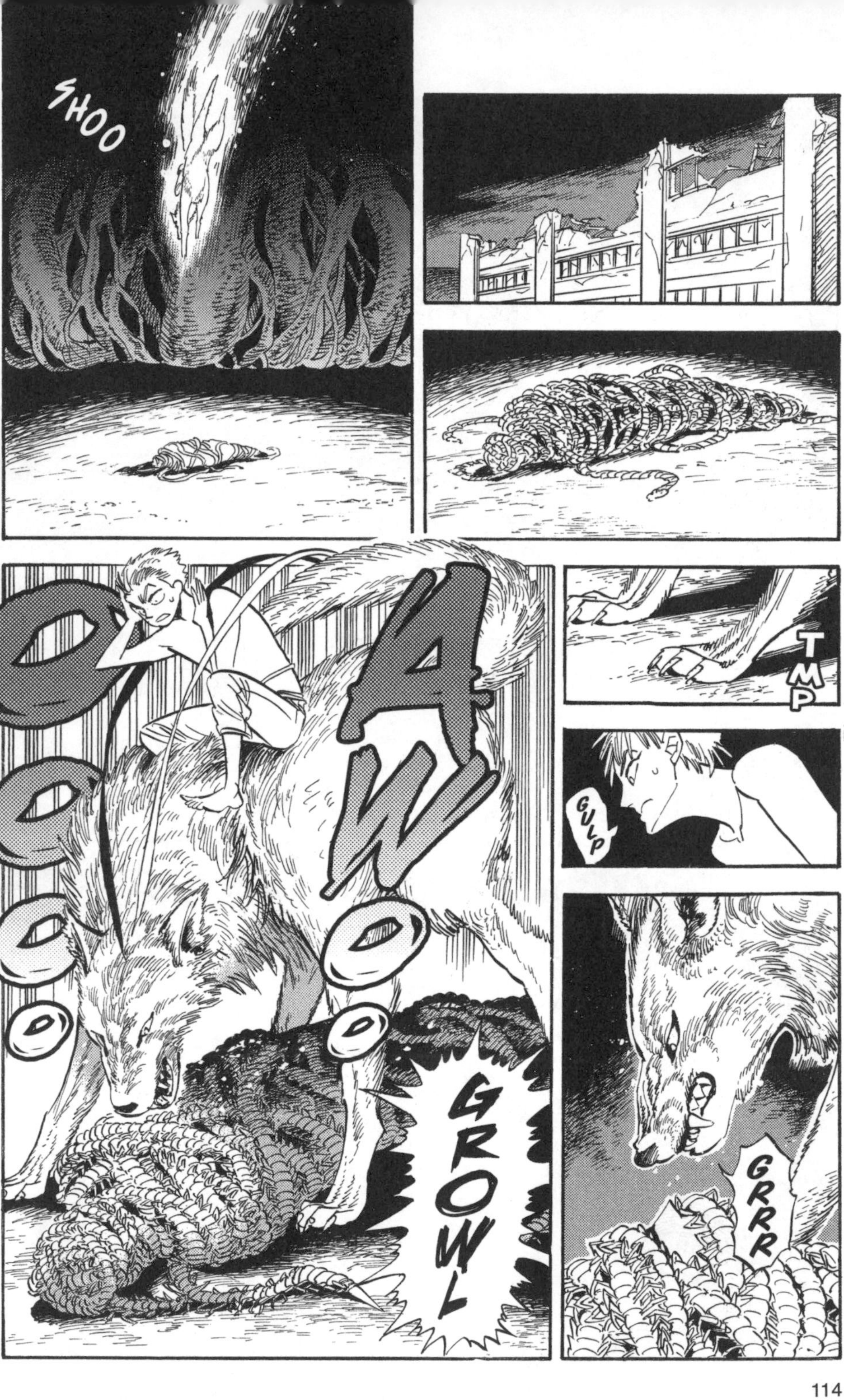
SHOO
TMP
GULP
GRRR
AWOOOOOO
GROWL

KRSH KRSH
CHOMP
RIP RIP
RIP
TAKE THAT!
RIP RIP
GET OFF...
...OF HER!
TWITCH
LOOK.
FWIP
THANK GOOD-NESS.
YOU'RE ...
... AWAKE ...

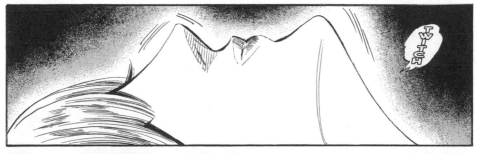

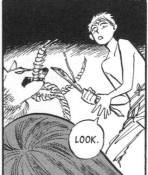

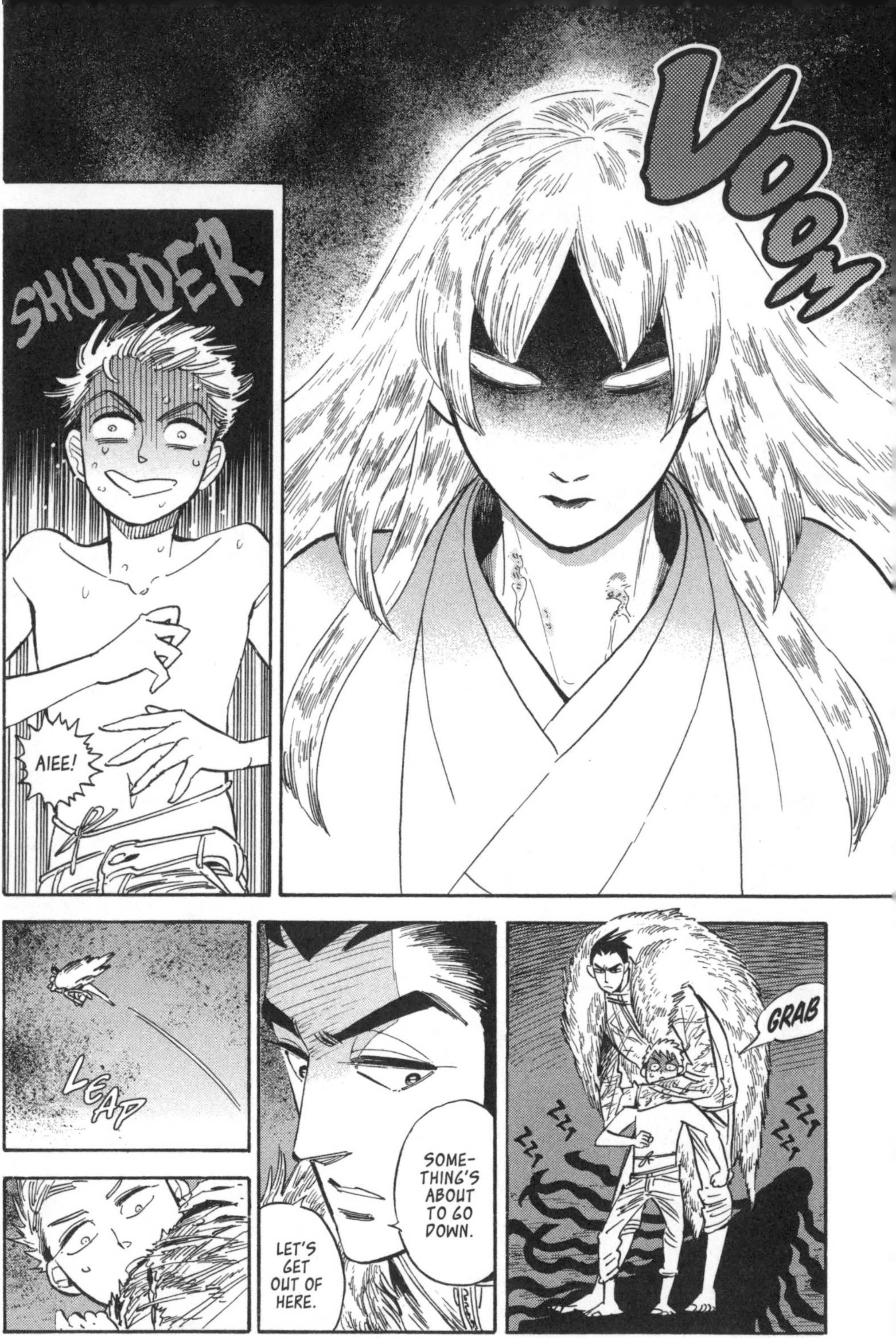
VOOM
SHUDDER
AIEE!
GRAB
SOME-THING'S ABOUT TO GO DOWN.
LET'S GET OUT OF HERE.
LEAP

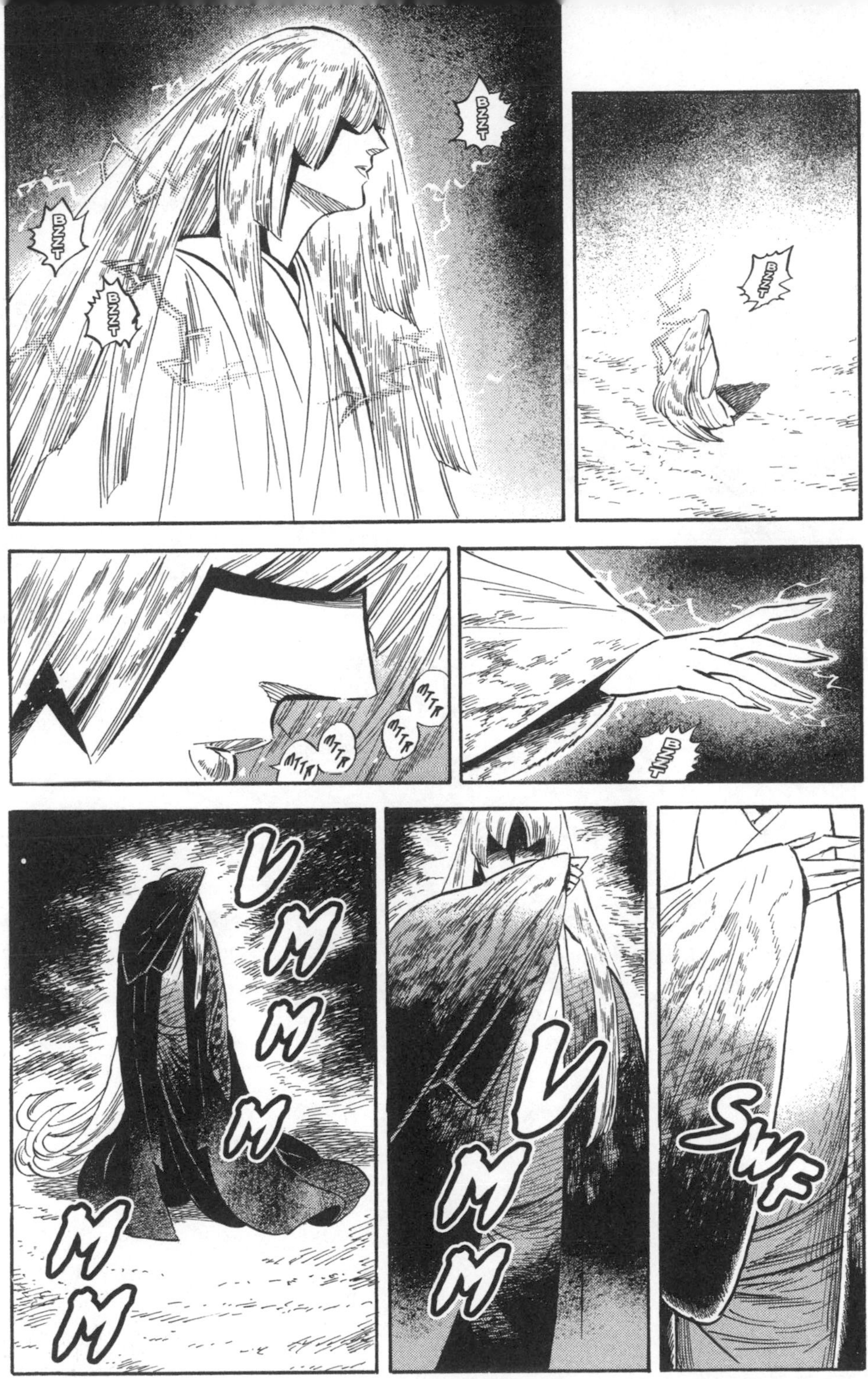
BZZT
BZZT
BZZT
BZZT
BZZT
MTTR
MTTR
MTTR
MTTR
SWF
VMMM
VMMMMM

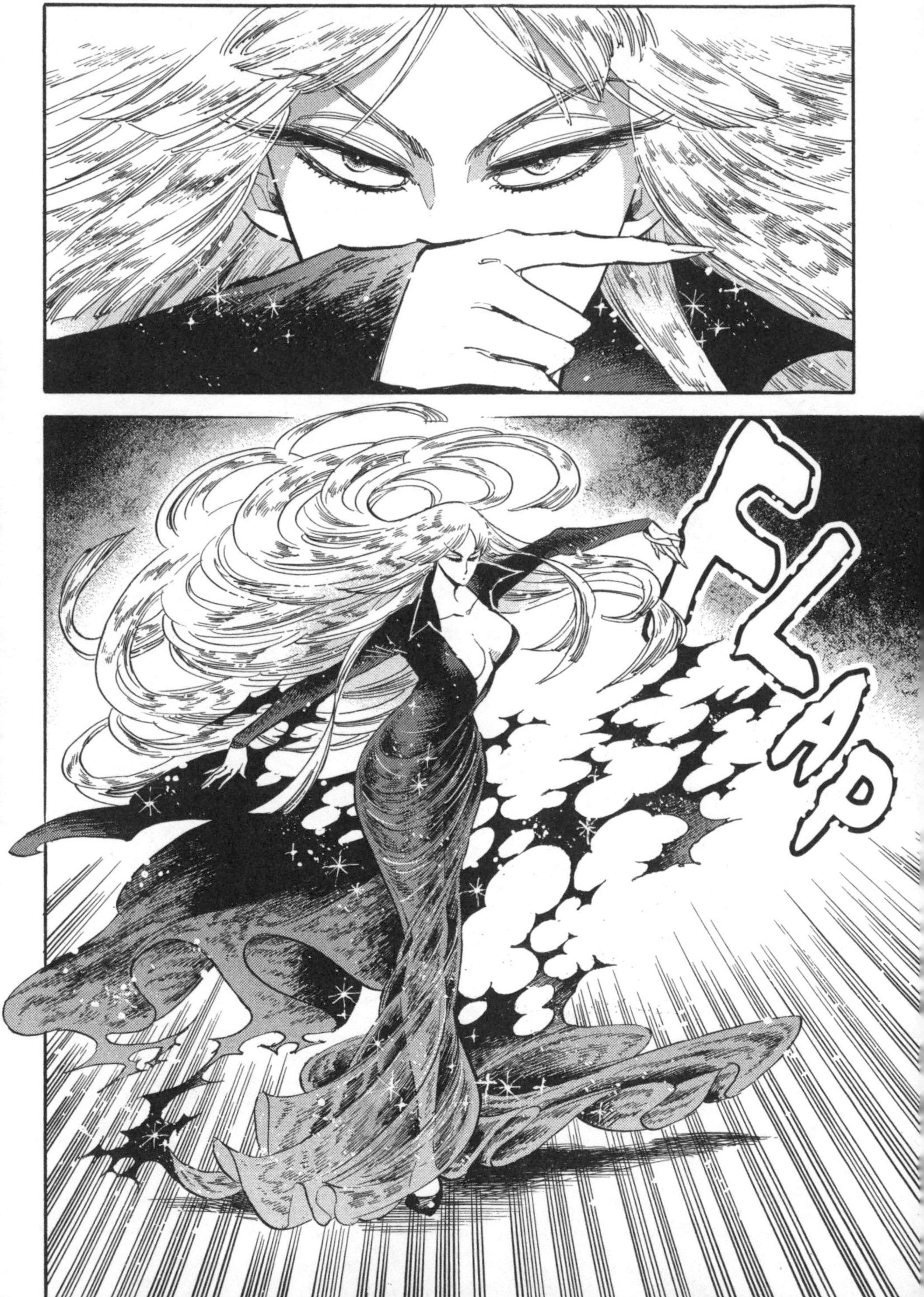
FLAP

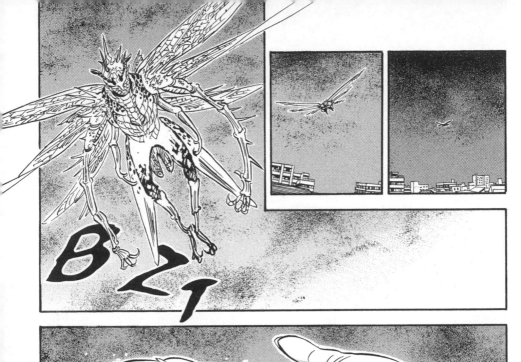

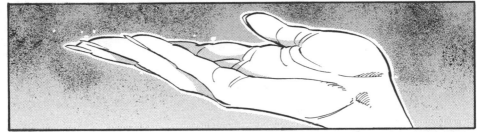

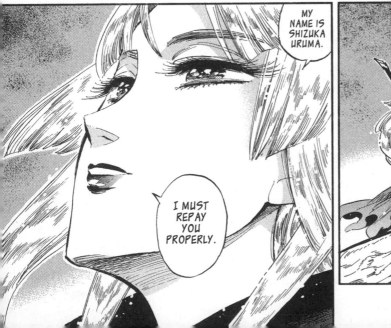

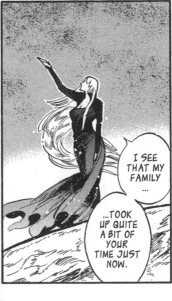

I SEE THAT MY FAMILY ...
...TOOK UP QUITE A BIT OF YOUR TIME JUST NOW.
MY NAME IS SHIZUKA URUMA.
I MUST REPAY YOU PROPERLY.

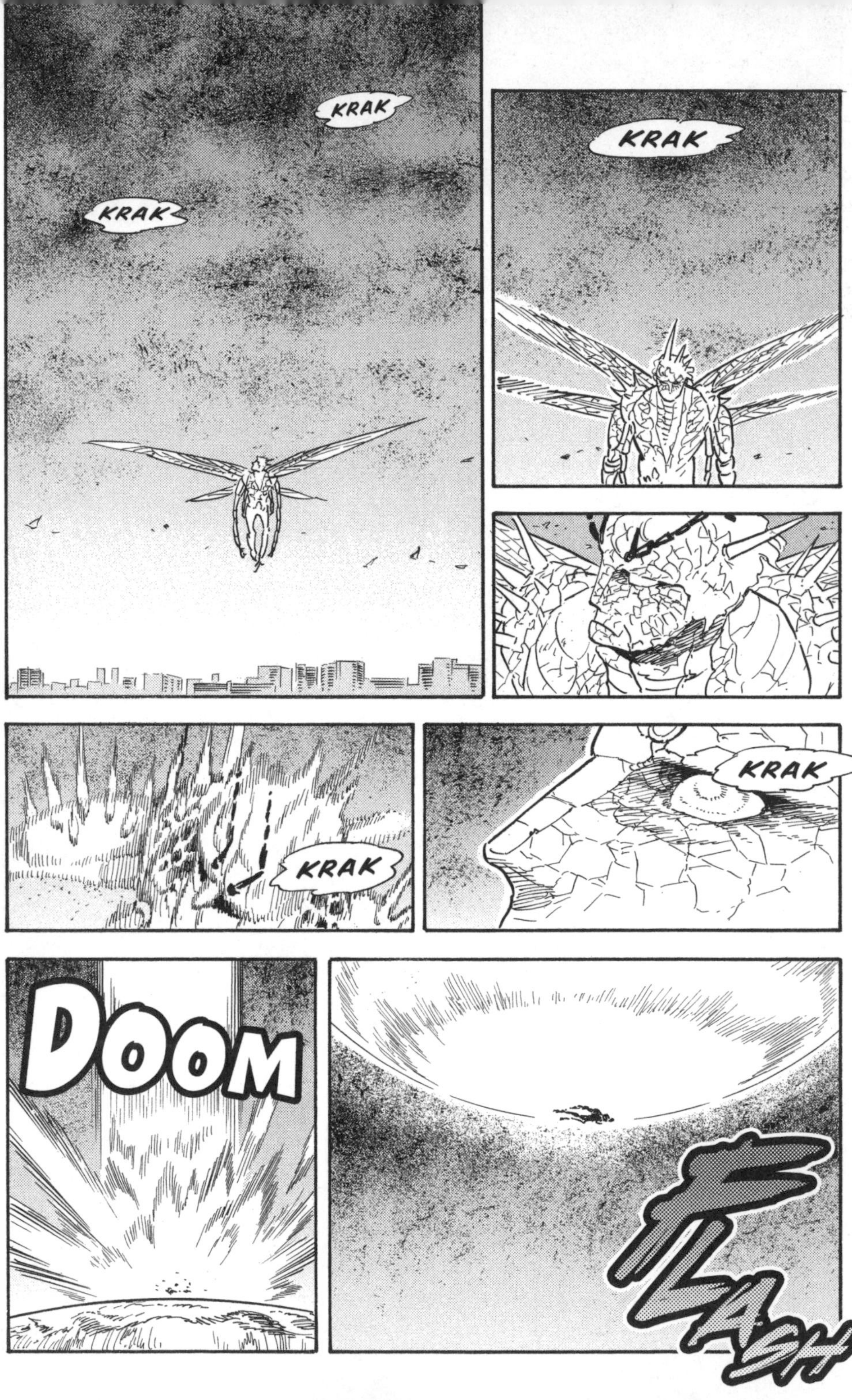
KRAK
KRAK
KRAK
KRAK
KRAK
FLASH
DOOM

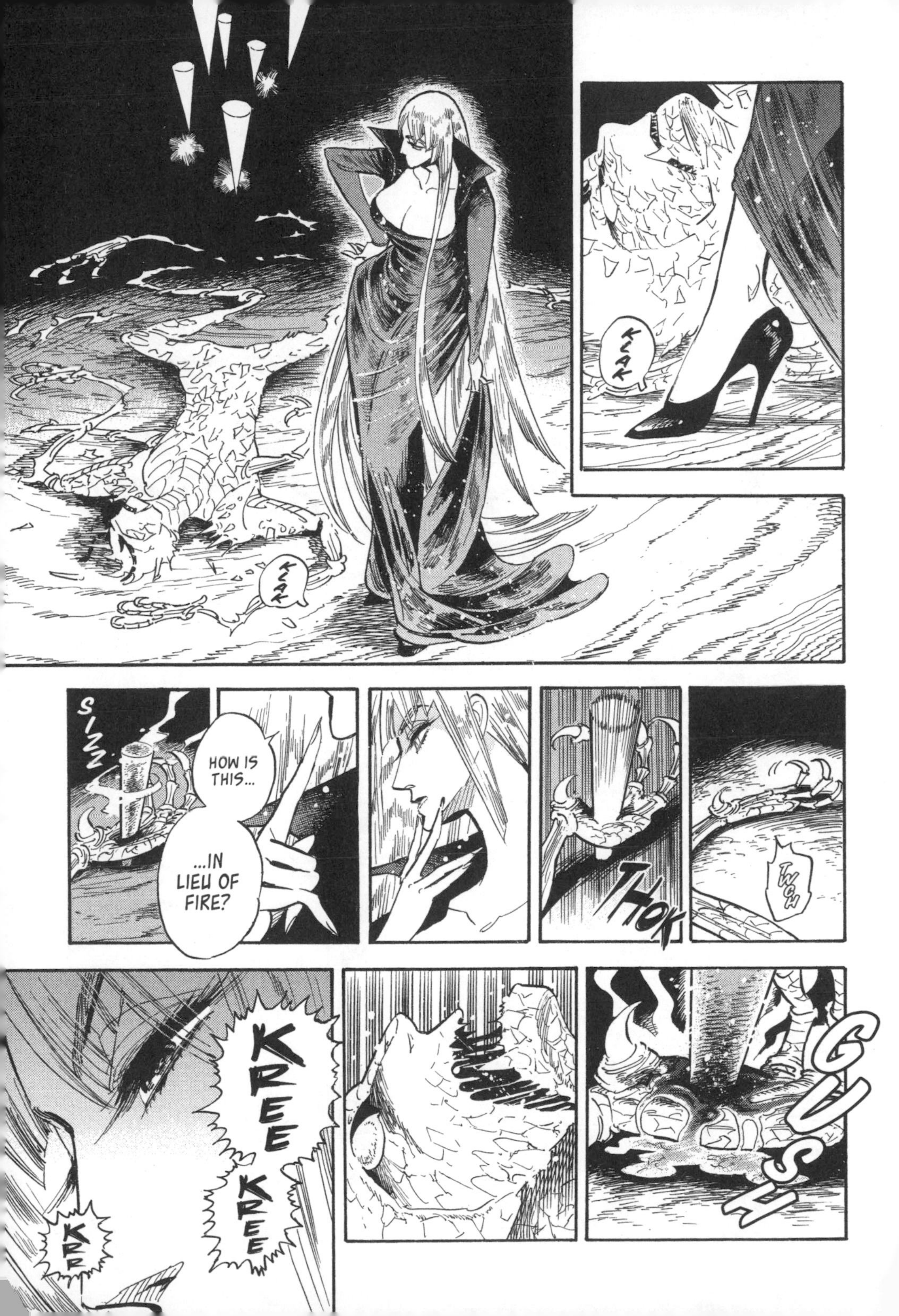
KRAK
KRAK
TWCH
THOK
HOW IS THIS...
...IN LIEU OF FIRE?
SIZZ
GUSH
KREE
KREE
KRR

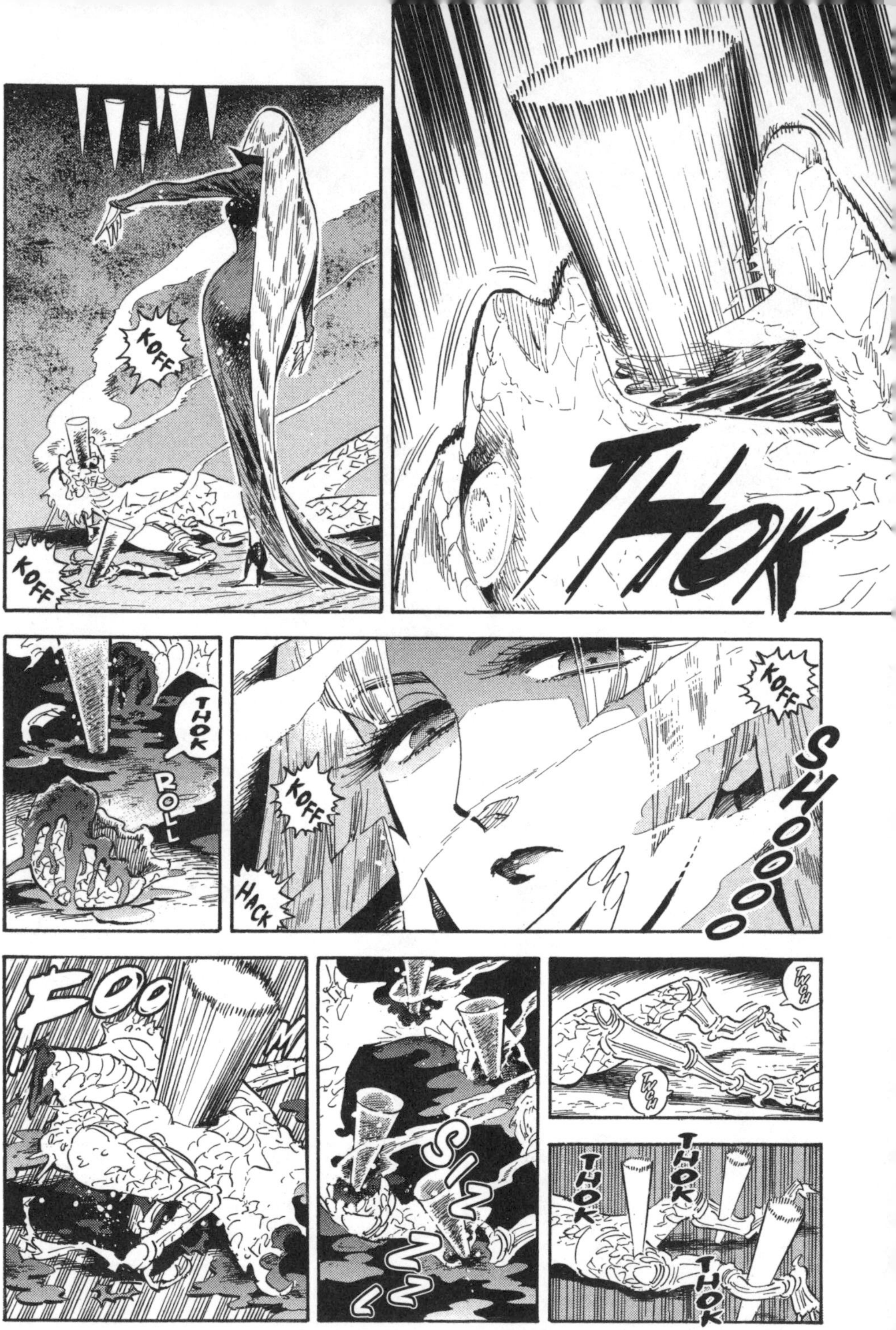
THOK
KOFF
KOFF
KOFF
KOFF
HACK
SHOOOOOO
THOK
ROLL
THOK
THOK
THOK
THOK
SIZZZ
FOOOM

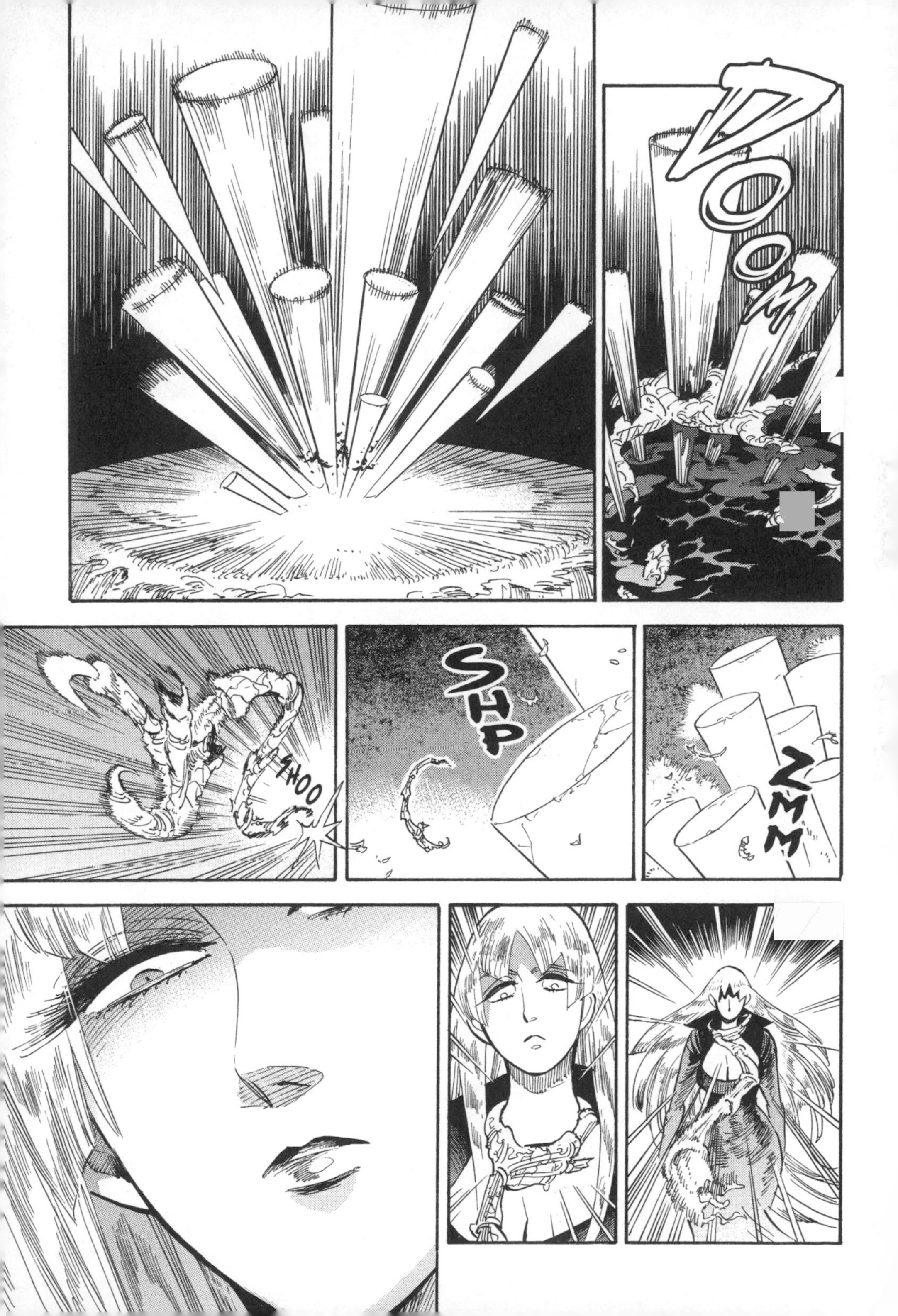
DOOM
ZMM
SHP
SHOO

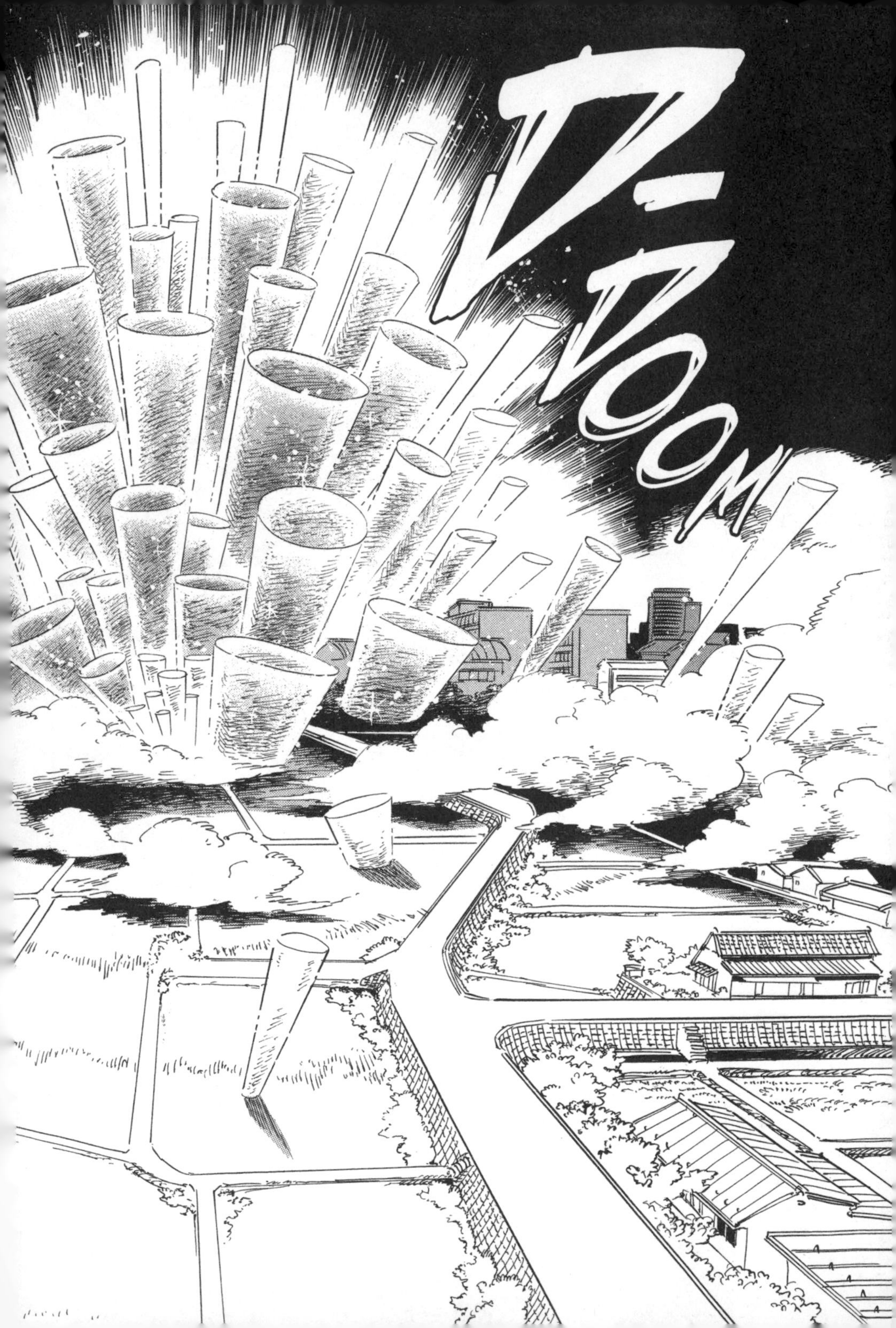
D-DOOM

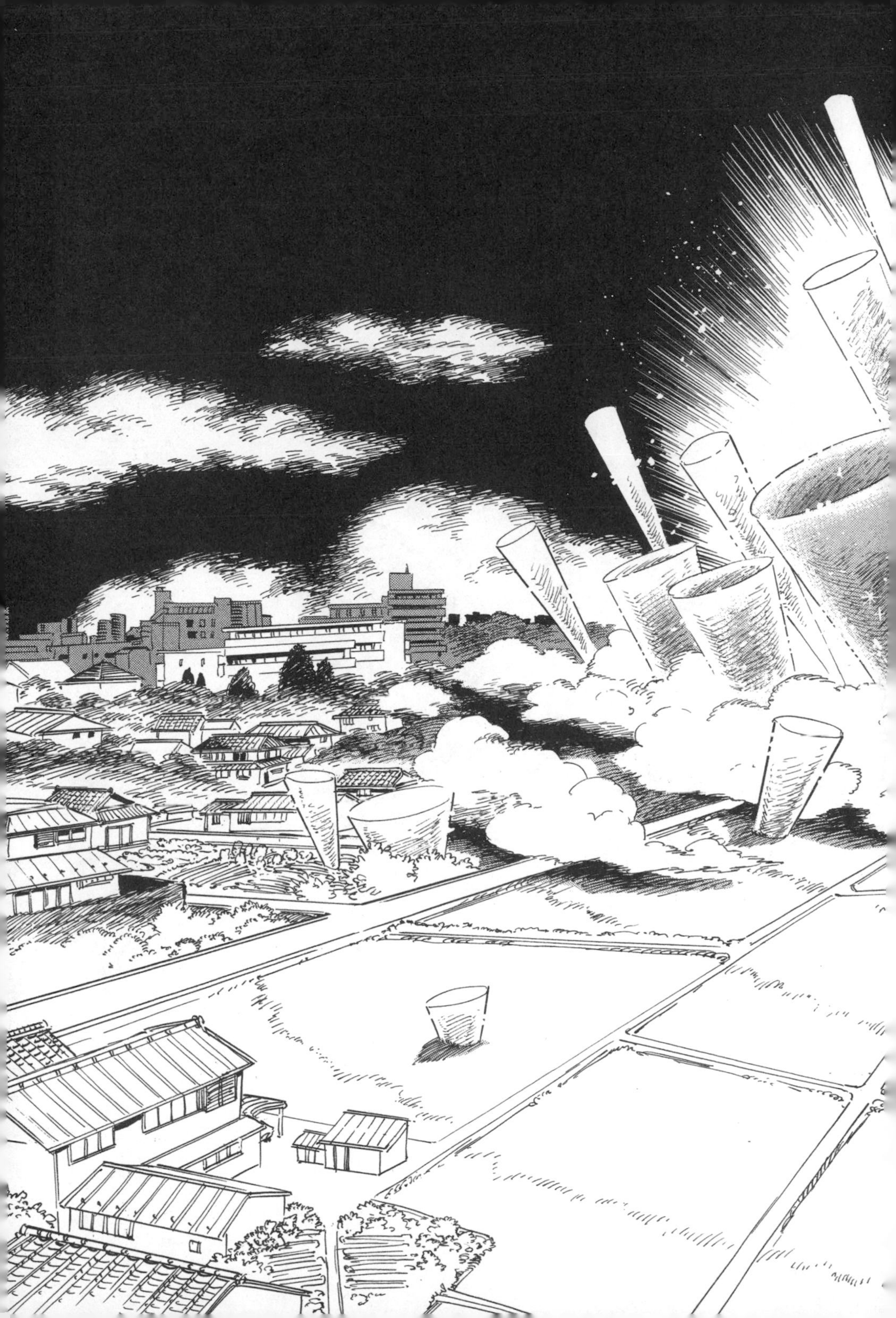

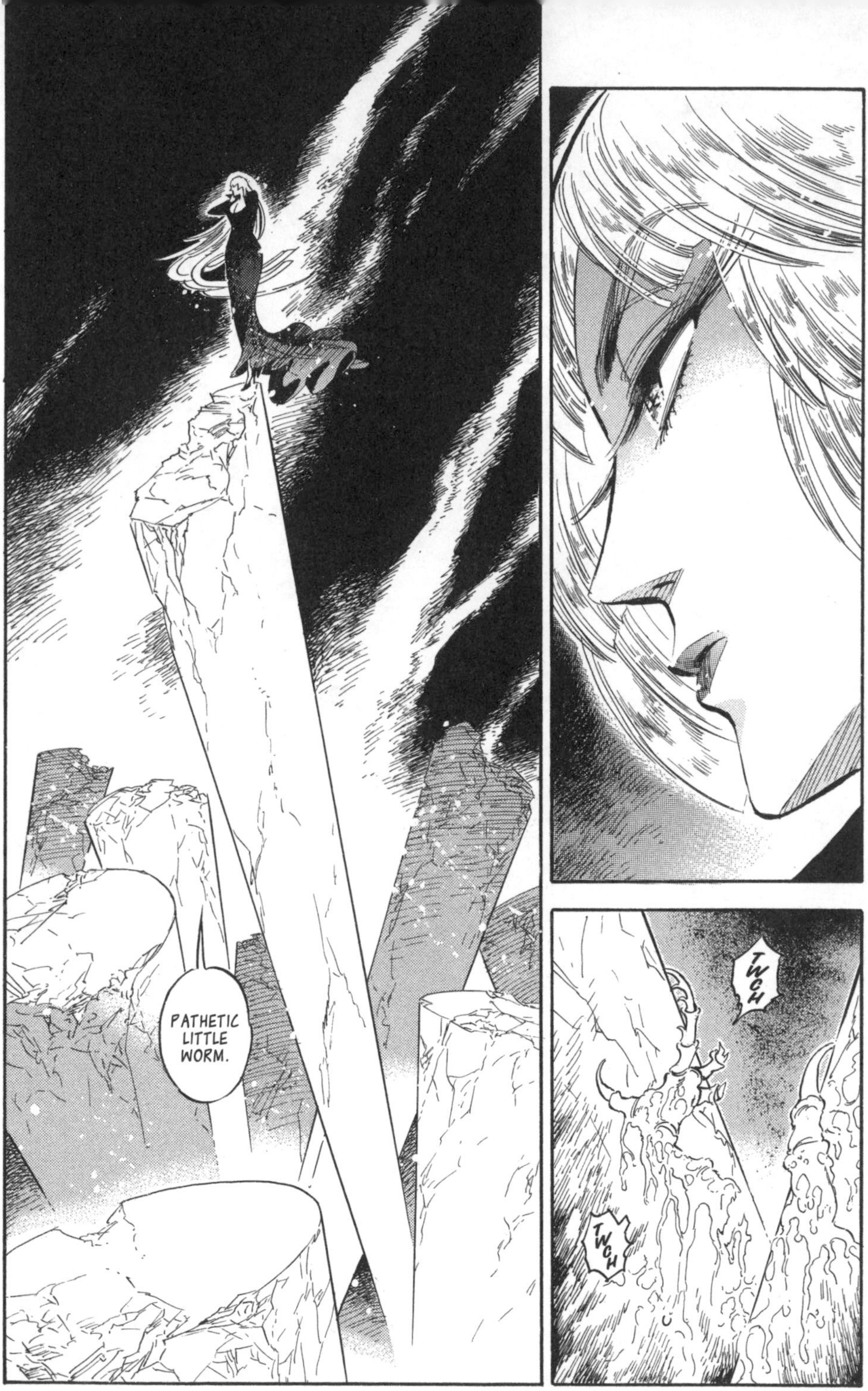
TWCH
TWCH
PATHETIC LITTLE WORM.

Chapter 34 / The End

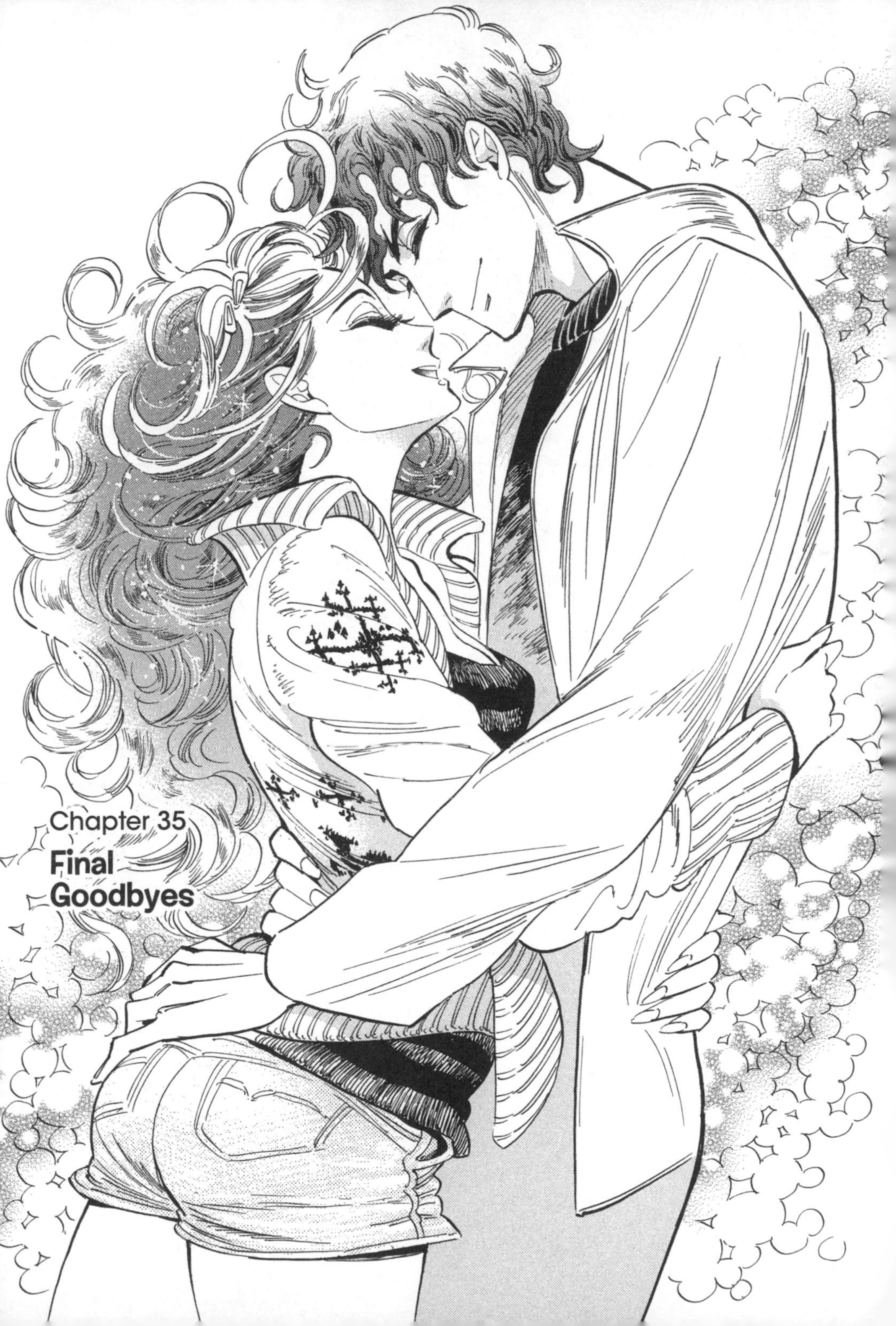
Chapter 35
Final Goodbyes

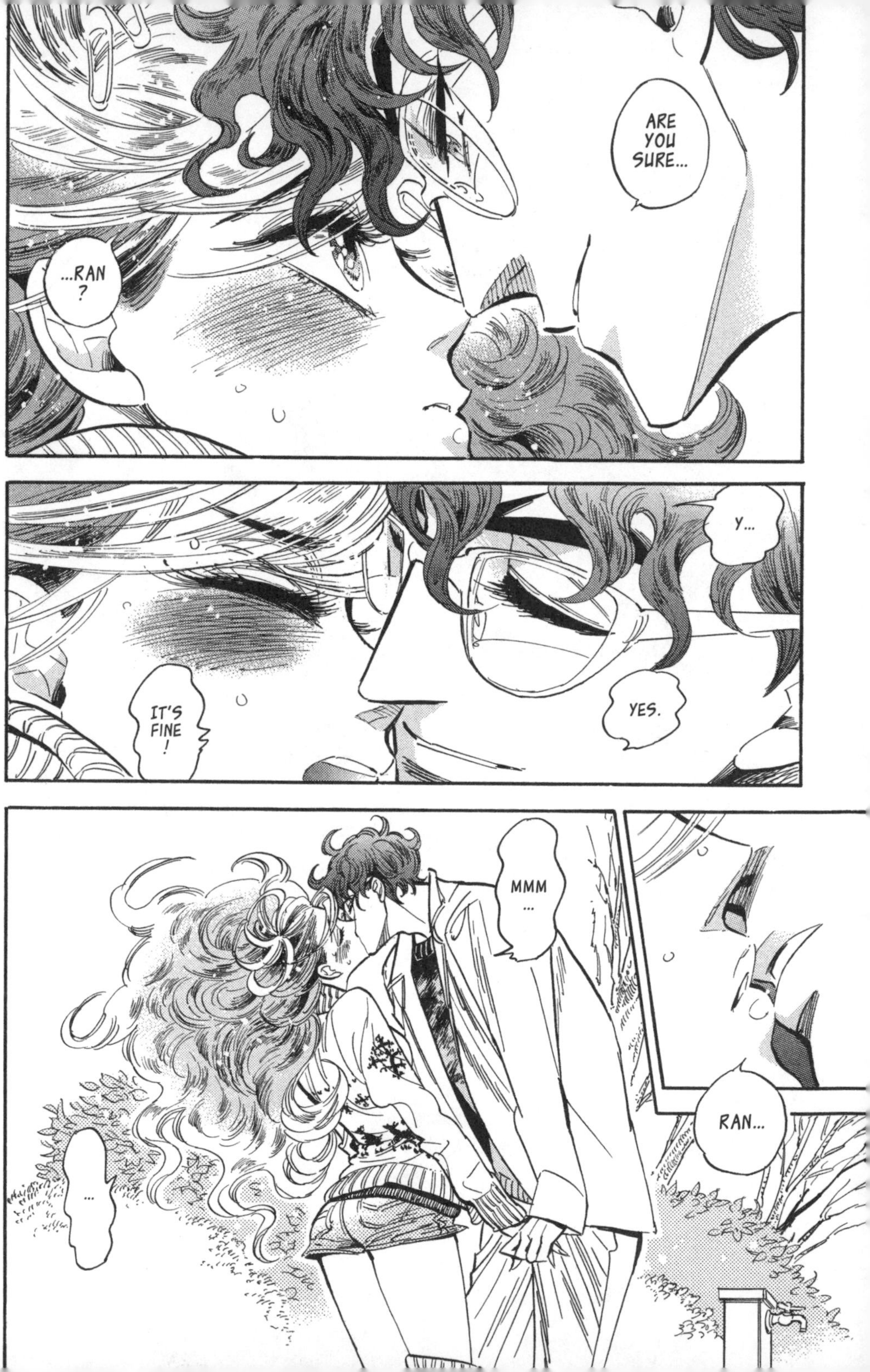
ARE YOU SURE...
...RAN ?
Y...
YES.
IT'S FINE !
RAN...
MMM ...
...

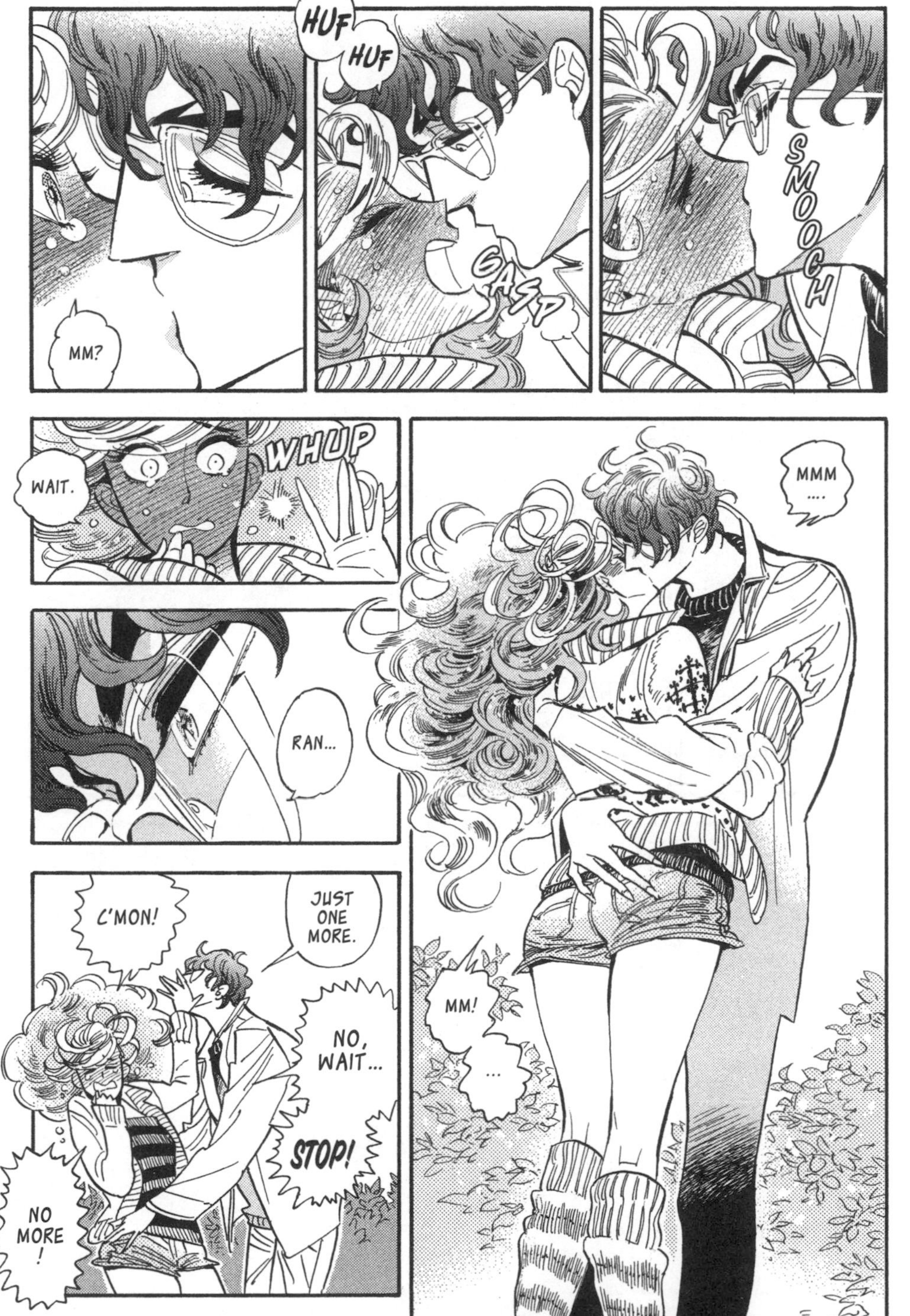
SMOOCH
HUF
HUF
GASP
MM?
MMM ....
MM!
...
WHUP
WAIT.
RAN...
JUST ONE MORE.
C'MON!
NO, WAIT...
STOP!
NO MORE!

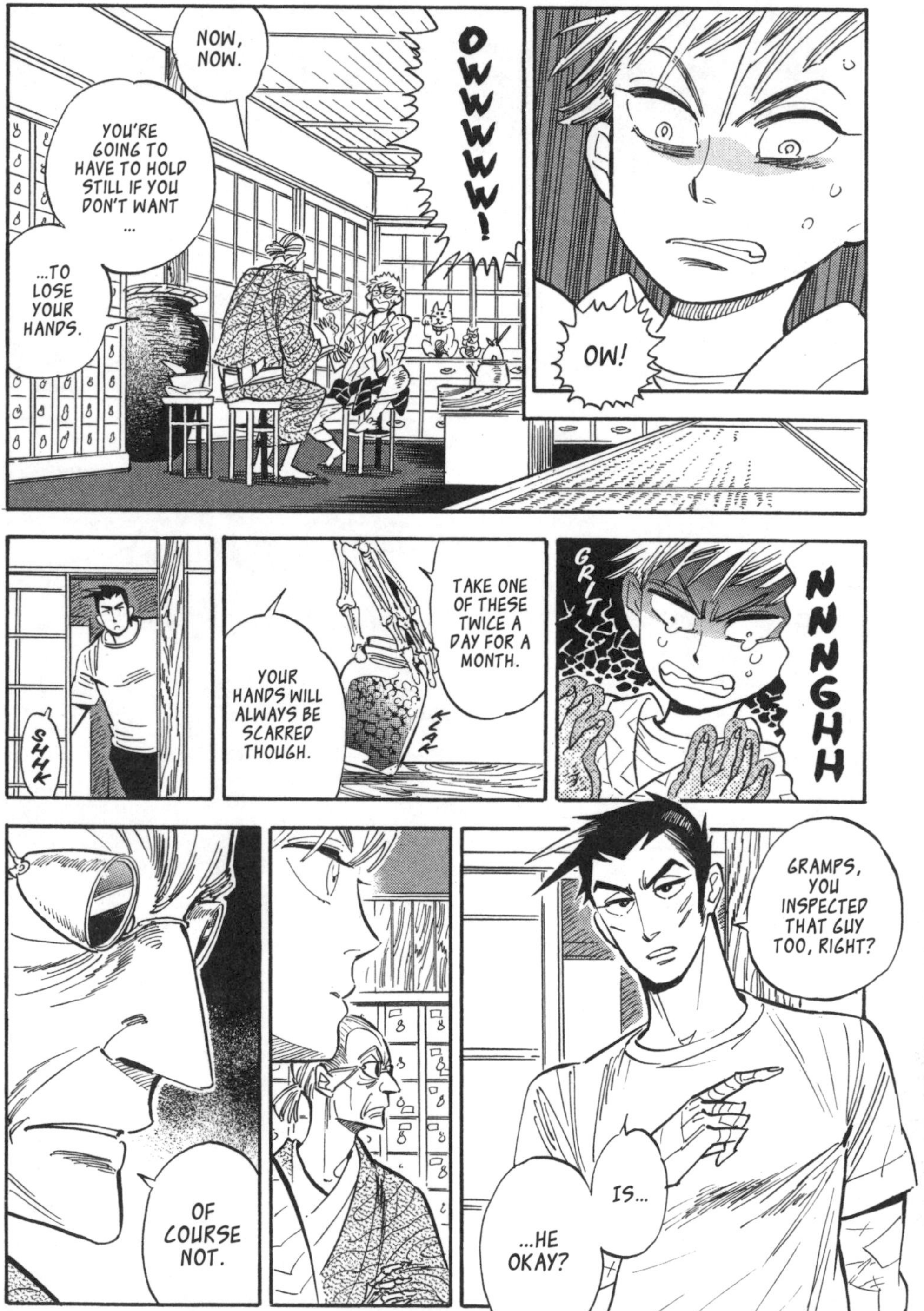
OW!
OWWWWWW!
NOW, NOW.
YOU'RE GOING TO HAVE TO HOLD STILL IF YOU DON'T WANT ...
...TO LOSE YOUR HANDS.
NNNGHH
GRIT
TAKE ONE OF THESE TWICE A DAY FOR A MONTH.
YOUR HANDS WILL ALWAYS BE SCARRED THOUGH.
KLAK
SHHK
GRAMPS, YOU INSPECTED THAT GUY TOO, RIGHT?
IS...
...HE OKAY?
OF COURSE NOT.

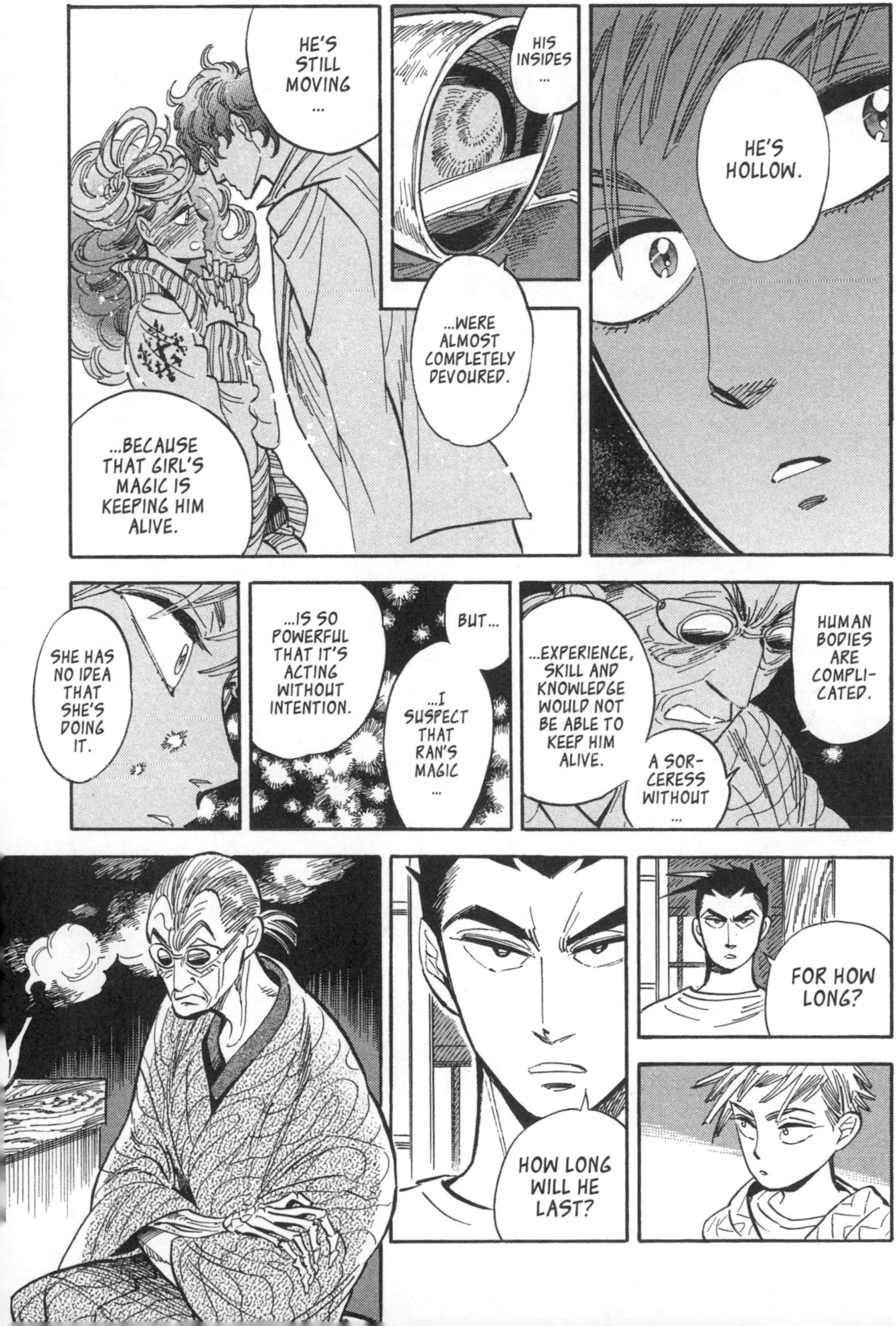
HE'S HOLLOW.
HIS INSIDES ...
...WERE ALMOST COMPLETELY DEVOURED.
HE'S STILL MOVING ...
...BECAUSE THAT GIRL'S MAGIC IS KEEPING HIM ALIVE.
HUMAN BODIES ARE COMPLI-CATED.
A SOR-CERESS WITHOUT ...
...EXPERIENCE, SKILL AND KNOWLEDGE WOULD NOT BE ABLE TO KEEP HIM ALIVE.
BUT...
...I SUSPECT THAT RAN'S MAGIC ...
...IS SO POWERFUL THAT IT'S ACTING WITHOUT INTENTION.
SHE HAS NO IDEA THAT SHE'S DOING IT.
FOR HOW LONG?
HOW LONG WILL HE LAST?

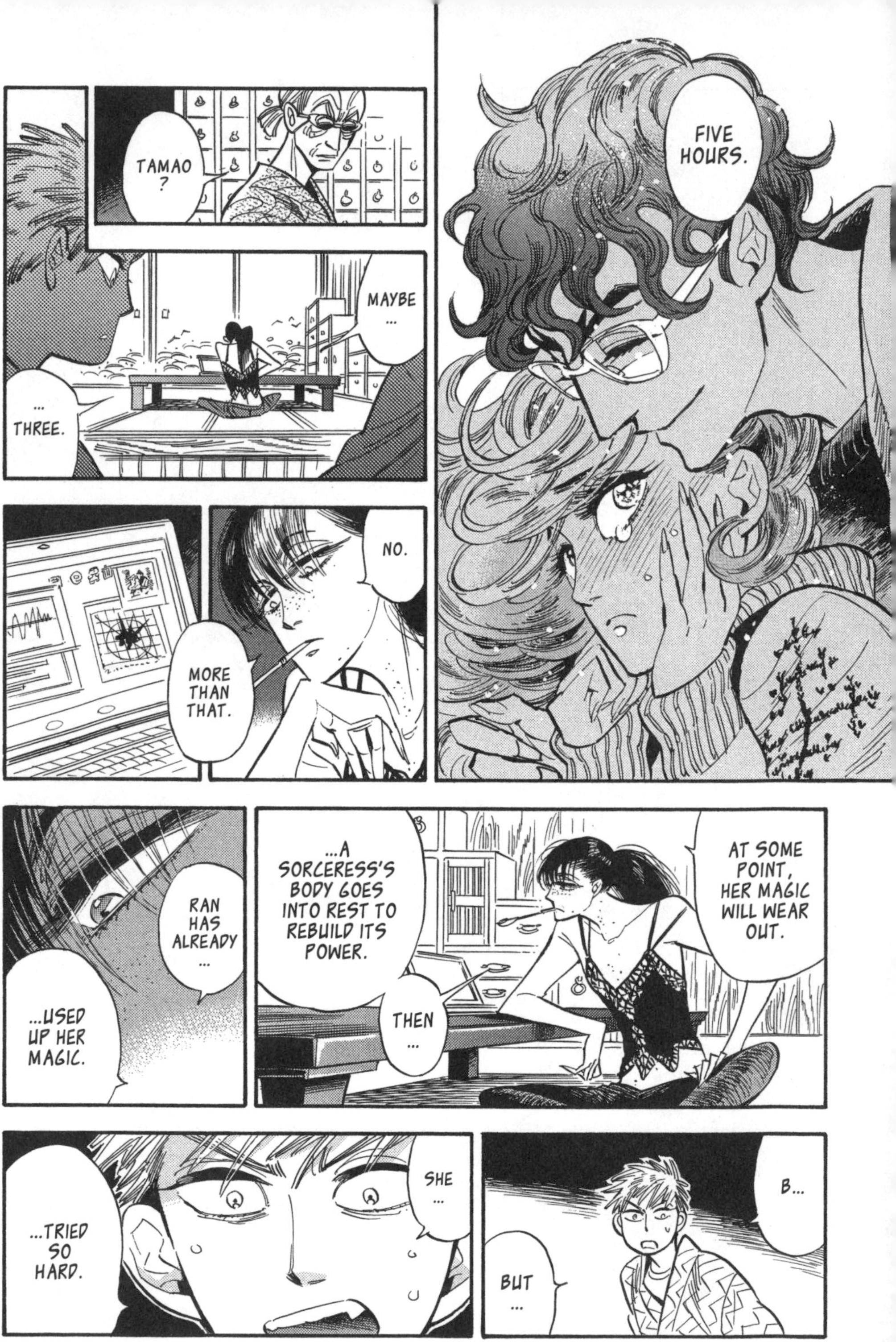
FIVE HOURS.
TAMAO?
MAYBE...
...THREE.
NO.
MORE THAN THAT.
AT SOME POINT, HER MAGIC WILL WEAR OUT.
...A SORCERESS'S BODY GOES INTO REST TO REBUILD ITS POWER.
THEN...
RAN HAS ALREADY...
...USED UP HER MAGIC.
B...
BUT...
SHE...
...TRIED SO HARD.

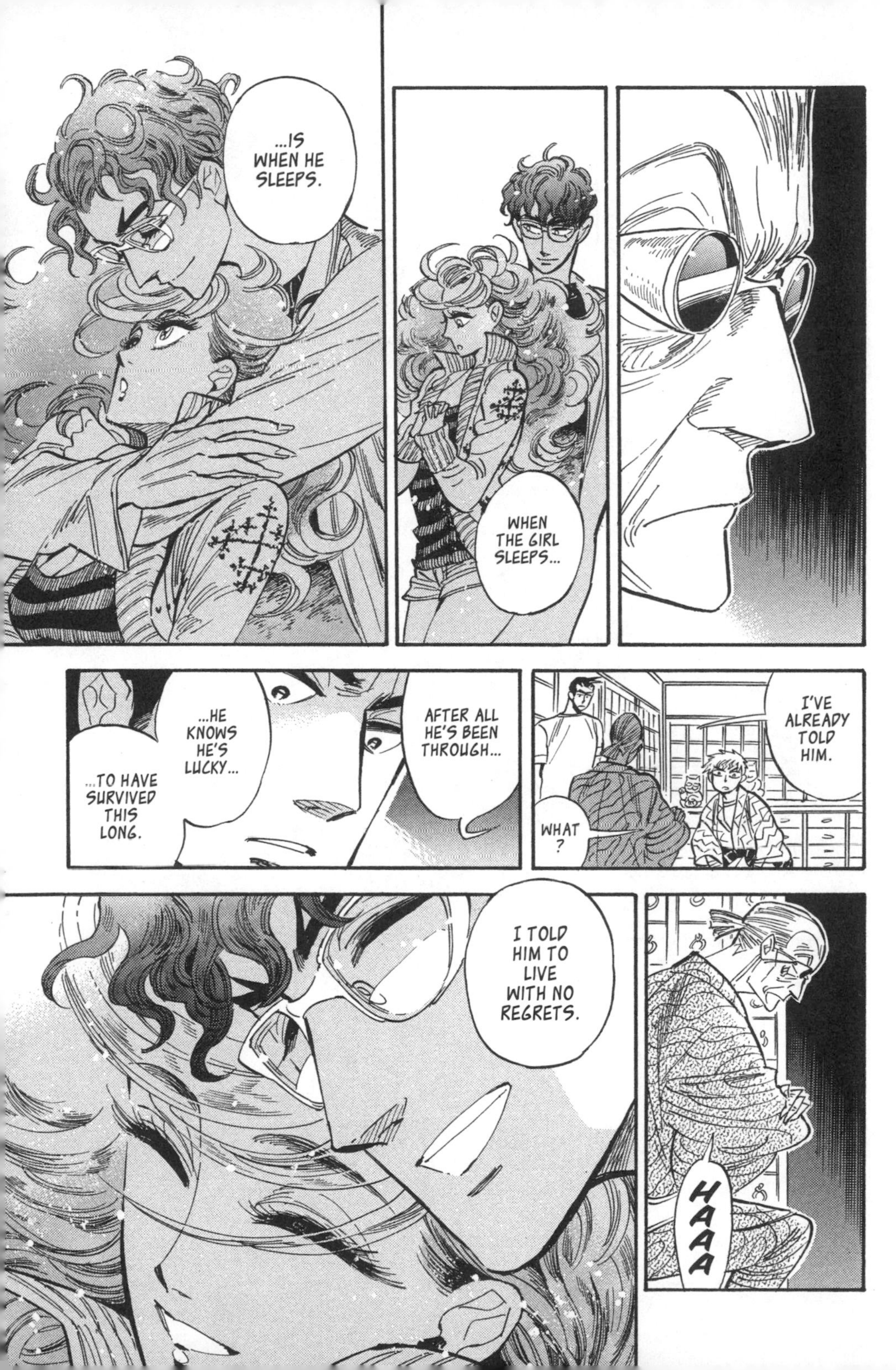
WHEN THE GIRL SLEEPS...
...IS WHEN HE SLEEPS.
I'VE ALREADY TOLD HIM.
WHAT?
AFTER ALL HE'S BEEN THROUGH...
...HE KNOWS HE'S LUCKY...
...TO HAVE SURVIVED THIS LONG.
HAAA
I TOLD HIM TO LIVE WITH NO REGRETS.

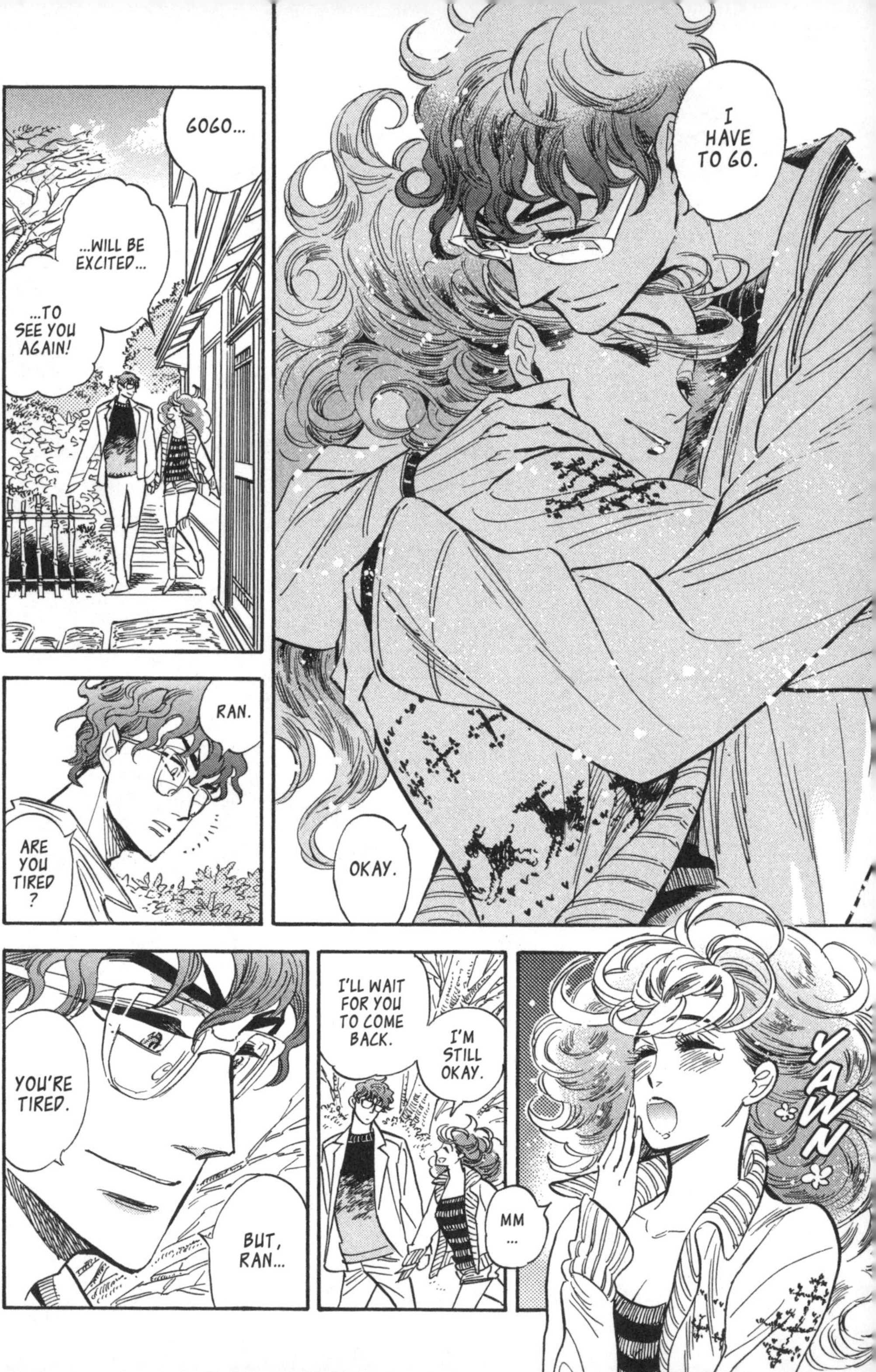
I HAVE TO GO.
OKAY.
GOGO...
...WILL BE EXCITED...
...TO SEE YOU AGAIN!
RAN.
ARE YOU TIRED?
YAWN
MM...
I'LL WAIT FOR YOU TO COME BACK.
I'M STILL OKAY.
YOU'RE TIRED.
BUT, RAN...

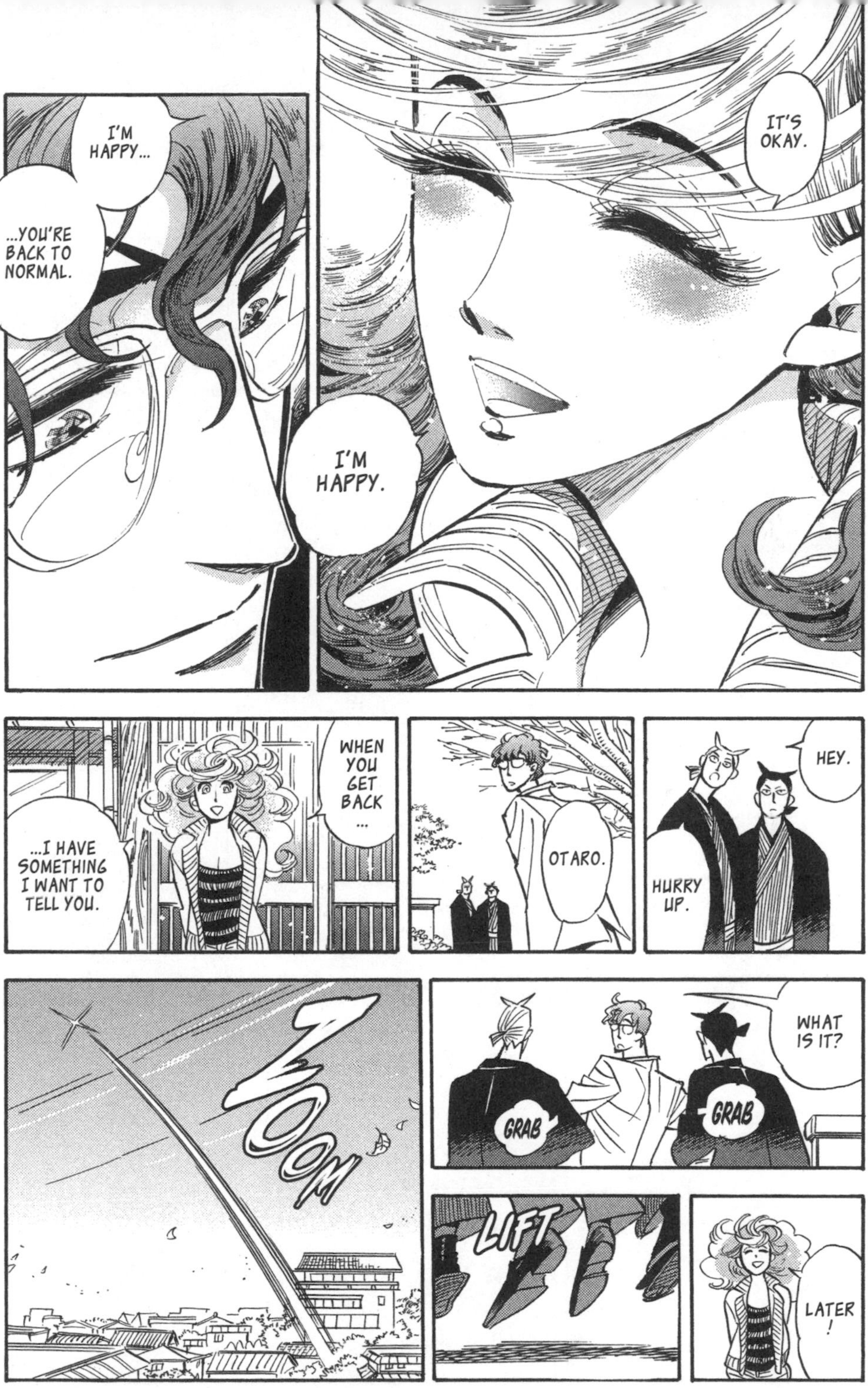
IT'S OKAY.
I'M HAPPY.
I'M HAPPY...
...YOU'RE BACK TO NORMAL.
HEY.
HURRY UP.
OTARO.
WHEN YOU GET BACK...
...I HAVE SOMETHING I WANT TO TELL YOU.
WHAT IS IT?
GRAB
GRAB
LATER!
LIFT
ZOOM

MASTER
OTARO
...

WELCOME
HOME.

YES.

...

YOU
KNOW
?

THEY'RE
GOOD AT
WHAT
THEY DO.

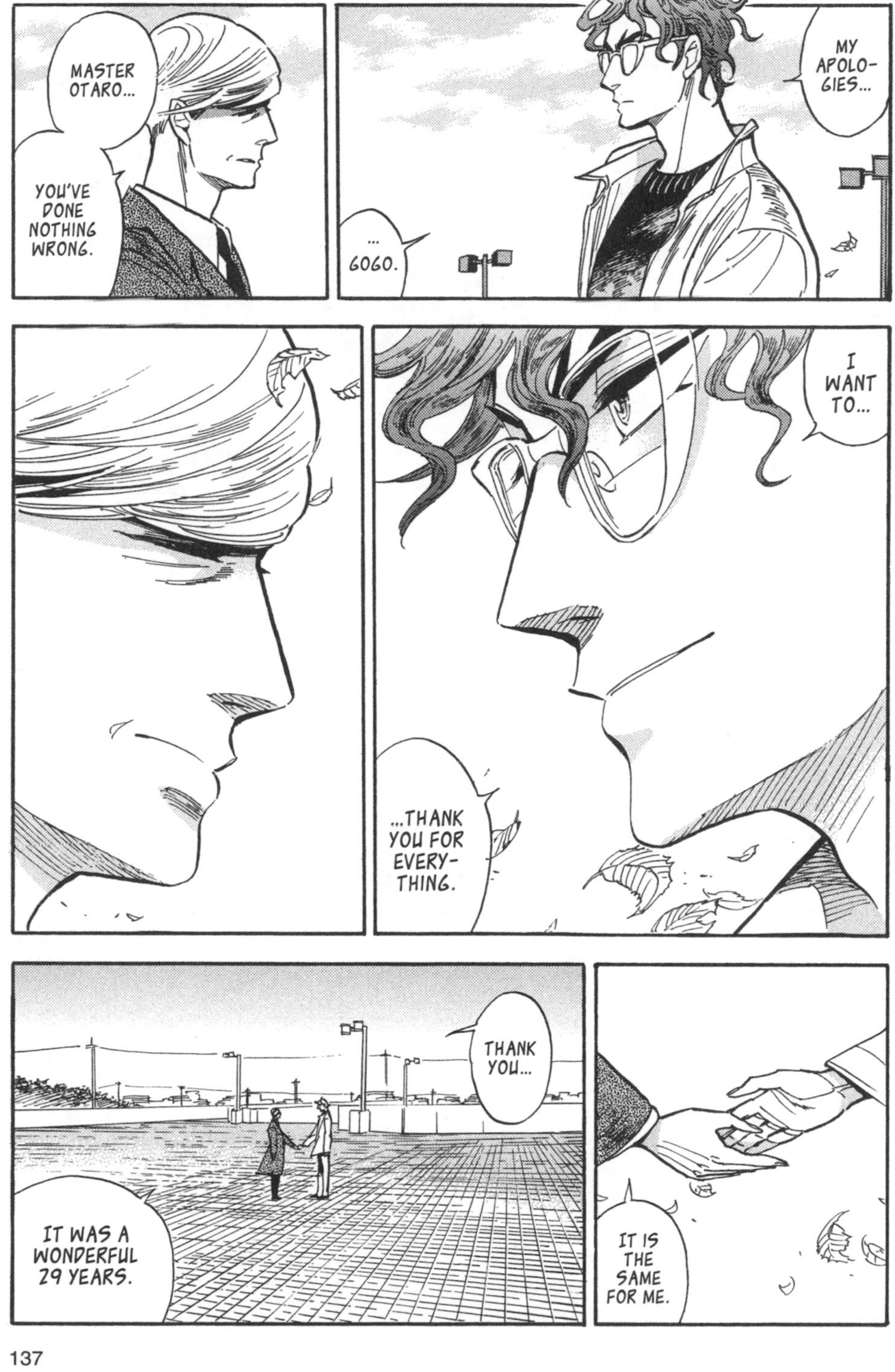
MY APOLOGIES...
... GOGO.
MASTER OTARO...
YOU'VE DONE NOTHING WRONG.
I WANT TO...
...THANK YOU FOR EVERYTHING.
IT IS THE SAME FOR ME.
THANK YOU...
IT WAS A WONDERFUL 29 YEARS.

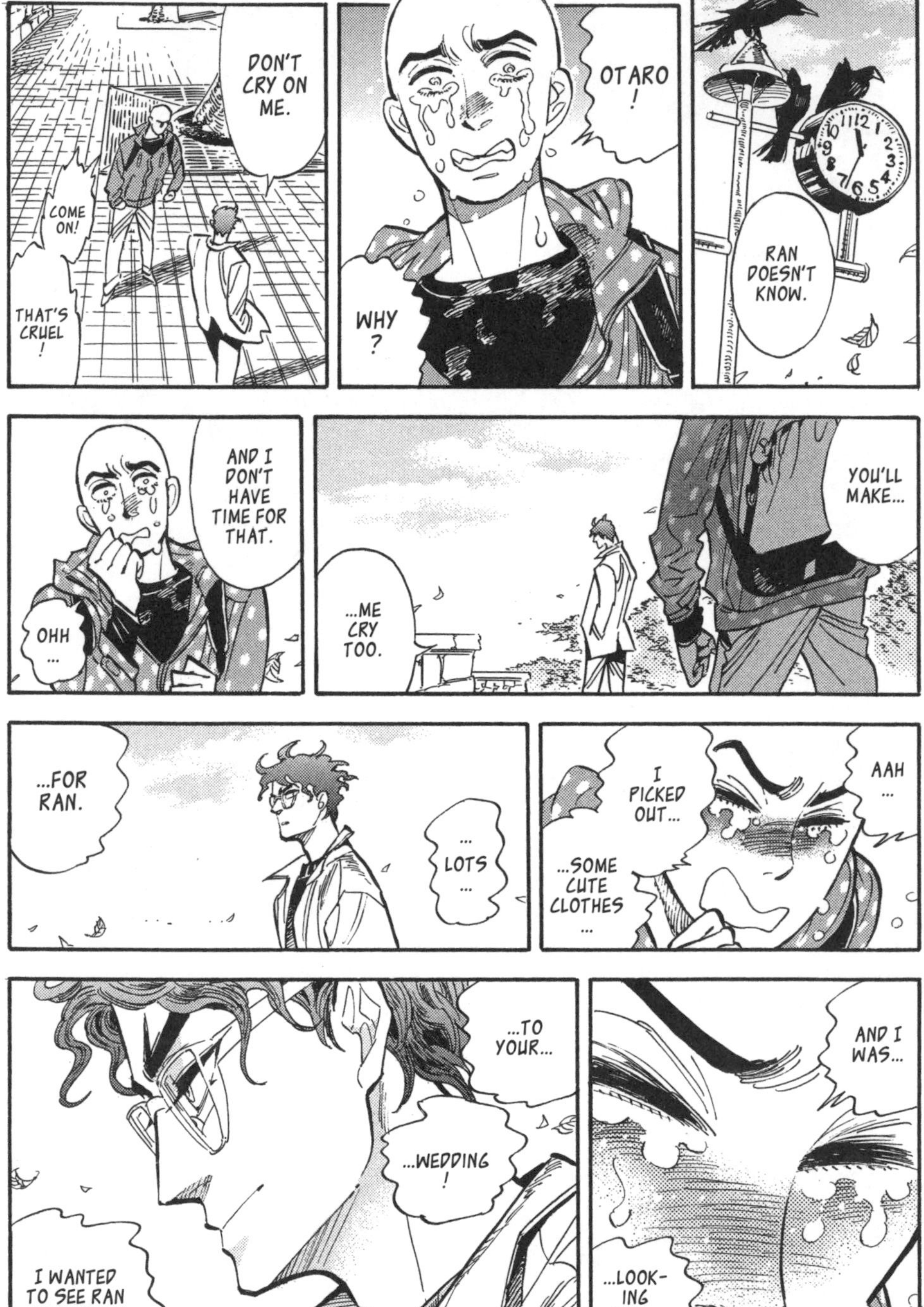
RAN DOESN'T KNOW.
OTARO!
WHY?
DON'T CRY ON ME.
COME ON!
THAT'S CRUEL!
YOU'LL MAKE...
...ME CRY TOO.
AND I DON'T HAVE TIME FOR THAT.
OHH...
AAH...
I PICKED OUT...
...SOME CUTE CLOTHES...
...LOTS...
...FOR RAN.
AND I WAS...
...LOOKING-ING FOR-WARD...
...TO YOUR...
...WEDDING!
I WANTED TO SEE RAN DRESSED IN WHITE...

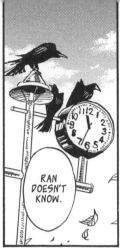

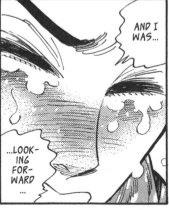

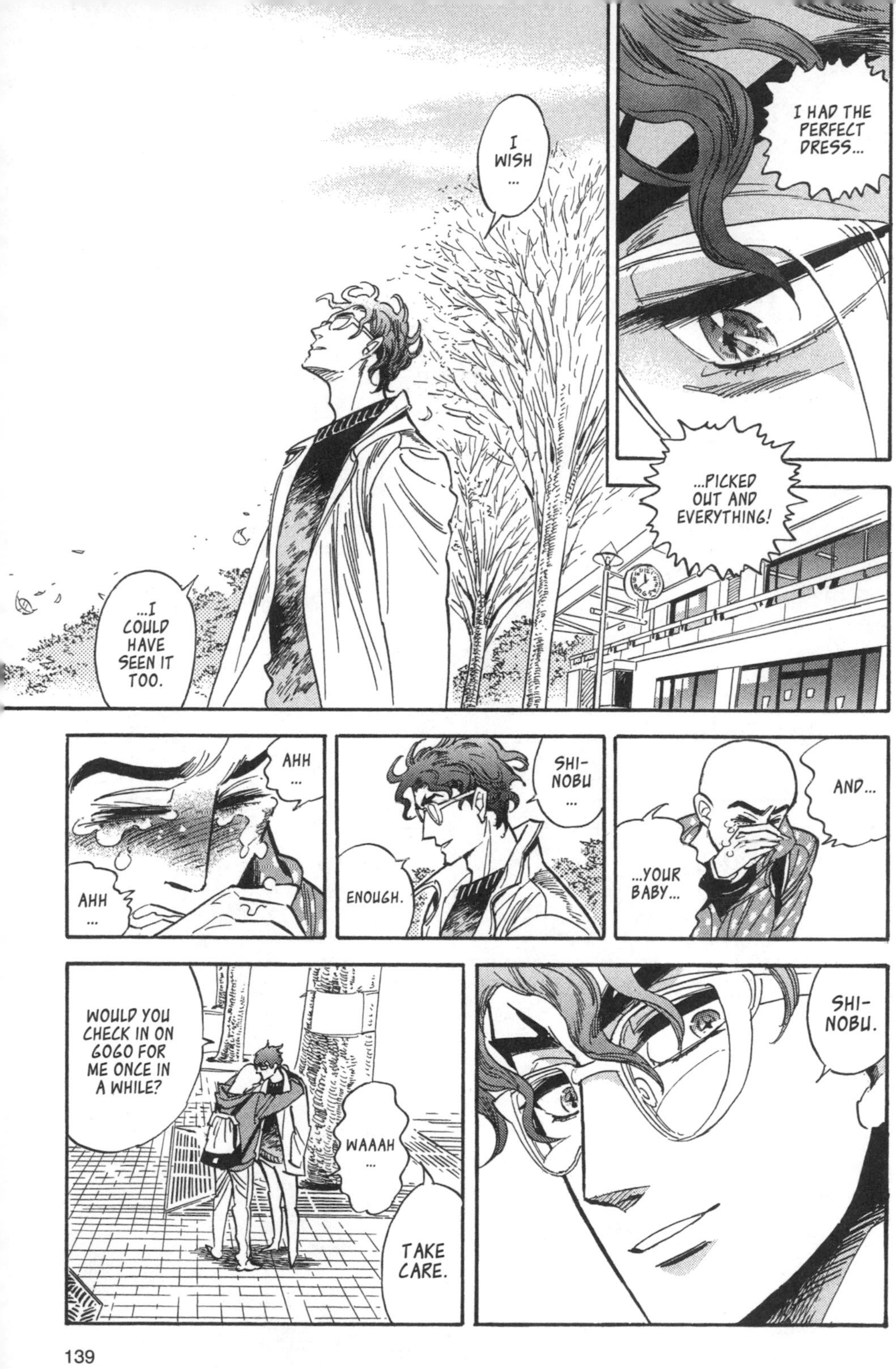
I HAD THE PERFECT DRESS...
...PICKED OUT AND EVERYTHING!
I WISH...
...I COULD HAVE SEEN IT TOO.
AND...
...YOUR BABY...
SHI-NOBU...
ENOUGH.
AHH...
AHH...
SHI-NOBU.
WOULD YOU CHECK IN ON GOGO FOR ME ONCE IN A WHILE?
WAAAH...
TAKE CARE.

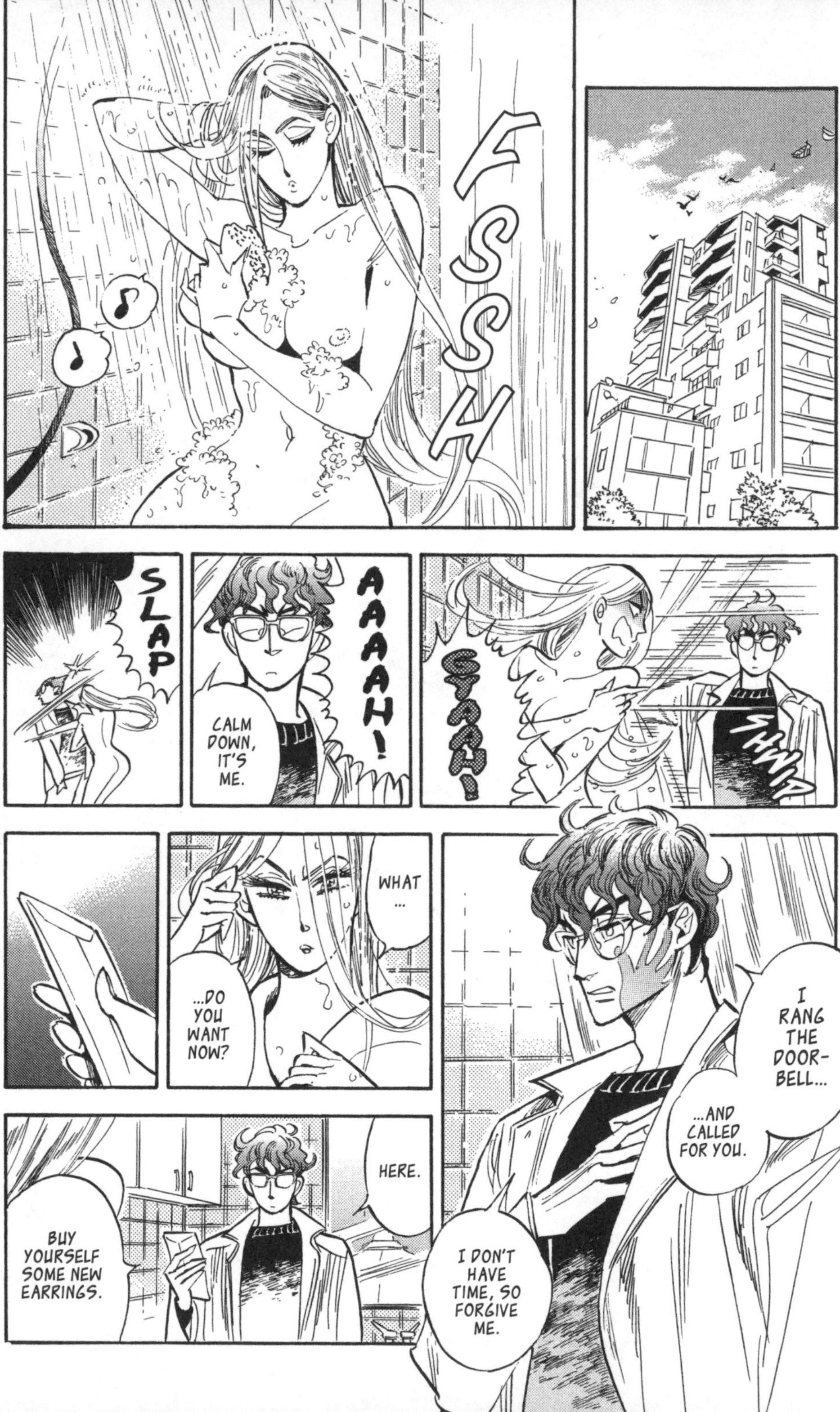
FSSH
GYAAH!
SHWIP
AAAAH!
CALM DOWN, IT'S ME.
SLAP
I RANG THE DOOR-BELL...
...AND CALLED FOR YOU.
I DON'T HAVE TIME, SO FORGIVE ME.
WHAT ...
...DO YOU WANT NOW?
HERE.
BUY YOURSELF SOME NEW EARRINGS.

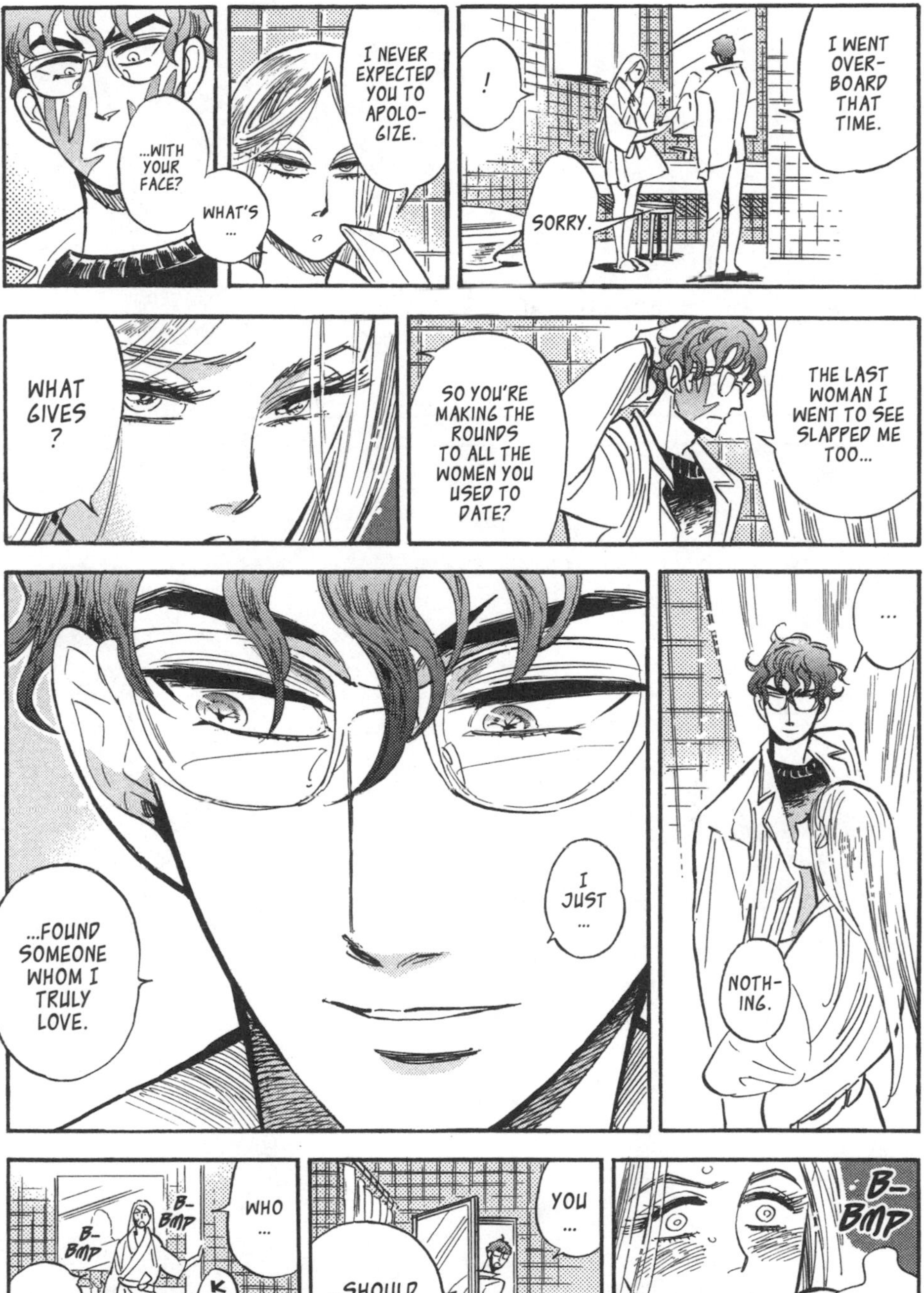
I WENT OVER-BOARD THAT TIME.
!
SORRY.
I NEVER EXPECTED YOU TO APOLO-GIZE.
WHAT'S ...
...WITH YOUR FACE?
THE LAST WOMAN I WENT TO SEE SLAPPED ME TOO...
SO YOU'RE MAKING THE ROUNDS TO ALL THE WOMEN YOU USED TO DATE?
WHAT GIVES?
...
NOTH-ING.
I JUST ...
...FOUND SOMEONE WHOM I TRULY LOVE.
B-BMP
WHAT?!
YOU ...
...SHOULD TRY IT TOO.
WHO ...
B-BMP
B-BMP
KCHAM
...WAS THAT?

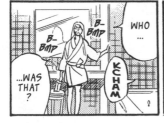

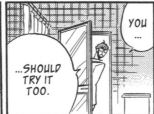

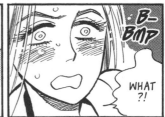

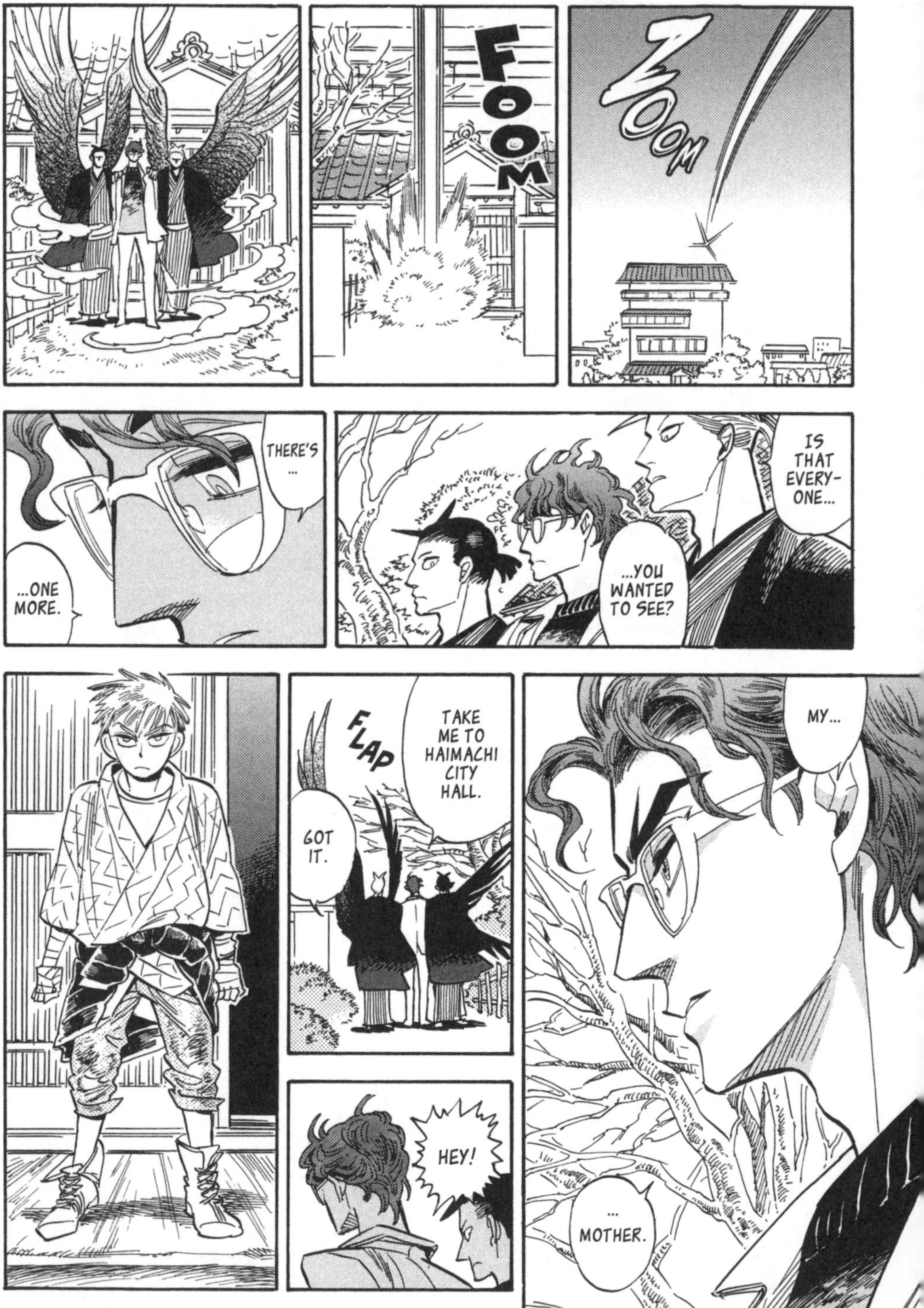
ZOOM
FOOM
IS THAT EVERY-ONE...
...YOU WANTED TO SEE?
THERE'S ...
...ONE MORE.
MY...
... MOTHER.
TAKE ME TO HAIMACHI CITY HALL.
FLAP
GOT IT.
HEY!

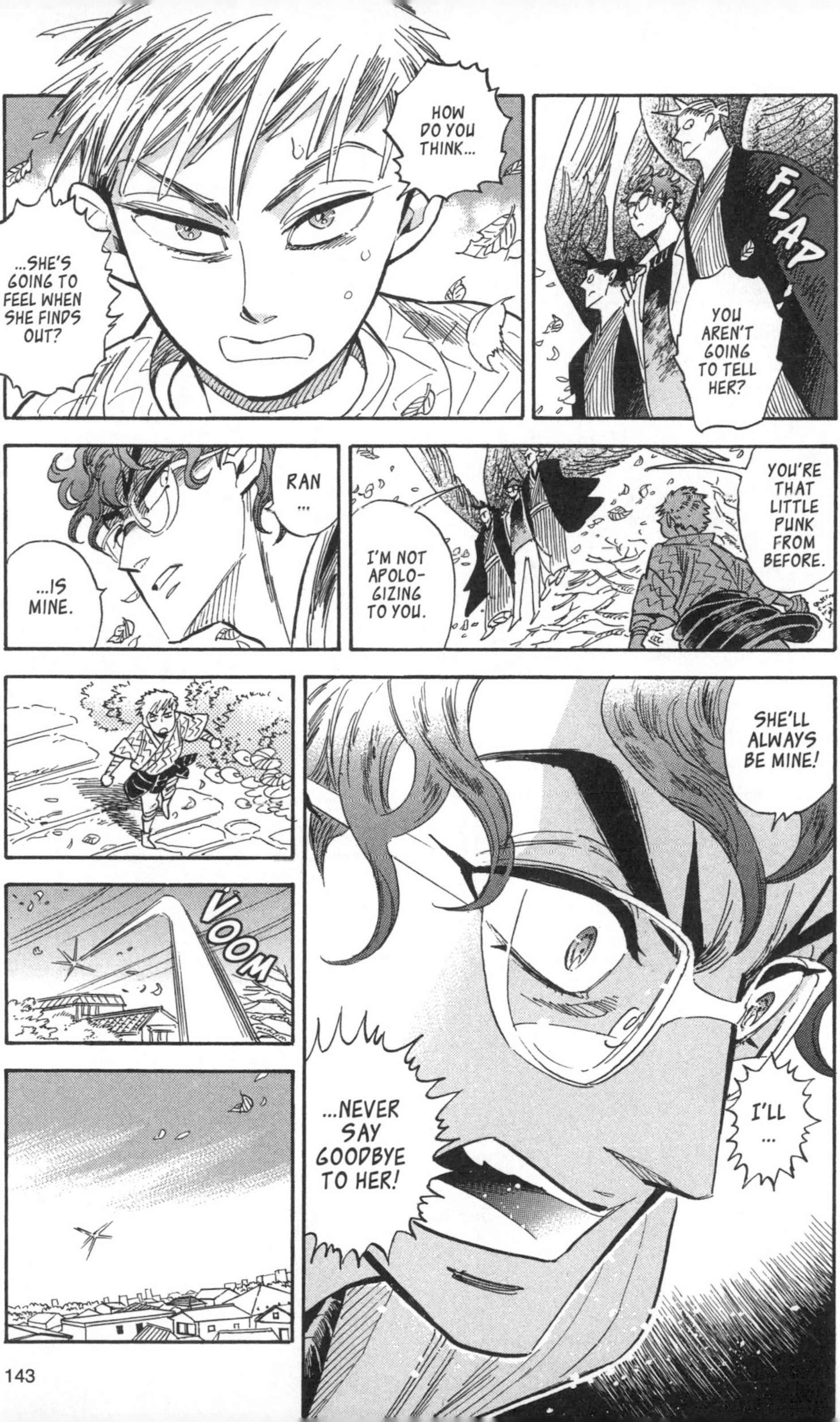
FLAP
YOU AREN'T GOING TO TELL HER?
HOW DO YOU THINK...
...SHE'S GOING TO FEEL WHEN SHE FINDS OUT?
YOU'RE THAT LITTLE PUNK FROM BEFORE.
I'M NOT APOLO-GIZING TO YOU.
RAN ...
...IS MINE.
SHE'LL ALWAYS BE MINE!
I'LL ...
...NEVER SAY GOODBYE TO HER!
VOOM

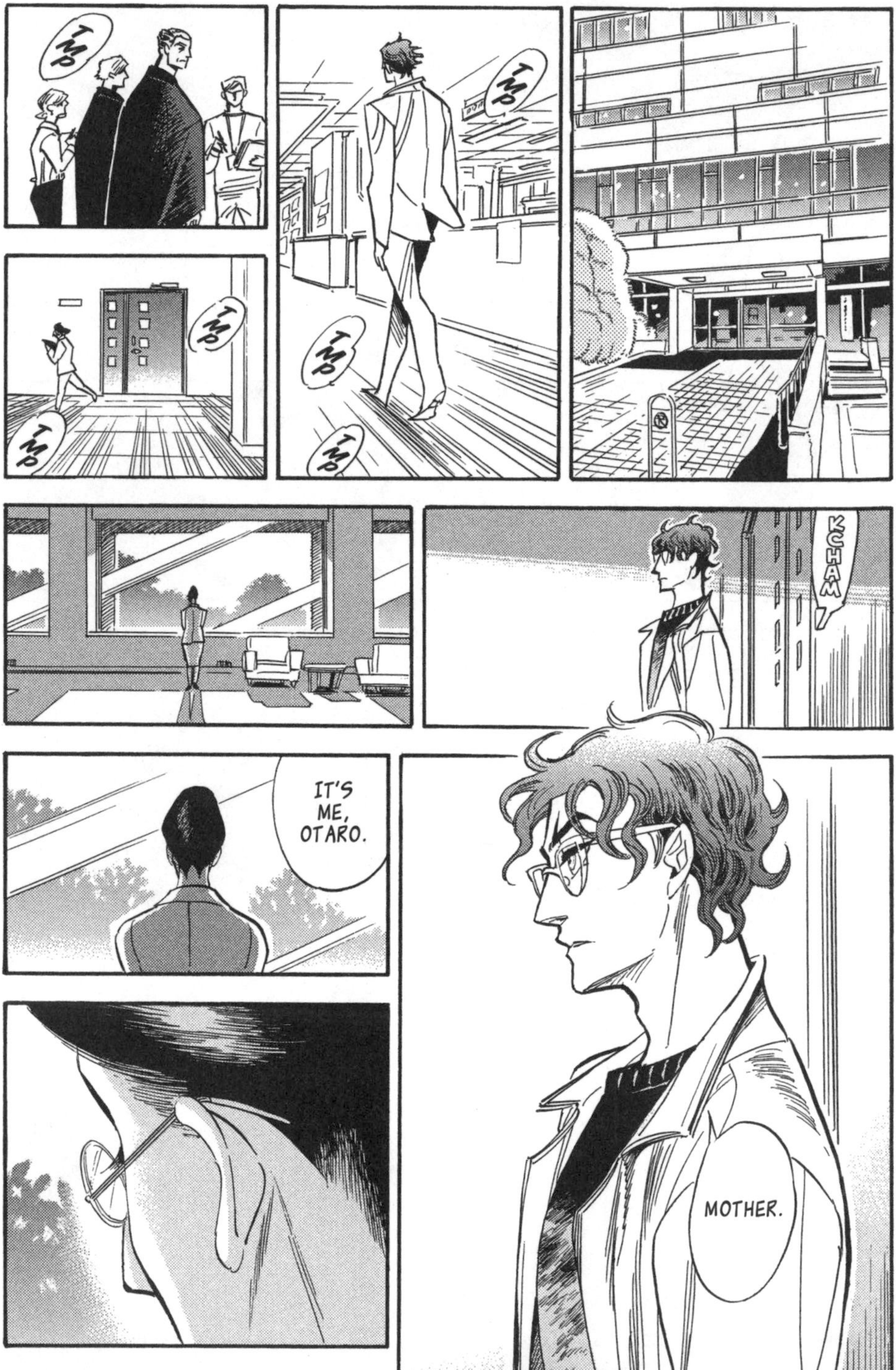
TMP
TMP
TMP
TMP
TMP
TMP
KCHAM
MOTHER.
IT'S ME, OTARO.

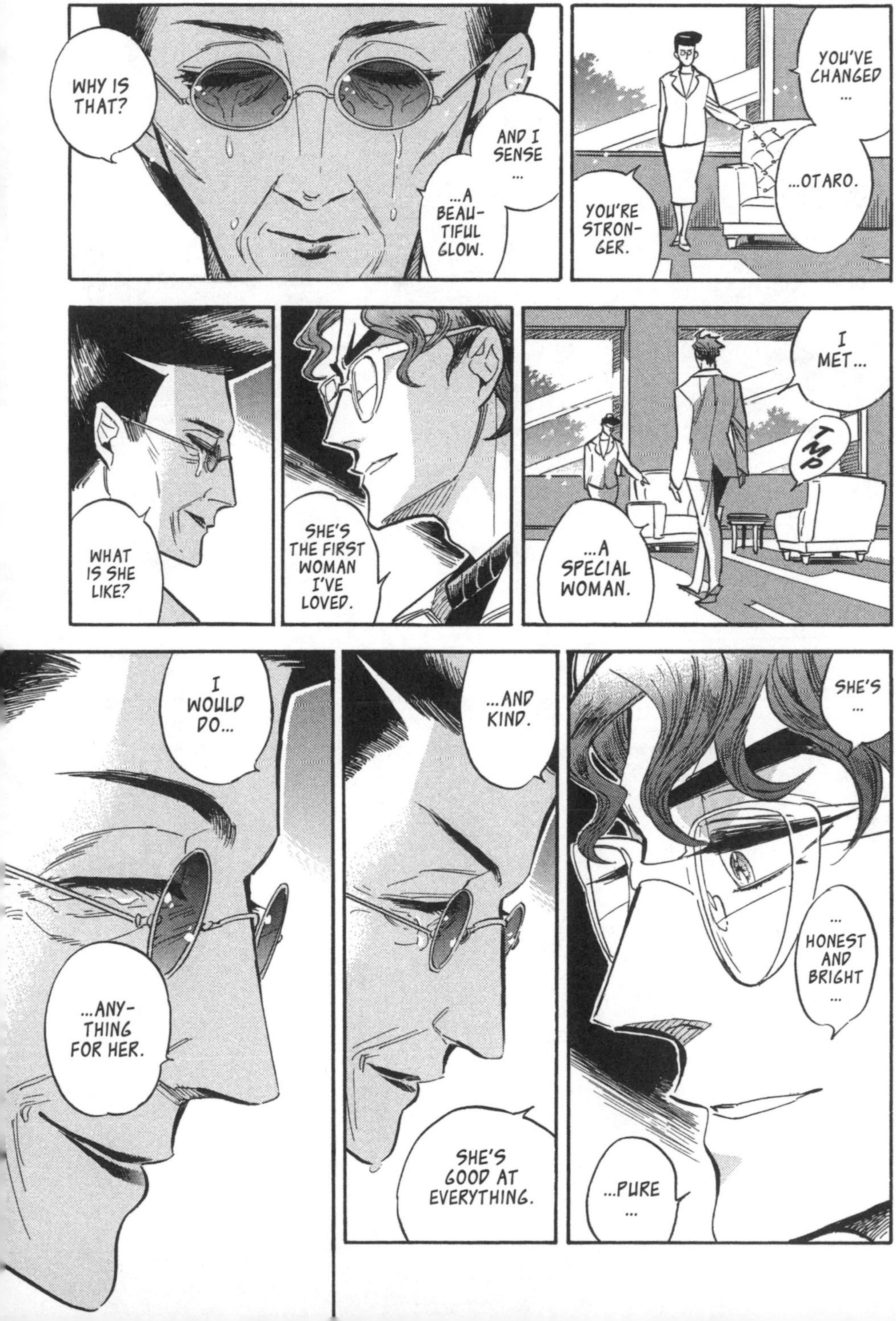
YOU'VE CHANGED ...
...OTARO.
YOU'RE STRONGER.
AND I SENSE ...
...A BEAUTIFUL GLOW.
WHY IS THAT?
I MET...
TMP
...A SPECIAL WOMAN.
SHE'S THE FIRST WOMAN I'VE LOVED.
WHAT IS SHE LIKE?
SHE'S ...
... HONEST AND BRIGHT ...
...PURE ...
...AND KIND.
SHE'S GOOD AT EVERYTHING.
I WOULD DO...
...ANYTHING FOR HER.

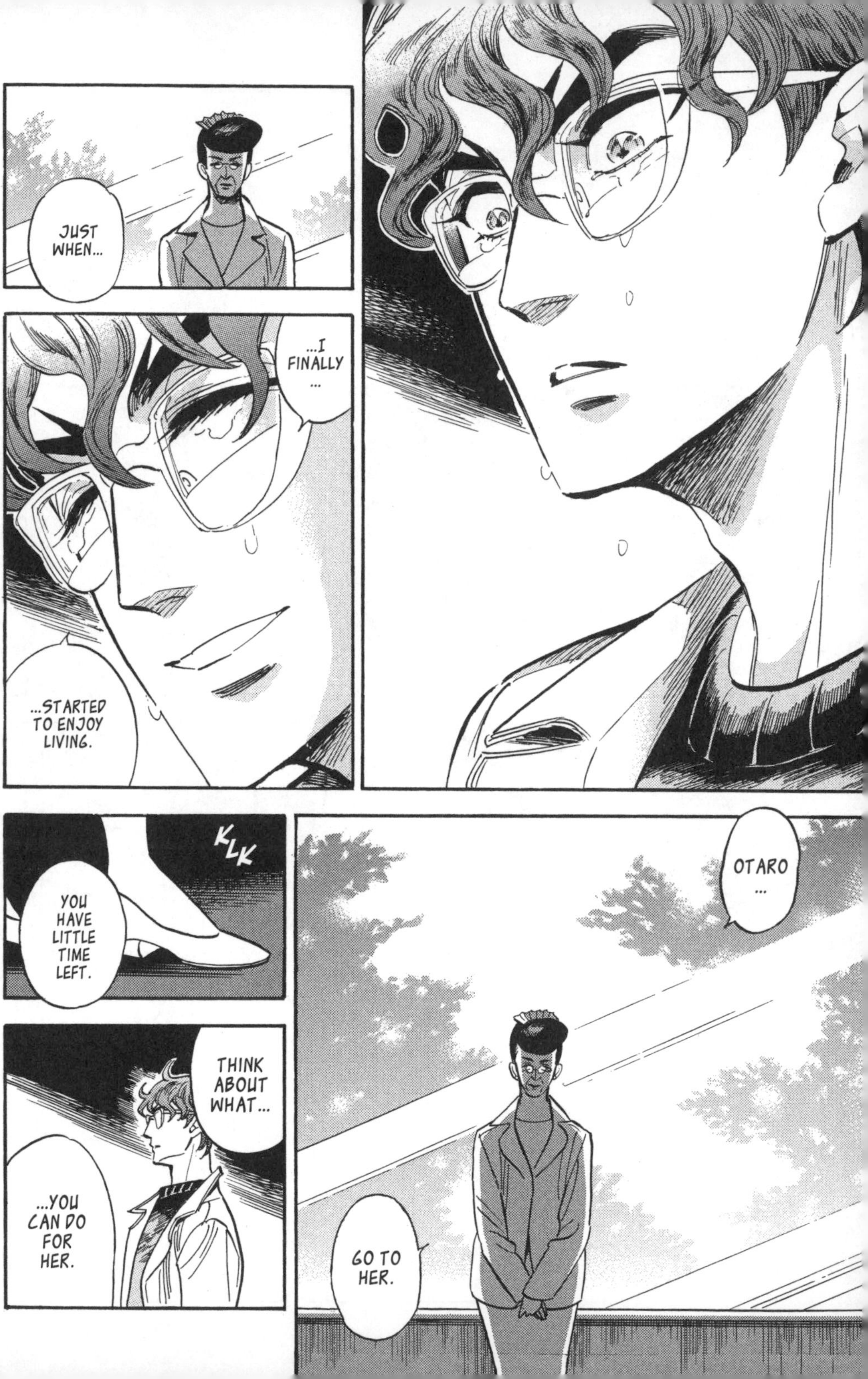
JUST WHEN...
...I FINALLY ...
...STARTED TO ENJOY LIVING.
OTARO ...
GO TO HER.
KLK
YOU HAVE LITTLE TIME LEFT.
THINK ABOUT WHAT...
...YOU CAN DO FOR HER.

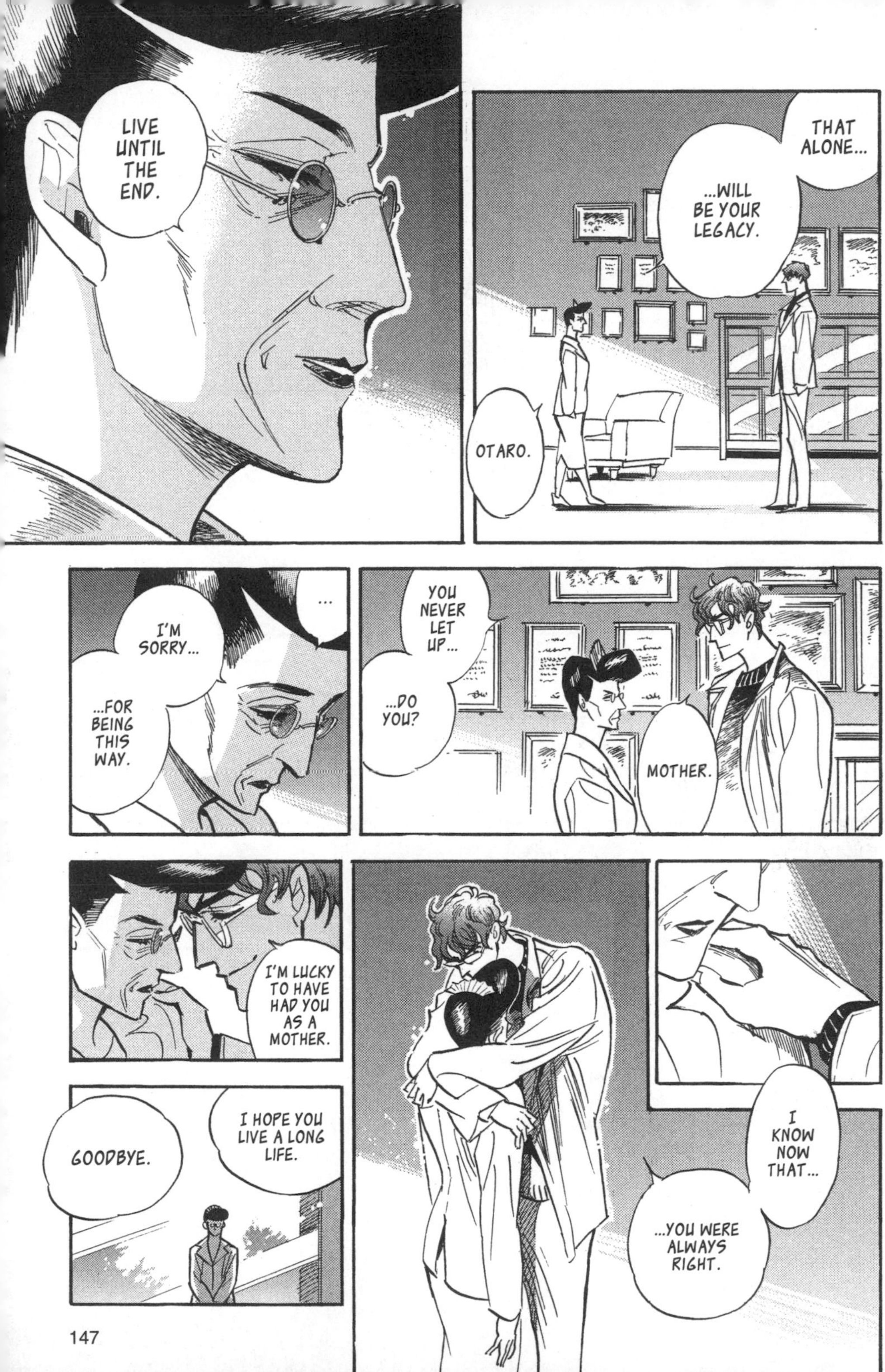
THAT ALONE...
...WILL BE YOUR LEGACY.
OTARO.
LIVE UNTIL THE END.
YOU NEVER LET UP...
...DO YOU?
MOTHER.
...
I'M SORRY...
...FOR BEING THIS WAY.
I KNOW NOW THAT...
...YOU WERE ALWAYS RIGHT.
I'M LUCKY TO HAVE HAD YOU AS A MOTHER.
I HOPE YOU LIVE A LONG LIFE.
GOODBYE.

KOFF

DOOT
DOOT

DOOT

DOOT

?!

WHAT DOES THAT MEAN ?!

PERFECT TIMING.

TELL YOUR GIRLFRIEND THAT I'M SORRY ABOUT WHAT HAPPENED.

OH, IT'S YOU.

HM?

GWCK

HELLO ?

RRING

LET HER KNOW THAT...

...I'M NOT COMING HOME.

I IMA- GINE...

...SHE'LL BE ASLEEP SOON.

FOR RAISING RAN TO BE SO WONDERFUL.

ALSO ...

I WANT TO THANK YOU.

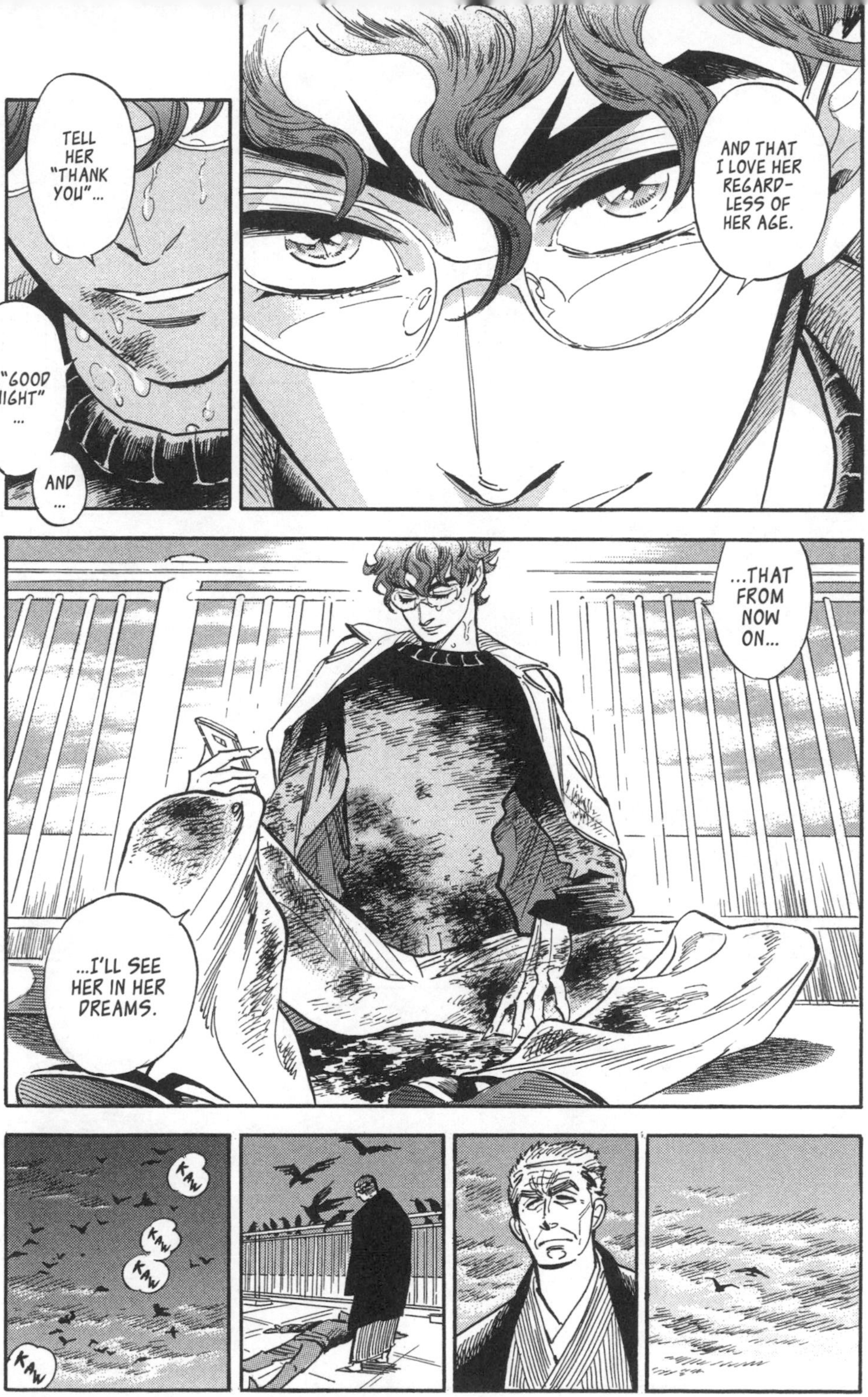
AND THAT I LOVE HER REGARD-LESS OF HER AGE.
TELL HER "THANK YOU"...
..."GOOD NIGHT" ...
AND ...
...THAT FROM NOW ON...
...I'LL SEE HER IN HER DREAMS.
KAW
KAW
KAW
KAW

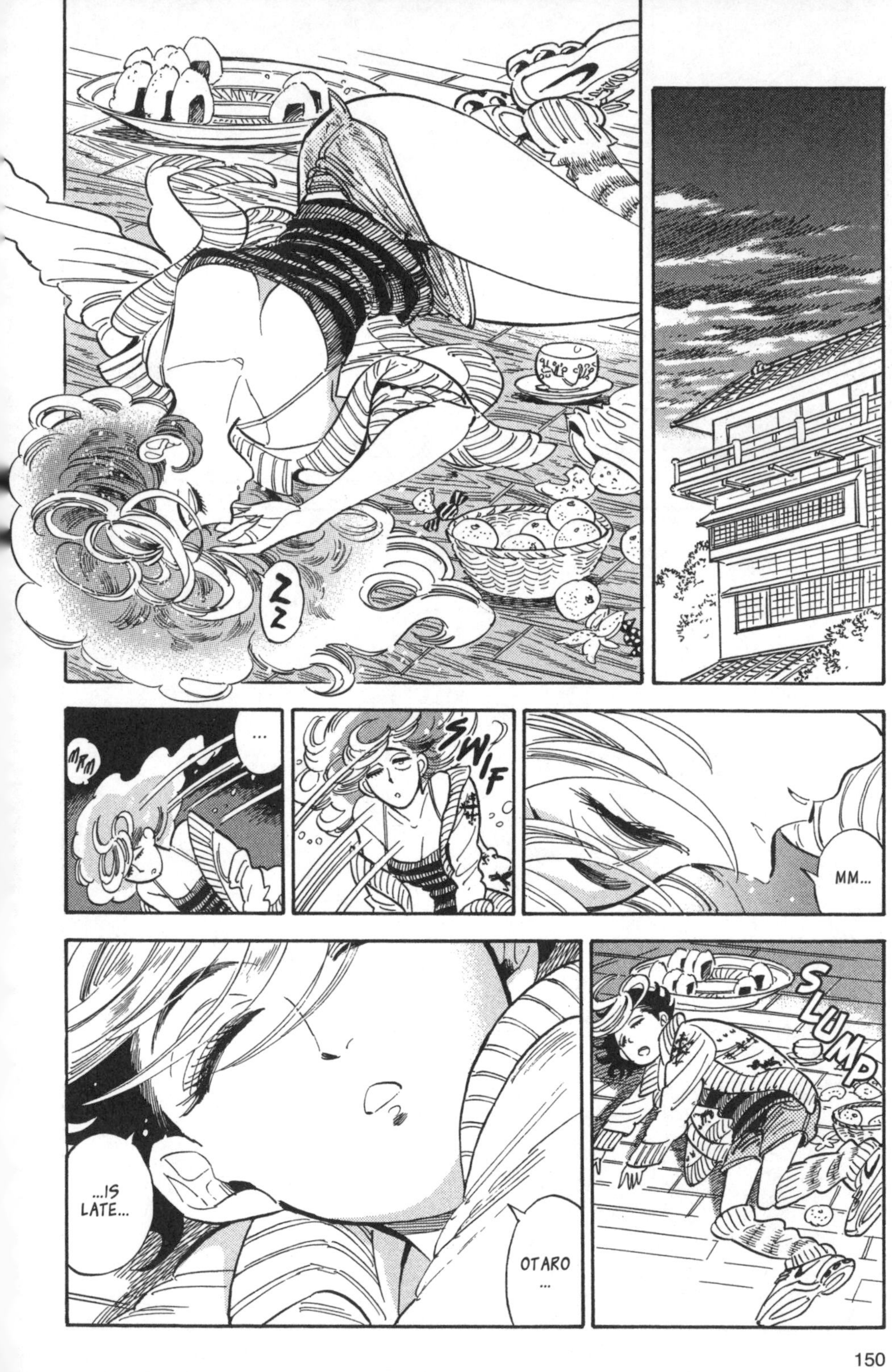
ZZ
MM...
SWIF
...
MRM
SLUMP
OTARO ...
...IS LATE...

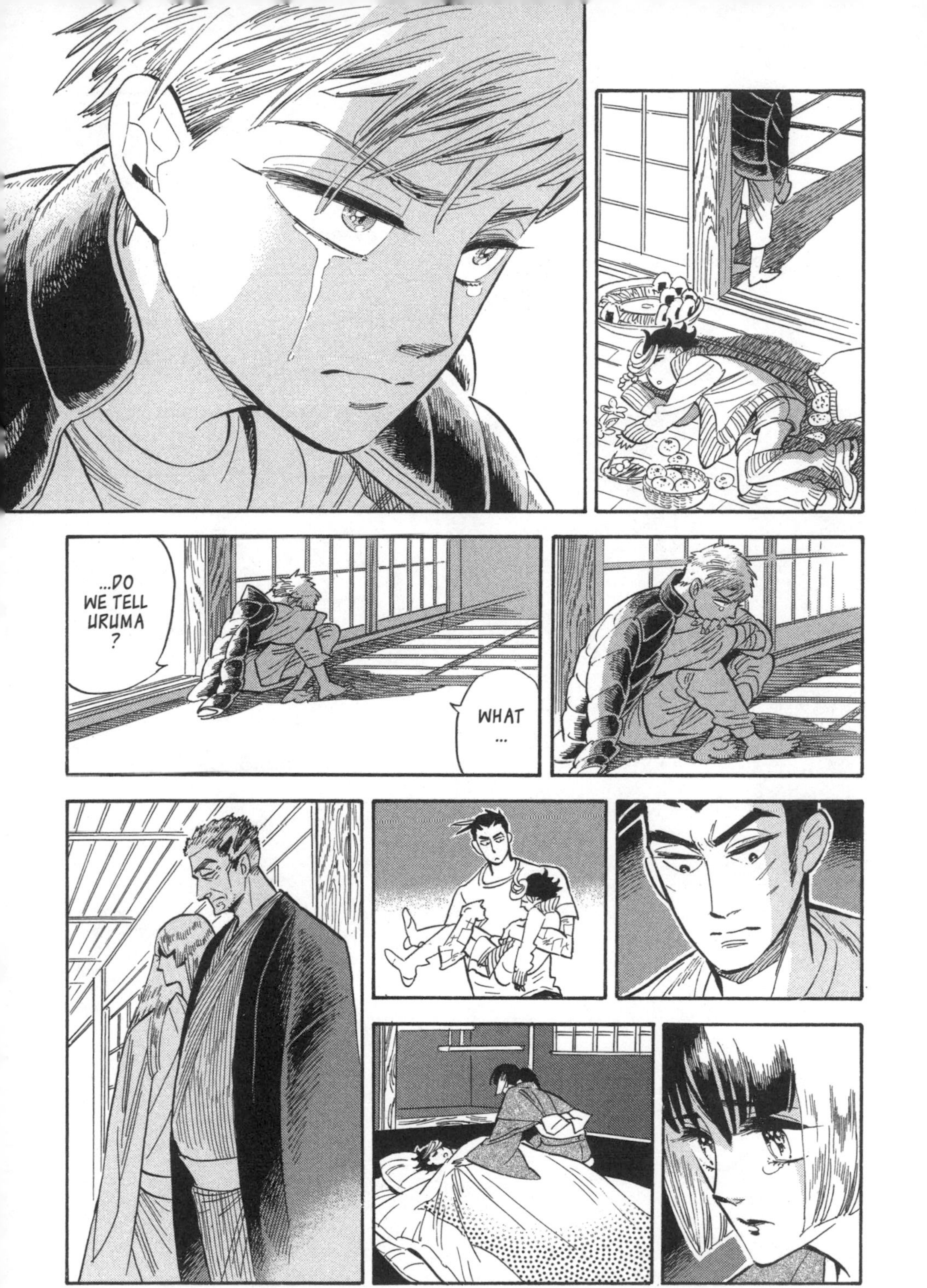
...DO WE TELL URUMA?
WHAT ...

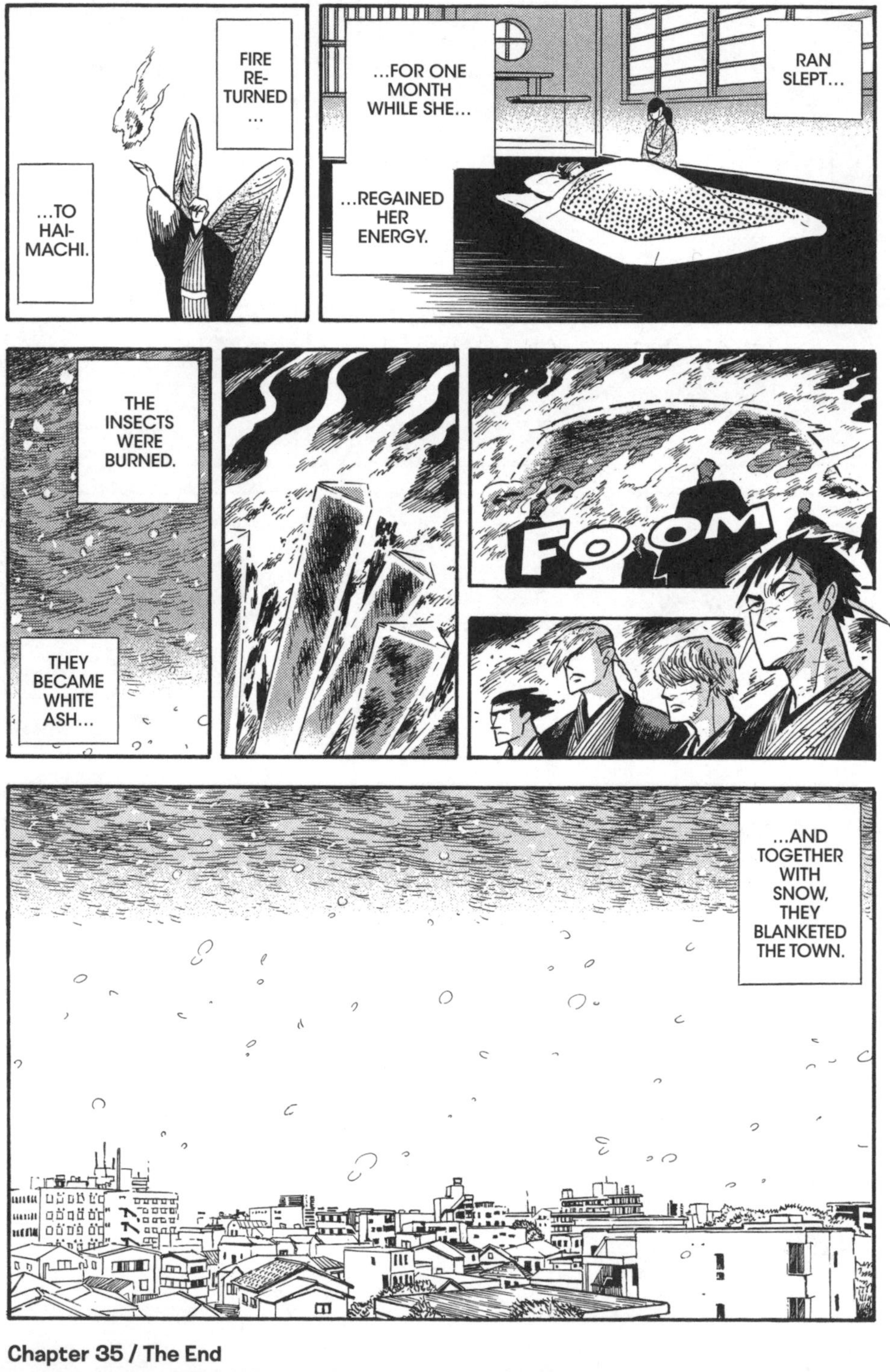
RAN SLEPT…
…FOR ONE MONTH WHILE SHE…
…REGAINED HER ENERGY.
FIRE RE-TURNED …
…TO HAI-MACHI.
FOOM
THE INSECTS WERE BURNED.
THEY BECAME WHITE ASH…
…AND TOGETHER WITH SNOW, THEY BLANKETED THE TOWN.

Chapter 35 / The End

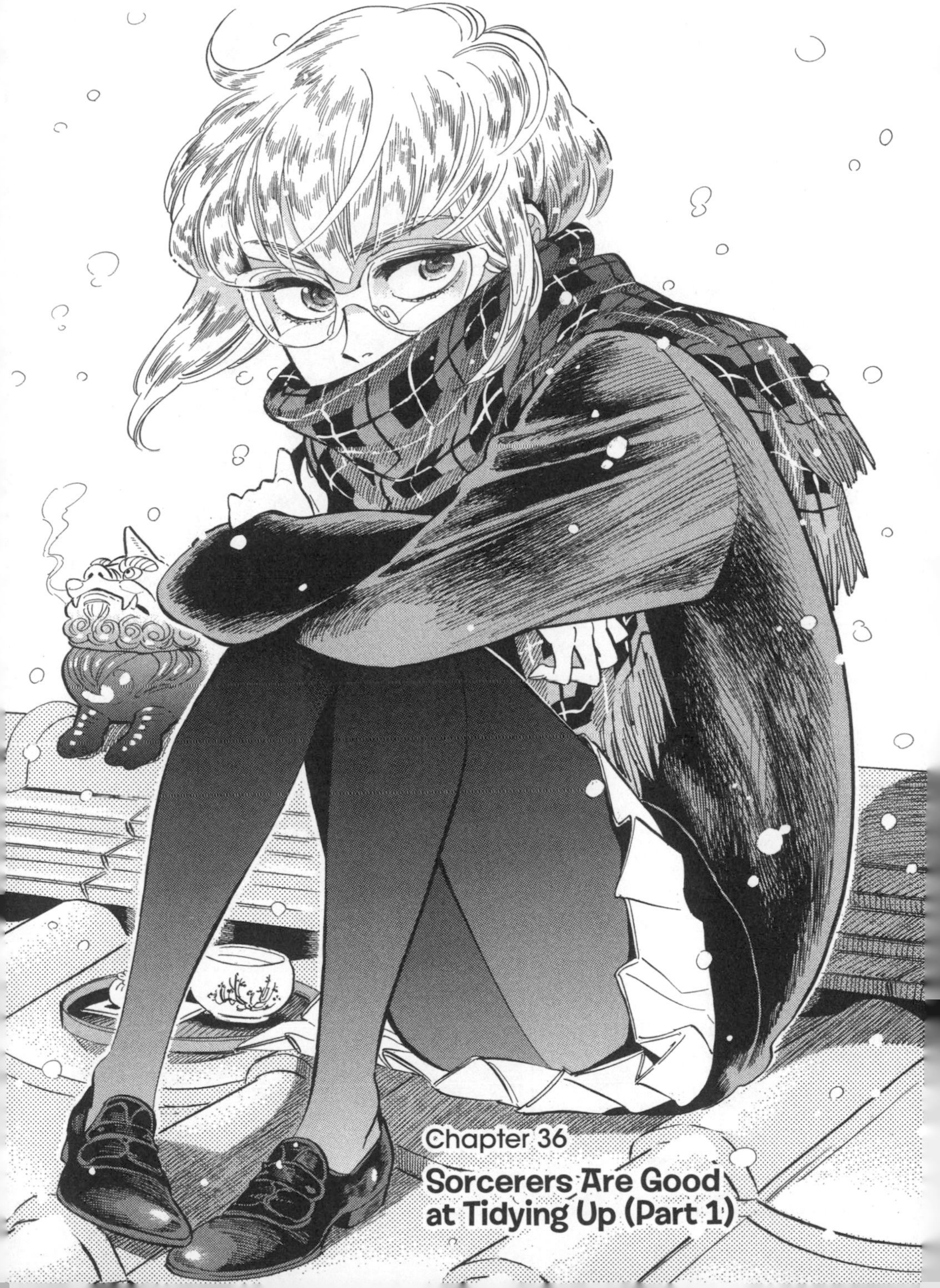

Chapter 36
Sorcerers Are Good at Tidying Up (Part 1)

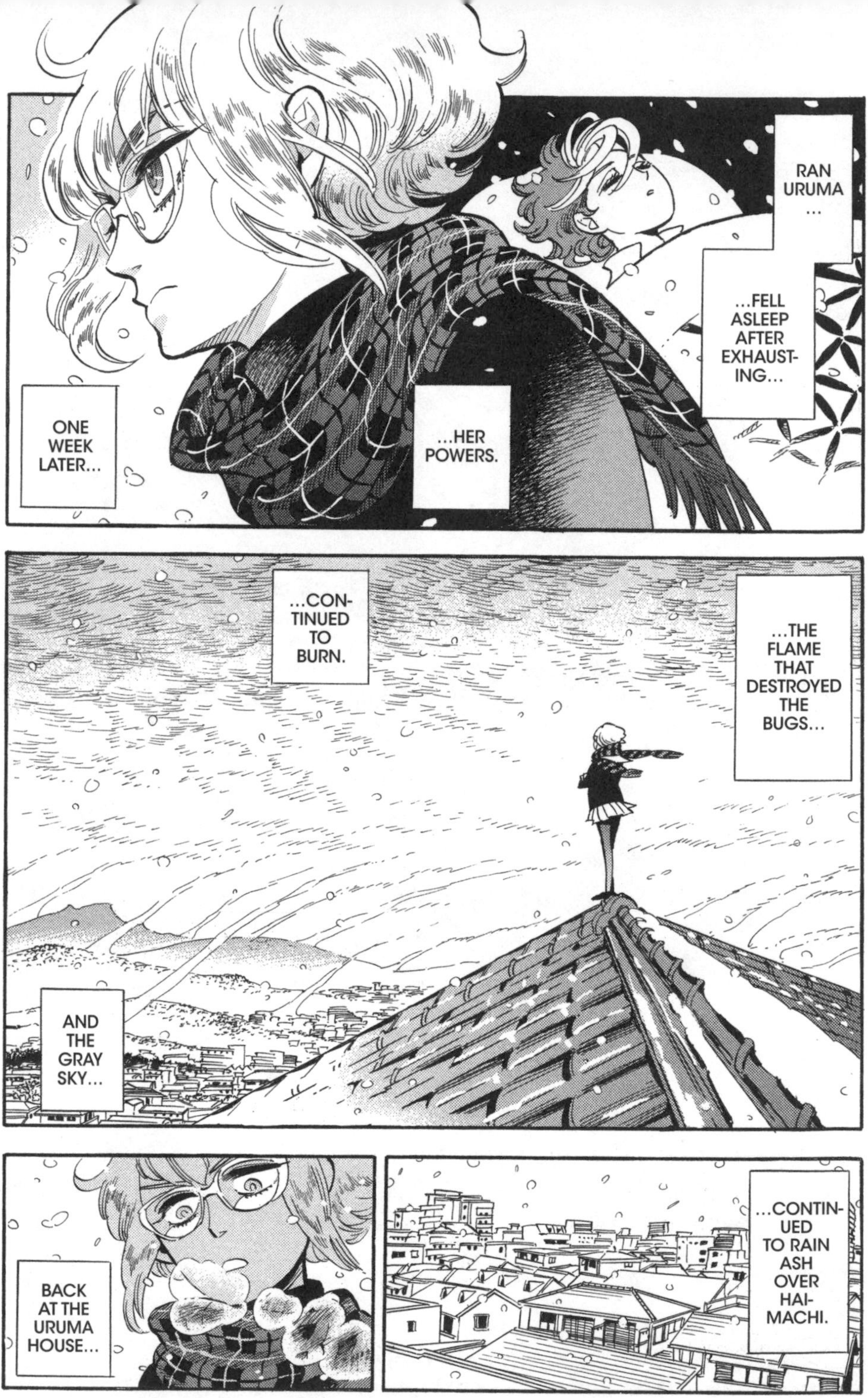
RAN URUMA ...
...FELL ASLEEP AFTER EXHAUST-ING...
...HER POWERS.
ONE WEEK LATER...
...THE FLAME THAT DESTROYED THE BUGS...
...CON-TINUED TO BURN.
AND THE GRAY SKY...
...CONTIN-UED TO RAIN ASH OVER HAI-MACHI.
BACK AT THE URUMA HOUSE...

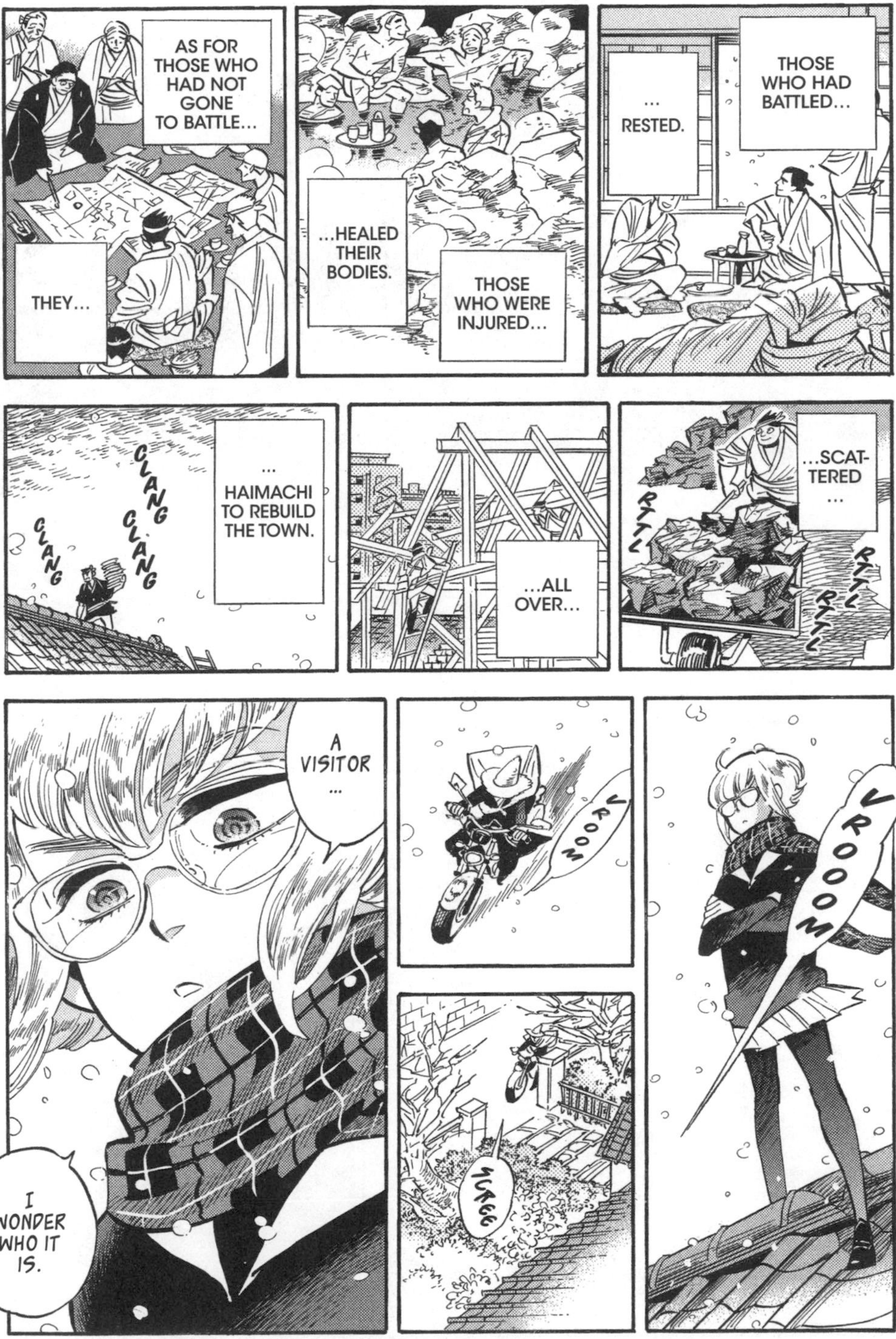
THOSE WHO HAD BATTLED...
...RESTED.
THOSE WHO WERE INJURED...
...HEALED THEIR BODIES.
AS FOR THOSE WHO HAD NOT GONE TO BATTLE...
THEY...
...SCAT-TERED ...
RTTL
RTTL
RTTL
...ALL OVER...
... HAIMACHI TO REBUILD THE TOWN.
CLANG
CLANG
CLANG
VROOOOM
VROOM
SCREEE
A VISITOR ...
I WONDER WHO IT IS.

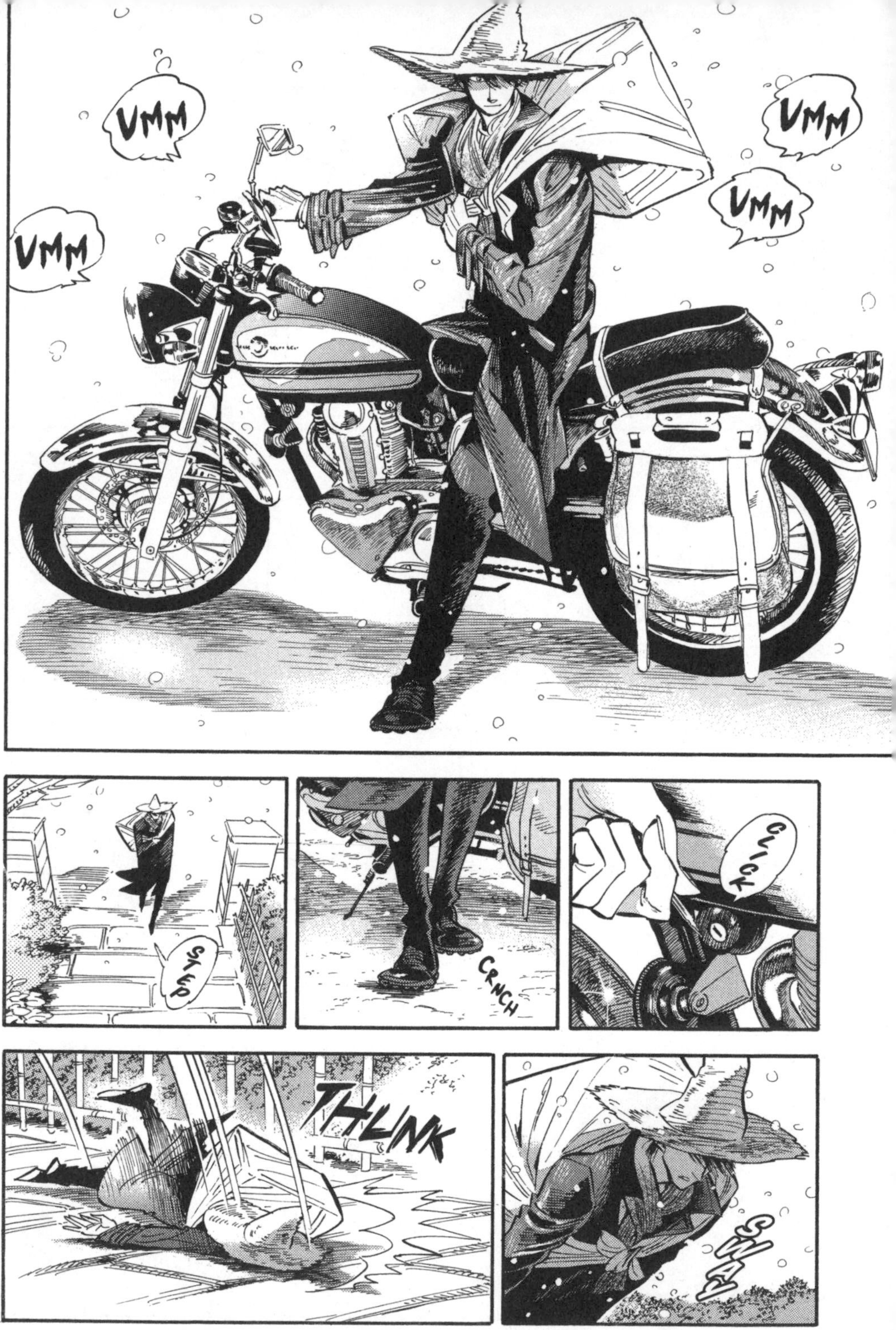
VMM
VMM
VMM
VMM
CLICK
CRNCH
STEP
SWAY
THUNK

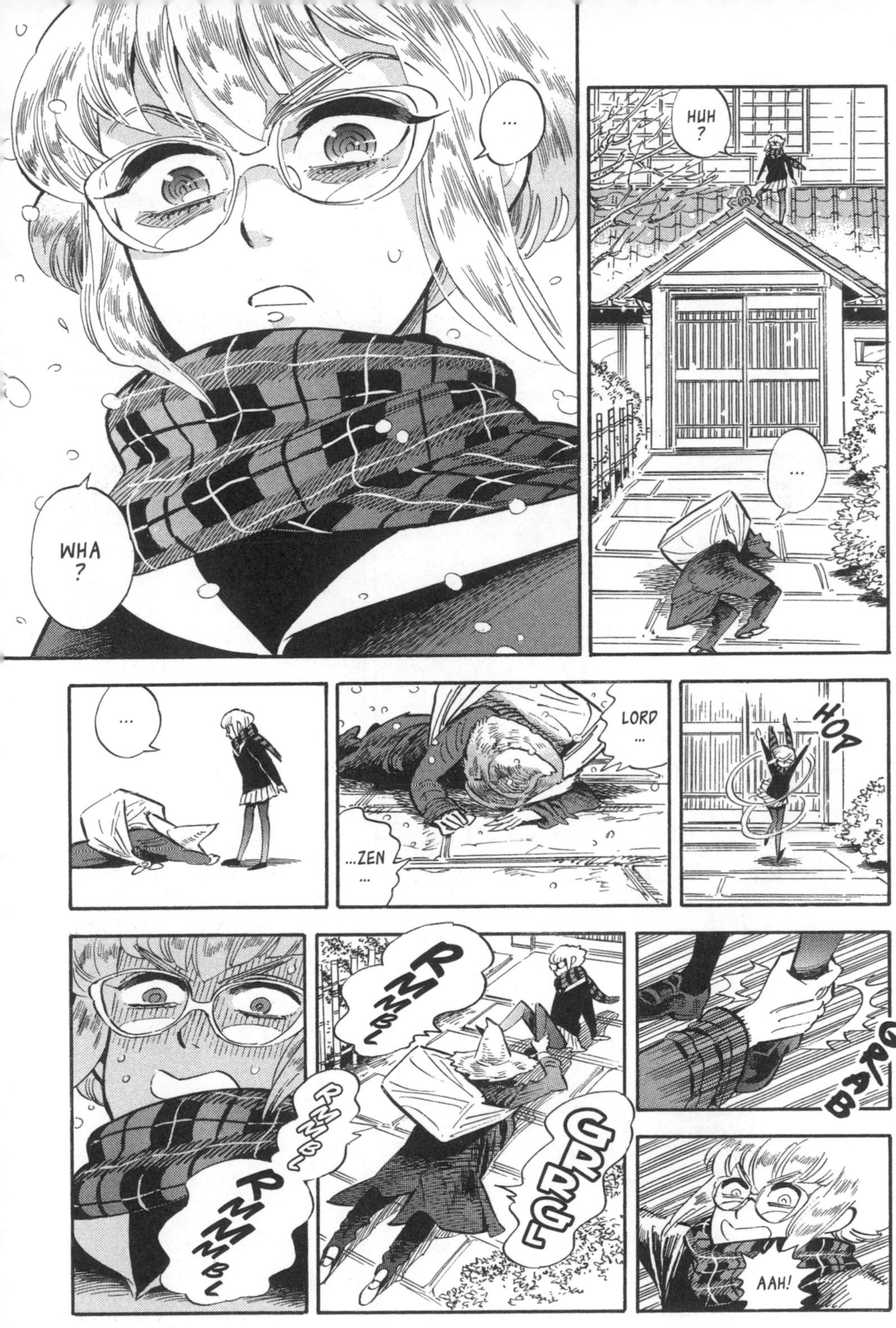
HUH?
...
...
WHA?
HOP
LORD...
...ZEN...
...
GRAB
AAH!
RMMBL
RMMBL
GRRGL
RMMMBL

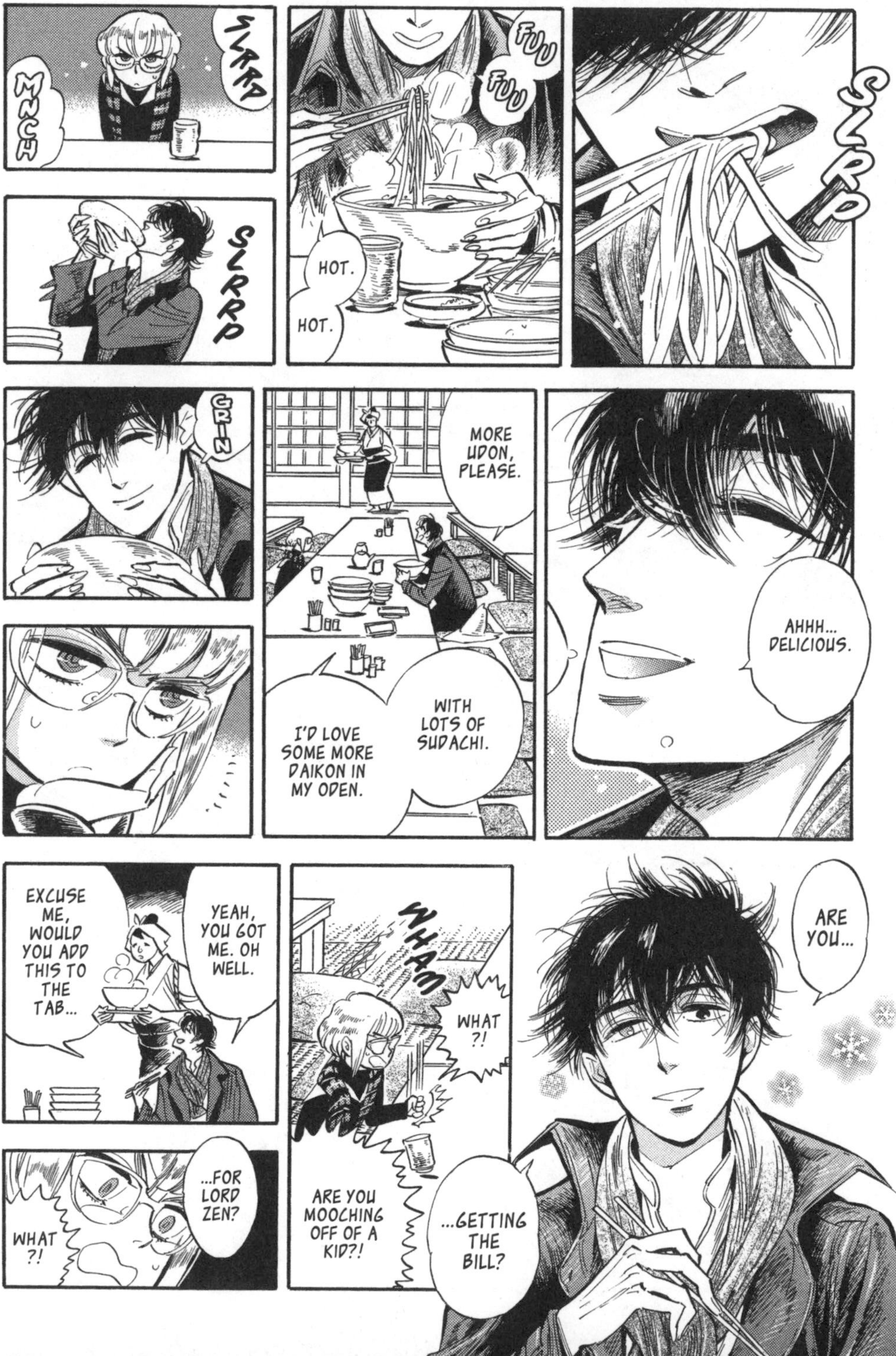
SLRP
FUU
FUU
HOT.
HOT.
SLRRP
MNCH
SLRRP
AHHH... DELICIOUS.
MORE UDON, PLEASE.
WITH LOTS OF SUDACHI.
I'D LOVE SOME MORE DAIKON IN MY ODEN.
GRIN
ARE YOU...
...GETTING THE BILL?
WHAM
WHAT?!
ARE YOU MOOCHING OFF OF A KID?!
YEAH, YOU GOT ME. OH WELL.
EXCUSE ME, WOULD YOU ADD THIS TO THE TAB...
...FOR LORD ZEN?
WHAT?!

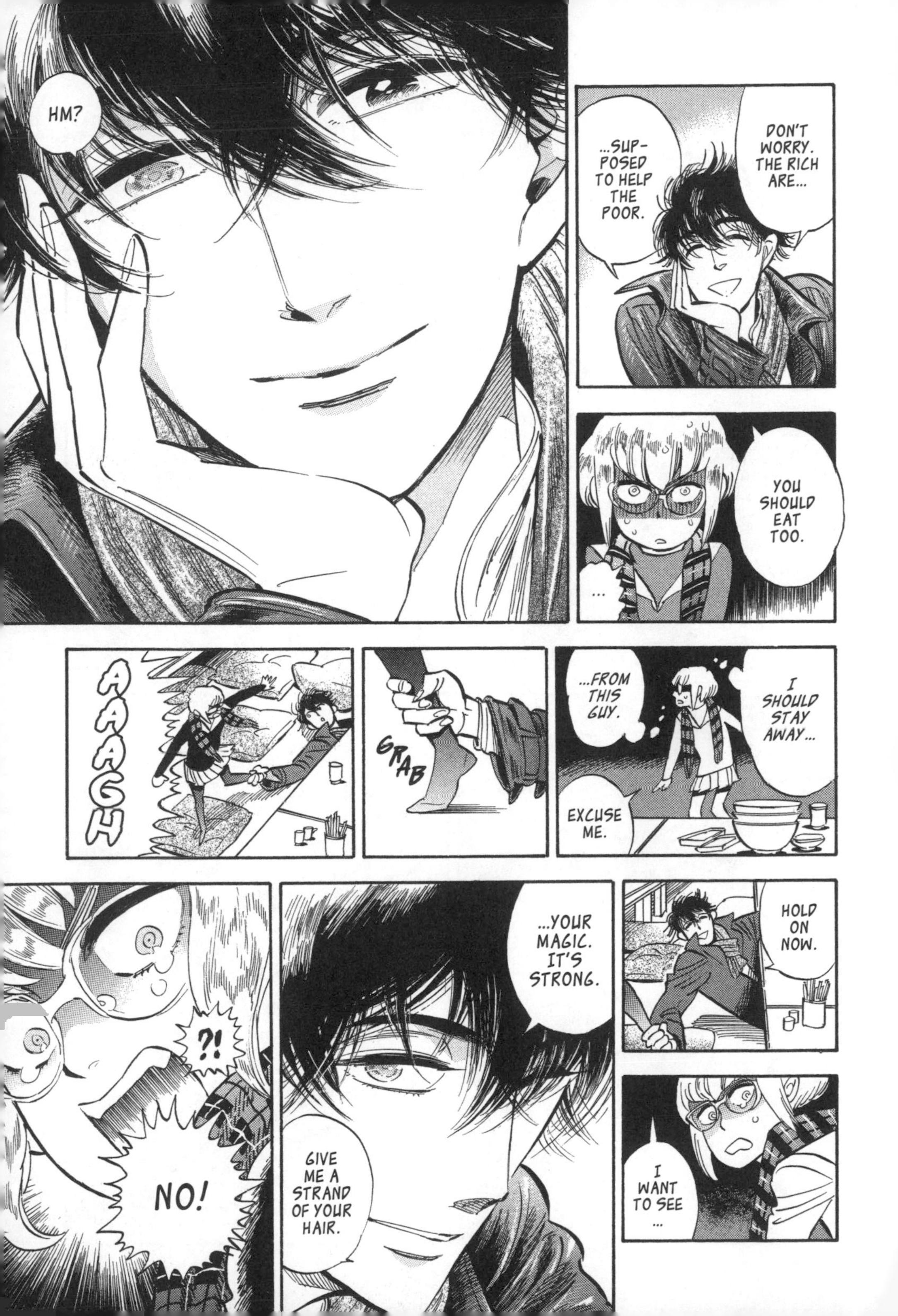
DON'T WORRY. THE RICH ARE...
...SUP-POSED TO HELP THE POOR.
YOU SHOULD EAT TOO.
...
HM?
I SHOULD STAY AWAY...
...FROM THIS GUY.
EXCUSE ME.
GRAB
AAAAGH
HOLD ON NOW.
I WANT TO SEE ...
...YOUR MAGIC. IT'S STRONG.
GIVE ME A STRAND OF YOUR HAIR.
?!
NO!

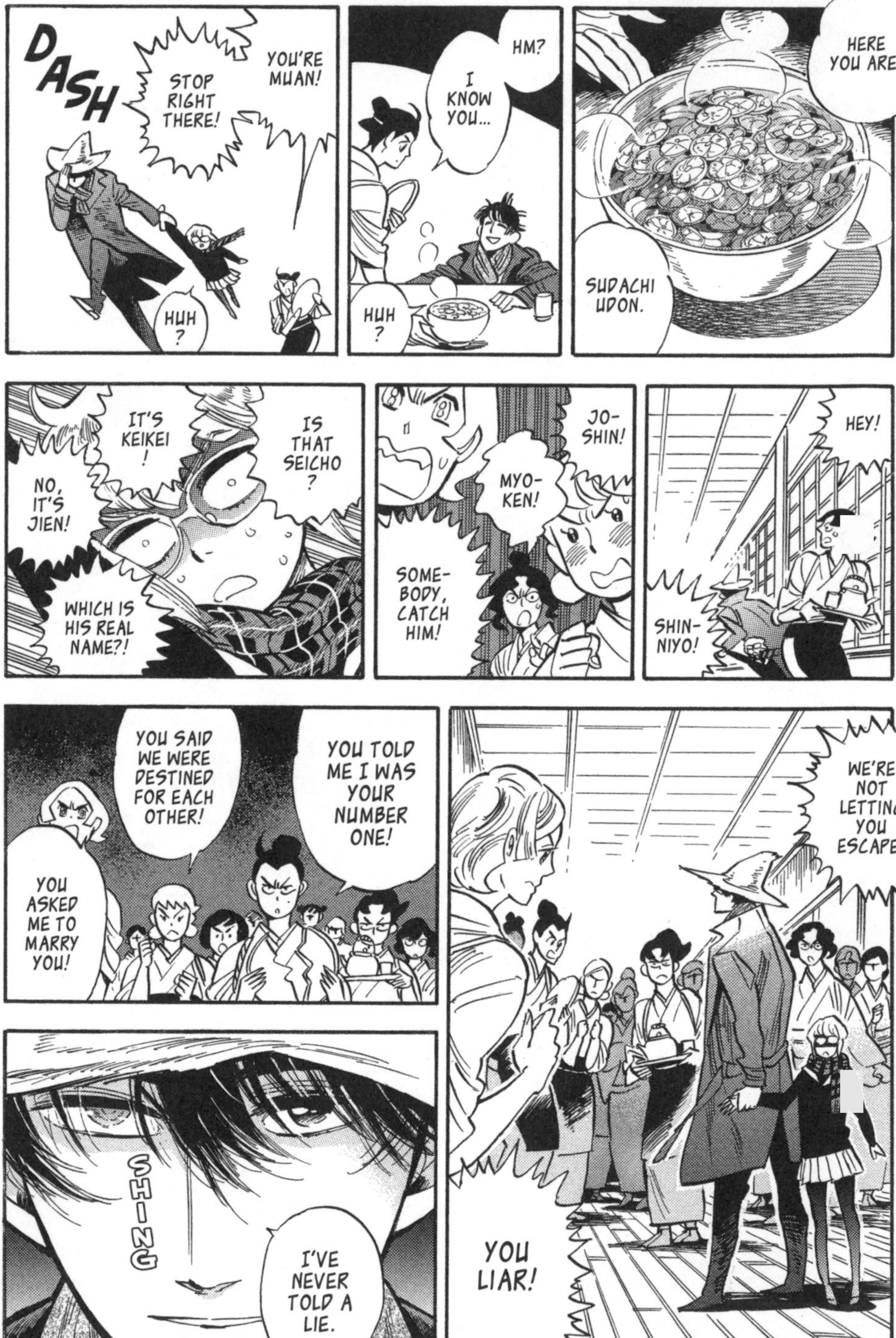
HERE YOU ARE.
SUDACHI UDON.
HM?
I KNOW YOU...
HUH?
YOU'RE MUAN!
STOP RIGHT THERE!
DASH
HUH?
HEY!
SHIN-NIYO!
JO-SHIN!
MYO-KEN!
SOME-BODY, CATCH HIM!
IS THAT SEICHO?
IT'S KEIKEI!
NO, IT'S JIEN!
WHICH IS HIS REAL NAME?!
WE'RE NOT LETTING YOU ESCAPE!
YOU LIAR!
YOU TOLD ME I WAS YOUR NUMBER ONE!
YOU SAID WE WERE DESTINED FOR EACH OTHER!
YOU ASKED ME TO MARRY YOU!
SHING
I'VE NEVER TOLD A LIE.

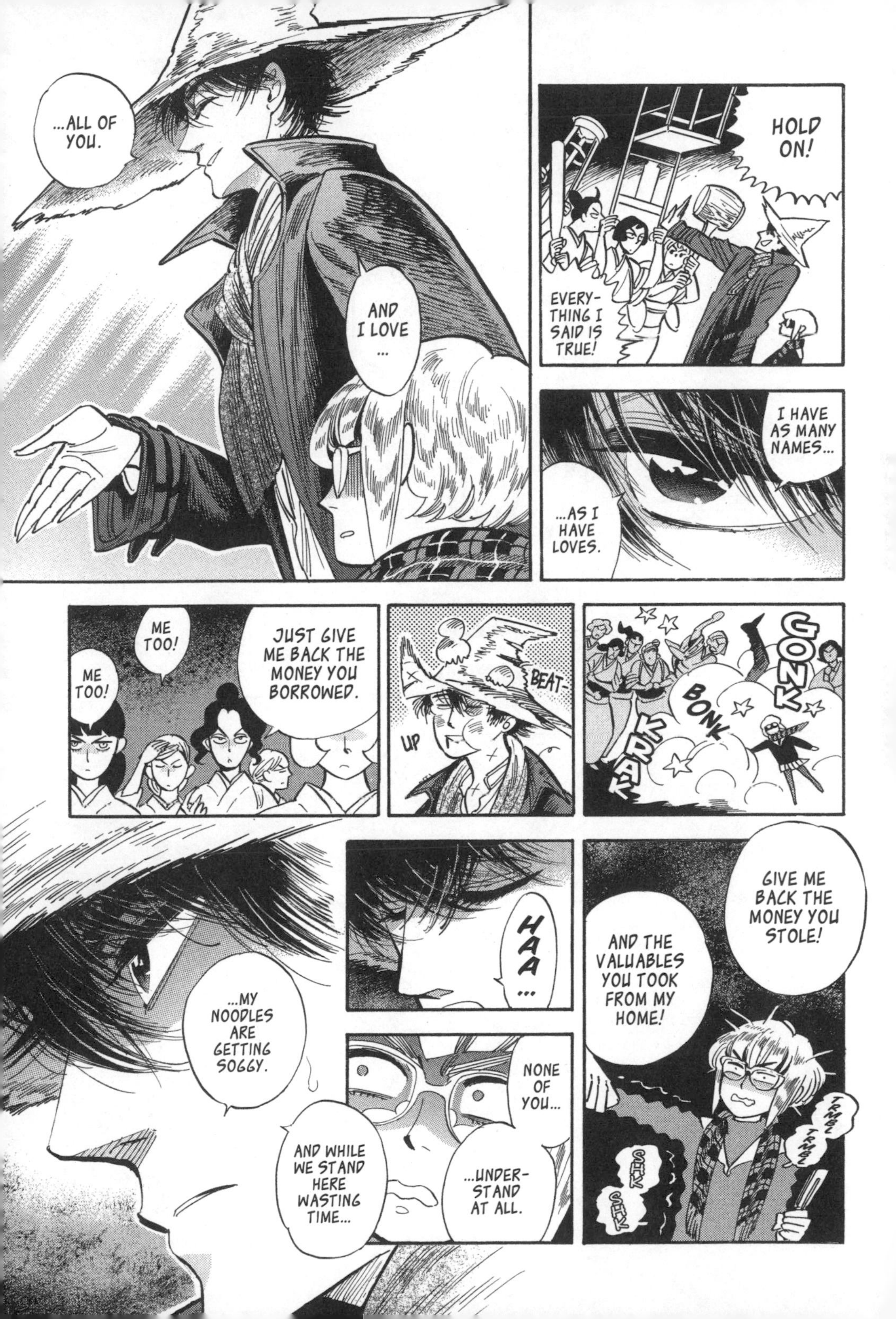
HOLD ON!
EVERY-THING I SAID IS TRUE!
I HAVE AS MANY NAMES...
...AS I HAVE LOVES.
AND I LOVE ...
...ALL OF YOU.
GONK
BONK
KPAK
BEAT-
UP
JUST GIVE ME BACK THE MONEY YOU BORROWED.
ME TOO!
ME TOO!
GIVE ME BACK THE MONEY YOU STOLE!
AND THE VALUABLES YOU TOOK FROM MY HOME!
TRMBL TRMBL
SHK SHK
HAA...
NONE OF YOU...
...UNDER-STAND AT ALL.
AND WHILE WE STAND HERE WASTING TIME...
...MY NOODLES ARE GETTING SOGGY.

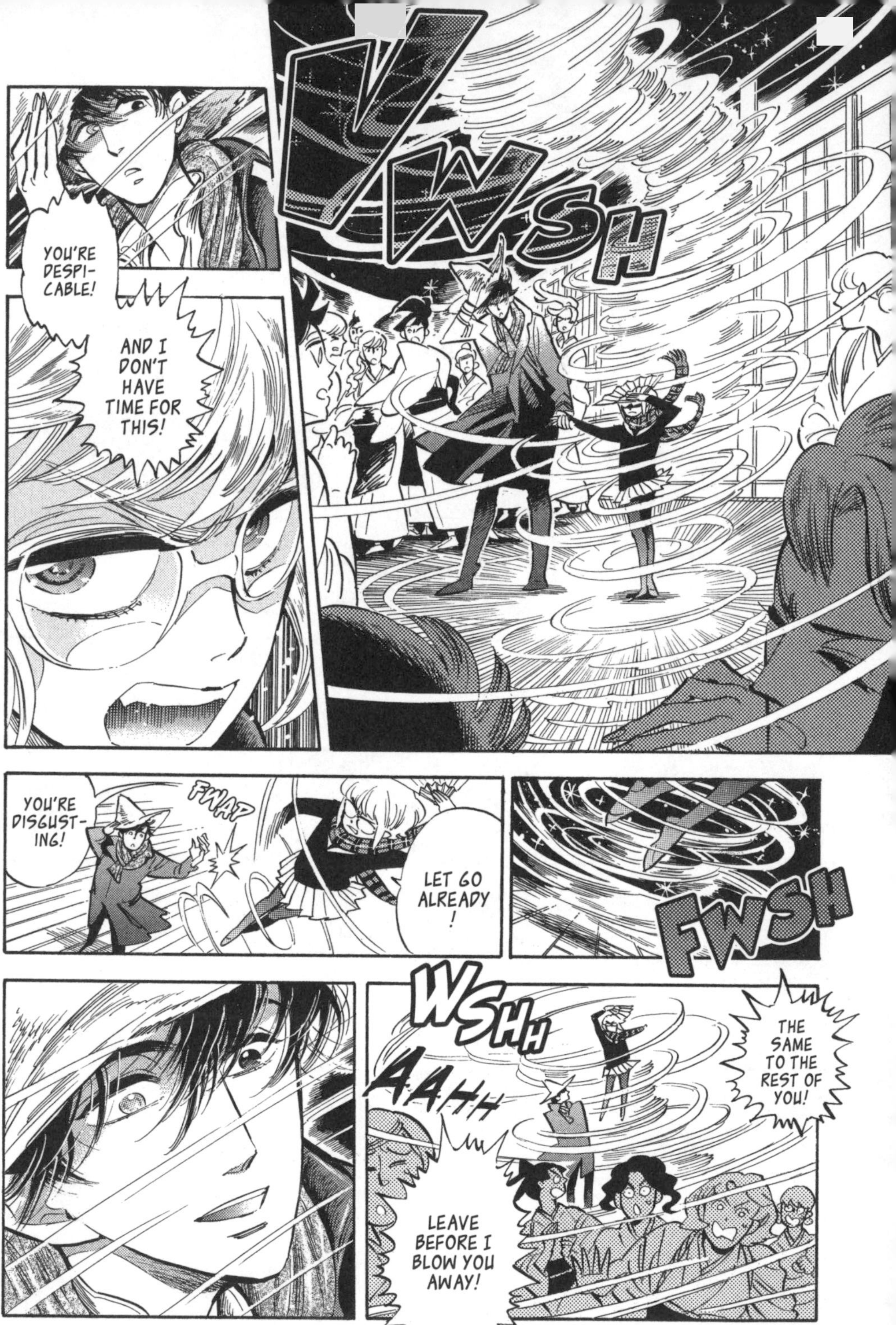
VWNSH
YOU'RE DESPI-CABLE!
AND I DON'T HAVE TIME FOR THIS!
FWSH
LET GO ALREADY!
FWAP
YOU'RE DISGUST-ING!
THE SAME TO THE REST OF YOU!
WSHH
AAHH
LEAVE BEFORE I BLOW YOU AWAY!

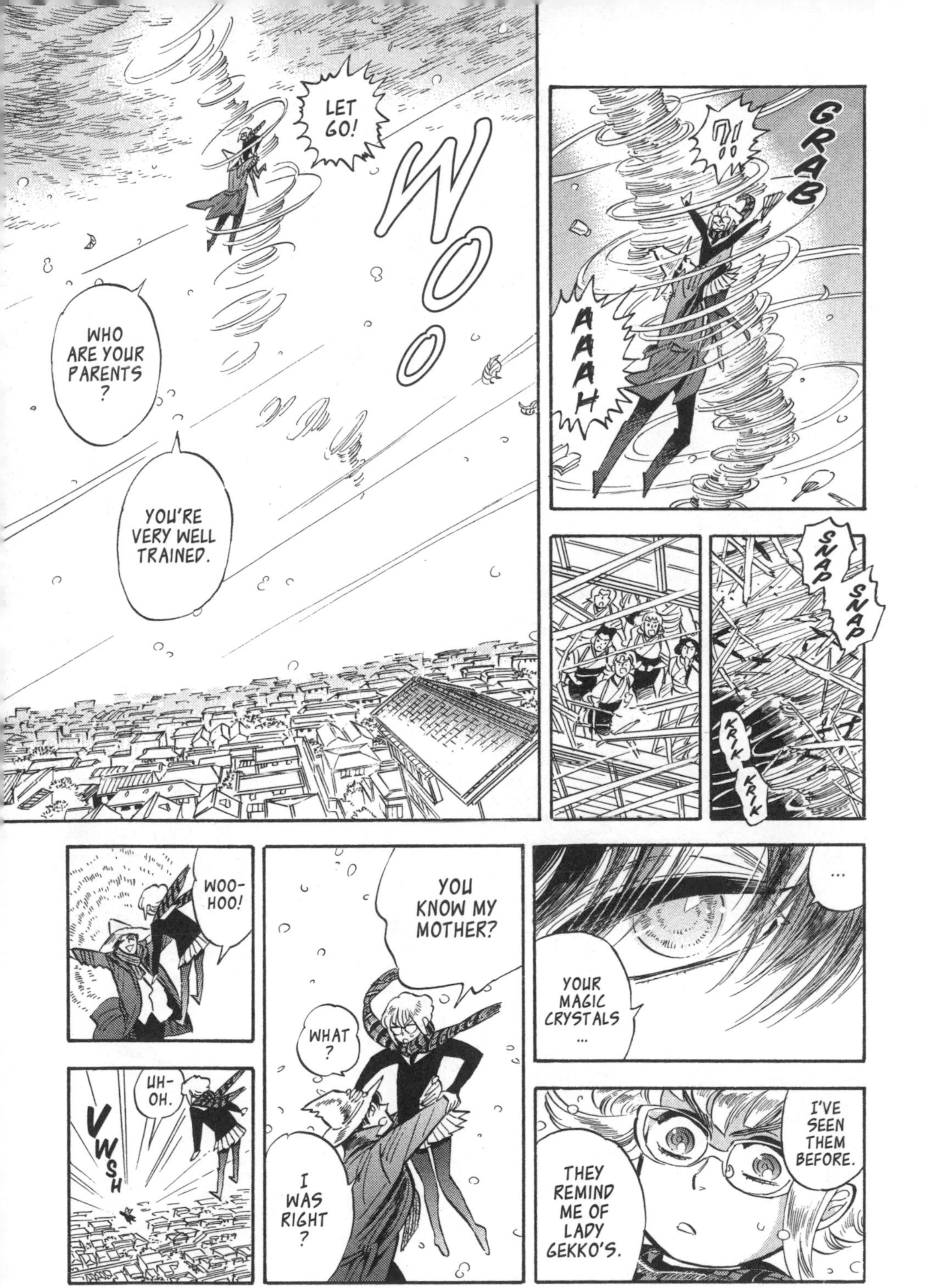
GRAB
?!!
AAAAH
SNAP
SNAP
KRIK
KRIK
LET GO!
WOOOO
WHO ARE YOUR PARENTS?
YOU'RE VERY WELL TRAINED.
...
YOUR MAGIC CRYSTALS ...
I'VE SEEN THEM BEFORE.
THEY REMIND ME OF LADY GEKKO'S.
YOU KNOW MY MOTHER?
WHAT?
I WAS RIGHT?
WOO-HOO!
UH-OH.
VWSH

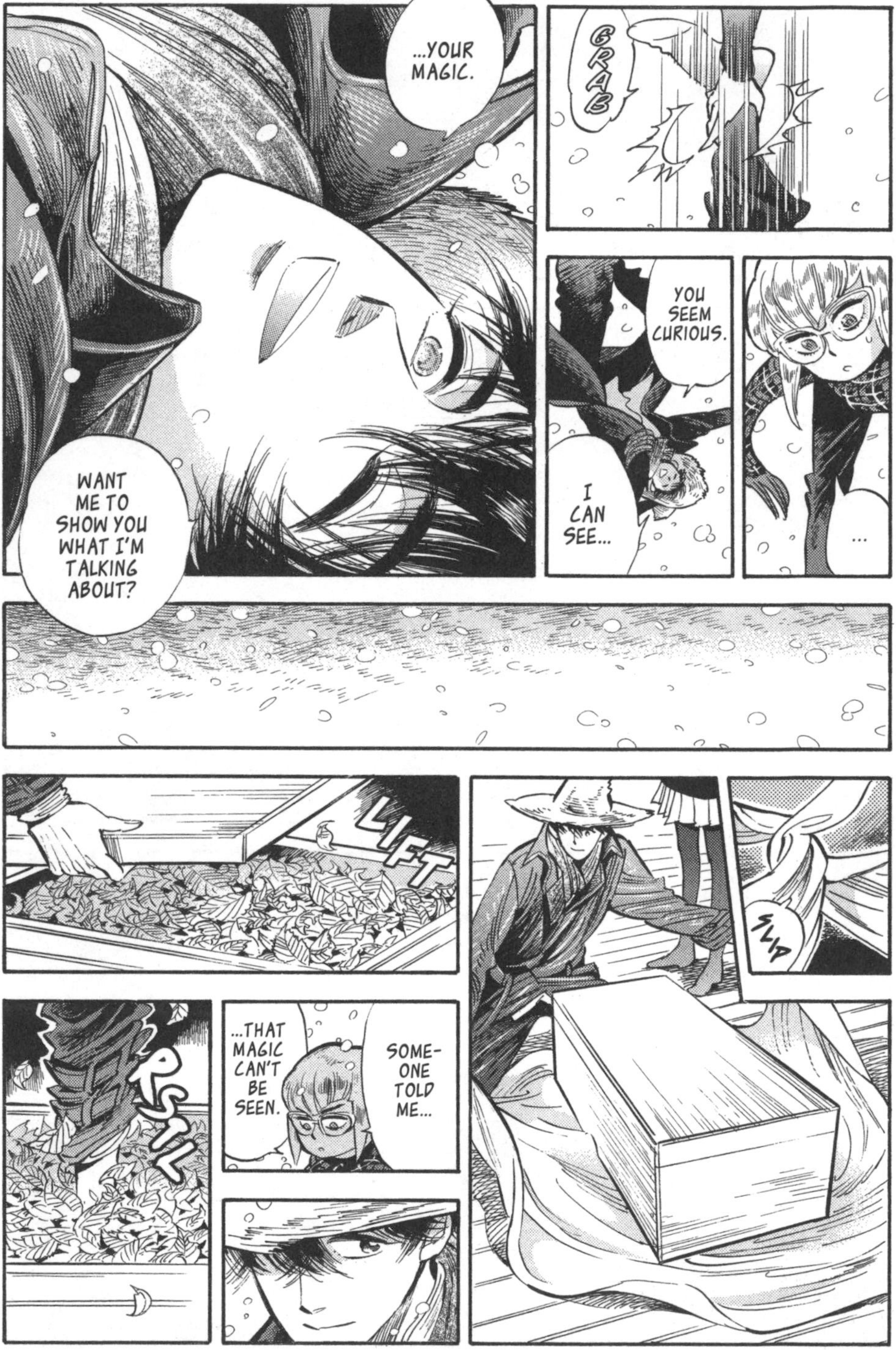
GRAB
...
YOU SEEM CURIOUS.
I CAN SEE...
...YOUR MAGIC.
WANT ME TO SHOW YOU WHAT I'M TALKING ABOUT?
SLIP
LIFT
SOME-ONE TOLD ME...
...THAT MAGIC CAN'T BE SEEN.
PSTL

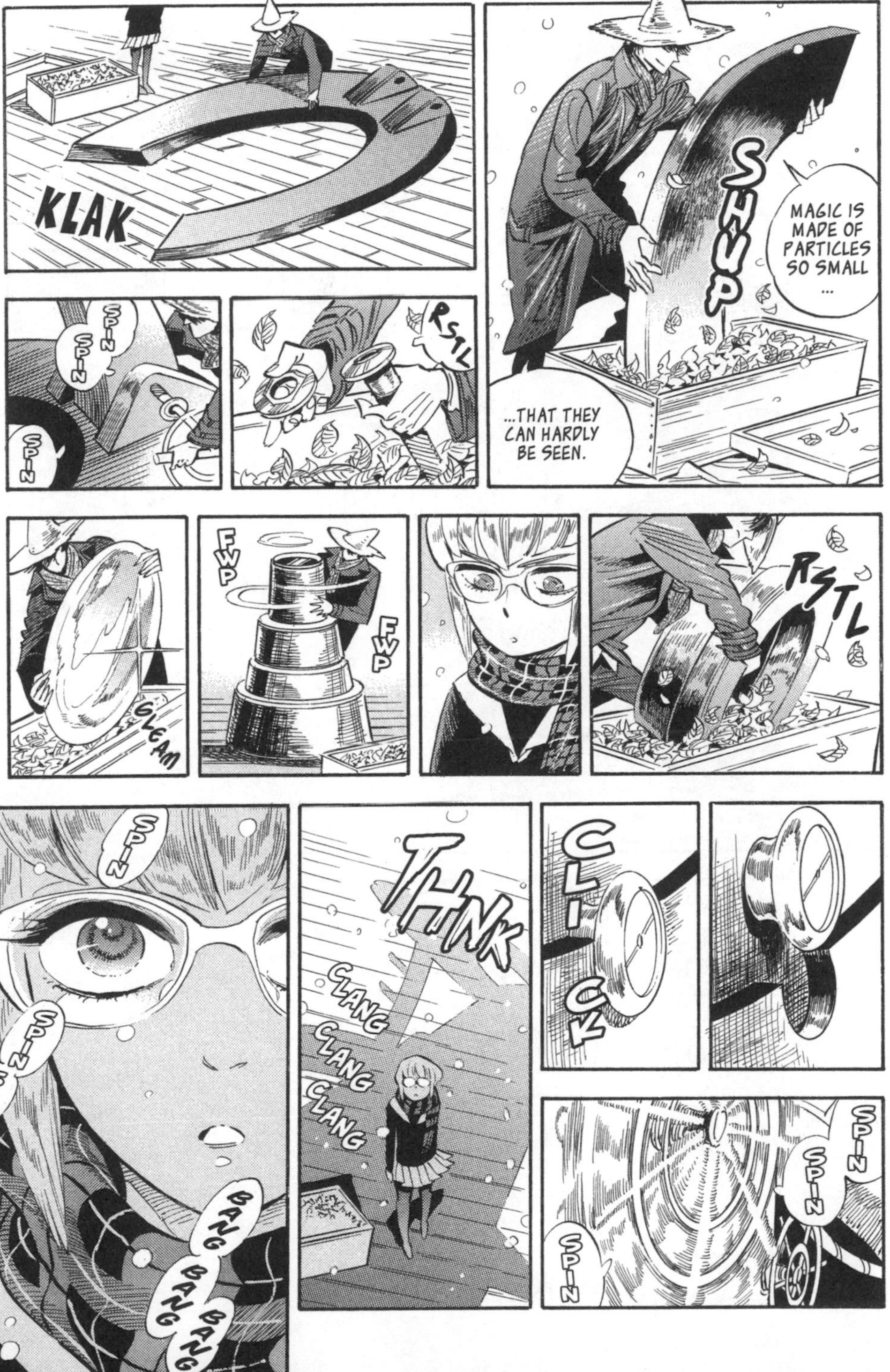
SHUP
MAGIC IS MADE OF PARTICLES SO SMALL ...
...THAT THEY CAN HARDLY BE SEEN.
KLAK
RSTL
SPIN
SPIN
SPIN
RSTL
FWP
FWP
GLEAM
CLICK
SPIN
SPIN
SPIN
THNK
CLANG
CLANG
CLANG
CLANG
SPIN
SPIN
SPIN
SPIN
BANG
BANG
BANG
BANG

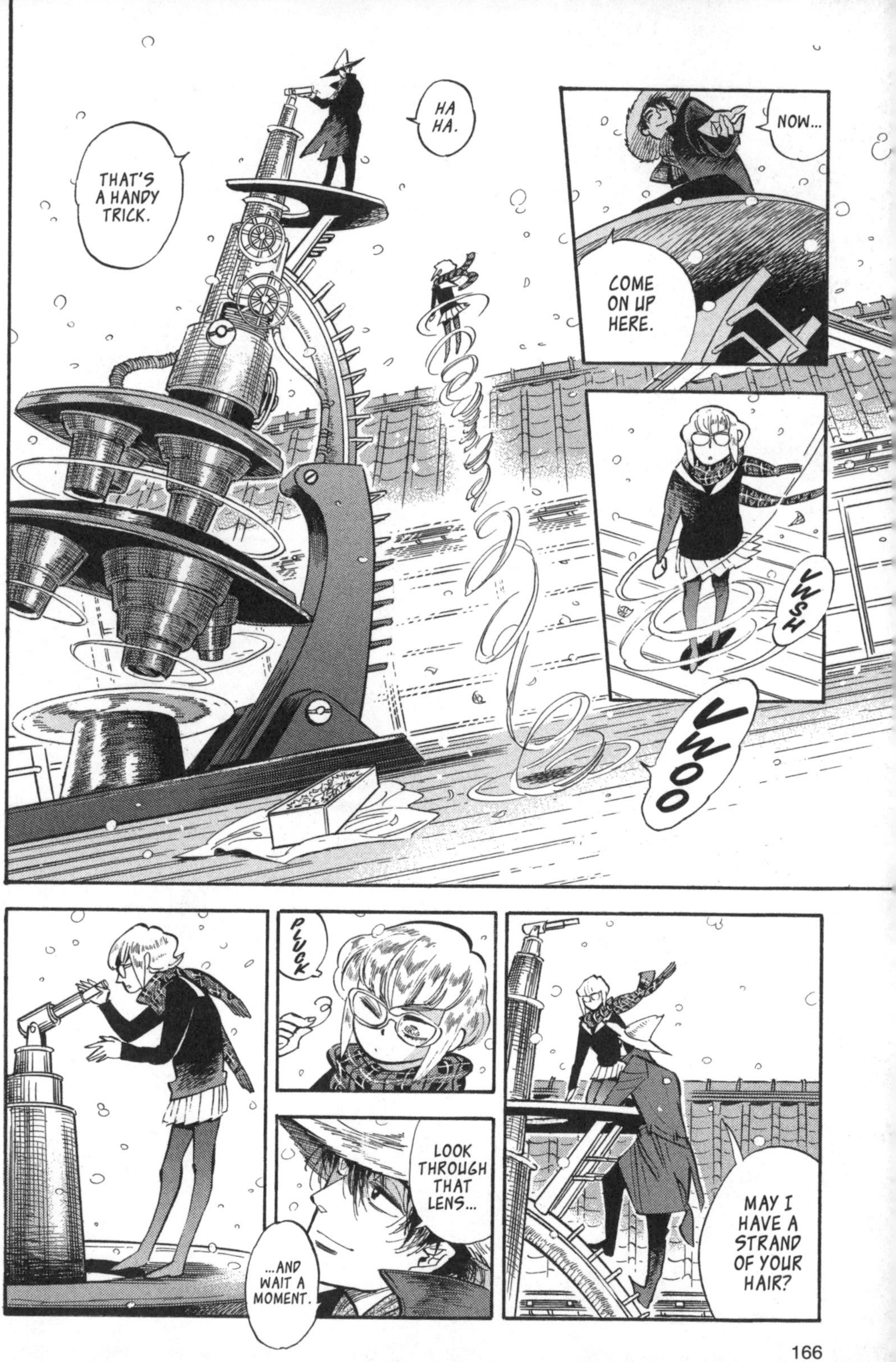
NOW...
COME ON UP HERE.
VWSH
VWOO
HA HA.
THAT'S A HANDY TRICK.
MAY I HAVE A STRAND OF YOUR HAIR?
PLUCK
LOOK THROUGH THAT LENS...
...AND WAIT A MOMENT.

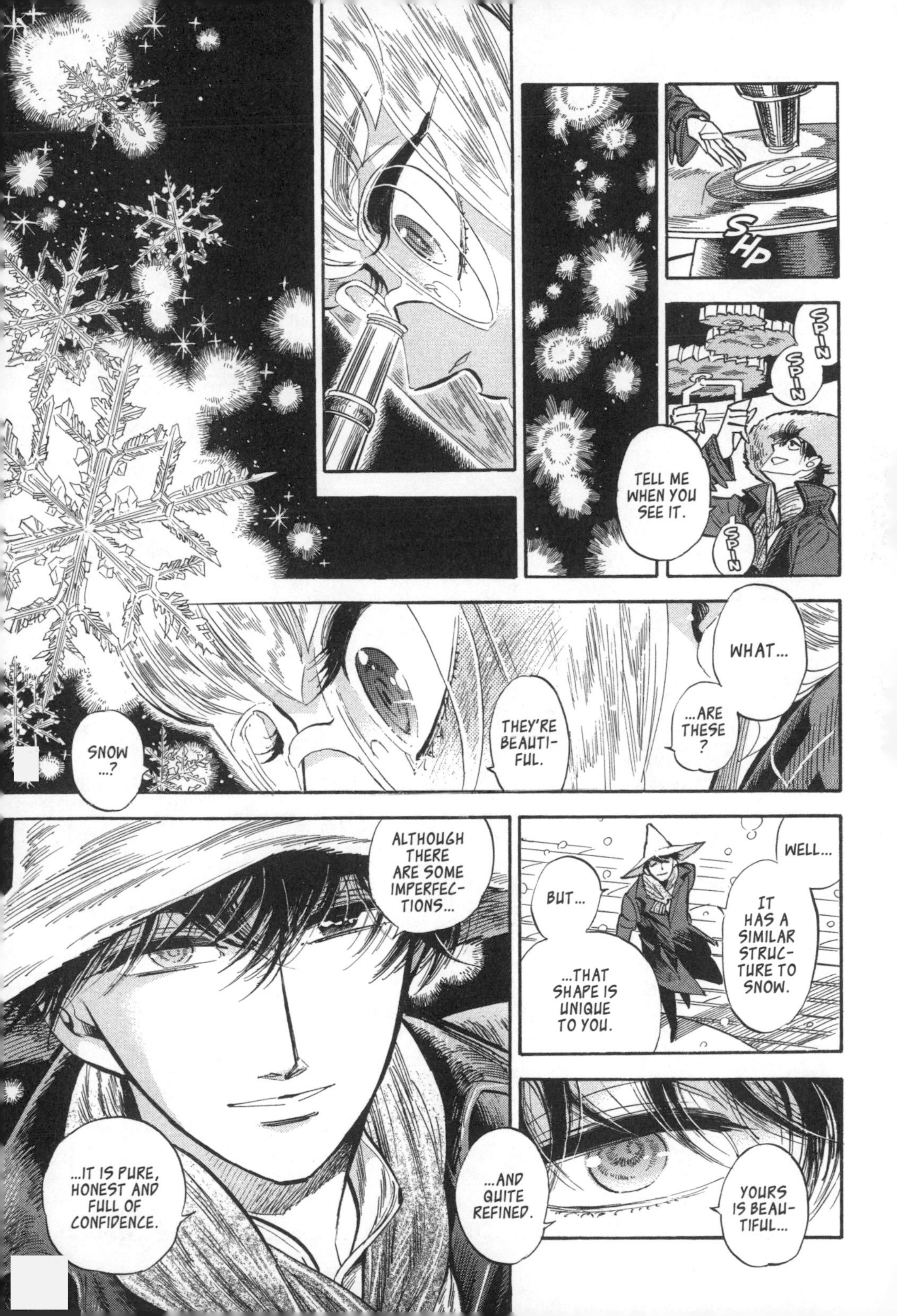
SHP
SPIN SPIN
TELL ME WHEN YOU SEE IT.
SPIN
WHAT...
...ARE THESE?
THEY'RE BEAUTIFUL.
SNOW...?
WELL...
IT HAS A SIMILAR STRUCTURE TO SNOW.
BUT...
...THAT SHAPE IS UNIQUE TO YOU.
YOURS IS BEAUTIFUL...
...AND QUITE REFINED.
ALTHOUGH THERE ARE SOME IMPERFECTIONS...
...IT IS PURE, HONEST AND FULL OF CONFIDENCE.

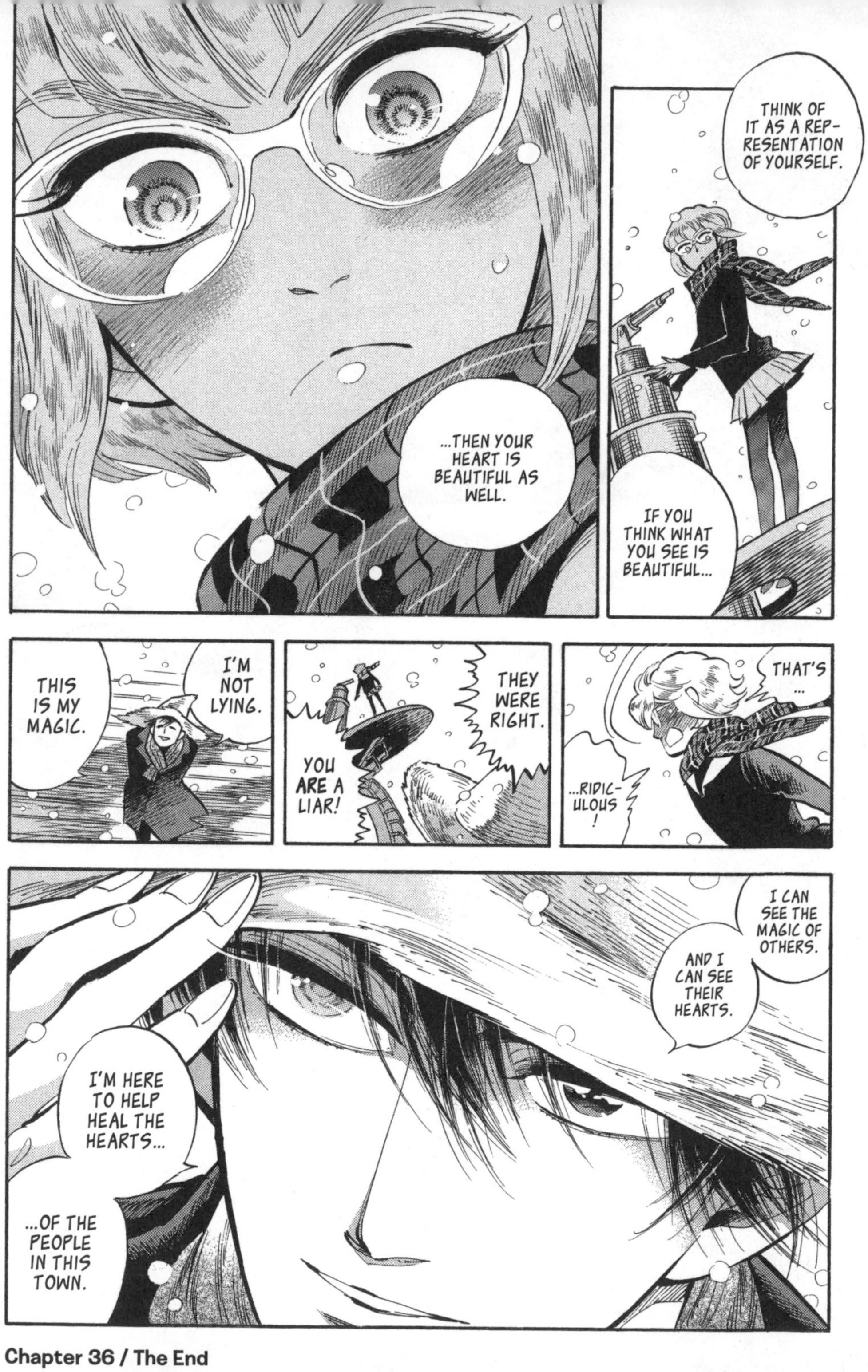
THINK OF IT AS A REPRESENTATION OF YOURSELF.
IF YOU THINK WHAT YOU SEE IS BEAUTIFUL...
...THEN YOUR HEART IS BEAUTIFUL AS WELL.
THAT'S...
...RIDICULOUS!
THEY WERE RIGHT.
YOU ARE A LIAR!
I'M NOT LYING.
THIS IS MY MAGIC.
I CAN SEE THE MAGIC OF OTHERS.
AND I CAN SEE THEIR HEARTS.
I'M HERE TO HELP HEAL THE HEARTS...
...OF THE PEOPLE IN THIS TOWN.

Chapter 36 / The End

Chapter 37
Sorcerers Are Good at Tidying Up (Part 2)

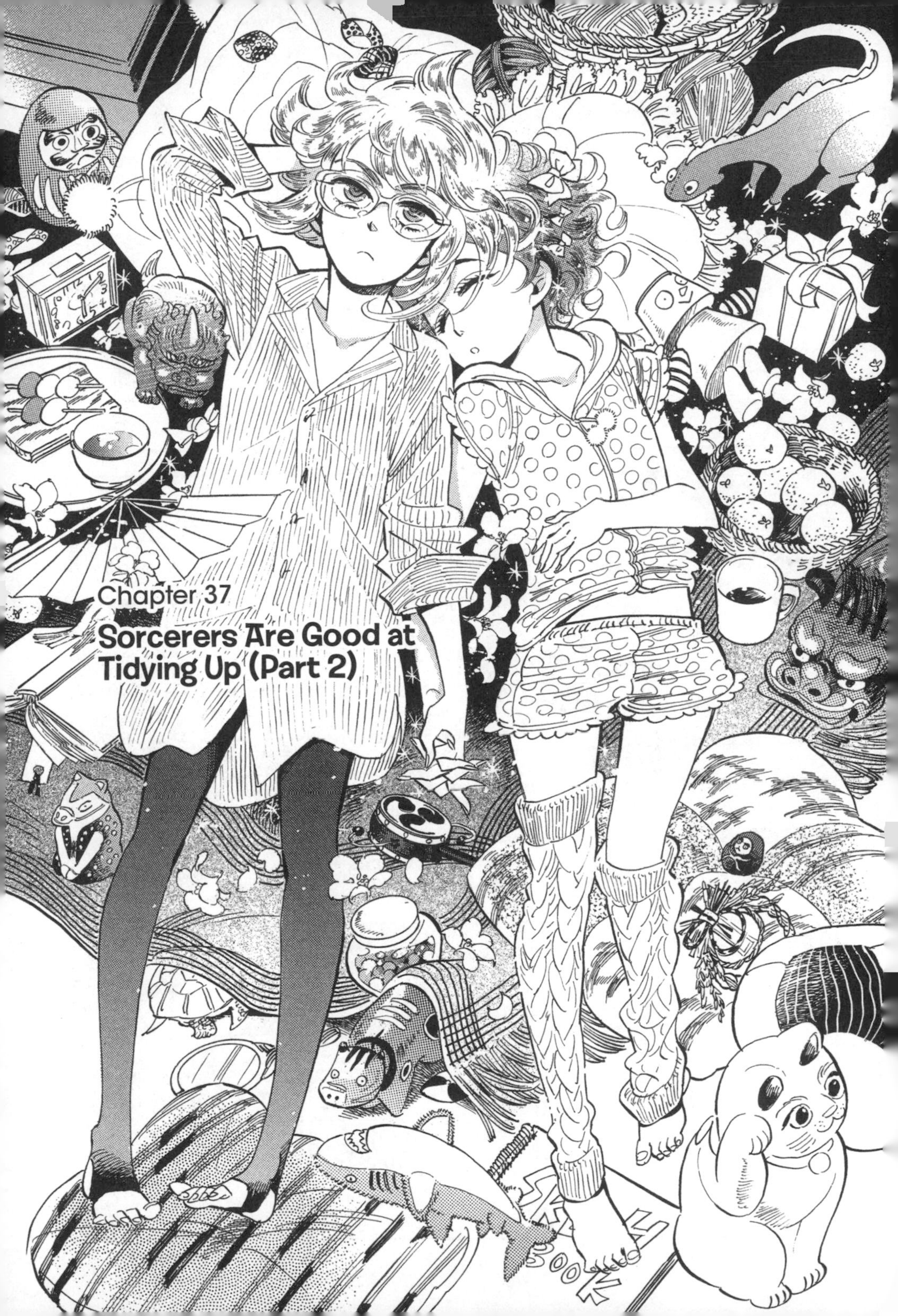

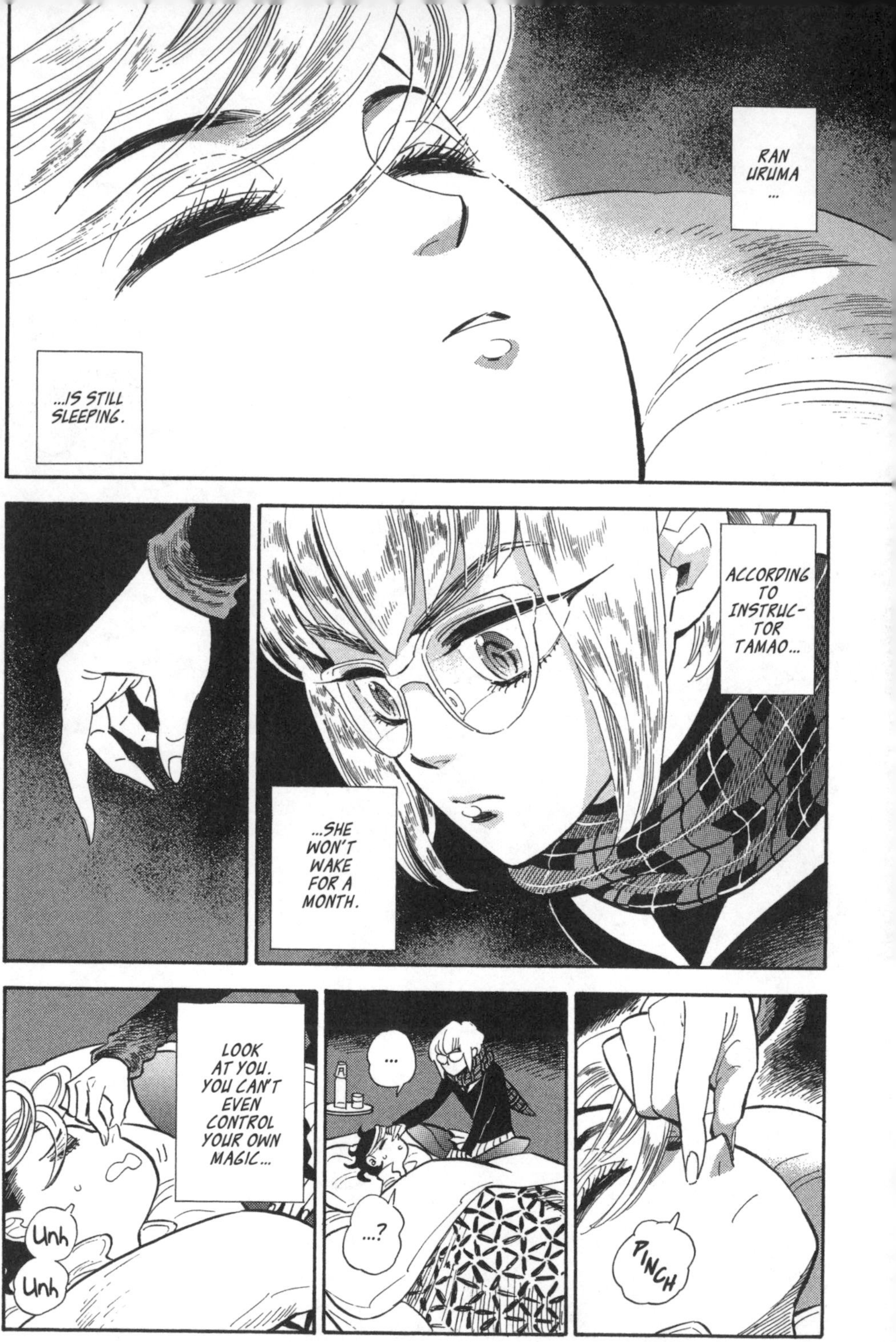
RAN URUMA ...
...IS STILL SLEEPING.
ACCORDING TO INSTRUC-TOR TAMAO...
...SHE WON'T WAKE FOR A MONTH.
PINCH
...
...?
LOOK AT YOU. YOU CAN'T EVEN CONTROL YOUR OWN MAGIC...
Unh
Unh

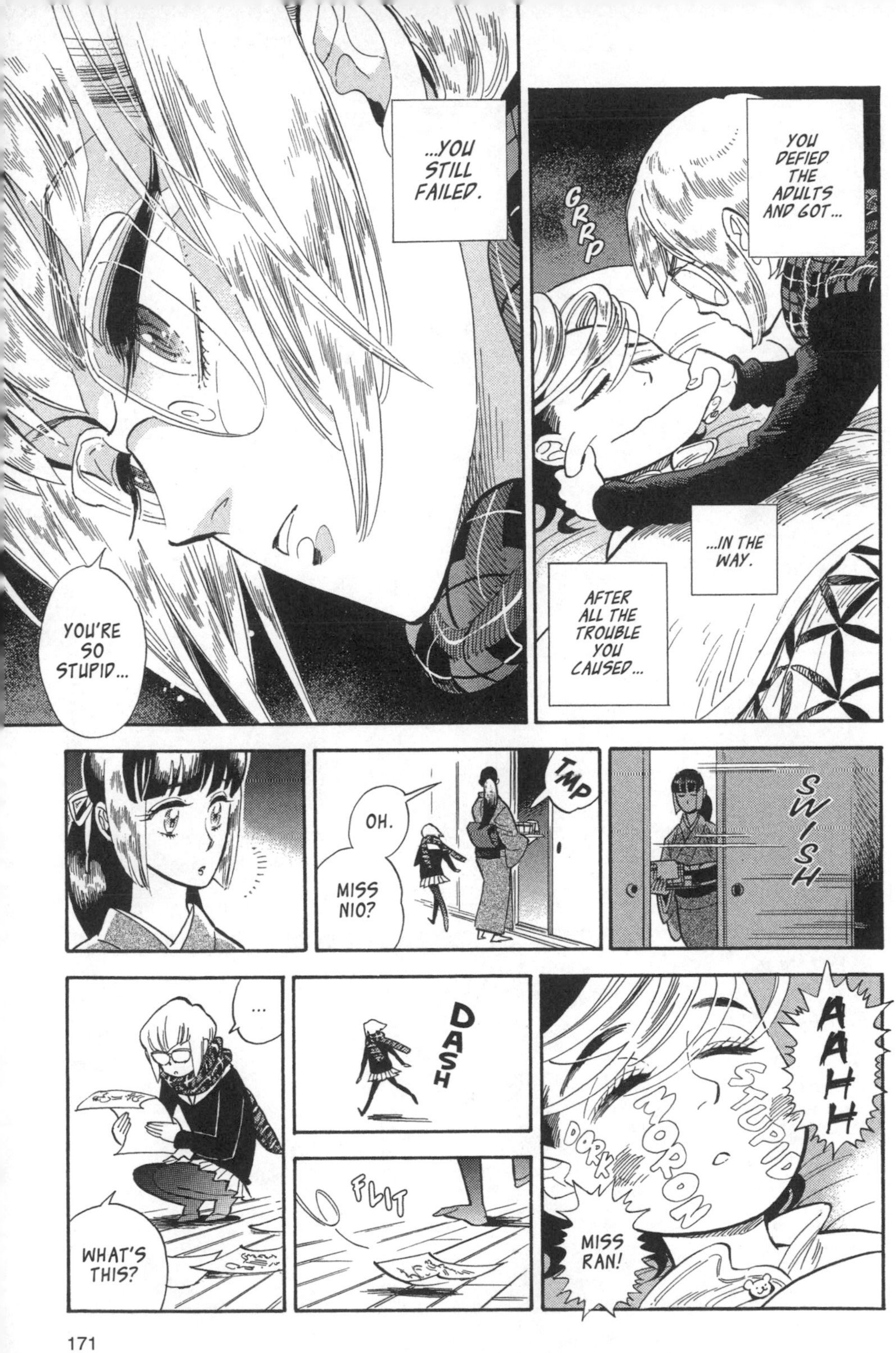
YOU DEFIED THE ADULTS AND GOT...
GRRP
...IN THE WAY.
AFTER ALL THE TROUBLE YOU CAUSED...
...YOU STILL FAILED.
YOU'RE SO STUPID...
SWISH
TMP
OH.
MISS NIO?
AAHH
STUPID
MORON
DORK
MISS RAN!
DASH
FLIT
...
WHAT'S THIS?

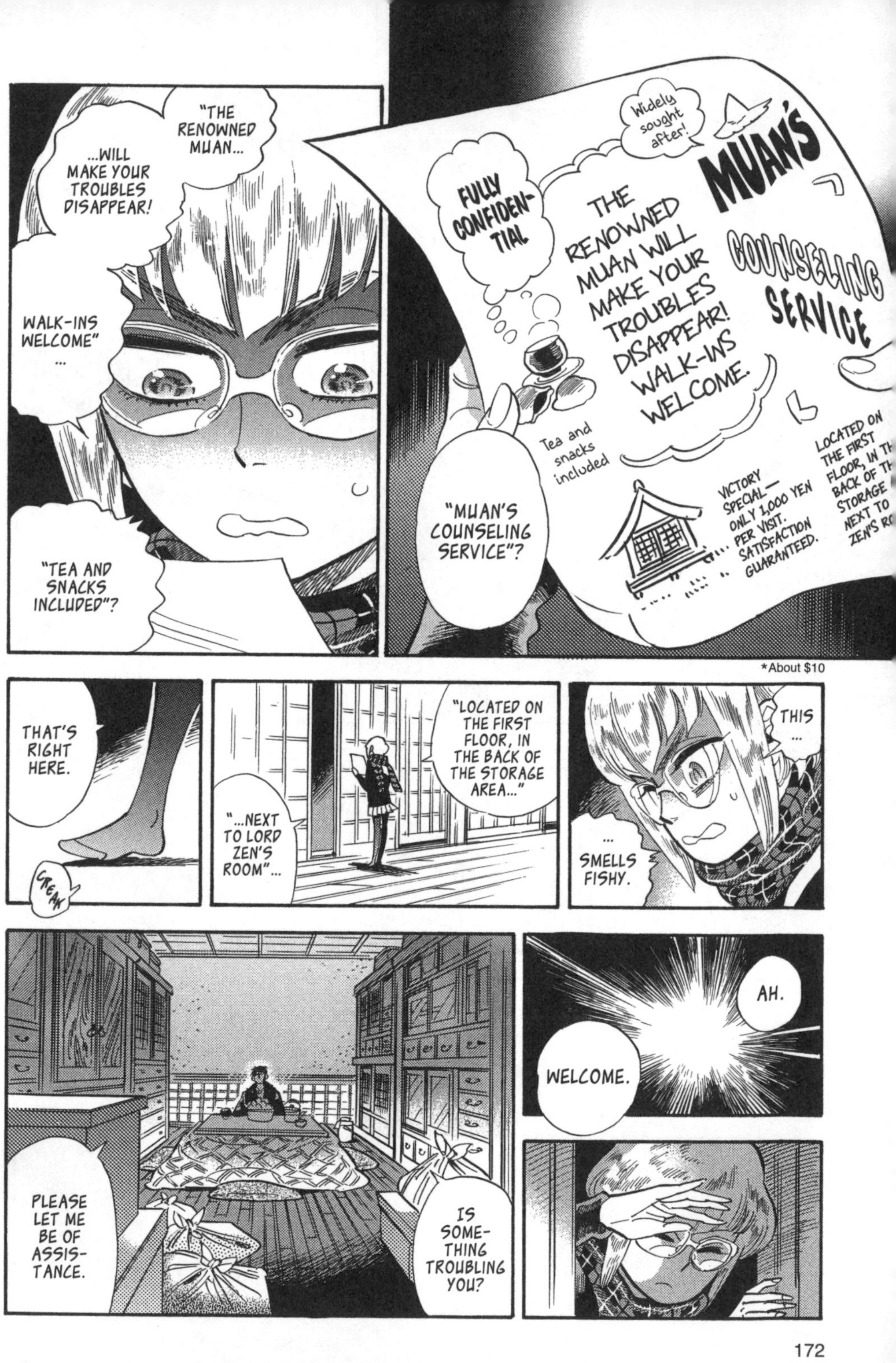
MUAN'S
COUNSELING SERVICE
Widely sought after!
FULLY CONFIDENTIAL
THE RENOWNED MUAN WILL MAKE YOUR TROUBLES DISAPPEAR! WALK-INS WELCOME.
Tea and snacks included
VICTORY SPECIAL—ONLY 1,000 YEN PER VISIT. SATISFACTION GUARANTEED.
"MUAN'S COUNSELING SERVICE"?
"THE RENOWNED MUAN...
...WILL MAKE YOUR TROUBLES DISAPPEAR!
WALK-INS WELCOME"...
"TEA AND SNACKS INCLUDED"?
THIS...
...SMELLS FISHY.
"LOCATED ON THE FIRST FLOOR, IN THE BACK OF THE STORAGE AREA..."
"...NEXT TO LORD ZEN'S ROOM"...
THAT'S RIGHT HERE.
CREAK
AH.
WELCOME.
IS SOMETHING TROUBLING YOU?
PLEASE LET ME BE OF ASSISTANCE.

*About $10

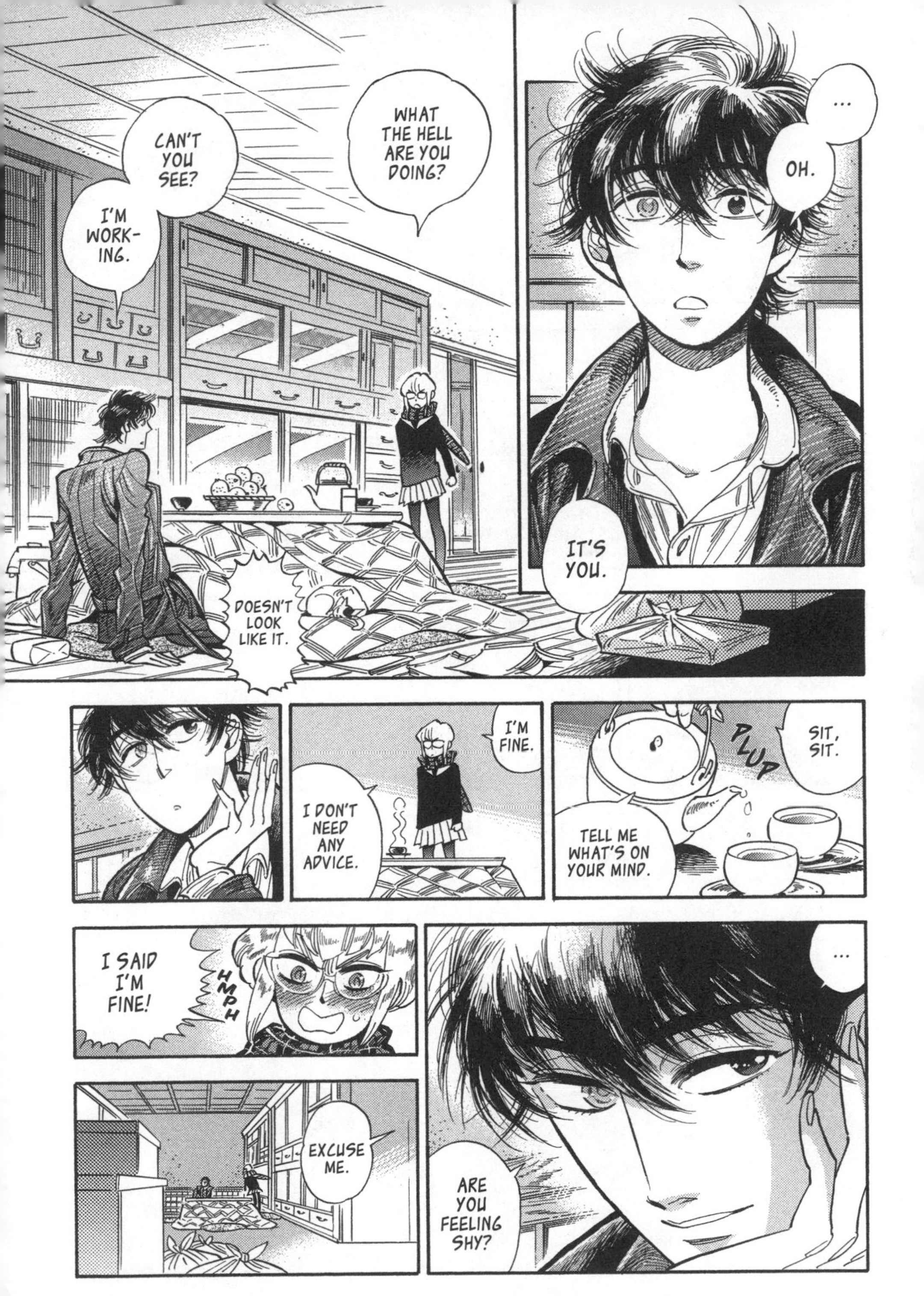
...
OH.
IT'S YOU.
WHAT THE HELL ARE YOU DOING?
CAN'T YOU SEE?
I'M WORKING.
DOESN'T LOOK LIKE IT.
SIT, SIT.
PLUP
TELL ME WHAT'S ON YOUR MIND.
I'M FINE.
I DON'T NEED ANY ADVICE.
...
ARE YOU FEELING SHY?
I SAID I'M FINE!
HMPH
EXCUSE ME.

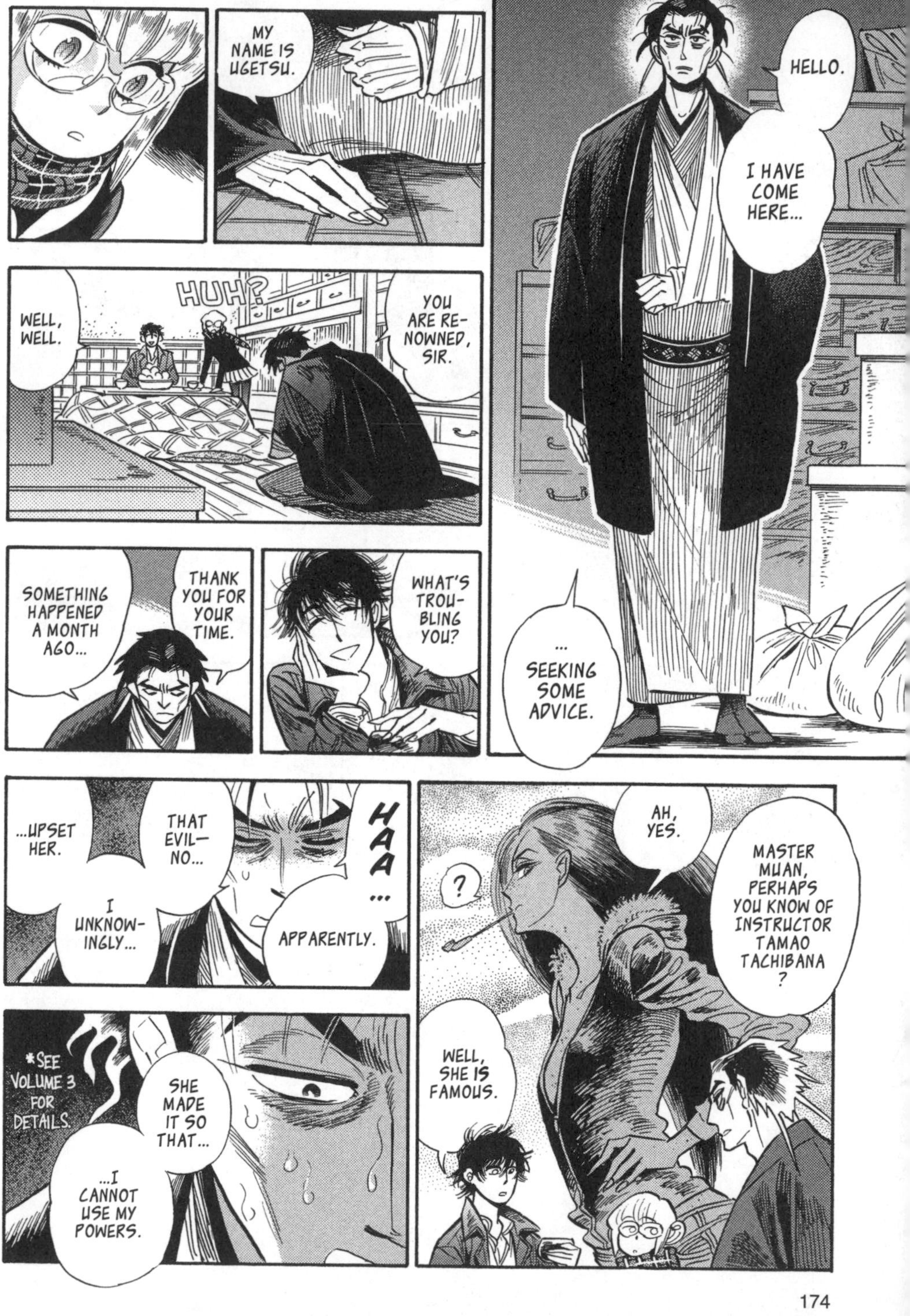
HELLO.
I HAVE COME HERE...
...SEEKING SOME ADVICE.
MY NAME IS UGETSU.
YOU ARE RE-NOWNED, SIR.
HUH?
WELL, WELL.
WHAT'S TROUBLING YOU?
THANK YOU FOR YOUR TIME.
SOMETHING HAPPENED A MONTH AGO...
AH, YES.
MASTER MUAN, PERHAPS YOU KNOW OF INSTRUCTOR TAMAO TACHIBANA?
?
WELL, SHE IS FAMOUS.
HAA...
APPARENTLY.
THAT EVIL—NO...
I UNKNOW-INGLY...
...UPSET HER.
SHE MADE IT SO THAT...
...I CANNOT USE MY POWERS.
*SEE VOLUME 3 FOR DETAILS.

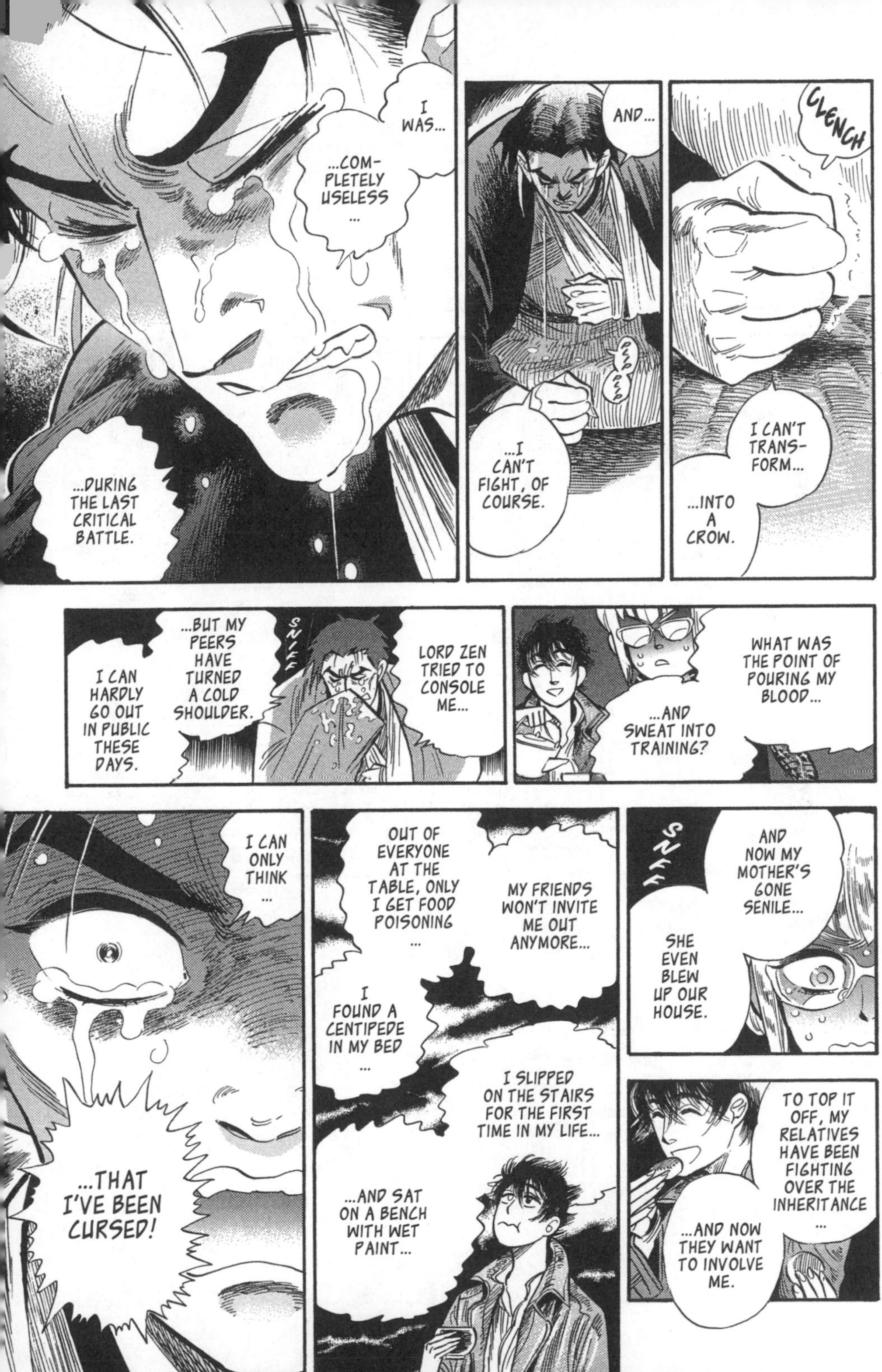
CLENCH
I CAN'T TRANS-FORM...
...INTO A CROW.
AND...
...I CAN'T FIGHT, OF COURSE.
I WAS...
...COM-PLETELY USELESS...
...DURING THE LAST CRITICAL BATTLE.
WHAT WAS THE POINT OF POURING MY BLOOD...
...AND SWEAT INTO TRAINING?
SNIFF
LORD ZEN TRIED TO CONSOLE ME...
...BUT MY PEERS HAVE TURNED A COLD SHOULDER.
I CAN HARDLY GO OUT IN PUBLIC THESE DAYS.
AND NOW MY MOTHER'S GONE SENILE...
SHE EVEN BLEW UP OUR HOUSE.
TO TOP IT OFF, MY RELATIVES HAVE BEEN FIGHTING OVER THE INHERITANCE...
...AND NOW THEY WANT TO INVOLVE ME.
MY FRIENDS WON'T INVITE ME OUT ANYMORE...
OUT OF EVERYONE AT THE TABLE, ONLY I GET FOOD POISONING...
I FOUND A CENTIPEDE IN MY BED...
I SLIPPED ON THE STAIRS FOR THE FIRST TIME IN MY LIFE...
...AND SAT ON A BENCH WITH WET PAINT...
I CAN ONLY THINK...
...THAT I'VE BEEN CURSED!

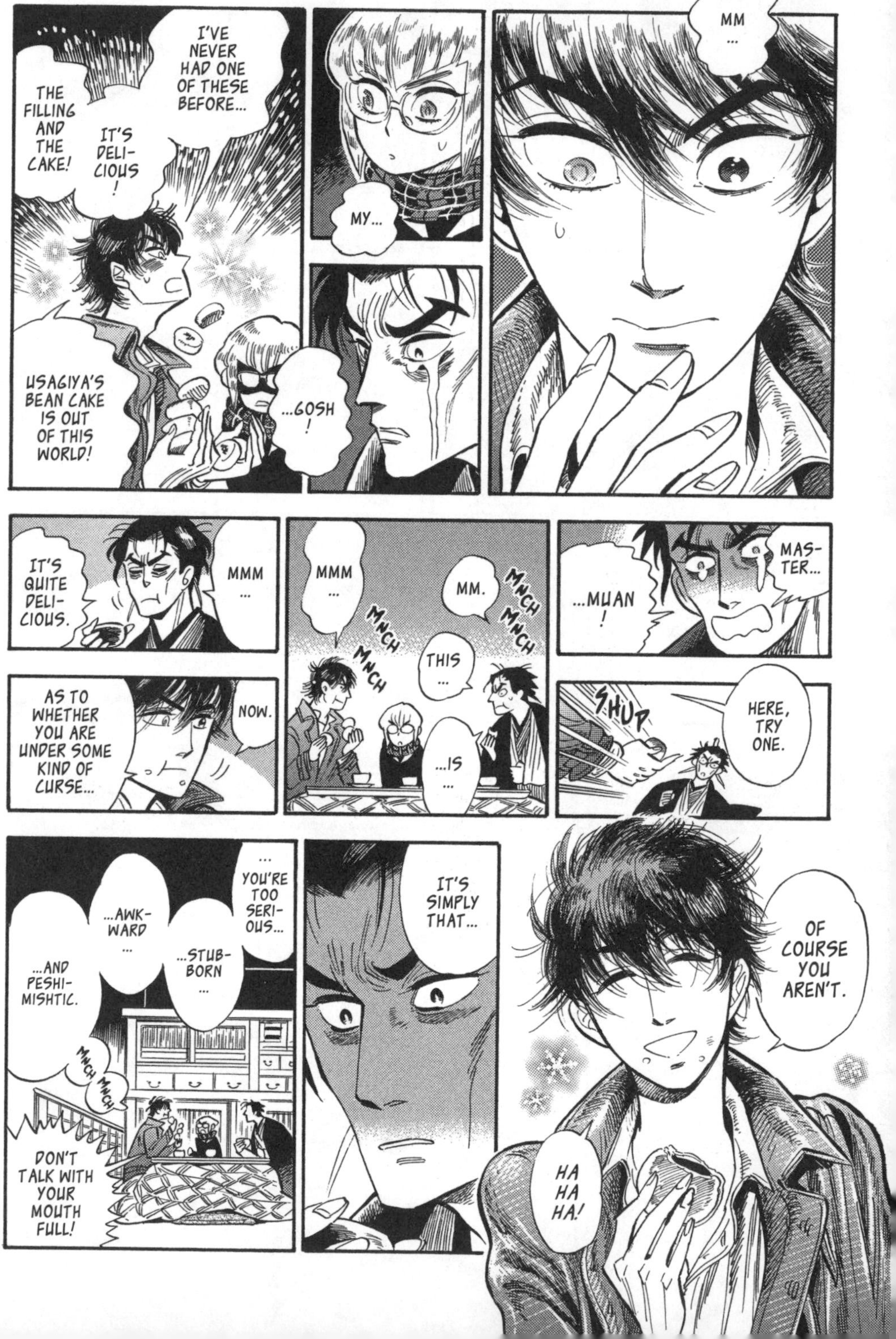
MM ...
MY...
...GOSH!
I'VE NEVER HAD ONE OF THESE BEFORE...
IT'S DELICIOUS!
THE FILLING AND THE CAKE!
USAGIYA'S BEAN CAKE IS OUT OF THIS WORLD!
MASTER...
...MUAN!
SHUP
HERE, TRY ONE.
MM.
MNCH MNCH
MMM ...
MNCH MNCH
THIS ...
...IS ...
MMM ...
IT'S QUITE DELICIOUS.
NOW.
AS TO WHETHER YOU ARE UNDER SOME KIND OF CURSE...
OF COURSE YOU AREN'T.
HA HA HA!
IT'S SIMPLY THAT...
... YOU'RE TOO SERIOUS...
...STUBBORN ...
...AWKWARD ...
...AND PESHIMISHTIC.
MNCH MNCH
DON'T TALK WITH YOUR MOUTH FULL!

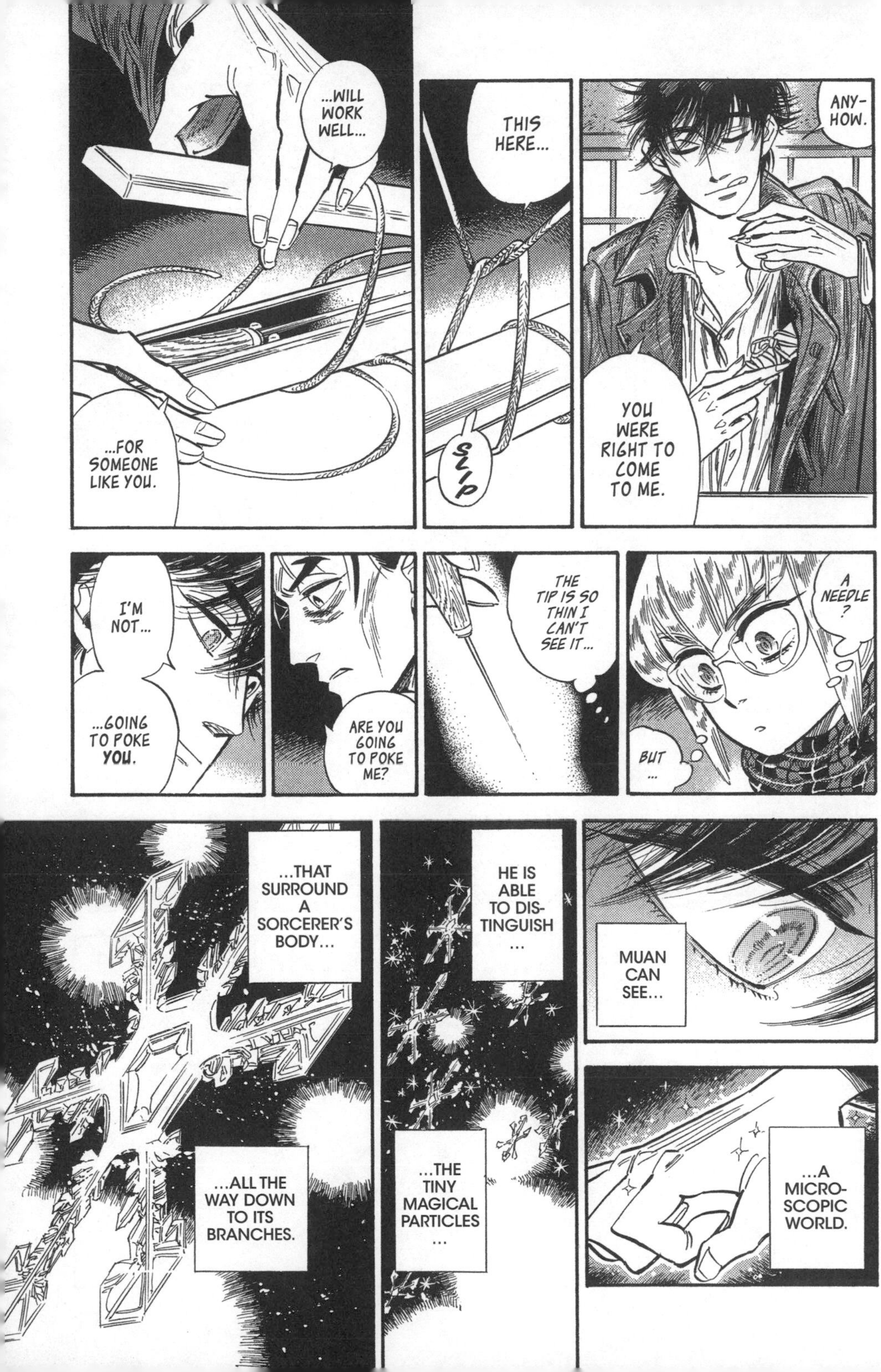
ANY-HOW.
YOU WERE RIGHT TO COME TO ME.
THIS HERE...
SLIP
...WILL WORK WELL...
...FOR SOMEONE LIKE YOU.
A NEEDLE?
BUT ...
THE TIP IS SO THIN I CAN'T SEE IT...
ARE YOU GOING TO POKE ME?
I'M NOT...
...GOING TO POKE **YOU**.
MUAN CAN SEE...
...A MICRO-SCOPIC WORLD.
HE IS ABLE TO DIS-TINGUISH ...
...THE TINY MAGICAL PARTICLES ...
...THAT SURROUND A SORCERER'S BODY...
...ALL THE WAY DOWN TO ITS BRANCHES.

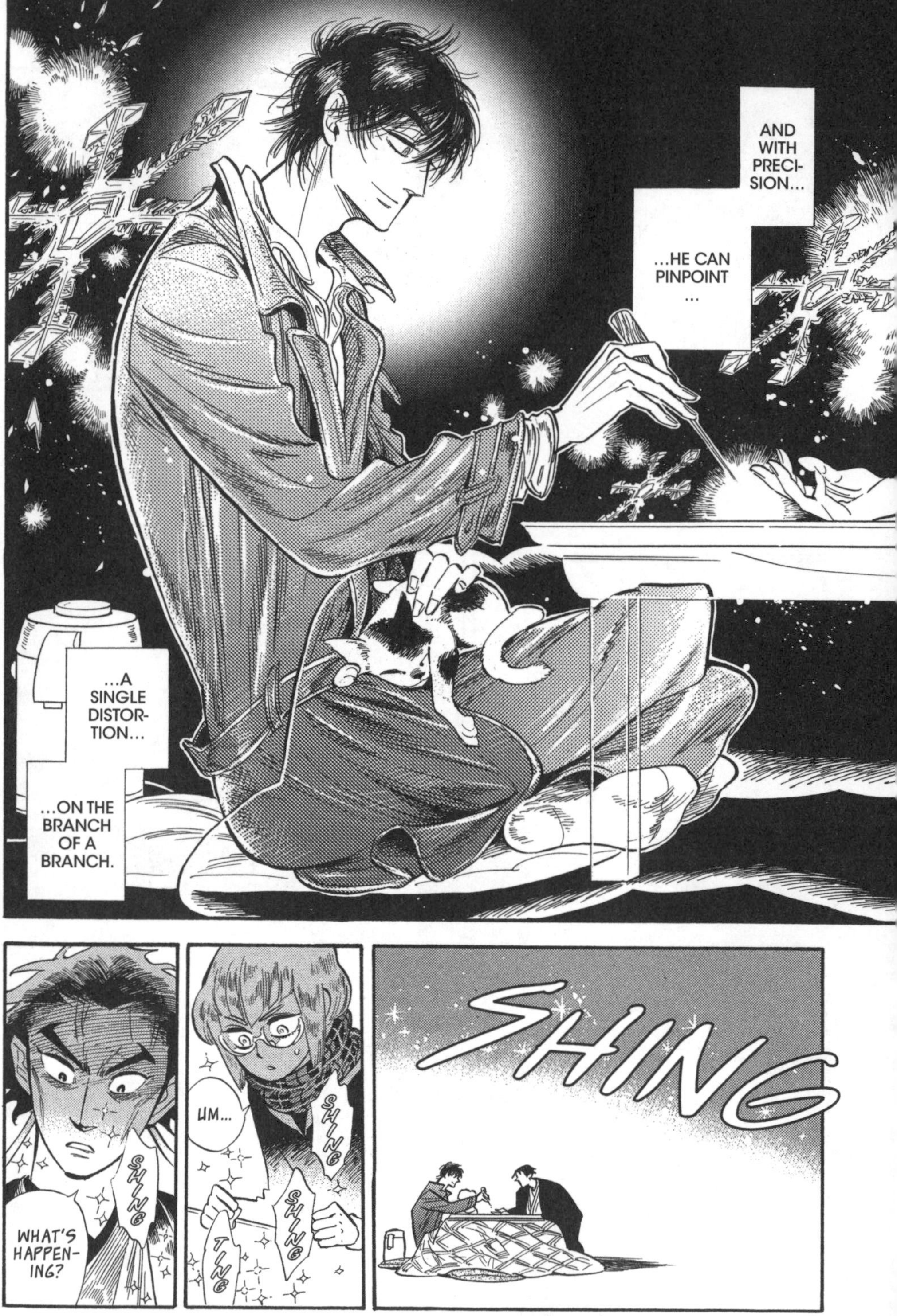
AND WITH PRECISION...
...HE CAN PINPOINT ...
...A SINGLE DISTORTION...
...ON THE BRANCH OF A BRANCH.
SHING
UM...
SHING
SHING
TING
SHING
WHAT'S HAPPENING?

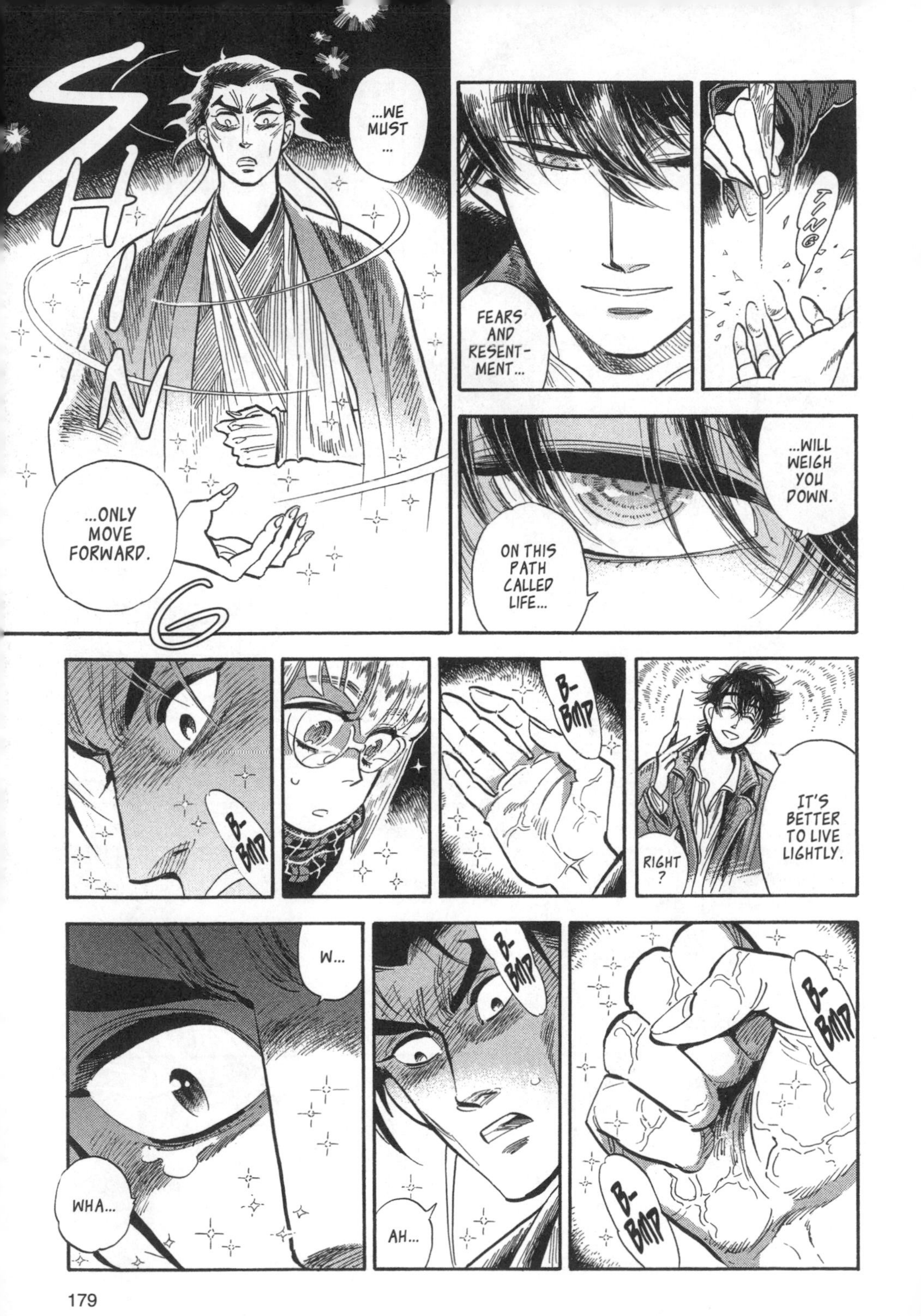
TING
FEARS AND RESENT-MENT...
...WILL WEIGH YOU DOWN.
ON THIS PATH CALLED LIFE...
...WE MUST ...
SHING
...ONLY MOVE FORWARD.
IT'S BETTER TO LIVE LIGHTLY.
RIGHT?
B-BMP
B-BMP
B-BMP
B-BMP
B-BMP
AH...
W...
WHA...

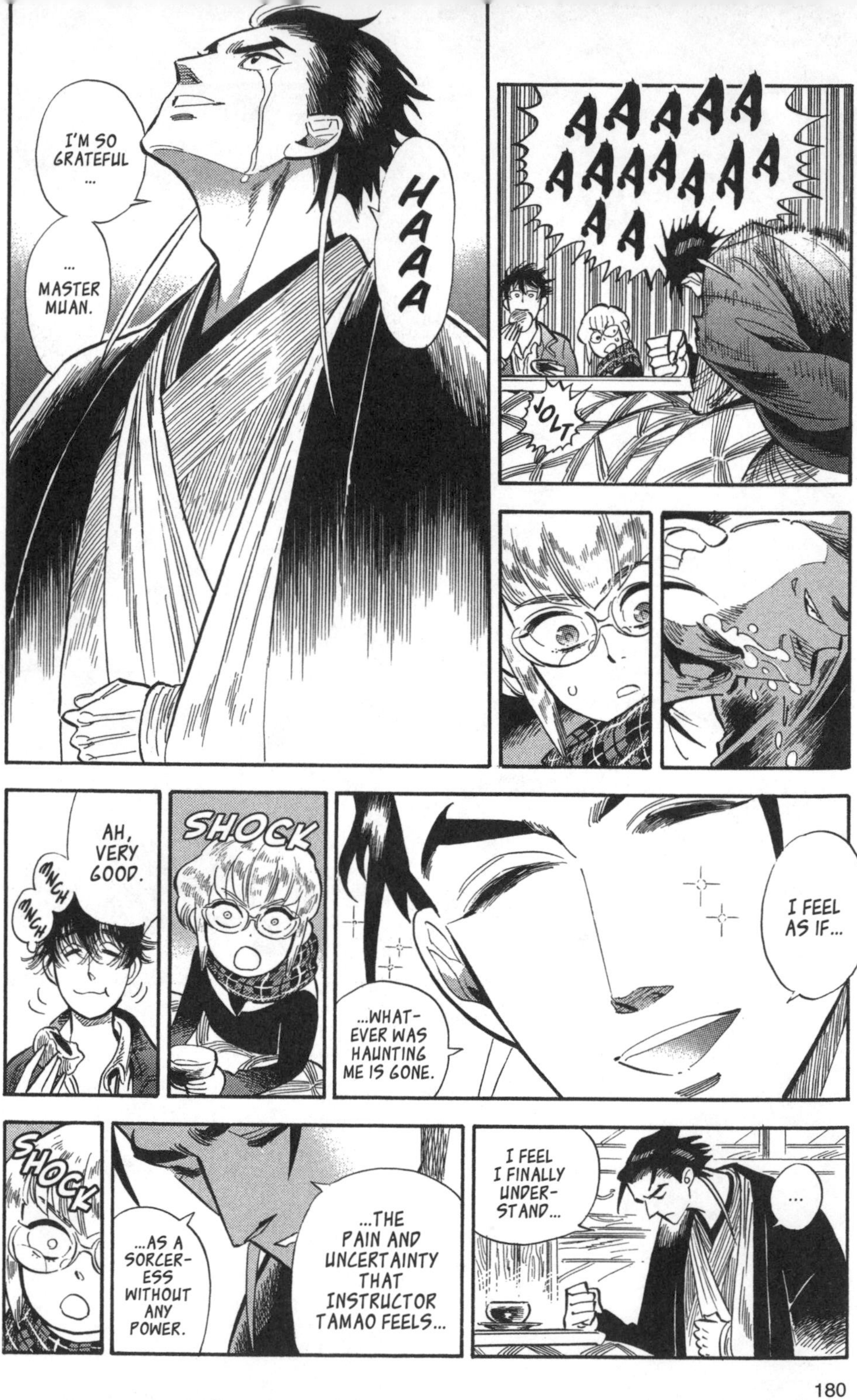
AAAAA AAAAAAA AA
JOLT
HAAAA
I'M SO GRATEFUL ...
... MASTER MUAN.
I FEEL AS IF...
...WHAT-EVER WAS HAUNTING ME IS GONE.
SHOCK
AH, VERY GOOD.
MNCH MNCH
...
I FEEL I FINALLY UNDER-STAND...
...THE PAIN AND UNCERTAINTY THAT INSTRUCTOR TAMAO FEELS...
...AS A SORCER-ESS WITHOUT ANY POWER.
SHOCK

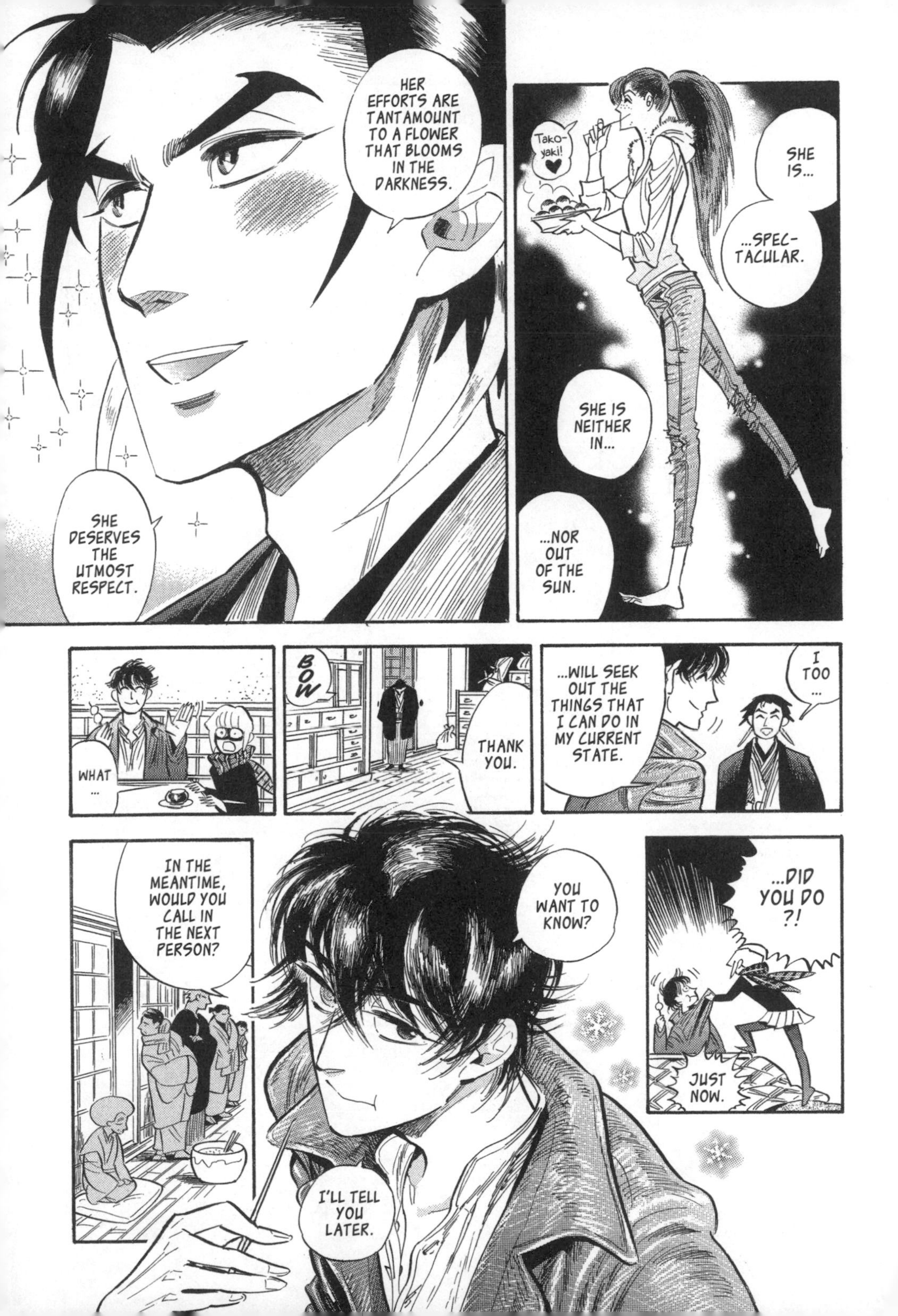
SHE IS...
...SPEC-TACULAR.
Tako-yaki! ♥
SHE IS NEITHER IN...
...NOR OUT OF THE SUN.
HER EFFORTS ARE TANTAMOUNT TO A FLOWER THAT BLOOMS IN THE DARKNESS.
SHE DESERVES THE UTMOST RESPECT.
I TOO ...
...WILL SEEK OUT THE THINGS THAT I CAN DO IN MY CURRENT STATE.
BOW
THANK YOU.
WHAT ...
...DID YOU DO ?!
JUST NOW.
YOU WANT TO KNOW?
IN THE MEANTIME, WOULD YOU CALL IN THE NEXT PERSON?
I'LL TELL YOU LATER.

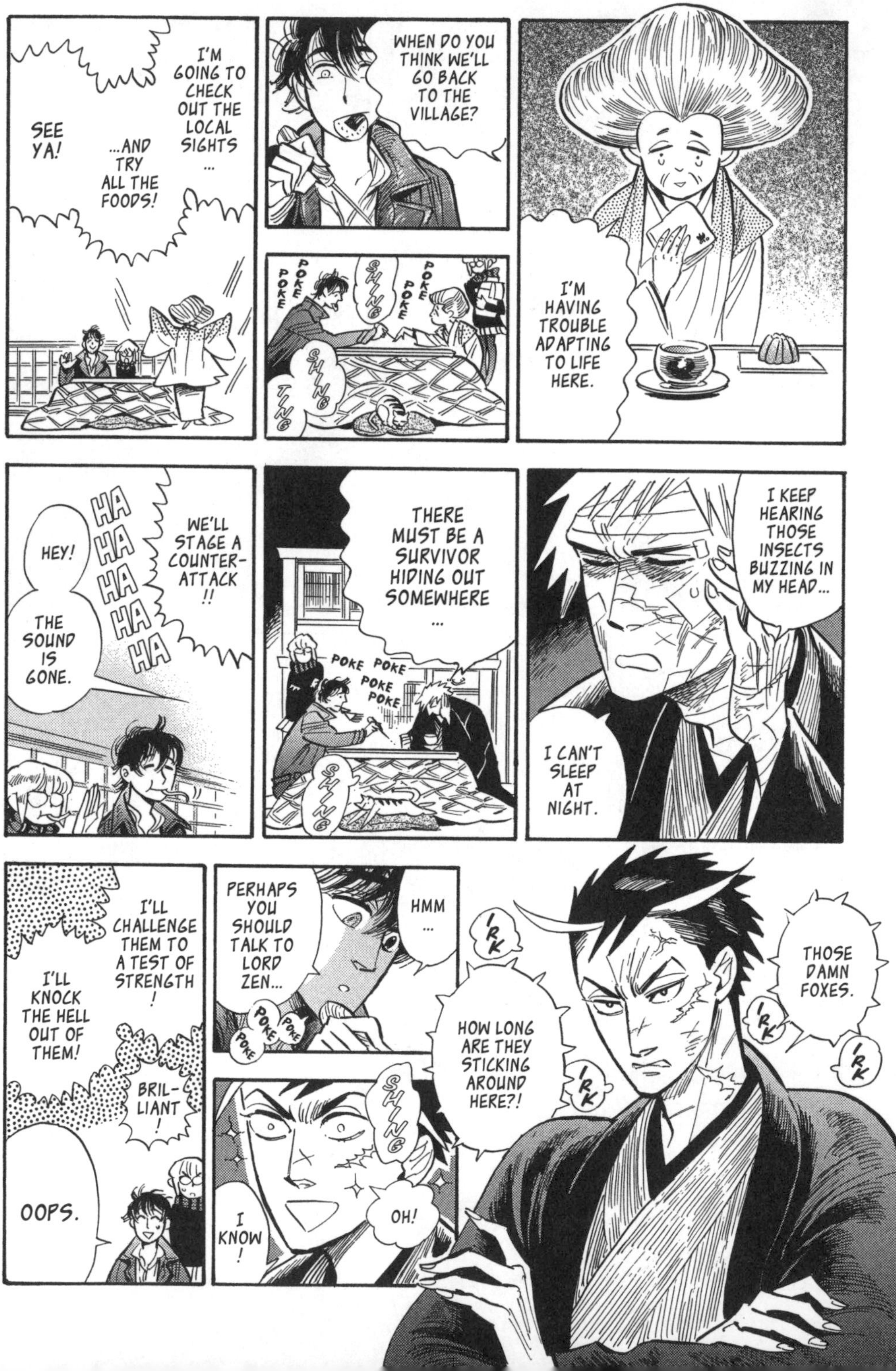
I'M HAVING TROUBLE ADAPTING TO LIFE HERE.
WHEN DO YOU THINK WE'LL GO BACK TO THE VILLAGE?
POKE POKE
SHING
POKE POKE
SHING
TING
I'M GOING TO CHECK OUT THE LOCAL SIGHTS ...
...AND TRY ALL THE FOODS!
SEE YA!
I KEEP HEARING THOSE INSECTS BUZZING IN MY HEAD...
I CAN'T SLEEP AT NIGHT.
THERE MUST BE A SURVIVOR HIDING OUT SOMEWHERE ...
POKE POKE
POKE POKE
SHING
WE'LL STAGE A COUNTER-ATTACK!!
HA HA HA HA HA HA
HEY!
THE SOUND IS GONE.
THOSE DAMN FOXES.
IRK
IRK
IRK
HOW LONG ARE THEY STICKING AROUND HERE?!
IRK
HMM ...
PERHAPS YOU SHOULD TALK TO LORD ZEN...
POKE POKE POKE
SHING
OH!
I KNOW!
I'LL CHALLENGE THEM TO A TEST OF STRENGTH!
I'LL KNOCK THE HELL OUT OF THEM!
BRILLIANT!
OOPS.

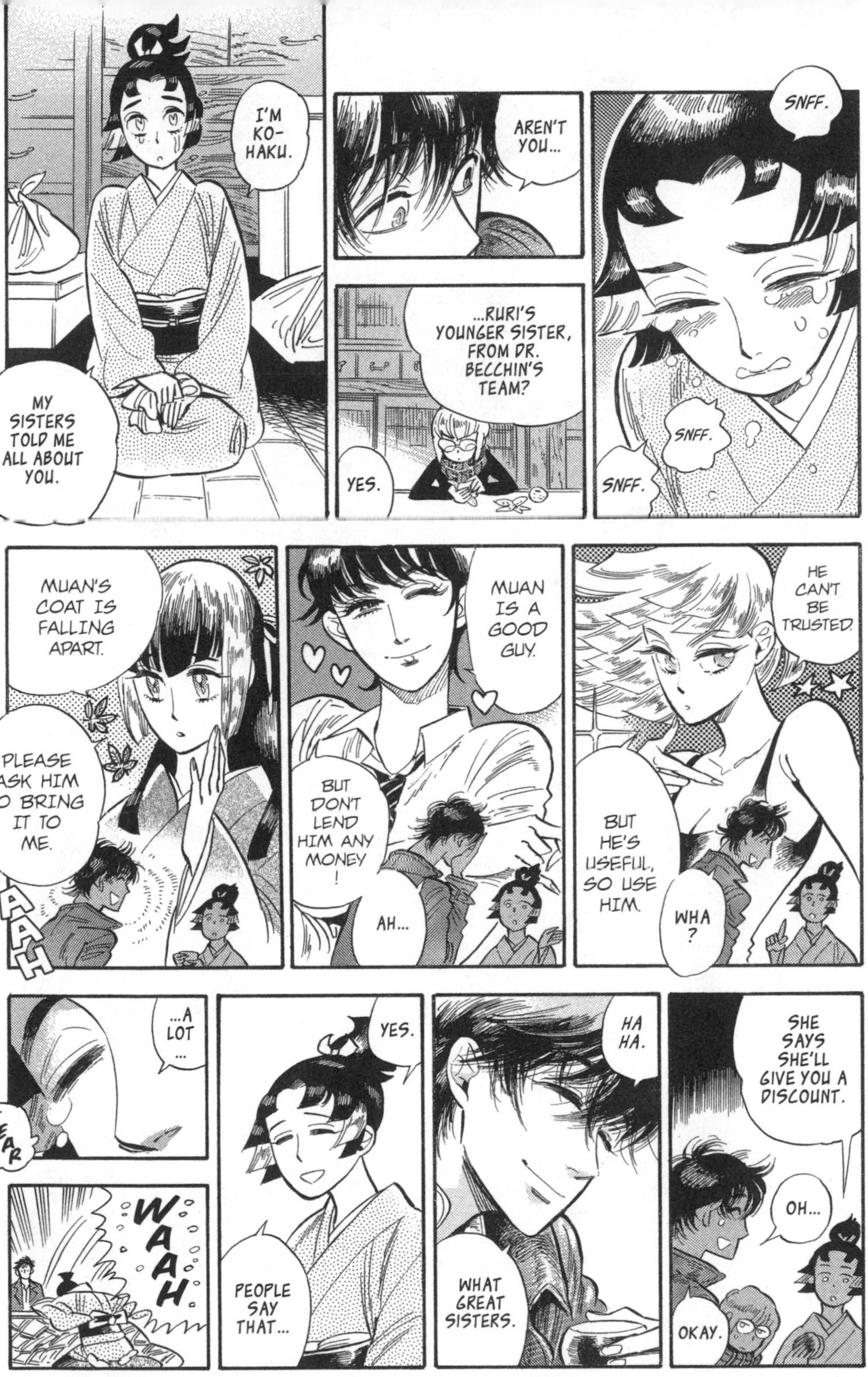
SNFF.
SNFF.
SNFF.
AREN'T YOU...
...RURI'S YOUNGER SISTER, FROM DR. BECCHIN'S TEAM?
YES.
I'M KO-HAKU.
MY SISTERS TOLD ME ALL ABOUT YOU.
HE CAN'T BE TRUSTED.
BUT HE'S USEFUL, SO USE HIM.
WHA?
MUAN IS A GOOD GUY.
BUT DON'T LEND HIM ANY MONEY!
AH...
MUAN'S COAT IS FALLING APART.
PLEASE ASK HIM TO BRING IT TO ME.
AAAH
SHE SAYS SHE'LL GIVE YOU A DISCOUNT.
OH...
OKAY.
HA HA.
WHAT GREAT SISTERS.
YES.
PEOPLE SAY THAT...
...A LOT...
TEAR
WAAAH

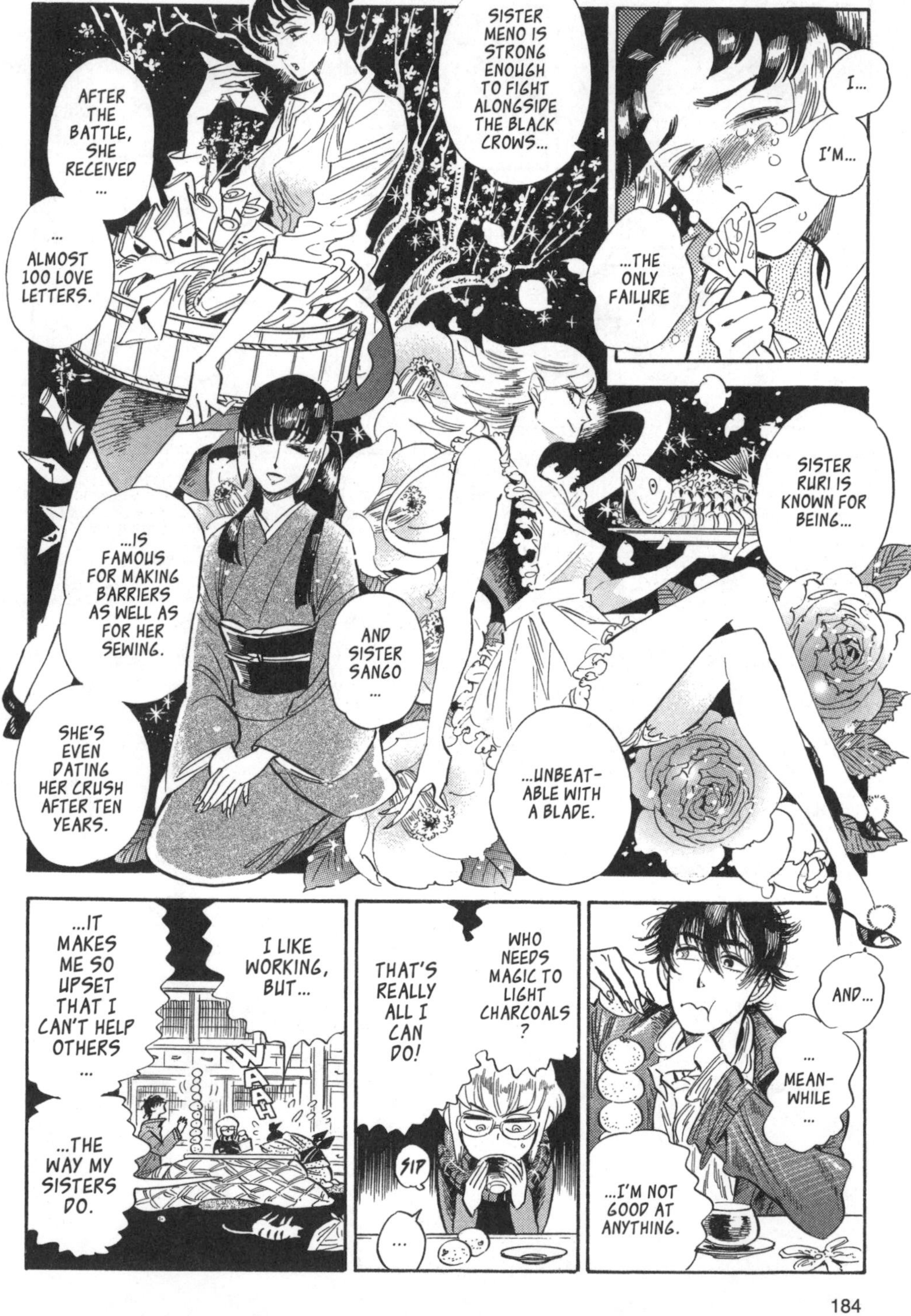
I...
I'M...
...THE ONLY FAILURE!
SISTER MENO IS STRONG ENOUGH TO FIGHT ALONGSIDE THE BLACK CROWS...
AFTER THE BATTLE, SHE RECEIVED...
...ALMOST 100 LOVE LETTERS.
SISTER RURI IS KNOWN FOR BEING...
...UNBEAT-ABLE WITH A BLADE.
AND SISTER SANGO...
...IS FAMOUS FOR MAKING BARRIERS AS WELL AS FOR HER SEWING.
SHE'S EVEN DATING HER CRUSH AFTER TEN YEARS.
AND...
...MEAN-WHILE...
...I'M NOT GOOD AT ANYTHING.
WHO NEEDS MAGIC TO LIGHT CHARCOALS?
THAT'S REALLY ALL I CAN DO!
SIP
...
I LIKE WORKING, BUT...
...IT MAKES ME SO UPSET THAT I CAN'T HELP OTHERS...
WAAAH
...THE WAY MY SISTERS DO.

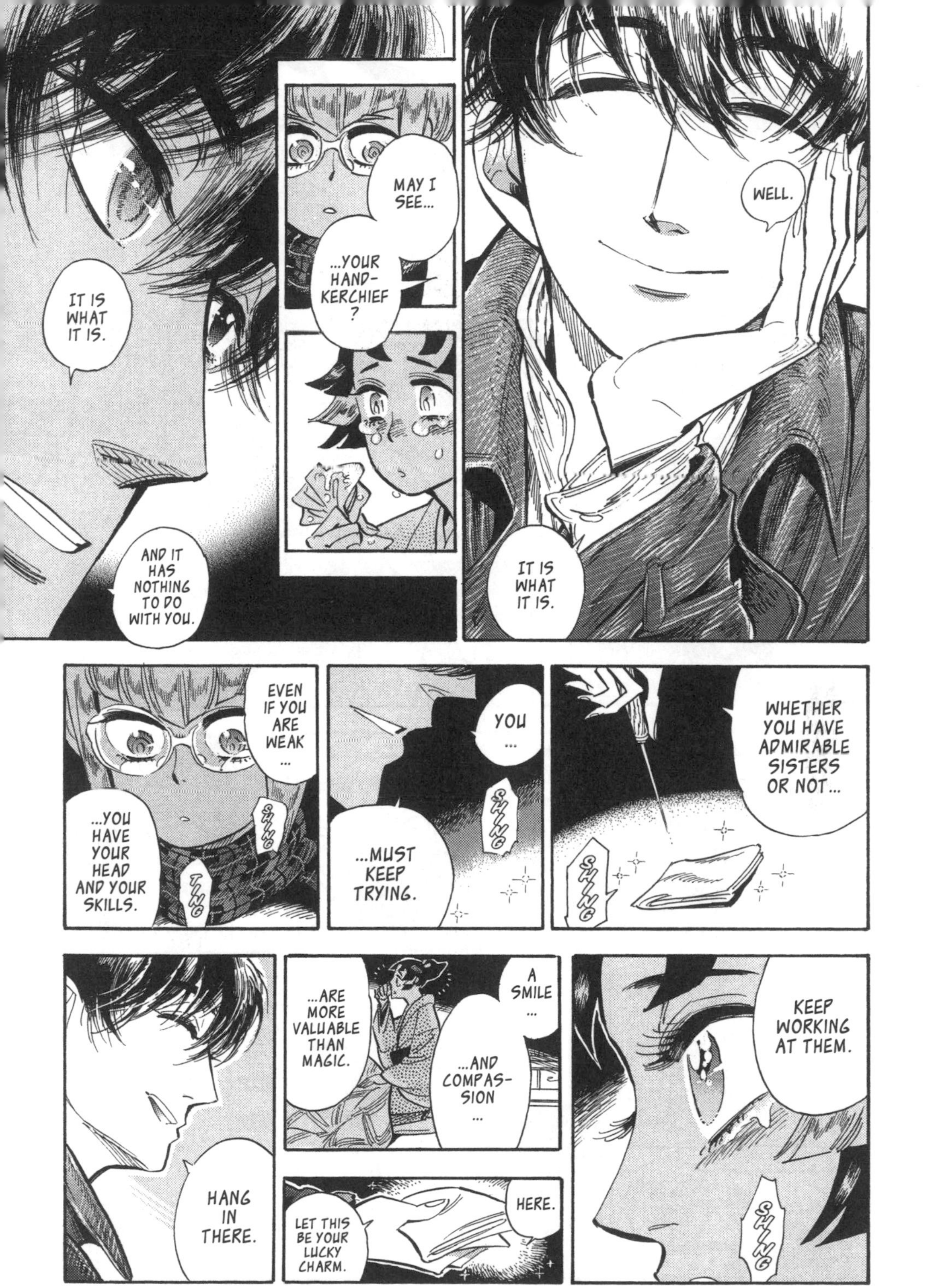
WELL.
IT IS WHAT IT IS.
MAY I SEE...
...YOUR HANDKERCHIEF?
IT IS WHAT IT IS.
AND IT HAS NOTHING TO DO WITH YOU.
WHETHER YOU HAVE ADMIRABLE SISTERS OR NOT...
SHING
SHING
YOU...
SHING
...MUST KEEP TRYING.
EVEN IF YOU ARE WEAK...
SHING
...YOU HAVE YOUR HEAD AND YOUR SKILLS.
TING
KEEP WORKING AT THEM.
SHING
A SMILE...
...AND COMPASSION...
...ARE MORE VALUABLE THAN MAGIC.
HERE.
LET THIS BE YOUR LUCKY CHARM.
HANG IN THERE.

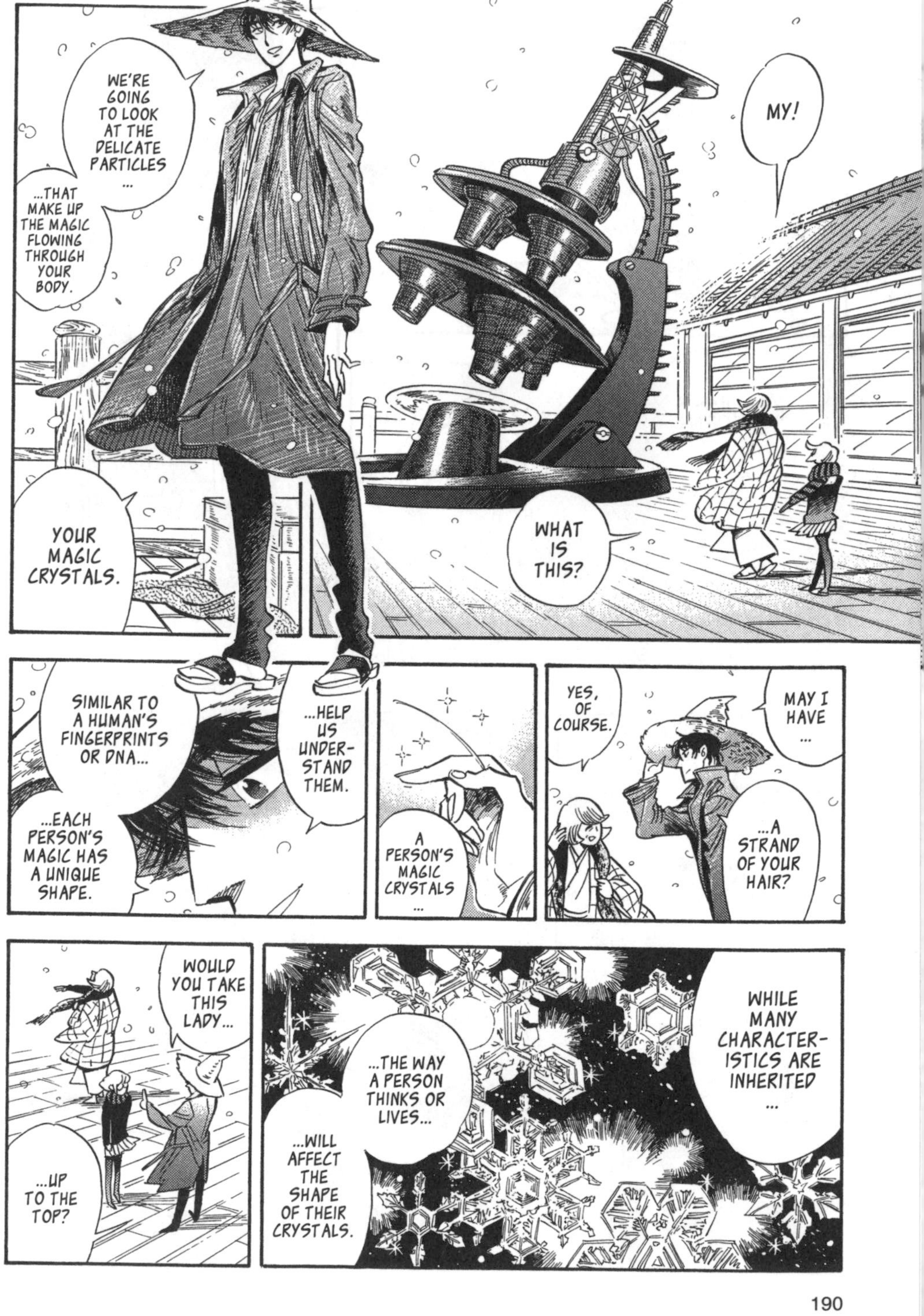
MY!
WHAT IS THIS?
WE'RE GOING TO LOOK AT THE DELICATE PARTICLES...
...THAT MAKE UP THE MAGIC FLOWING THROUGH YOUR BODY.
YOUR MAGIC CRYSTALS.
MAY I HAVE...
...A STRAND OF YOUR HAIR?
YES, OF COURSE.
A PERSON'S MAGIC CRYSTALS...
...HELP US UNDER-STAND THEM.
SIMILAR TO A HUMAN'S FINGERPRINTS OR DNA...
...EACH PERSON'S MAGIC HAS A UNIQUE SHAPE.
WHILE MANY CHARACTER-ISTICS ARE INHERITED...
...THE WAY A PERSON THINKS OR LIVES...
...WILL AFFECT THE SHAPE OF THEIR CRYSTALS.
WOULD YOU TAKE THIS LADY...
...UP TO THE TOP?

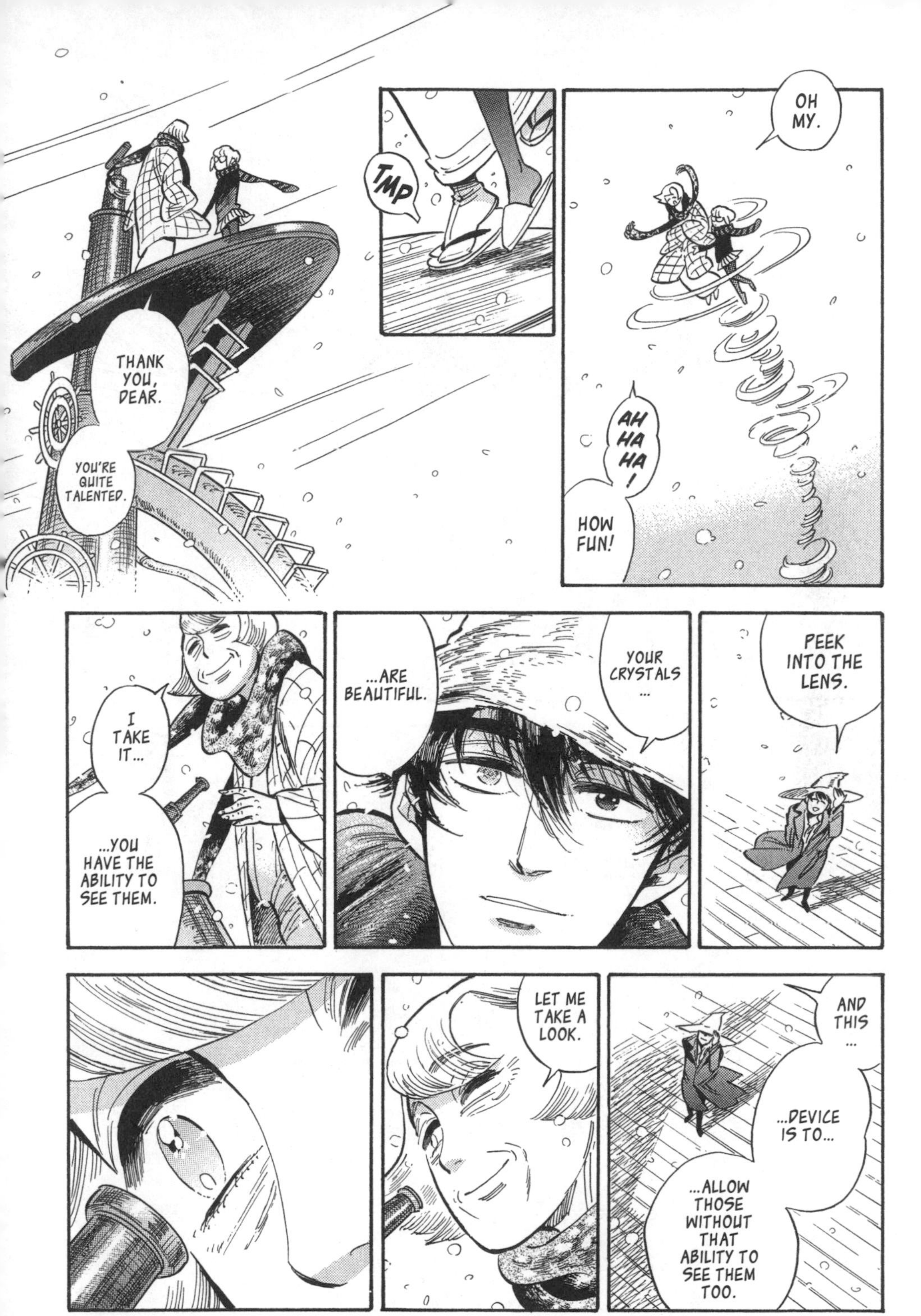
OH MY.
AH HA HA!
HOW FUN!
TMP
THANK YOU, DEAR.
YOU'RE QUITE TALENTED.
PEEK INTO THE LENS.
YOUR CRYSTALS ...
...ARE BEAUTIFUL.
I TAKE IT...
...YOU HAVE THE ABILITY TO SEE THEM.
AND THIS ...
...DEVICE IS TO...
...ALLOW THOSE WITHOUT THAT ABILITY TO SEE THEM TOO.
LET ME TAKE A LOOK.

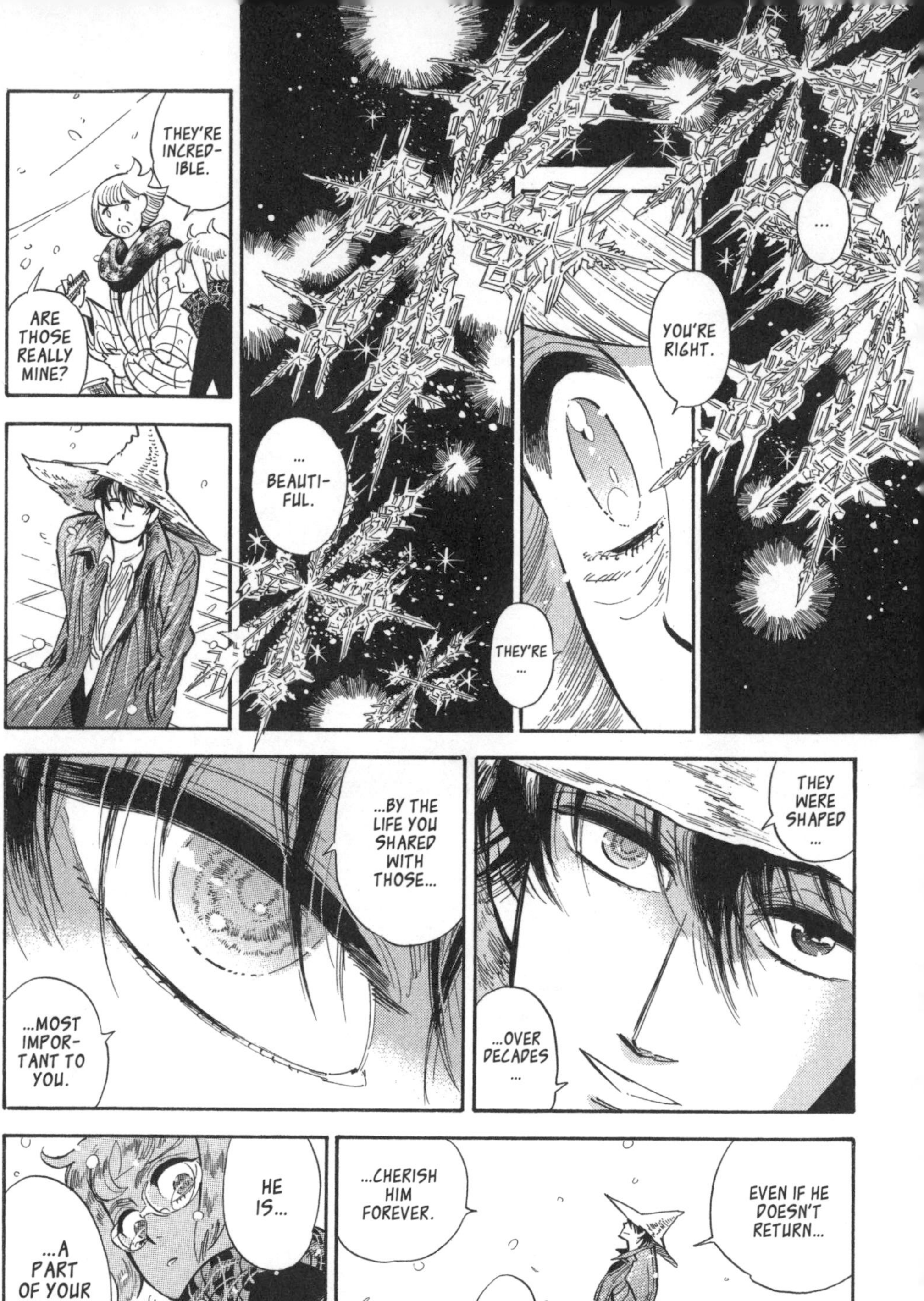
...
YOU'RE RIGHT.
THEY'RE ...
... BEAUTIFUL.
THEY'RE INCREDIBLE.
ARE THOSE REALLY MINE?
THEY WERE SHAPED ...
...OVER DECADES ...
...BY THE LIFE YOU SHARED WITH THOSE...
...MOST IMPORTANT TO YOU.
EVEN IF HE DOESN'T RETURN...
...CHERISH HIM FOREVER.
... PLEASE ...
HE IS...
...A PART OF YOUR BEAUTY.

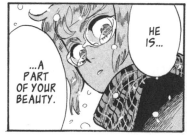

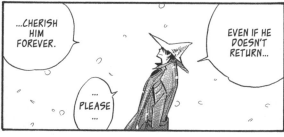

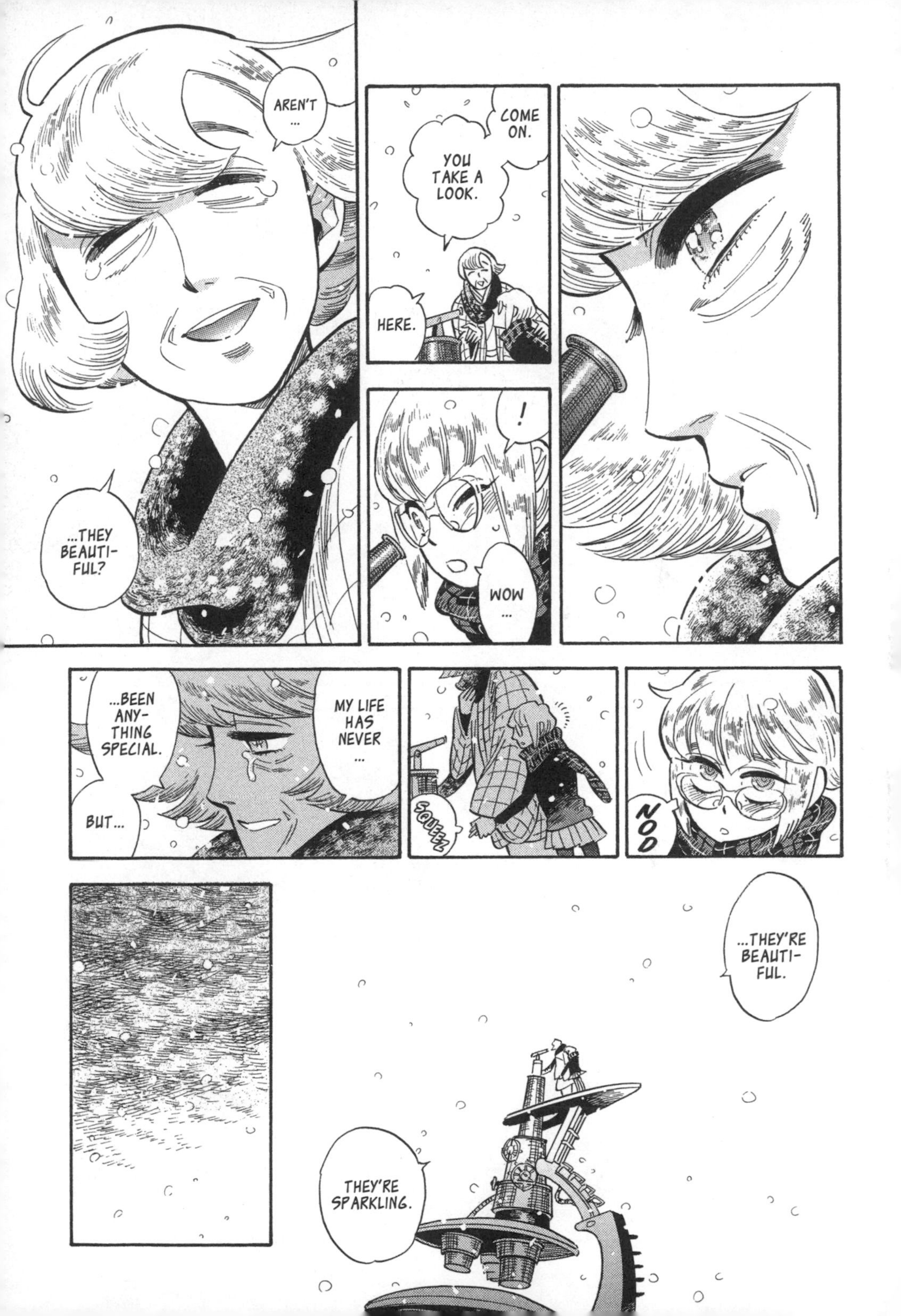
COME ON.
YOU TAKE A LOOK.
HERE.
!
WOW ...
AREN'T ...
...THEY BEAUTIFUL?
NOD
SQUEEZ
MY LIFE HAS NEVER ...
...BEEN ANYTHING SPECIAL.
BUT...
...THEY'RE BEAUTIFUL.
THEY'RE SPARKLING.

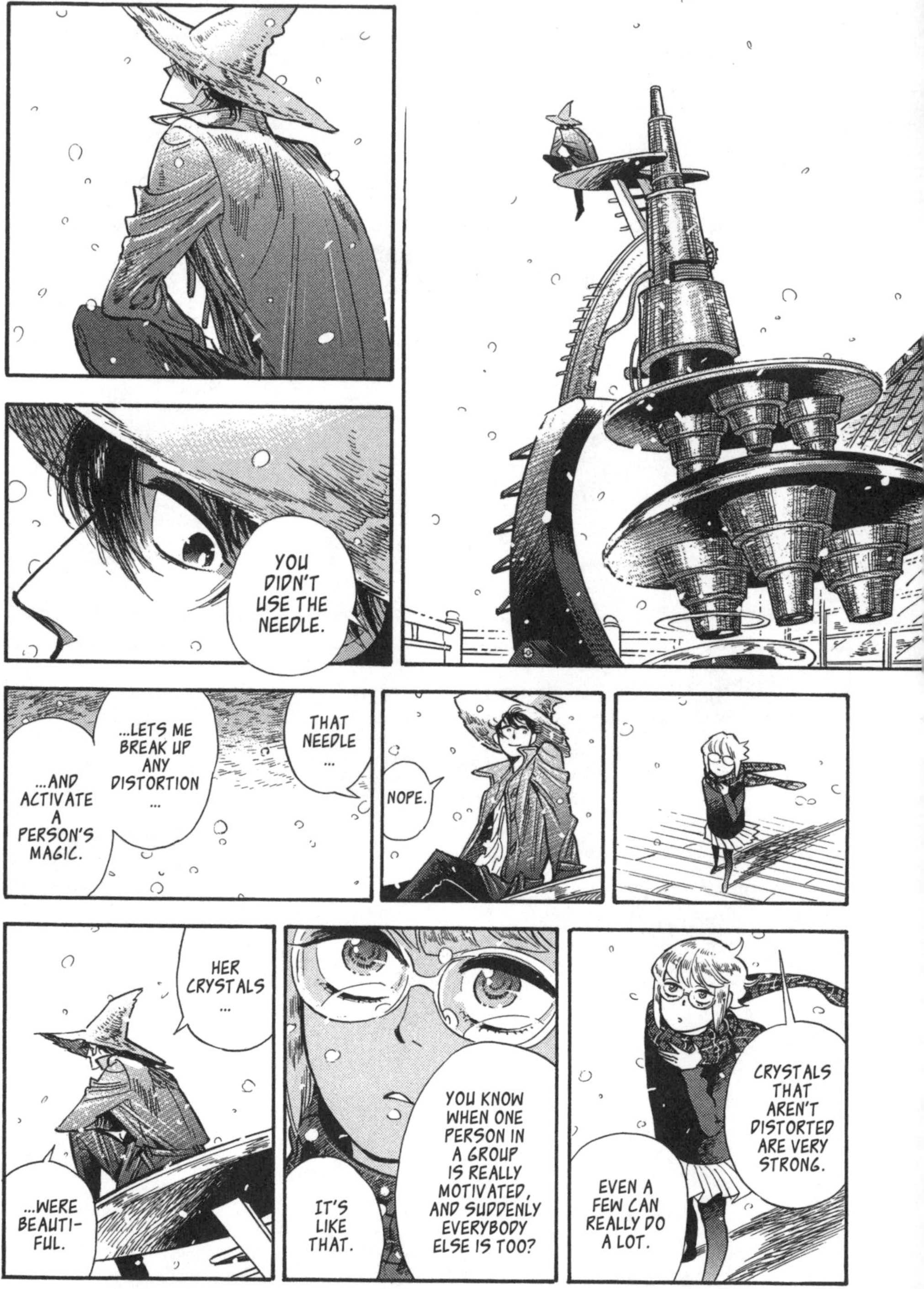
YOU DIDN'T USE THE NEEDLE.
NOPE.
THAT NEEDLE ...
...LETS ME BREAK UP ANY DISTORTION ...
...AND ACTIVATE A PERSON'S MAGIC.
CRYSTALS THAT AREN'T DISTORTED ARE VERY STRONG.
EVEN A FEW CAN REALLY DO A LOT.
YOU KNOW WHEN ONE PERSON IN A GROUP IS REALLY MOTIVATED, AND SUDDENLY EVERYBODY ELSE IS TOO?
IT'S LIKE THAT.
HER CRYSTALS ...
...WERE BEAUTI-FUL.

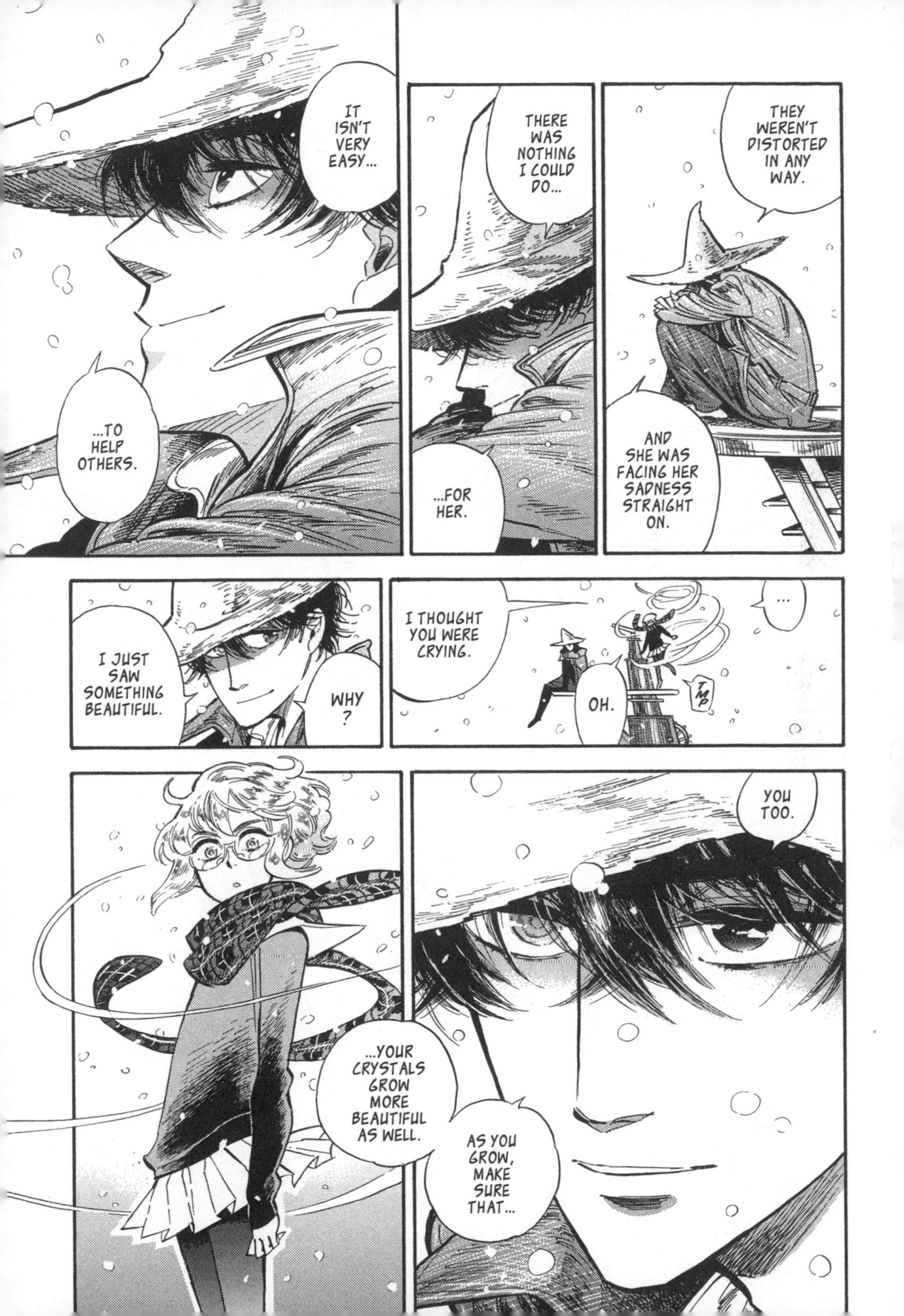
THEY WEREN'T DISTORTED IN ANY WAY.
AND SHE WAS FACING HER SADNESS STRAIGHT ON.
THERE WAS NOTHING I COULD DO...
...FOR HER.
IT ISN'T VERY EASY...
...TO HELP OTHERS.
...
I THOUGHT YOU WERE CRYING.
OH.
TMP
WHY?
I JUST SAW SOMETHING BEAUTIFUL.
YOU TOO.
AS YOU GROW, MAKE SURE THAT...
...YOUR CRYSTALS GROW MORE BEAUTIFUL AS WELL.

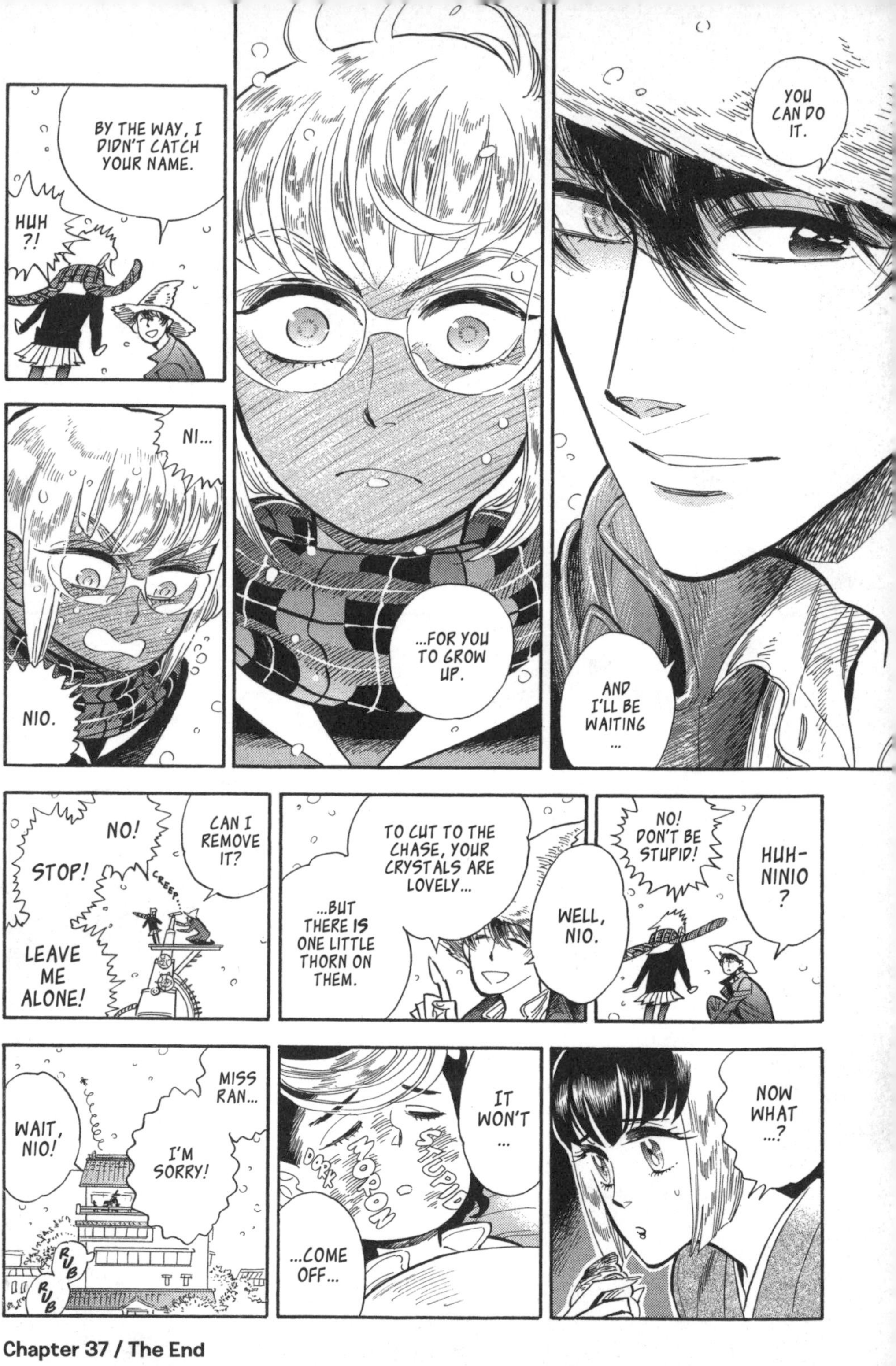
YOU CAN DO IT.
AND I'LL BE WAITING ...
...FOR YOU TO GROW UP.
BY THE WAY, I DIDN'T CATCH YOUR NAME.
HUH ?!
NI...
NIO.
HUH-NINIO ?
NO! DON'T BE STUPID!
WELL, NIO.
TO CUT TO THE CHASE, YOUR CRYSTALS ARE LOVELY...
...BUT THERE IS ONE LITTLE THORN ON THEM.
CAN I REMOVE IT?
NO!
STOP!
CREEP...
LEAVE ME ALONE!
NOW WHAT ...?
IT WON'T ...
STUPID
MORON
DORK
...COME OFF...
MISS RAN...
I'M SORRY!
WAIT, NIO!
RUB
RUB

Chapter 37 / The End

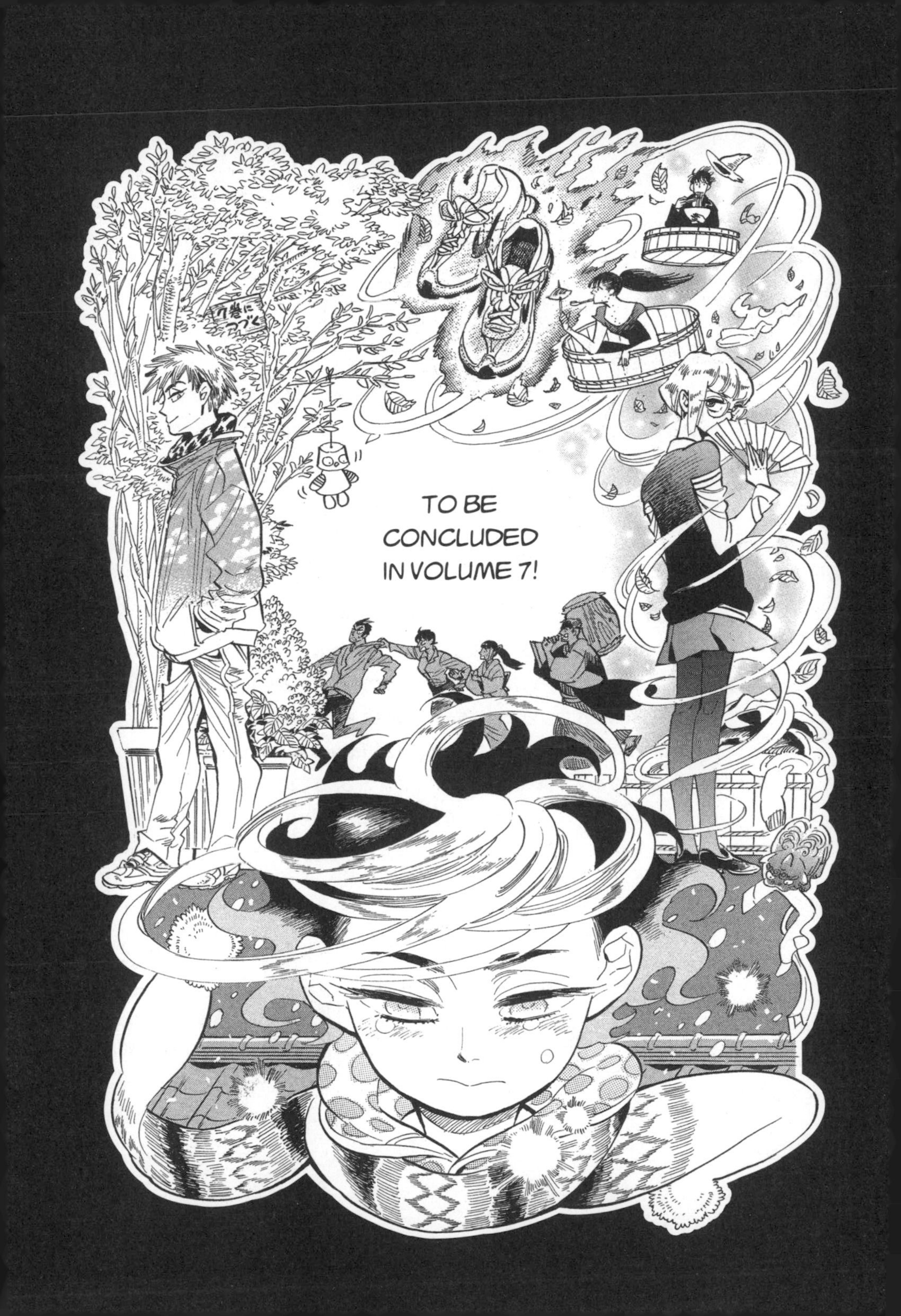
7巻に
つづく
TO BE
CONCLUDED
IN VOLUME 7!

Aki Irie was born in Kagawa Prefecture, Japan. She
began her professional career as a manga artist in
2002 with the short story "Fuku-chan Tabi Mata Tabi"
(Fuku-chan on the Road Again), which was published in
the monthly manga magazine *Papu*. *Ran and the Gray
World*, her first full-length series, is also the first
of her works to be released in English.

RAN AND THE GRAY WORLD
VOL. 6
VIZ Signature Edition

Story & Art by
AKI IRIE

English Translation & Adaptation / Emi Louie-Nishikawa
Touch-Up Art & Lettering / Joanna Estep
Design / Yukiko Whitley
Editor / Amy Yu

RAN TO HAIIRO NO SEKAI Vol. 6
© Aki Irie 2014
First published in Japan in 2014 by KADOKAWA CORPORATION, Tokyo.
English translation rights arranged with KADOKAWA CORPORATION, Tokyo.

Printed in Canada

Published by VIZ Media, LLC
P.O. Box 77010
San Francisco, CA 94107

10 9 8 7 6 5 4 3 2 1
First printing, February 2020

viz.com   vizsignature.com